THE MONUMENTAL NATION

AUSTRIAN AND HABSBURG STUDIES

General Editor: Gary B. Cohen, Center for Austrian Studies,
University of Minnesota

Before 1918, Austria and the Habsburg lands constituted an expansive
multinational and multiethnic empire, the second largest state in Europe and
a key site for cultural and intellectual developments across the continent. At
the turn of the twentieth century, the region gave birth to modern psychology,
philosophy, economics, and music, and since then has played an important
mediating role between Western and Eastern Europe, today participating as
a critical member of the European Union. The volumes in this series address
specific themes and questions around the history, culture, politics, social, and
economic experience of Austria, the Habsburg Empire, and its successor states
in Central and Eastern Europe.

For a full volume listing, please see back matter

THE MONUMENTAL NATION

Magyar Nationalism and Symbolic Politics
in Fin-de-siècle Hungary

Bálint Varga

berghahn
NEW YORK · OXFORD
www.berghahnbooks.com

First published 2016 by

Berghahn Books

www.berghahnbooks.com

© 2016, 2020 Bálint Varga
First paperback edition published in 2020

Library of Congress Cataloging-in-Publication Data
A C.I.P. cataloging record is available from the Library of Congress

British Library Cataloguing in Publication Data
A catalogue record for this book is available from the British Library

ISBN 978-1-78533-313-2 hardback
ISBN 978-1-78920-519-0 paperback
ISBN 978-1-78533-314-9 ebook

CONTENTS

ILLUSTRATIONS AND TABLES

❦

Illustrations

Tables

ACKNOWLEDGMENTS

❧

This book could not have been written without the help of numerous people and institutions. The initial idea to write this study came from Gábor Sonkoly, who has accompanied me on the long intellectual journey I have traveled in the past few years. Discussions with Balázs Trencsényi in Budapest, Elena Mannová in Bratislava, and Hans-Christian Maner in Mainz were always fruitful in shaping my ideas. Beyond them, I could always rely on the advice of Nándor Bárdi, Cristian Cercel, Gábor Czoch, Peter Haslinger, Gabriela Kiliánová, Csaba Gy. Kiss, Szonja Komoróczy, Jan Kusber, Gernot Nussbächer, Thomas Şindilariu, and Csaba Zahorán. Stevo Đurašković, Danilo Sarenac, and György B. Lukács generously helped me to organize research in Zagreb and Belgrade, and with the translations from Serbian and Croatian. László Sebők generously provided help with cartography. Besides these, many others shared their ideas with me and did me favors; to all of them I am likewise grateful. The final manuscript was significantly improved by the feedback of András Cieger, Gábor Egry, Zoltán Fónagy and Gábor Gyáni. The most critical reader of the manuscript was my wife Réka. Finally, the anonymous reviewers at Berghahn Books pointed out many shortcomings of the book; I appreciate their balanced opinion, which was of crucial importance. The virtues of this book are thus largely the outcome of my collaboration with numerous people; needless to say that all the mistakes are my own.

This research project was supported by a number of institutions, including the Loránd Eötvös University of Budapest, the Johannes Gutenberg University of Mainz, the Slovak Academy of Sciences, the University of Vienna, the Pro Renovanda Cultura Hungarie Foundation, and the Southeast Europe Association. Their support proved crucial in collecting the documents this study is built on.

I dedicate this book to the memory of my grandmother. She was always most proud to see her grandson becoming a historian; I regret I was not quick enough to complete this project during her lifetime.

TERMINOLOGY

❦

Naming places in Central Europe is a complicated issue, since all name variants carry a national significance. The most correct method would be to include all variations, but this is impossible for practical reasons. The capital of Slovakia illustrates this challenge: it should be referred to as Posonium/Pressburg/Pozsony/Prešpurk/Bratislava/בראטיסלאווא, just to mention the most common Latin, German, Magyar, old Slovak, current Slovak, and Yiddish names. Even this solution omits some older Slavonic, Ruthenian, Serbian, Czech, and Croatian variants and some other vernacular forms. For the sake of simplicity, places will be referred to according to the largest group of mother tongue, as recorded in the 1890 census, the last before the millennial year. In citations, place names will appear as in the original. Appendix 2 helps to identify current names.

The distinction between Magyar and Hungarian is emphasized throughout this book. Hungarian is used as a neutral term for the entire country, while the term Magyar is applied to the ethnic group and its language. The term Hungary has also various meanings; in this work Hungary refers to the lands under the direct control of the Budapest government (excluding Croatia-Slavonia, Transylvania until 1867, and the Military Frontier until its dissolution in 1881). The Greek Catholic population of northeastern Hungary is labeled as Rusyn rather than Ruthenian or Ukrainian. A difference between German and Saxon is kept, reserving Saxon for the Lutheran German-speaking population of Transylvania and using German to refer to any other German-speaking group of Hungary.

Except otherwise noted, all translations are mine.

ABBREVIATIONS

⬥

AH	Archiv der Honterusgemeinde A. B. in Kronstadt (Archives of the Honterus Lutheran Parish in Braşov)
AJ	Arhiv Jugoslavije (Archives of Yugoslavia, Belgrade)
DAZO	Derzhavnii Arhiv Zakarpatskoi Oblasti (State Archives of the Transcarpathian County, Beregovo)
DJBAN	Direcţia Judeţeană Braşov a Arhivelor Naţionale (Braşov County Filiale of the National Archives, Braşov)
FMKE	Felsőmagyarországi Közművelődési Egylet (Upper Hungarian Cultural Association)
GYÉL	Gyulafehérvári Érseki Levéltár (Archives of the Alba Iulia Diocese, Alba Iulia)
HDA	Hrvatski državni arhiv (Croatian State Archives, Zagreb)
HSDP	Hungarian Social Democratic Party
IAB	Istorijski arhiv Beograda (Historic Archives of Belgrade)
MNL CSML	Magyar Nemzeti Levéltár Csongrád Megyei Levéltár Szentesi Levéltára (Archives of Csongrád County, Szentes)
MNL OL	Magyar Nemzeti Levéltár Országos Levéltára (National Archives of Hungary, Budapest)
OSZK K	Országos Széchényi Könyvtár Kézirattár (Manuscript Collection of the Széchényi Hungarian National Library, Budapest)
PFL	Pannonhalmi Főapátság Levéltára (Archives of the Pannonhalma Archabbey, Pannonhalma)
ŠANPN	Štatny archív v Nitre pobočka Nitra (Nitra Filial of the Nitra State Archives)
SNA	Slovenský národný archív (Slovak National Archives, Bratislava)
ŠOAB	Štátny oblastný archív v Bratislave (State County Archives in Bratislava)
ŠOAN	Štátny oblastný archív v Nitre (State County Archives in Nitra)

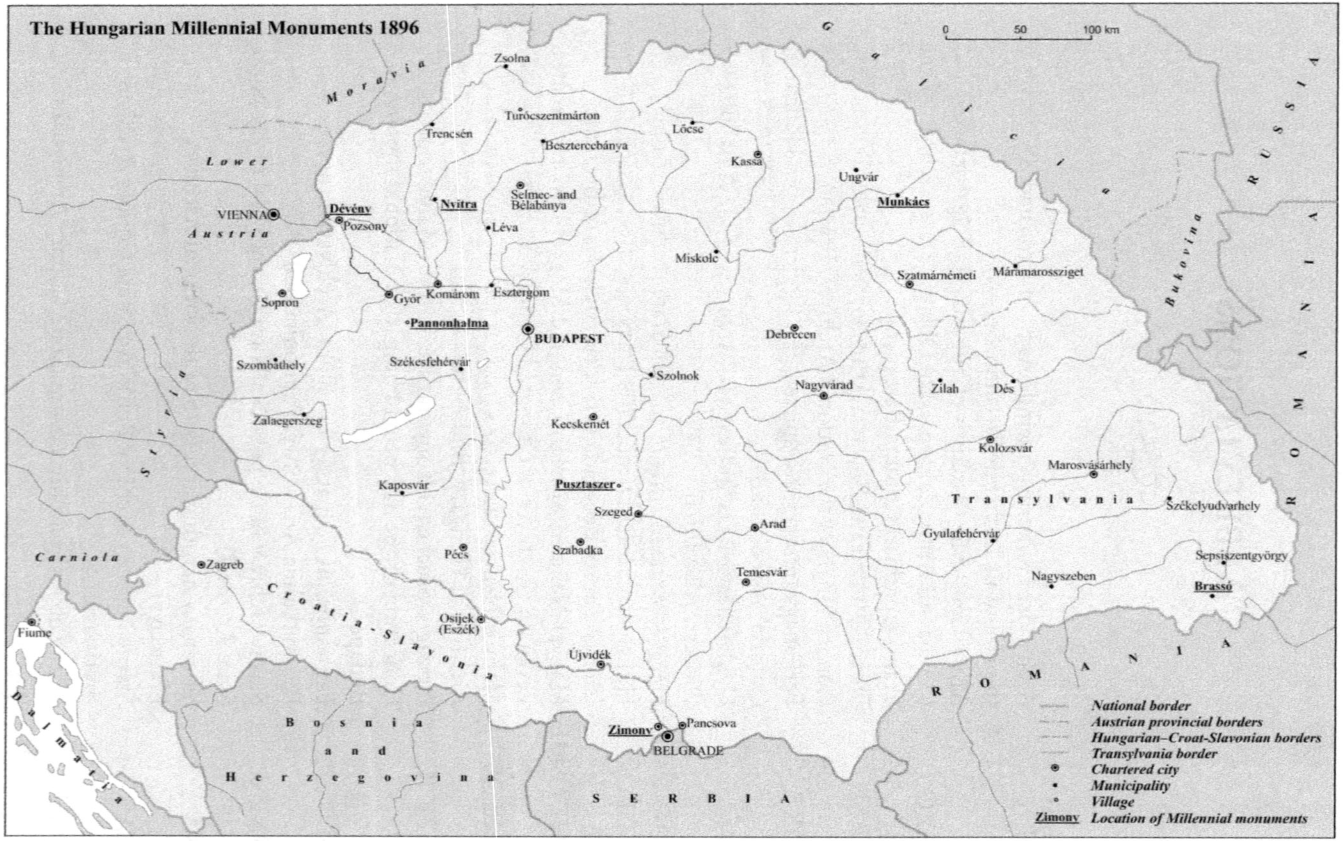

Figure 0.1. The Kingdom of Hungary and the millennial monuments, 1896. Map by László Sebők

INTRODUCTION

❦

Conqueror and Founder of the Homeland—these were the most common epitaphs dedicated to Árpád, the late ninth-century Magyar prince, in fin-de-siècle Hungary. Prince Árpád, who led the Magyar tribes from their genuine homeland somewhere in present-day Ukraine to the Carpathian Basin in the 890s, became one of the most important national heroes in late nineteenth-century Hungary. The figure of Árpád and the story of the conquest (*honfoglalás*) provided convenient material with the potential to be developed into a powerful national myth. The *Gesta Hungarorum*, a chronicle written at the turn of the twelfth century, explained how Árpád's Magyars fought the original population of the Carpathian Basin and conquered their new homeland. A century later, Árpád's successor St. Stephen established the Christian Kingdom of Hungary. The frame of the myth was thus given but the more precise content varied greatly. These variations derived from the fact that little was known for certain about either Árpád or the conquest. The very details of the conquest remained in the shadow of the past; even such basic data as the exact chronology and the very territory of the Magyars could not be established, giving much space to myth inventors.

Most members of the Magyar elite liked to fill this frame with the so-called Hungarian state doctrine (*magyar állameszme*), the official political-historical dogma of dualist Hungary, which promoted a liberal and united nation under ethnic Magyar leadership. In the sense of the Hungarian state doctrine, the military victory of the Magyars over the indigenous peoples was stressed, and the foundation of the Christian monarchy was ascribed solely to the Magyars. This reading of the past was unacceptable for a number of non-Magyar national activists in Hungary. Slovak leaders in the north of the country, Romanians in the east, and Serbs in the south were particularly concerned about the political consequences of the Magyar historical narrative: if Árpád's Magyars alone founded Hungary, there was no place for other peoples except the Magyar. Therefore, they offered alternative readings of the past, stressing their aboriginality, their high cultural standards compared to pagan Magyars, and various historic forms of self-government, which stood in sharp contrast to the unifying and ethnically Magyar agenda of the Hungarian state doctrine. Catholic leaders were also concerned about the cult of Árpád, since a pagan figure was hardly compatible with Christian values.

Nonetheless, the cult of Árpád flourished in the nineteenth century. The *Gesta Hungarorum*, a manuscript hidden for centuries in a library in Vienna, was published in Latin in 1746 and in 1790 in Magyar translation. Its discovery "made Árpád, the leader of that campaign, the central figure of ancestry [and] moved the center of the narrative to the ninth-century foundation of the kingdom."[1] Beginning with the late eighteenth century, historians elaborated the story of the conquest and their authority "guaranteed" its accuracy. During the *Vormärz*, the "Panther-Skinned" Árpád became a central hero in Magyar epic poetry.[2] Árpád also found his way into textbooks and popular chapbooks; the rising standards of education and literacy brought him to the widest possible audience of the age.[3] Still, by the end of the nineteenth century, the myth of Prince Árpád was to be found on paper only: it did not materialize yet.

The Magyar national elite of the country was dissatisfied with both the intangibleness of Árpád and the incomplete "national consciousness" of the Hungarians. To solve these matters, in the year 1896, the Hungarian government organized large-scale celebrations to commemorate the 1000th anniversary of the conquest. The scale of these festivities was grandiose; they certainly reached millions of Hungarian citizens. Before this year, symbolic politics in Hungary was designed and consumed mostly by members of the middle class; now the designers remained the same but the audience became far larger. The message of the millennial festivities was developed in concert with the Hungarian state doctrine.

The uniform message symbolized by Prince Árpád was received, digested, and conceptualized by the diverse Hungarians in a number of ways. This book aims to illustrate how this transpired, through the analysis of seven government-sponsored monuments erected in provincial Hungarian cities during the millennial year.

Two of these monuments were built in northwestern Hungary: one at the castle of Theben (today Devín) near Pressburg (Bratislava), and another on Zobor Hill next to Nitra. Both of these locations belong to Slovakia today; at the end of the nineteenth century they had a mixed Magyar-German-Slovak-Jewish population. The third memorial was at the Munkács castle (today Mukachevo in Ukraine), built in a then Magyar-Rusyn-Jewish environment on the northeastern border of the country. The fourth monument was located on Cenk (Tâmpa) Hill in Brassó (Brașov), today a city in Romania, then a stronghold of Transylvanian Saxons, Romanians, and Magyars facing the Romanian border. The fifth millennial monument was erected at the castle of Semlin (Zemun), a town today part of the Serbian capital, Belgrade, but then bordering on Serbia and inhabited by a Serbian-Croatian-German-Jewish population. Two other memorials were located in the Hungarian "inland," at Pannonhalma Archabbey in western Hungary, and in Pusztaszer, not far from Szeged. Both of them still belong to Hungary; now, like a century ago, they are located in a predominantly Magyar-speaking environment.

The seven locations reflected the enormous heterogeneity of late nineteenth-century Hungary, whose inhabitants spoke a number of vernaculars (Magyar, German, Romanian, Slovak, Rusyn, Serbian, Croatian, Yiddish, etc.), worshiped God according to various denominations (Roman Catholic, Greek Catholic, Orthodox, Calvinist, Lutheran, reformed Jew, Orthodox Jew, etc.), and lived in diverse environments ranging from the booming metropolis of Budapest to remote villages in the Carpathians. They had various concepts of the past and their loyalties went to various communities, based on religion, social status, and a sense of ethnicity. All in all, they were quite different from the ideal Hungarians imagined in the framework of the Hungarian state doctrine.

Decorated with images of Prince Árpád, his Magyar warriors, and their totemic bird, the *turul*, the seven millennial monuments made the already invented but so far only written tradition of Árpád tangible. The monuments were meant to inscribe a Magyar ethnic reading of the past into cityscapes and landscapes and by that to anchor the Hungarian state doctrine in the minds of the population of the Hungarian provinces. The univocal content of the millennial monuments fit into the diverse spaces and minds incidentally. Conflicts between the central government and various local actors, and among the local actors themselves, arose. These conflicts were, of course, not unique to the Hungarian case. Scholars studying commemorative culture agree that "[c]elebrations often exacerbated divisions within societies,"[4] since "[c]ommemorative activity is by definition social and political, for it involves the coordination of individual and group memories, whose result may appear consensual when they are in fact the product of processes of intense contest, struggle, and, in some instances, annihilation."[5]

This was the case for the millennial monuments, too, which indeed provoked conflicts. They were built above the discussed localities and their huge size was meant to dominate the cityscape or the surrounding landscape. Their uniform message was understood and negotiated in various local milieus by different groups in a number of ways. Prince Árpád was built above the cities to rule them, but was genuinely accepted in only a few cases.

Later on, local elites also built monuments to express local values and to locate themselves in the symbolic body of the nation. If national and local identities coincided, the message of local monuments was identical to the state-sponsored ones. If this was not the case, then there were profound differences between the governmental and local monuments. In these cases, monuments built by local actors were more successful than the governmental memorials in representing a past meaningful for urban communities. These differences were dependent on local social factors; thus, the analysis of these is the central issue discussed in this study. Local middle classes were the core targets of the monuments: their voice was the most crucial in the reception of the memorials, they utilized the monuments after their inauguration, and they were in the position to build artifacts to express their identities. They will be also the main subjects of this book.

Being built in a statuomanic age, the monuments provoked passionate responses and these reactions unfold various identities in given moments. Identities are certainly situational: the millennial memorials were events that forged groups around themselves by forcing people to choose sides. National activists wished to see these groups clear-cut and eternal. In fact, they were neither; what one finds are social structures shaping these groups.

The analysis of the reception of these monuments and the mechanism that led to their success or failure is beneficial in many ways. First, on a macro-level, it allows us to shed light on the contrast between the Magyar national integration project supported by a central governmental will and the competing visions of integration offered by the country's other elites. Second, on a micro-level, the millennial festivities identify national, denominational, and political cleavages in provincial towns of late nineteenth-century Hungary in a comparative way. The third and probably most important contribution of this project is the establishment of the link between the macro- and the micro-levels, the government and "high politics" and the local interests. It may broaden our knowledge and understanding of local milieus in Hungary, whose study has been rather neglected in scholarship.

The first part of the book will briefly introduce fin-de-siècle Hungary and the macro-conditions of symbolic politics. It will discuss the millennial idea and its implementation in Budapest and will explain how it was to be extended to provincial Hungary by historian and politician Kálmán Thaly. This part will show Thaly's reasons for choosing the seven locations that are at the heart of this book. Part II will guide us through these five towns and two non-urban locations. Social structures, local milieus and identities, and national integration processes will be introduced here. Each chapter will reflect on the local self-image and the usage of urban space. It will be shown that religious, class, and regional identities shaped fin-de-siècle Hungary far more than previous scholarship, often focusing on ethnic and national belonging, has supposed. Part III will meticulously examine the local millennial experiences. First, the celebrations in the spring of 1896 will show how local actors acted when they had the chance to organize the millennial festivities for themselves. Second, the inauguration of the millennial monuments will be examined. This will show how locals reacted to the highly centralized attempt by the government to distribute a uniform identity to provincial Hungarians. The third chapter in this part will analyze the usage of the millennial monuments in the period up to the Great War, the initiatives to represent local values, and the complex relationship between these.

Notes

1. János M. Bak, "From the Anonymous *Gesta* to the *Flight of Zalán* by Vörösmarty," in *Manufacturing a Past for the Present: Forgery and Authenticity in Medievalist Texts and Objects in Nineteenth-Century Europe*, ed. János M. Bak, Patrick J. Geary and Gábor Klaniczay (Leiden and Boston: Brill, 2015), 98.
2. Ibid., 103–6.
3. László L. Lajtai, *"Magyar nemzet vagyok": Az első magyar nyelvű és hazai tárgyú történelemtankönyvek nemzetdiskurzusa* (Budapest: Argumentum, 2013); Éva Mikos, Árpád pajzsa: A magyar honfoglalás-hagyomány megszerkesztése és népszerűsítése a XVIII–XIX. században (Budapest: MTA Néprajzi Kutatóintézete—PTE Néprajz–Kulturális Antropológia Tanszék—L'Harmattan, 2010).
4. Patrice M. Dabrowski, *Commemorations and the Shaping of Modern Poland* (Bloomington: Indiana University Press, 2004), 6.
5. John R. Gillis, "Memory and Identity: The History of a Relationship," in *Commemorations: The Politics of National Identity*, ed. John R. Gillis (Princeton: Princeton University Press, 1994), 5.

Part I

A MILLENNIUM-OLD PAST

Chapter 1

THE CHALLENGE OF INTEGRATION

Hungary in the Nineteenth Century

By the end of the nineteenth century, the liberal and Magyar nationalist government of Hungary was determined to make a modern Hungary by foster-
ing the national economy and culture and by turning the diverse Hungarians
into loyal Magyars. In the 1890s, Magyar statesmen believed that progress
would almost automatically fulfill their dream of national integration. It seemed
that only a few obstacles stood in the way of their goal, and the government
believed in its ability to master these difficulties.

The political autonomy of the Kingdom of Hungary within the Austro-
Hungarian Monarchy was a key element in this process. Imperial integration
attempts, which reached their climax during the reign of Joseph II (1780–90)
and the neo-absolutist government of the 1850s, had failed by the 1867 Austro-
Hungarian Compromise (*Ausgleich, kiegyezés*). The Compromise gave Hungary
a special status within the Empire, enabling an effective internal integration in
terms of administration, legislation, and economy; only the foreign, military,
and certain financial policies remained imperial. As a result, the decades following the Compromise witnessed not only the internal integration of Hungary, but
also a certain divergence between the two halves of the monarchy.[1]

The administrative and legislative integration of Hungary was a result of
the liberal idea of government, which held that local privileges were feudal and
backward institutions, but believed in the idea of unity. This process started
in 1848 by introducing equality before the law and finished with administrative reforms lasting from the 1860s to 1881. In 1868, Transylvania[2] was united
with Hungary proper, and in 1876 territories with special status, including the
autonomous Saxon Royal Land,[3] were abolished. Finally, in 1881, the Military
Frontier was integrated into civil Hungary and Croatia. All feudal autonomous

territories were replaced by the unitary county system governed by a lord lieutenant (*főispán, Obergespan*) appointed by the central government.[4] The 1868 Croatian-Hungarian Compromise (*nagodba*) reframed and modernized relations between Zagreb and Budapest, and guaranteed limited autonomy to Croatia. The Croatian government, led by the *banus*, had more say in administrative, cultural, educational, and social issues but a limited power in economic matters.[5]

Economic integration of the country was a more difficult task, as the entire Habsburg monarchy formed a single customs union from 1850. Due to the 1867 Austro-Hungarian Compromise, however, the Hungarian government was in a position to influence its economic policies by supporting underdeveloped industries, nationalizing the railway network, and setting laws concerning economic issues in Hungary only. The Hungarian economy can be described partly as a national economy, partly as an integrated member of the Habsburg economic system.[6]

While the administrative-legislative integration of Hungary was completed by the 1880s and economic integration was also on its way, the mental integration of the Hungarians was a more challenging task. The feudal heritage and the significance of religion prevailed well into the liberal period in Hungary, as convincingly demonstrated by Zoltán Tóth.[7] Equality before the law theoretically abolished feudal differences, but did not challenge religious and ethnic-linguistic diversity, as Table 1 demonstrates.

Table 1.1. Mother tongue and religion of the civil population of Hungary (without Croatia-Slavonia and Fiume), 1880–1900.
Source: Magyar statisztikai közlemények 27 (1909): 86–87, 120–121.

	1880		1900	
Total population	**13,728,622**		**16,683,517**	
According to mother tongue				
Magyar	6,397,651	46.6%	8,586,022	51.5%
German	1,866,212	13.6%	1,978,537	11.9%
Slovak	1,858,017	13.5%	1,991,375	11.9%
Romanian	2,411,447	17.6%	2,784,703	16.7%
Rusyn	355,265	2.6%	423,159	2.5%
Croatian	(together with Serbian)		181,754	1.1%
Serbian	628,575	4.6%	434,592	2.6%
Other	211,454	1.5%	303,375	1.8%

According to religion				
Roman Catholic	6,482,595	47.2%	8,100,554	48.6%
Greek Catholic	1,486,598	10.8%	1,830,749	11.0%
Orthodox	1,937,105	14.1%	2,186,859	13.1%
Lutheran	1,107,515	8.1%	1,250,030	7.5%
Calvinist	2,023,257	14.7%	2,409,561	14.4%
Unitarian	55,787	0.4%	67,978	0.4%
Jew	624,737	4.6%	825,055	4.9%
Other	11,028	0.1%	12,731	0.1%

Censuses, of course, not only recorded but also created linguistic categories by establishing clear-cut vernaculars and ignoring multilingualism. Each Hungarian subject had to declare his or her mother tongue; the statistical office then put these answers into larger categories (Saxon, Swabian, and Yiddish, for instance, all fell into the category "German"). Declaring multiple mother tongues was not possible. Inconsistent policies in the case of people living in linguistic contact zones and direct pressure on governmental employees hijacked census results but these manipulations should not be overestimated, as Ágoston Berecz argues in his nuanced investigation.[8]

Out of the two, the question of denominations proved to be the easier task. Being one of the religiously most heterogeneous countries on the European continent and having long traditions of religious tolerance, the denominational divisions remained, but a policy recognizing their equality was introduced. By establishing the equal status of the Catholic, Protestant, and Orthodox Churches and Judaism and by introducing civil marriage in a series of laws in 1867, 1894, and 1895, "all Hungarian citizens could embrace a common public allegiance to the Hungarian state."[9]

This allegiance, however, remained a dream for a long time. Just like its European counterparts, the early modern Hungarian population was characterized by particular and heterogeneous identities based on social and legal status, religion, clan membership, gender, profession, and the narrow geographic environment. Loyalty to the monarch and a certain identification with the Kingdom of Hungary were common; nevertheless, a sense of community with the entire population of the extended territory of the country was absent.[10] Being rooted in feudalism, this pre-national pattern of identity became anachronistic by the late eighteenth and early nineteenth century. A new concept, the so-called *Hungarus* idea emerged, which "extended the nation down the social hierarchy, resulting in a multi-ethnic, socially-inclusive vision of Hungarian nationalism."[11] The

Enlightenment-inspired concept of *Hungarus* identity flourished in the early decades of the nineteenth century.[12]

However, the *Hungarus* concept was unable to meet the demands of the emerging nationalisms, which were heavily influenced by the ideas of Johann Gottfried Herder.[13] For liberal nationalists, a homogeneous culture was increasingly seen as the primary binding material of a society.[14] The various identities of the Hungarians seemed anachronistic and were viewed as obstacles to progress and modernity. The integration of the Hungarian citizens into a community of conscious Magyars sharing the same culture, memory, and vision of the future, and being loyal to the Hungarian state, seemed to be a crucial task. According to nationalist politics, national identity is dominant among other loyalties: nationalists believed that first and foremost, everyone is member of a nation and any affiliation with a social, professional, religious group, a region or city or any other group of belonging may be subordinate only. Nationalists dreamt that everyday decisions, such as choosing schooling or buying products from particular vendors, were made on a national basis. This dream, however, never came true, as national indifference and everyday pragmatism proved to be resilient to nationalist agitation.[15]

The process of national integration was driven by the top level of national activists: well-educated intellectuals, professors, artists, politicians, high-ranking clerics, industrial and financial leaders. They used literature, ethnography, historiography, and some other disciplines to convert both the already existing and the recently invented components into elements of a new identity. These components defined the borders of the nation, regarding people and territory.

The content constructed on the macro-level reached "ordinary people" through institutionalized channels, such as school, church congregations, associations, and even cooperatives. These institutions were dominated by members of a vaguely defined middle class.[16] They were teachers, lawyers, priests, town and village mayors, local businessmen, and journalists. In general, they were more educated and wealthy than those in their immediate environments, they were male, and they had leverage in the local administration, church congregations, and local economy. They did not merely distribute the national agenda that they learned from the macro-level national ideologists. Instead, they reinterpreted and renegotiated it and adapted it to local circumstances. The agenda of nationalism had as many shapes as there were local interest groups in the country. It bore different, sometimes confusing meanings in the various social contexts.

Nation building was a phenomenon most common in nineteenth-century Europe. However, as Joachim von Puttkamer argues, Hungary was a special case in one respect: unlike most Western European states, the pre-national and *Hungarus* identities of the Hungarian population were challenged by numerous national elite groups.[17] The most powerful elite group of the country, protagonists of the Magyar national idea, developed the concept of Magyar national integration. On the one hand, this concept was integrative, since it meant forging a mass society, divided by flexible cleavages that replaced the former stable, hardly trespassable, feudal and confessional social divisions. On the other hand, the concept was exclusive, since the binding material of this new society was a modern Magyar national identity. The dominant Magyar national activists aimed at disseminating a modern national idea among the entire population of Hungary, despite their ethnic understanding of the "Magyar nation." The Magyar national integration was challenged by a number of competitors. The earliest projects were the Serbian and the Romanian nationalisms, which emerged in the late eighteenth century.[18] A Slovak nationalism developed from pan-Slavic and Czecho-Slovak national concepts in the mid nineteenth century.[19] A German nationalism appeared on the eve of the Great War, mostly in southern Hungary.[20] (Transylvanian Saxon identity had some national components but cannot be described as a purely German national phenomenon.[21]) The non-Magyar national elites defined their target along cultural lines only, thus limiting their endeavors to a particular group of Hungarian citizens. Beside the emerging nationalisms, two movements appeared that were theoretically nationally indifferent but in reality were not devoid of nationalism, either. The Catholic Church developed an attractive program of Christian socialism during the 1890s, which was particularly popular with Catholics in northwestern Hungary.[22] Social democracy appeared in the last decades of the nineteenth century mostly in Budapest and spread to other cities and industrial plants.[23]

The Magyar national integration formed an essential part of the policy of all governments in office between 1867 and 1918, yet it underwent a profound change during these decades.[24] The theoretical background of Magyar national integration was the so-called Hungarian state doctrine (*magyar állameszme*). The "state doctrine," as the second word literally means, was derived from a centuries-old legal tradition claiming that the sovereignty and constitutionalism of Hungary were rooted in a series of feudal compromises between the monarch and the estates, symbolized by the Holy Crown of St. Stephen. This tradition served as ammunition for the demand for Hungarian home rule within the Habsburg Empire, and in the eyes of some radical commentators, for complete independence from Vienna.[25] This set of legal concepts was accompanied by growing ideas of exclusive Magyar supremacy over the other ethnic groups of the country, inspired by social Darwinism and relying on historical, ethnographic, and other cultural arguments.[26]

The founding fathers of the dualist system, representatives of the great liberal generation, Ferenc Deák and József Eötvös, believed in a politically united, but culturally and linguistically diverse nation. Their intentions can be seen in the nationality and elementary education laws of 1868. The law of nationalities defined the Hungarian nation as a single body of all the citizens of the country, denying the existence of any nation defined in cultural terms. At the same time, the law of elementary education enabled wide cultural autonomy on a local level, sustained in particular by church congregations.[27]

This cultural tolerance was gradually challenged starting in the 1870s. The Magyar political class learned a crucial lesson in 1848: it had to choose between Vienna or the competing national elites as prospective negotiation partners. In 1867, the liberal Magyar political elite opted for the former, making the toleration of non-Magyar political demands less and less necessary. Deák and Eötvös passed away in the 1870s, leaving the government to a younger generation. Unlike their predecessors, several members of this new generation were convinced that in case of conflict, the national interest was to be given preference over liberal values, so they promoted a solid increase and centralization of state power. They aimed at using this power for Magyar national purposes.[28] In 1878, Béla Grünwald, deputy lord lieutenant of the northern Zvolen County and a prominent member of this new centralist generation, published the pamphlet *The Upper Land: A Political Study*, claiming that Magyar national integration was completely ineffective and proposing aggressive national integrative measures.[29] This pamphlet alarmed Magyar national activists, and from the 1890s the Budapest governments put radically increasing pressure on competing national elites and non-Magyar speakers in the spirit of Grünwald. The aggressive national integration policy culminated during the governments of Dezső Bánffy (1895–99) and Sándor Wekerle (1906–10).[30]

Still, contests among national integration projects did not exclusively rule the political arena in the 1880s and early 1890s. The "standard issue" of Hungarian politics was the relation to Vienna: the governing Liberal Party insisted on the dualist system and was open to minor corrections only, while the Party of Independence, the major liberal oppositional party, strove for a mere personal union between Hungary and Cisleithanian parts of the Empire. The most vividly discussed topic was the increase in size of the Hungarian army at the expense of the imperial (*k. u. k.*) army; this idea was completely rejected by Emperor Francis Joseph and the Austrian politicians. The other issue provoking public interest in the 1880s was the "Jewish question," i.e. emancipation and Jewish integration into the gentile society. This culminated in the infamous Tiszaeszlár blood libel in 1882/83 and the emergence of the Antisemitic Party.[31] A further often-discussed problem was the *Kulturkampf* between the liberal government and the churches, which reached its climax in 1894 and 1895 with the introduction of civil marriage, governmental control over birth certificates, the equality of Christian churches and Jewry, and the right to belong to no religion. These measures poisoned relations between liberal politics and the Catholic Church; the Liberal Party and the Party of Independence formed an alliance against the Catholic People's Party (established in 1895) and launched a bitter fight in the press and Parliament. The liberal policy-makers' fear of political Catholicism overshadowed even that of the non-Magyar national parties.

The increasing Magyar national integrative attempts also radicalized the non-Magyar national elites to such an extent that a reconciliation of the different national goals became impossible after the 1870s. Still, the "nationality question" became a central political issue as late as in the second half of the 1890s. Reflecting on the increasing national tensions, Prime Minister Baron Dezső Bánffy was the first to explicitly address the "nationality question" in detail when delivering his program speech in January 1895. Bánffy, who proudly called himself a chauvinist,[32] set up a special department to analyze the "nationality question" and ordered the lord lieutenants to keep an eye on the local non-Magyar national activists and to report on their activity frequently. Being a former lord lieutenant in the remote and underdeveloped northern Transylvanian counties of Solnoc-Dăbâca and Bistriţa-Năsăud, Bánffy regularly employed cheap practices to control his subordinates and he followed the same measures as prime minister. He was strongly convinced that the "nationality question" was solely the outcome of some Russia- and Romania-backed troublemakers and that the problem could be solved by isolating them, meaning, in practice, persecuting them.[33]

It is not by accident that the Hungarian government increased pressure on the non-Magyar national integration processes during the 1890s. The very person of Bánffy was certainly of high importance but the same significance should be ascribed to the changing relationship between society and government that took place in the last decades of the nineteenth century. The concept of the night-watchman state, dominant in Hungarian liberalism in the mid nineteenth century, was increasingly overshadowed by an ideal of a government more active in social questions. Until 1894, major events of private life, such as birth and marriage, were regulated by the churches. In that year the government curtailed these rights and took over the control over birth certificates and registration of marriages and granted everyone the right to divorce. From 1897 onward, the government launched a large-scale economic and social transformation project in northeast Hungary, followed by another one in Transylvania (1902) and later projects in some other regions. Taking over tasks which had been responsibilities of businessmen, governmental agencies now re-shaped the structure of local properties and banks and promoted modern technologies and organizational forms, such as cooperatives, in order to create a healthier peasantry. Bánffy's active policies against the non-Magyar national elites thus fit well into a concept of a government expanding its responsibilities.

While the governmental policy radicalized and extended, the political representatives of the non-Magyar national movements sought various strategies to construct their alternative national communities. Until the turn of the nineteenth century, they mostly withdrew from parliamentary politics, viewing the Hungarian Parliament as a hostile, even illegitimate institution. With the exception of the Saxon People's Party, non-Magyar national parties had boycotted elections since the 1870s. However, even when non-Magyar national candidates ran for parliamentary mandates, they had to face governmental manipulation and gerrymandering. Thus, most non-Magyar elites were deprived of the most important tool in articulating their interests in the political arena.[34]

Due to the lack of political success, the first half of the 1890s witnessed an increasing crisis in the policy of passivity of the non-Magyar national parties. The last attempt by these parties to achieve a breakthrough without modifying their passive program was that of closer cooperation. In 1895, the Slovak, Romanian, and Serbian national parties organized the so-called Conference of Nationalities, but the outcome of this meeting was a mere manifesto repeating the parties' already known demands.[35] By the end of the century, they had to realize that the long boycott of parliamentary elections did not bring results but rather hindered their goals. The passivity of the non-Magyar national parties and the demands of territorial autonomy did not bring fruitful results but rather led to isolation and decay. The non-Magyar national activists also had to accept that, contrary to their hopes, the dualist system had undergone a successful stabilization process in the two decades following the Compromise. The Hungarian government was able to prevent a trialistic restructuring of the Habsburg Empire, settled the Croatian demands, and integrated Transylvania and all the formerly privileged territories. Three decades after the Compromise, demands to modify the very basis of the dualist system seemed anachronistic and unrealistic. Still, it took one more decade for all the non-Magyar national parties to accept the results of the Compromise and decide on a political program within the framework of the Kingdom of Hungary.

The mid 1890s were an unfavorable period for all non-Magyar national integration projects in the European context too. The stability of the Habsburg Empire was seen, particularly by Great Britain and Germany, as a cornerstone of the balance of power on the continent. Following the failure of Eduard Taaffe as prime minister of the Cisleithanian part of the monarchy (1893) and the ongoing crisis of Austrian politics marked by short-lived governments, the Hungarian half of the dual monarchy was even seen as the more stable and developing part of the Habsburg Empire. The European public still had a definite sympathy for the Magyars, resulting from the 1848 revolution and the image of the "gentle, constitutional" Magyar gentry.[36] This positive picture was challenged, and then completely changed, mainly by the "nationality question."[37] In 1896, the Slovak, Romanian, and Serbian national parties tried to draw the attention of the European public to their sufferings, hidden under the shine of the millennial festivities,[38] but the negative image of Hungary and the Magyar political elite did not become dominant until the 1900s. Only the 1907 Černova massacre[39] and some strikingly manipulated elections turned the former prestigious image of Magyars as a nation of gentlemen into a picture of violent, antidemocratic and elitist oppressors, mostly due to the works of influential publicists such as Wickham Steed, the Viennese correspondent of *The Times*, and the London-based historian and regional expert Robert William Seton-Watson.[40]

Beyond the lack of the largely moral support of the European public, a more painful shortcoming of the non-Magyar national endeavors was the absence of direct external supporters. The majority of Czech national activists were rather ignorant of Slovak issues until 1907.[41] Ukrainian or Russian support was even more fragile. Even the Hungarian Romanian national activists had to temporarily give up their hopes for help from the Bucharest government in the 1890s. The Conservative Party, governing Romania between 1891 and 1895, sought a strong alliance with Austria-Hungary, even at the cost of withdrawing support for the Romanian speakers of Hungary. Its major rival, the Liberal Party, accused the Conservatives of betraying Romanian national interests and promised a more active policy to support the Hungarian Romanians. However, when the liberal Dmitrie Sturdza was appointed prime minister in October 1895, he immediately suspended the financial support of Hungarian Romanians and declared their issue the exclusive domain of Austria-Hungary.[42] The Serbian government also had to limit its support of the Hungarian Serbians, as the kings of the Obrenović dynasty followed a pro-Habsburg foreign policy until their removal in 1903.[43]

The Catholic People's Party, enjoying considerable support from the largest non-governmental institution of the country, the Catholic Church, found itself in a defensive position too, attacked by the dominant liberals. Hungarian social democracy also had to cope with serious challenges. A restricted voting franchise, laws promoting the interests of the upper classes, and penalizing socialist agitation, all prevented large-scale political activity by the Hungarian Social Democratic Party (established in 1890).

The stability of the Hungarian government, the weakness and internal controversies of the non-Magyar national elites, the Catholic Church and social democracy movement, and the favorable international conditions thus resulted in beneficial circumstances for the implementation of the Magyar national goals—at least on a symbolic level.

Notes

1. Peter Haslinger, *Hundert Jahre Nachbarschaft: Die Beziehungen zwischen Österreich und Ungarn 1895–1994* (Frankfurt am Main: Peter Lang, 1996), 1–15.

2. Judit Pál, *Unió vagy "unificáltatás"? Erdély uniója* és *a királyi biztos működése (1867–1872)* (Kolozsvár: Erdélyi Múzeum Egyesület, 2010).

3. Carl Göllner, "Die Auflösung der Sächsischen Nationsuniversität (1876): Vorgeschichte und Folgen," in *Gruppenautonomie in Siebenbürgen: 500 Jahre siebenbürgisch-sächsische Nationsuniversität*, ed. Wolfgang Kessler (Cologne: Böhlau, 1990), 355–66.

4. András Cieger, "A közigazgatás autonómiájának nézőpontjai 1848–1918," in *Autonómiák Magyarországon 1848–2000*, ed. Jenő Gergely (Budapest: ELTE Történettudományi Doktori Iskola—L'Harmattan, 2005), 1: 25–62.

5. Fernando Veliz, *The Politics of Croatia-Slavonia 1903–1918: Nationalism, State Allegiance and the Changing International Order* (Wiesbaden: Harrasowitz, 2012), 92.

6. John Komlos, *The Habsburg Monarchy as a Customs Union: Economic Development in Austria-Hungary in the Nineteenth Century* (Princeton: Princeton University Press, 1983).

7. Zoltán Tóth, "A rendi norma és a "keresztény polgárosodás": Társadalomtörténeti esszé," *Századvég* no. 2–3 (1991): 75–130.

8. Ágoston Berecz, *The Politics of Early Language Teaching: Hungarian in the Primary Schools of the Late Dual Monarchy* (Budapest: Pasts, Inc., Central European University, 2013), 23–30.

9. Paul A. Hanebrink, *In Defense of Christian Hungary: Religion, Nationalism, and Antisemitism, 1890–1944* (Ithaca: Cornell University Press, 2006), 12.

10. On the European context, see Anthony D. Smith, *National Identity* (London: Penguin Books, 1991), 1–8.

11. Alexander Maxwell, "Multiple Nationalism: National Concepts in Nineteenth-Century Hungary and Benedict Anderson's 'Imagined Communities'," *Nationalism and Ethnic Politics* 11 (2005): 387.

12. Moritz Csáky, "'Hungarus' oder 'Magyar': Zwei Varianten des Nationalbewusstseins zu Beginn des 19. Jahrhunderts," *Annales Universitatis Scientiarium Budapestinensis: Sectio Historica* 22 (1982): 71–84.

13. Holm Sundhausen, *Der Einfluss der Herderschen Ideen auf die Nationsbildung bei der Völkern den Habsburgermonarchie* (Munich: Oldenbourg, 1973).

14. On the development of Hungarian national liberalism see: János Gyurgyák, *Ezzé lett magyar hazátok…: A magyar nemzeteszme és nacionalizmus története* (Budapest: Osiris, 2007), 21–133.

15. Tara Zahra, "Imagined Noncommunities: National Indifference as a Category of Analysis," *Slavic Review* 69, no. 1 (2010): 93–119.

16. György Kövér, "A magyar középosztály-teremtés programjai és kudarcai: Fogalomtörténeti áttekintés a reformkor végétől a nagy válság kezdetéig," in *Zsombékok: Középosztályok és iskoláztatás Magyarországon a 19. század elejétől a 20. század közepéig*, ed. György Kövér (Budapest: Századvég, 2006), 77–160.

17. Joachim von Puttkamer, "Kein europäischer Sonderfall: Ungarns Nationalitätenproblem im 19. Jahrhundert und die jüngere Nationalismusforschung," in *Das Ungarnbild der deutschen Historiographie*, ed. Márta Fata (Stuttgart: Franz Steiner, 2004), 84–98.

18. Emanual Turczynski, *Konfession und Nation: Zur Frühgeschichte der serbischen und rumänischen Nationsbildung* (Düsseldorf: Pädagogischer Verlag Schwann, 1976).

19. Alexander Maxwell, *Choosing Slovakia: Slavic Hungary, the Czechoslovak Language and Accidental Nationalism* (London: Tauris Academic Series, 2009).

20. Gerhard Seewann, *Geschichte der Deutschen in Ungarn* (Marburg: Herder Institut, 2012), 2: 122–40.

21. Gerhard Seewann, "Siebenbürger Sachse, Ungarndeutscher, Donauschwabe? Überlegungen zur Identitätsproblematik des Deutschtums in Südosteuropa," in *Minderheitenfragen in Südosteuropa: Beiträge der internationalen Konferenz: The Minority Question in Historical*

Perspective 1900–1990. Inter University Center, Dubrovnik, 8–14 April 1991, ed. Gerhard Seewann (Munich: Oldenbourg Verlag, 1992), 139–55.

22. Dániel Szabó, "A Néppárt 1895–1914" (PhD diss., Magyar Tudományos Akadémia, Budapest, 1983).

23. Lajos Varga, ed., *A magyar szociáldemokrácia kézikönyve* (Budapest: Napvilág Kiadó, 1999), 29–39.

24. A non-national program was offered by only two parties, the ultra-conservative Catholic People's Party (which, however, relied on the most advanced political repertoire, such as mass media) and the HSDP. The former was part of the government between 1906 and 1910, but even then was outnumbered by its liberal allies, while the latter never managed to win any electoral seat, thus its influence was limited.

25. János M. Bak and Anna Gara-Bak, "The Ideology of a 'Millennial Constitution' in Hungary," *East European Quarterly* 15, no. 3 (1981): 307–26; László Péter, "The Holy Crown of Hungary, Visible and Invisible," *Slavonic and East European Review* 81, no. 3 (July 2003): 421–510.

26. Monika Baár, *Historians and Nationalism: East-Central Europe in the Nineteenth Century* (Oxford: Oxford University Press, 2010), 242–48; Oscar Jászi, *The Dissolution of the Habsburg Monarchy* (Chicago: University of Chicago Press, 1929), 317–27; Marius Turda, *The Idea of National Superiority in Central Europe, 1880–1918* (Lewiston: Edwin Mellon Press, 2004), 67–142. The Hungarian state doctrine inspired contemporaries to dream of Hungarian imperialism in the Balkans, too. See Iván Bertényi Jr, "A 'magyar birodalmi gondolatról'—az I. világháború előtt," *Kommentár*, no. 4 (2007): 40–56.

27. Ludwig von Gogolák, "Ungarns Nationalitätengesetze und das Problem des magyarischen National- und Zentralstaates," in *Die Völker des Reiches*, vol. 3 of *Die Habsburgermonarchie 1848–1918*, ed. Adam Wandruszka and Peter Urbanitsch (Vienna: Verlag der Österreichischen Akademie der Wissenschaften, 1980), 1270–88.

28. András Cieger, "A hatalomra jutott liberalizmus és az állam a dualizmus első felének magyar politikai gondolkodásában," *Századvég*, no. 20 (2001): 95–118.

29. Béla Grünwald, *A Felvidék: Politikai tanulmány* (Budapest: Ráth Mór, 1878).

30. von Gogolák, "Ungarns Nationalitätengesätze," 1288–99.

31. Andrew Handler, *An Early Blueprint for Zionism: Győző Istóczy's Political Anti-Semitism* (Boulder, CO: East European Monographs, 1989); Nathaniel Katzburg, *Antisemitism in Hungary, 1867–1914* (Tel-Aviv: Dvir, 1969); György Kövér, *A tiszaeszlári dráma: Társadalomtörténeti látószögek* (Budapest: Osiris, 2011).

32. Iván Bertényi Jr., "A nevetségesség öl? Adalékok a magyarországi sovinizmusfogalom századfordulós értelmezéséhez," in *Magyar-szlovák terminológiai kérdések*, ed. Barna Ábrahám (Piliscsaba: Pázmány Péter Katolikus Egyetem Bölcsészettudományi Kar Szlavisztika Közép-Európa Intézet Szent Adalbert Közép-Európa Kutatócsoport, 2008), 118–36.

33. Iván Bertényi Jr., "Bánffy Dezső és a nemzetiségi kérdés" (PhD diss., Eötvös Loránd Tudományegyetem, Budapest, 2005).

34. András Gerő, *The Hungarian Parliament, 1867–1918: A Mirage of Power* (Boulder, CO: Social Science Monographs, 1997).

35. Lucian Boia, *Relationships between Romanians, Czechs and Slovaks 1848–1914* (Bucharest: Edituria Academiei Republicii Socialiste România, 1977), 126–29; Keith Hitchins, "The Romanians of Transylvania and the Congress of Nationalities," *The Slavonic and East European Review* 48, no. 112 (July 1970): 388–402; Milan Krajčovič, *Slovenská politika v Strednej Európe 1890–1901: Spolupráca Slovákov, Rumunov a Srbov* (Bratislava: Vydavateľstvo Slovenskej Akadémie Vied, 1971).

36. The most emblematic piece is John Paget, *Hungary and Transylvania; with Remarks on their Condition, Social, Political and Economical* (London: John Murray, 1839). For the fin-de-siècle period, see Géza Jeszenszky, *Az elveszett presztízs: Magyarország megítélésének változása Nagy-Britanniában (1894–1918)* (Budapest: Magvető, 1986).

37. The first issue to pique the interest of the Western European public was the Memorandum Trial in 1894, during which Romanian national protagonists were sentenced to prison for issuing a manifesto of their most important demands in 1892. Keith Hitchins, "Austria-Hungary, Rumania, and the Nationality Problem in Transylvania, 1894–1897," *Rumanian Studies* 4 (1979): 75.

38. *La question des trois nationalités en Hongrie* (Paris: Édition du Comité des Trois Nationalités, 1896); Peter Haslinger, "Das Ungarnbild der Wiener Presse am Vorabend des Millenniums: Der Nationalitätenkongress 1895 und die kroatische Frage," in *Nationalitäten und Identitäten in Ostmitteleuropa: Festschrift aus Anlaß des 70. Geburtstages von Richard Georg Plaschka*, ed. Walter Lukan and Arnold Suppan (Vienna: Böhlau Verlag, 1995), 133–46.

39. The Hungarian police shot some Slovak-speaking demonstrators in the village of Černova (today on the outskirts of Ružomberok in central Slovakia), who protested against the consecration of their church in the absence of their imprisoned priest, the later influential politician Andrej Hlinka. See József Demmel, *"Egész Szlovákia elfért egy tutajon…:" Tanulmányok a 19. századi Magyarország szlovák történelméről* (Pozsony: Kalligram, 2009), 187–210; Roman Holec, *Tragédia v Černovej a slovenské spoločnosť* (Martin: Matica slovenská, 1997).

40. Scotus Viator [Robert William Seton-Watson], *Racial Problems in Hungary* (London: Archibald Constable, 1908); R. W. Seton-Watson, *Corruption and Reform in Hungary: A Study of Electoral Practice* (London: Constable, 1911); Jeszenszky, *Az elveszett presztízs*, 211–33.

41. Peter Haslinger, *Nation und Territorium im tschechischen politischen Diskurs 1880–1938* (Munich: Oldenbourg, 2010), 100–106; Marie L. Neudorfl, "Slovakia in the Czech Press at the Turn of the Nineteenth and Twentieth Centuries," in *The Czech and Slovak Experience: Selected Papers from the Fourth World Congress for Soviet and East European Studies, Harrogate, 1990*, ed. John Morrison (New York: St. Martin's Press, 1992), 38–61.

42. Hitchins, "Austria–Hungary, Rumania, and the Nationality Problem," 81–83.

43. Branislav Vranešević, "Die aussenpolitische Beziehungen zwischen Serbien und der Habsburgermonarchie," in *Die Habsburgermonarchie im System der internationalen Beziehungen*, vol. 6 of *Die Habsburgermonarchie 1848–1918*, ed. Adam Wandruszka and Peter Urbanitsch (Vienna: Verlag der Österreichischen Akademie der Wissenschaften, 1989), 358–63.

Chapter 2

ANCHORING A MILLENNIUM-OLD PAST IN THE HUNGARIAN MINDS

∽⟨⟨⟩⟩∼

Inventing Pasts, Building Monuments: The Making of National Cultures in Nineteenth-Century Europe

The nineteenth century was the age of "backward-looking prophets" (*rückwärts gekehrter Propheten*, an aphorism coined by Friedrich Schlegel). Romantic intellectuals ventured into writing new national and democratic histories, whose subject was the national community.[1] These writings became the cornerstone of nationalist politics, as, in the words of Stefan Berger, they were able "to mobilize people by giving them an identity and orientation."[2] By the end of the nineteenth century, the appeal of romanticism had already vanished and was replaced by a more critical sense of historical scholarship, marked by the Rankean method of *Quellenkritik*. However, the methodological innovation did not challenge the very subject of history writing: the nation remained at the center of historical inquiries. The culture of the nineteenth century was profoundly shaped by the past. As Donald J. Olsen argues:

> A sense of history gave the nineteenth century the organizing principle—a way of relating discrete facts, ideas, and images one to another—that Christian Aristotelianism had given the High Middle Ages, a vision of classical antiquity had given the Renaissance, and Euclidean geometry the seventeenth century. … History for the nineteenth century was no mere field of research, still less a way of escaping from the present, but a pervasive mode of thinking, a world view, a means of coping with and mastering the multitudinous facts, images, and ideas with which the contemporary consciousness was being bombarded.[3]

This sense of the past was shared not only by politicians and members of the middle class but it even spread beyond. All in all, the past was endowed with a power unknown in former ages and the belief in this power was shared by politicians, members of the educated middle class, and beyond.[4]

National historians particularly searched for the origins of their communities and the medieval histories. These endeavors were, however, limited by the available pasts. "Greek and Italian historians eagerly plundered the legacy of ancient civilizations,"[5] whereas Northern European historians traced their histories back to "barbaric" ages, using the Tacitean topos of the noble savage to attribute enough appeal to barbarians to make them worthy forefathers of the nation.[6] Ancient histories were brought alive by being personalized: the nineteenth century was also the age of the hero cult, in particular due to Thomas Carlyle's well-read essay *On Heroes*.[7] From Portugal to Russia, ancient and medieval heroes populated the national pantheon. Prince Árpád found himself in distinguished society: among his fellow forefathers were the once Gallic, now French Vercingetorix, the Germanic-German Hermann, the Moravian-Slovak Svatopluk, and many others.

The past not only had to be conquered for the nation on the pages of the new history books, but it also had to be represented to the masses. As Peter Burke states:

> The main use of non-academic representations of the past in this period was to assist what the late George Mosse described as the "nationalization of the masses" … to encourage national sentiments and national loyalties among as high proportion as possible including the working classes as well as the middle classes, peasants as well as townspeople and women, children as well as adult males and the inhabitants of national peripheries, often speaking a language of their own.[8]

Among the means of these non-academic representations was the monument, a beloved artifact of the nineteenth century.[9] The nineteenth century was the age of statuomania: throughout Europe, monarchs, national governments, local authorities, and grassroots organizations raced to inscribe their heroes into landscapes and cityscapes. Monuments dedicated to national and local heroes became a standard feature of both urban and rural spaces.[10]

The most obvious function of these monuments was thus to "anchor the national myths and symbols in the consciousness of the people."[11] The reason behind monuments was simple: discourse alone was not enough to achieve this anchoring, so the nation had to be shown to the people; "not imagination alone, but substantiality and materiality characterized such efforts."[12] As monuments, in particular those built in urban environments, were encountered by a large number of people, national activists ascribed them an important role.

Germany, whose cultural practices had been traditionally appealing in Hungary, was a prominent example of the statuomania of the nineteenth century. As early as the late eighteenth century, monuments to significant representatives of German culture were built, such as memorials to Gottfried

Leibniz in Hannover and to Gotthold Ephraim Lessing in Wolfenbüttel. They were followed by hundreds of similar structures during the next century: during the *Vormärz*, monuments were erected in honor of, among others, Martin Luther in Wittenberg, Johannes Gutenberg in Mainz, Friedrich Schiller in Stuttgart, Albrecht Dürer in Nuremberg, Johann Sebastian Bach in Leipzig, Johann Wolfgang Goethe in Frankfurt am Main, and Ludwig van Beethoven in Bonn. These monuments celebrated pioneers of German culture who at the same time were relevant for local communities too: all the above-listed figures were either citizens of or had strong ties to the towns hosting the monuments. These memorials could express local pride and local contributions to the German culture, thus they were initiated and financed by the local bourgeoisie rather than monarchs. They were built in the heart of urban environments, typically in busy downtown squares.[13]

The wave of monuments celebrating German cultural achievements did not shrink during the second half of the century. The novelty of this period was the emergence of monuments representing a more direct political message. The creation of the German Reich inspired a number of public monuments celebrating the unification of Germany and its central figures, Emperor William I and the Iron Chancellor, Otto von Bismarck. As a result, by the end of the nineteenth century, German townscapes were flooded by public monuments.[14]

At the same time, the German landscape also became a target of the statuomania. The first remarkable structure was the Walhalla, a Germanic hall of fame erected above the Danube near Regensburg by Bavarian king Ludwig I in 1842. After 1871, gigantic structures occupying hilltops were built to celebrate German unity. The Hermannsdenkmal near Detmold honored the victory of Germanic tribes over the Romans (1875) and the Niederwalddenkmal at Rüdesheim am Rhein was dedicated directly to the unification of Germany (1883). In the year of the Hungarian millennium, two hilltop memorials were inaugurated to celebrate the emperor: the Barbarossa Monument at the Kyffhäuser range in Thuringia and the Emperor William Monument above the Weser gorge of Porta Westfalica. Among the Bismarck monuments one could find both urban structures and towers built in the countryside.[15]

Beside the monument-boom, nineteenth-century cities witnessed a radical, twofold change. First, cities were laboratories of modernity. Municipalities had to provide their booming population with new and more hygienic housing, organize new methods of urban transport and had to take over an increasing number of tasks, such as social care and schooling, from the churches.[16] At the same time, cities were subjects to historicization, too. Using the apt words of Donald J. Olsen, nineteenth-century cities became themselves historical monuments, represented best by the architectural language of the age.[17]

The emergence of monuments inspired new rituals, through which these monuments and, in a broader sense, the public space were used. Festive culture changed radically after 1815 in Western Europe, first of all in terms of deepening politicization. Dominated by middle class males, the new festive culture of the century displayed liberal and national values, often within the framework of local or urban pride. The first national festival in the German lands was held in 1814, commemorating the first anniversary of the Battle of Leipzig. This was followed during the *Vormärz* by individual (i.e. non-sequential) festivities, such as the Wartburg festival in 1817, commemorating the Reformation, and the 1832 Harmbach festival, a gathering having a democratic and national agenda. During the 1848 revolution, festivities promoting a united and democratic Germany were held in various cities throughout the German Confederation.[18] The institutionalization of national festive culture gathered momentum in November 1859. For the first time in German history, festivities approximately on the same day commemorated the same person: Friedrich Schiller and the hundredth anniversary of his birth. Schiller festivals were organized in each major German-speaking city, from Hamburg to Vienna, and they attracted a large audience, making the impression of a united German cultural space ranging from the Alps to the North Sea.[19] By the end of the nineteenth century, rituals became standard practices of national integration both in Germany and in Austria.[20] Yet, the initiators and the core audience of national festivities remained limited to mostly urban, middle class males.

Similarly to the reconfiguration of urban space, the nationalist rituals were partly based upon already existing mass events (such as carnivals, Catholic processions, torchlight processions) and were in some cases entirely new inventions which nonetheless pretended to be authentic and ancient. The historical procession, a popular genre of the day, is an apt example. Processions had been held to celebrate military victories in ancient Rome and to cheer royal marriages or funerals in Renaissance and Baroque Europe. The historical procession of the late nineteenth century added a new element by evoking glorious times of the nation. The best known procession in the Habsburg Monarchy took place in 1879. Celebrating the twenty-fifth wedding anniversary of Francis Joseph and Empress Elisabeth, painter Hans Makart designed the most spectacular event which featured eight thousand participants in medieval costumes and was seen by roughly half a million people.[21]

Contemporaries were aware that these practices were not just simply copied from older times but serious inventiveness was needed. Hungarian art historian and archeologist Flóris Rómer, for instance, delivered a lengthy lecture at the 1885 convention of the Hungarian Historical Association in which he discussed earlier manifestations of Hungarian festive culture and argued for their incorporation into present practices of national integration: "We want to make the people willingly identify themselves as Magyars and to think of national history on these occasions [festivities] with reminiscence of the good old ways."[22] Rómer complained about the lack of national festivals in Hungary which he compared to "foreign lands" by which he certainly meant Austria and Germany. Although his death in 1889 prevented him from seeing a major change, his contemporaries witnessed his wish granted in just a decade.

The Millennial Idea

The Europe-wide transformation of commemorative culture became tangible in Hungary with a delay of a few decades. From the mid nineteenth century, national activists consciously filled former religious cults, first of all the Catholic cult of St. Stephen, with national content.

Hungarian Catholics had celebrated 20 August, the day of St. Stephen, since the Middle Ages. In 1771, Queen Maria Theresa (1740–80) ordered a festive mass in each Catholic church in the country, and since 1818, all public authorities had participated in the spectacular procession in Buda. The procession became a popular event with the citizens of Buda and Pest. During the *Vormärz*, the national content started to overshadow the religious, slowly turning St. Stephen into a national hero, disregarding confessional boundaries.[23]

At the same time, genuine political and national commemorations appeared, too. From the mid nineteenth century, occasional feasts were held venerating contemporary cultural stars, such as Franz Liszt, and the leading figures of contemporary Magyar nationalism. Students were often responsible for organizing these events. Commemorative feasts were also held, remembering anniversaries of important figures. For instance, in 1860 the death of István Széchenyi was commemorated throughout the country. An annual national holiday honoring a purely political event was introduced as late as 1898, when the commemoration of the 1848 revolution was sanctioned by law. The very day of the revolution, 15 March, could not be commemorated, to avoid an open conflict with Francis Joseph. Instead, 11 April, the day of the April Laws, the liberal foundation of the constitutional monarchy, became a national holiday.[24]

The conquest did not fit into this framework smoothly. The Magyars originated from Asia and wandered through Eastern Europe, both of which territories were regarded as backward and barbaric in the nineteenth century. During the conquest, Árpád's pagan and nomadic Magyars fought the Christian Moravians and Bavarians, who were already settled. The conquest was followed by a series of military campaigns against the organized states of Christian Europe (mostly Germany and northern Italy) for five more decades. Since in the eyes of late nineteenth-century intellectuals, the state meant the framework for progress and, despite the gradual process of secularization, morals were understood mostly in Christian terms, the interpretation of the ancient Magyars, still living in a tribal organization, proved to be a rather difficult task for the creators of modern national history.[25]

The pagan Magyars were obviously not venerated in any form by any church and the dim story of Árpád was intangible compared to the figures of the *Vormärz*. However, as early as the 1830s, ideas emerged about commemorating the Magyar conquest's 1000th anniversary,[26] and, as time went on, demand for celebrations grew steadily. By the 1880s it became clear that the millennium of the conquest could not be overlooked.[27] In 1882 Sándor Hegedűs, a liberal MP and future minister of trade, brought the attention of the government to the forthcoming anniversary.[28] Benedek Göndöcs, a Catholic priest and liberal MP, even brought forth a large-scale plan. He suggested that the government should have built a pantheon of Hungarian heroes on a spectacular hill in Budapest and a monument to the Hungarian constitution in Pusztaszer.[29] However, the exact details, such as the date, the content, and the form of the millennial festivities, were not yet defined.

The millennial idea was challenged by two ambiguities. First, the exact date of the conquest was unknown, therefore a clear date for the celebrations could not be established. To solve this problem, after the interpellation of Hegedűs, the government requested the expert opinion of the Hungarian Academy of Sciences. A committee of distinguished medievalists (Gyula Pauler, Ferenc Salamon, Károly Szabó) was set up to determine the year of the conquest. Despite a detailed source analysis, the committee's report was only able to establish a broad period between 888 and 900 as the start and end years of the conquest.[30] In 1884, the Academy proposed 1894 as the festive year, claiming that a decade should be enough for the preparations.[31] In the following years, however, the interest in the cause dropped. In 1889 Bereg County petitioned the prime minister and demanded that the government decided the festive year and started the preparations. This petition was joined by more than fifty other counties and cities.[32] In 1890 Kálmán Thaly, a historian and representative of the Party of Independence, also addressed the prime minister regarding the same issue.[33] By the early 1890s it became clear that the commemoration of the millennium was an important issue for the Hungarian political class both in Budapest and in the provinces, therefore it was decided that the festivities should be organized by the government. This meant that the government had to engage in festive culture—a field which had been previously the domain of associations and municipalities. Satisfying the public demand, in 1892 the Parliament decided to hold the millennial festivities in 1895 and initiated a national exhibition to present the economic and cultural development of the country as the main forum of commemoration.[34] For purely practical reasons (the lack of time for preparations, and other large-scale exhibitions planned for the same year in other European cities), the festive year was postponed to 1896.[35]

The other striking challenge was the exact content of the millennial celebrations. Before the millennial year, the first Christian monarch of Hungary,

St. Stephen, was regarded as the founder of the state. In a historical narrative that was rooted in medieval historiography, St. Stephen was considered the representative of universal and pro-Western values, with Hungary's multiethnicity playing a relevant role. This reading was canonized by mostly Western Hungarian, Catholic, pro-Habsburg intellectuals. In contrast, Prince Árpád represented the ethnic Magyar nation that was born in the East and always strove for independence, a topos often used by Calvinist, mostly Transylvanian or Eastern Hungarian, intellectuals.[36] To make things even more complicated, Attila the Hun was also often regarded as the first Magyar ruler and the predecessor of Árpád's Magyars, reinforcing the Magyars' Eastern origin and their 'legitimate' rule over Hungary. Even though official historiography in the late nineteenth century refuted the link between the Huns and the Magyars, based on works by some earlier authors the Huns were regarded by the public as potential relatives, even forefathers of the Magyars, forming a fundamental myth of origin.[37]

The pagan Attila the Hun, and Árpád and his military victory over the indigenous population were well known in historiography and in subsequent popular publications, but were never celebrated in an organized way. The millennial festivities were the first to commemorate *per definitionem* Árpád and the conquest. Plenty of practical arguments were made in favor of choosing Árpád over St. Stephen: the very number of one thousand years was appealing and elegant; Árpád represented the beginning of Magyar history in the current territory of Hungary; and his figure could unite Catholic and Protestant Magyars. Even though the celebration of the pagan Árpád led to some discrepancies with the established view of St. Stephen, this distinction was successfully absorbed into a single national narrative, disregarding the contradictory details. In this narrative, Árpád and his Magyars were regarded as proto-Christians of high morality, therefore the conquest was seen as a necessary step toward the formation of a Hungarian state and the subsequent Christianization of the country. The ambiguous allegories of the millennial festivities illustrate the overlaps well; the pagan Árpád was occasionally shown in the company of Protestant "freedom fighters" such as István Bocskay, Gabriel Bethlen, and Lajos Kossuth, but was also sometimes represented together with St. Stephen and Francis Joseph (who was occasionally called the second Árpád).[38]

Since celebrations of Árpád had never been held before the millennial year, the government could design the content of the millennial festivities freely. As András Gerő states, "the Millennial celebration was not just an occasion of revelry: it was an historic opportunity for the Hungarian government to construct an integrated national and historical ideology depicting the *de facto* imperfect state as *de jure* a whole."[39]

Turning the Idea into Reality: The Millennial Achievements

Until the millennial year, nationalist commemorative culture mostly passed without tangible traces and failed to make the target population conscious of the ideal past on an everyday basis. The enduring usage of urban space for national purposes started in Hungary as late as the last decades of the nineteenth century. Compared to Western Europe, the Hungarian elites were quite late in demonstrating their historical narratives in the urban space through public monuments. While the German statuomania started as early as the 1830s, Hungary's first modern public monument, dedicated to General Heinrich Hentzi, was erected in Buda in 1852. This monument provoked Magyar national sentiments, as it celebrated the Austrian commander of Buda Castle during its siege by the revolutionary army in 1849 and represented the intentions of the neo-absolutist Viennese government. Until its replacement in 1899, the Hentzi memorial brought about a series of conflicts with Magyar politicians and the wider public.[40] The first Magyar national monuments were erected in the Hungarian capital in the early 1860s, but until the millennial year only a dozen memorials were built.[41] This number clearly fell behind contemporary international trends. According to an anecdote, German emperor William II was impressed by the modernity of Budapest when visiting the Hungarian capital in 1897; the only shortcoming he allegedly saw was the lack of monuments.[42]

The comprehensive use of urban space, including the building of large-scale monuments, was deeply desired and planned for by national activists. The dominant national elite of the country, the Magyar, finally found that the millennial year provided a good excuse to address the alleged shortcoming and to carve the Hungarian state doctrine in stone and bronze. From the 1880s, an endless number of ideas emerged on the proper formalities of celebrations. As the emotions about the millennium heated up, the magnitude of the festive program gradually expanded, too. In December 1893, Prime Minister Wekerle (1892–95) issued the first program draft. First, this draft included infrastructural projects (some of them had been started earlier, while others were inspired by the festive year only), such as the new building of the Parliament and the Supreme Court, two new bridges in Budapest, the completion of the long-planned Iron Gate project (a Danube gorge on the Hungarian–Romanian–Serbian border where rocks had to be removed to ensure safe navigation) and the opening of four hundred elementary schools run by the government and teaching in Magyar only. Furthermore, in Budapest a festive procession, an exhibition and a festive session of the Parliament were initiated and commemorations were to be held in each church congregation.[43] The festivities were supervised by a committee, comprised of sixty members of the Parliament and chaired by MP and later prime minister Kálmán Széll but in fact the real decisions were made by an executive committee, with the participation of nine members under the leadership of Széll.

Increasing public demand led to festivities and achievements on a scale hitherto unknown in Hungarian history. Opened by Francis Joseph on 2 May 1896, the Millennial Exhibition in the Budapest City Park[44] was the most important attraction of the millennial year. Fin-de-siècle world fairs, in particular the World's Columbian Exposition in Chicago three years before and the Vienna World Exhibition in 1873, served as models for the Hungarian Millennial Exhibition. The Millennial Exhibition proudly demonstrated the advanced economy and culture of the country by displaying Hungarian products, technological advancement, and achievements in Hungarian arts and sciences. Thousands of companies used the exhibition for marketing, and public institutions were also present to demonstrate their contribution to the development of the nation.[45] Modernity was thus a key concept in the Millennial Exhibition, similar to any fin-de-siècle fair.

There was, however, a striking difference to other fairs: in Budapest, the past also had a definite role. Organizers of world fairs often tried to symbolize their advancement by remarkable architectural achievements, such as the Crystal Palace in London and the Eiffel Tower in Paris. In contrast, the symbolic buildings of the Millennial Exhibition were purely retrospective. In order to create a Magyar architectural heritage, existing buildings were copied to host the historic section of the exhibition. In the center of this section stood the copy of the castle of John Hunyadi and Matthias Corvinus in Hunedoara.[46] For a Gothic courtyard, the fountain on the Main Square in Pressburg served as a model while the Catherine Gate in Brassó was used for the early Renaissance building; both buildings were designed by Ignác Alpár, an outstanding representative of Hungarian historicist architecture.[47] As Alice Freifeld states, "[w]hile this architectural historicism was supposed to spur the creation of an indigenous Hungarian architecture, what it actually did was mimic the eclecticism that was fashionable at that time."[48] This eclectic structure was filled with artifacts of the Hungarian past, such as original documents, weapons, historic handicrafts, etc. Among these, several valuable artifacts of the Pannonhalma Archabbey were displayed, including the monastery's foundation document and a mantle believed to have served St. Stephen at his coronation.[49] Another spectacle of the exhibition was Árpád Feszty's monumental panoramic painting showing the conquest of the victorious Magyar tribes.

An ethnographic section displayed rural environments of all the regions of Hungary, including the non-Magyar-speaking parts. In order to be as realistic as possible, peasants from the respective regions were hired to live in the exhibition area. The highlight of the section was a series of marriages where real couples got married, showing the wedding customs of the Hungarian countryside. The diverse agenda behind the millennial festivities is illustrated by the fact that while the political and historical discourse was dominated by an ethnic Magyar perspective, the ethnographical section of the Millennial Exhibition displayed the peoples of Hungary proportionally (12 Magyar and 12 non-Magyar houses were built and populated by villagers).

Finally, the exhibition had a strong amusement character. A gaiety center named "Old Buda" was created. This structure mocked the Ottoman period of Budapest; even a mosque was built, and Turks were hired to act as muezzins. Among other attractions was an airship, which took people on flights above the exhibition, and an electric light railway. An endless number of souvenirs could be bought; among these, a Pusztaszer pavilion sold souvenirs of Pusztaszer, including small portions of land around the ruins of the monastery.

Due to intensive governmental propaganda and discounts, the exhibition was visited by more than 3 million people, approximately one-fifth of the entire population of the country. Foreign journalists were invited, too, to spread news of Hungary's glorious past and promising present worldwide.[50]

During May and June, several elite celebrations took place in Budapest. On 3 May, Francis Joseph, the Habsburg family, and the Hungarian elite listened to the *Te Deum* and Franz Liszt's *Hungarian Coronation Mass* in the Our Lady Church in Buda Castle, the church where Francis Joseph was crowned in 1867. Archbishop Kolos Vaszary praised the unity of the Hungarian nation and its monarch and the divine providence in the country's past.[51]

The most splendid event took place on 8 June, the day of the coronation of Francis Joseph. The Holy Crown of Hungary was brought first to the Our Lady Church, then to Parliament, and finally returned to the Royal Palace. The crown was escorted by a historical procession, featuring the political elite of the country wearing the most splendid historical robes. In the Our Lady Church, the crown was placed on the altar. In the new and still incomplete Parliament building, the crown was greeted by a festive session of both houses. In the Royal Palace, the crown and the escorting procession were received by Francis Joseph. This procession had a sophisticated symbolical dimension. First, by putting the crown at the center of the festivities, and by the historical flags and robes, the procession displayed the autonomous and glorious history of Hungary. Second, placing the crown on the altar of a church referred to the divine dimension of Hungarian history. Finally, the date and the route of the process represented the renowned alliance between monarch and nation. The process departed from the castle (traditionally symbolizing the monarchy) to Parliament, which embodied the will of the nation. While marching through the streets of the city, the grandiose process was seen by hundreds of thousands.[52]

Beside the Millennial Exhibition and the spectacular festivities, infrastructure projects were completed during the festive year. Governmental buildings, the Francis Joseph (today Liberty) Bridge in Budapest, and the new building of the Museum of Applied Arts were inaugurated. In the presence of Francis

Joseph, Serbia's Alexander I, and Romania's Charles I, the modernized Danube route at the Iron Gate was inaugurated, which regulated a dangerous part of the river and thus enabled large-scale shipping on the Danube. As probably the most important cultural achievement, four hundred new elementary schools instructing only in Magyar were established throughout the country.[53]

The costs of the millennial celebrations cannot be precisely given due to the various financing institutions. Yet, without question, they were enormous. Having a planned budget of 4.3 million florins, the exhibition produced a deficit of 550,000 florins.[54] The other governmental projects, the achievements initiated by counties, municipalities, church congregations, and private donations must have cost tens of millions of florins, making the millennium by far the most expensive event in the history of festive culture and symbolic politics in Hungary.

Conquering the Province for the Millennium: Kálmán Thaly and His Monuments

Almost all the above-discussed millennial achievements, whether monuments or other projects, were located in the national capital Budapest. Since the 1880s various institutions and individuals had lobbied for the expansion of the festivities to other parts of the country. Among them a key figure was veteran historian and politician Kálmán Thaly (1839–1909) who was the initiator and supervisor of the seven monuments discussed here. Thaly's guidelines were decisive in this project: the monuments' location, content, and form were heavily influenced by Thaly's personality, interests, and taste.

Kálmán Thaly was born into an impoverished Calvinist gentry family in 1839. He completed his secondary education at the Calvinist College in Pápa, and for a few terms he studied law in Pest but never earned a degree. The intellectual milieu Thaly socialized in was that of romantic nationalism. In that cultural setting, "the interdependence between the poetical and the political" (art inspired by nationality and instrumentalized for the national cause) was seen as self-evident.[55] In his youth, Thaly pursued a literary career. His poems, mostly imitations of the great Magyar romantic poetry, were published in the late 1850s and early 1860s. They sold well due to their easy-to-consume language but literary critics criticized them as banal and unworthy. Disappointed by his failure as a poet, Thaly turned to historical scholarship. He collaborated with László Szalay, the great liberal historian, was elected as the secretary of the Hungarian Historical Society, and was appointed editor of its journal *Századok* (both established in 1867). His own research was focused on the *kuruc* insurrections (the *kuruc* were anti-Habsburg rebels in the late seventeenth and early eighteenth centuries) and on Transylvanian Prince Francis

II Rákóczi (1676–1735) in particular, who led an anti-Habsburg uprising between 1703 and 1711. From 1878 until his death, Thaly was a member of the Hungarian Parliament, representing the Party of Independence.

Thaly diligently collected sources of the *kuruc* age and published a number of source collections. However, he did not apply source criticism, the method developed by Leopold von Ranke. Instead, his method was selection: he used sources that helped him to draw the demigod national hero Rákóczi and a few figures around him or to depict the traitors and ill-wishers to the nation. He liked to call himself the "scrivener of the Prince." His historical works, among them biographies of the *kuruc* leaders János Bottyán, László Ocskay, and Miklós Bercsényi, and studies discussing some *kuruc* campaigns, resemble his early poetic attempts. They are superficial, black and white only; they are more like heroic epics than serious historical study. He praised the middle gentry and criticized the pro-Vienna orientation in early modern Hungarian politics; this historical vision certainly fed the agenda of the Party of Independence. As a major representative of the neo-romantic school in Hungarian historical scholarship, Thaly presented the audience with what it wanted: romantic, adventurous heroes who sacrificed their lives on the altar of the nation. Contemporary historians criticized Thaly for the methodological weakness of his work, but could not challenge his popularity with the audience. His diligence in organizing Hungarian historical scholarship and his patriotic commitment were recognized by membership of the Hungarian Academy of Sciences and by his election as chairman of its Section of History.

A few years after his death, it turned out that Thaly had not only ignored sources that did not fit into his vision, but he had explicitly forged them. One of his early works that brought him fame was a collection of *kuruc* songs. Thaly, however, did not find the existing material inspiring enough and included some of his own poems in the collection. This act can be seen as revenge for his artistic failure: the poems written by him were now among the early treasures of Hungarian literature. The Thaly case, discovered only in 1913, has been the most important forgery scandal in Hungarian literary history ever since.[56]

Yet, in the 1890s, Thaly was at the peak of his career. As a politician, he urged the spread of Magyar national identity, mostly by cultural advancement and symbolic politics. He vehemently protested against the introduction of St. Stephen's Day as a national holiday, insisting on Árpád being the founder of Hungary.[57] Thaly was one of the earliest advocates of the millennial celebrations in Parliament. In a speech in the Parliament in 1891, he proposed to include a historical and ethnographic section in the Millennial Exhibition to give it a retrospective character.[58] The arguments of Thaly, a person whose commitment to Magyar nationalism was commonly known, were accepted by the government and he became member both of the broader parliamentary committee and the executive committee. As the only historian among the committee members, he could lend his arguments the illusion of expertise and historical objectivity and, at least according to his own account, he was frequently consulted in symbolic matters.[59] He also became a member of the board of the historical section of the Millennial Exhibition and in 1893 the government commissioned him to draft the concept of the *kuruc* sub-section.[60]

Before that, in 1890, Thaly initiated the erection of seven monuments in the Hungarian provinces. Before the millennial year, practically no Hungarian provincial town had a modern national memorial (the only significant exception was the memorial to the 1848 revolution in Arad).[61] Thaly aimed at utilizing the millennial ardor to address this "shortcoming." According to him, memorials built on lonely hilltops are particularly apt to raise national consciousness. He initiated simple and robust memorials, which impress people "less by their artistic elaboration but rather by their solid size."[62] His model was the monument dedicated to the fallen Bavarian soldiers in the Napoleonic Wars on Munich's Karolinenplatz, which is in fact a simple black obelisk. The locations initiated originally were slightly different from the final project: instead of Theben, they included Esztergom, and in northeastern Hungary, Munkács or Ungvár were proposed, while in Transylvania, Thaly suggested either the Felek Hill near Kolozsvár or the Budvár Hill at Székelyudvarhely.[63] The simple appearance of the monuments was not only an esthetic choice but was also a means to keep costs low. Thaly hoped that the Archbishop of Esztergom, the Bishop of Nitra, and the Abbot of the Pannonhalma Monastery would finance the monuments built there, while the county assemblies and donations would cover the costs of the other memorials.

In 1891 Thaly presented his idea in the Parliament. Citing German examples, such as the Niederwalddenkmal, the Walhalla and the Berlin Victory Column, he claimed that the most dignified way to commemorate the historical dimension of the millennial festivities was building monuments. The locations were still uncertain: Esztergom was dropped in the favor of Theben, while in the northeast, his proposal still included Munkács and Ungvár, and in Transylvania his opinion now oscillated between Brassó and the Budvár Hill. In a slight contrast to his 1890 proposal, a new element had been added to the concept: not only would the conquest be commemorated by the memorials, but the very territory of Hungary would be marked, and all non-Magyar peoples would be reminded of the Hungarian state doctrine: "It would be useful to mark some historically known events of the conquest in frontier and nationality [non-Magyar] regions where visible signs of the Hungarian state idea are anyway highly desired for national reasons,"[64] argued Thaly in the Parliament. The number seven, the number of the old Magyar tribes, was, of course, kept.

Yet, the genuine millennial program of the government, drafted in December 1893, did not contain Thaly's monuments. When the Parliament discussed the draft in early 1894, Thaly took his chance to convince Prime Minister Wekerle of the necessity of the seven monuments.[65] His efforts were successful and a few days later the second governmental program already included the project (although at this point, the Transylvanian location was still uncertain).[66] Finally, the Millennial Act in 1896 sanctioned the project and ensured its costs being paid from the central budget.[67]

Meanwhile, several important people lobbied for a monument. The influential aristocrat, writer, and politician Count Jenő Zichy proposed to locate the Transdanubian monument in his home town of Székesfehérvár instead of Pannonhalma, but Thaly insisted on his original choice.[68] Similarly, after choosing Brassó as the Transylvanian location, Udvarhely County demanded its relocation to Budvár Hill next to the county seat Székelyudvarhely to commemorate the "real" Transylvanian Magyar past instead of placing the memorial in a Saxon town irrelevant for Magyar national history. Thaly rejected this idea, as the monument had to represent the Hungarian state doctrine to the Saxons and Romanians and not to the purely Magyar-speaking Szeklers.[69] The final locations were determined by Thaly himself, and no lobby could alter his decision.

The first location was the Castle of Theben, west of Pressburg. The castle ruins were just a few meters away from the Austro-Hungarian border. The monument was built on the highest point of the castle ruins, and as the figure was looking toward Vienna, this monument was intended to represent Hungary as an independent state and to be a message to Austria. The choice of Theben over the original Esztergom is most probably related to the border: the central Hungarian town of Esztergom could not qualify to represent Hungarian independence from Austria, and Thaly preferred Árpád to St. Stephen anyway. Furthermore, Thaly had a solid connection to Pressburg: he lived there for a number of years during his gymnasium studies and then in the 1870s, and he frequently advocated the city's interests in the Hungarian Parliament.

The second monument was erected on Zobor Hill, in the vicinity of Nitra. The main reason for choosing Nitra was the Slovak-speaking environment, justified by the story of a certain Slavic Prince Zobor, who allegedly fell victim to the conqueror Magyars:

> I have also taken care of our Slovak kinsmen ("tót atyafiak"): its sign is on the top of Zobor Hill. There are plenty of good patriots among them, for them this monument must serve as a reminder of the centuries they spent happily and peacefully here and it also encourages them for the future; but for those who would riot against the Hungarian state doctrine: their ways must be led by the memorial on Zobor Hill, on that very rock where the traitor prince of the Slovaks was hanged by the homeland-founder, victorious Magyars, as it was told by the anonymous chronicler of King Béla.[70]

The justification for the third location, the Munkács castle, was the easiest. According to the *Gesta Hungarorum*, Árpád's Magyars crossed the Carpathians at the nearby Veretsky Pass and it was exactly at Munkács where they first settled. Due to its profound historical role, the castle had already been settled as a Magyar shrine well before the millennial year. Since the castle belonged to the Rákóczi family, Thaly felt a strong personal tie to the town. A further argument for locating a millennial monument in Munkács was the presence of the Rusyn-speaking population. The proximity of the Hungarian-Galician border was also taken into consideration. As the Lwów–Budapest railway line passed Munkács, the traveler arriving from the north and descending to the Hungarian plain saw the monument first, explained Thaly.[71]

The fourth monument, located on Cenk Hill directly above Brassó, represents the other end of the scale. This town was completely meaningless for the Magyar national imagination. Even Thaly was well aware of the fact that the conquering Magyar tribes did not enter Brassó. The only reason to locate a millennial monument in the town was purely political, as the memorial was:

> meant as a warning for the Romanians and the Brassó Saxons and in general for all the Saxons to respect the Hungarian state, whose land gave you homeland, and also speaks encouragingly to the Szeklers living on the Háromszék plain lying below the monument that the Magyar homeland will not forsake you.[72]

Furthermore, the monument reminded travelers entering the country from Romania by the Bucharest–Budapest railway line that they were crossing the Hungarian state border.

Similar to Brassó, the fifth monument in Semlin could not be directly connected to the history of the conquest. Semlin was not even on proper Hungarian soil, because this town belonged to the autonomous Croatia-Slavonia. Following the logic utilized at Brassó, Thaly chose Semlin to host a millennial memorial, which

> stands there proudly in front of the Serbs on the territory of the Croat-Slavones to represent the Hungarian state doctrine for them, too. … The Zimony monument is meant for Serbs living under the protecting arms of the Hungarian state but also for Serbs abroad: they must keep in mind [that Serbia extends] only to the Sava river [the border river between Serbia and the Austro-Hungarian monarchy] but not further.[73]

The monument was built in the castle ruins above the downtown.

The sixth monument, located near the Benedictine Monastery of Pannonhalma, could be justified far more easily. According to the *Gesta Hungarorum*, after winning a decisive battle over the Moravians and completing the conquest of Western Hungary, Árpád enjoyed the panorama of the new homeland from Pannonhalma. The monastery commemorating this was founded by his descendant, St. Stephen. The undeniable historical role of the archabbey was completed by the idea of Magyar supremacy and the concept of Hungarian territory, making Pannonhalma an ideal location for a millennial monument.[74]

The seventh monument was placed in the Hungarian Great Plain at the ruins of the Pusztaszer abbey, approximately thirty kilometers north of Szeged. The *Gesta Hungarorum* claimed that the Magyars won a decisive battle against a certain Prince Zalán nearby. Furthermore, the chronicle states that after the complete conquest of the Carpathian Basin, Árpád's Magyars convened at Pusztaszer to establish the constitution of their new homeland. The constitutional assembly of the early Magyars became a powerful national myth during the nineteenth century; it was not even dismantled by the fact that positivist historians proved that the story was fabricated by the chronicler.[75]

The seven locations displayed the multifaceted intentions of Thaly. They represented the borders of Hungary and were meant as a message to the neighboring countries (Theben to Austria, Munkács to Russia, Brassó to Romania, and Semlin to Serbia); they recalled the conquest and the glorious Magyar victories over the indigenous peoples; Pusztaszer reminded people of the ancient constitutional legacy of Hungary; while Pannonhalma was related to the Christian heritage. To provide the project with historical accuracy, Thaly related most locations to the *Gesta Hungarorum*. The fact that positivist scholarship raised serious doubts about the accuracy of the *Gesta Hungarorum* did not disturb him.[76]

Out of the seven locations, only one, the Semlin castle, was within a town. To reach the Zobor Hill, the Cenk Hill and the Munkács castle, one needs to walk for approximately an hour from Nitra, Brassó and Munkács, respectively. A visit to Theben, Pannonhalma and Pusztaszer took even more time and was an excursion of at least half a day. Thaly obviously chose hills on the margins of urban spaces to erect monuments on their tops, visible from a large distance. Hilltop monuments which ruled the surrounding landscape were popular artifacts of Romanticism and neo-Romanticism (take the example of the Walhalla), as they merged the cult of the past with the desire for nature. Thaly stated that "vast monuments visible from far … enhance the national consciousness;"[77] furthermore, he was convinced that his monuments would be destinations for national pilgrimages and these acts would affirm the Magyar identity of the visitors. By making an only recently elaborated myth tangible, these monuments are thus perfect examples of nineteenth-century statoumania and the state-driven invention of tradition. Since they were built in environments which were devoid of monuments and any political artifacts, they could distribute their message without any rivals.

The Hungarian millennial monuments thus represent a perfect example of the nineteenth-century statuomania. They carried a recently invented and ambiguous tradition: that of Prince Árpád and the Magyar conquest, which was—at least theoretically—apt to unite Magyars of any religion and social status. The monuments made the Árpád tradition, and by that the Hungarian state doctrine, visible and tangible for a large audience. When built in 1896, at most locations they were the very first national monuments, so they dominated the modern memory landscape until the construction of other memorials.

Carrying exclusively the Hungarian state doctrine, the monuments and the inauguration rituals served to legitimize social order at a moment when this order was being challenged from several sides. In order to understand how these monuments functioned in the public space, and whether they could fulfill the intentions of their initiators, first the meticulous examination of the particular locations is needed.

Notes

1. Baár, *Historians and Nationalism*, 46.
2. Stefan Berger, "The Invention of European National Traditions in European Romanticism," in *The Oxford History of Historical Writing, vol. 4: 1800–1945*, ed. Stuart Macintyre, Juan Maiguashca, and Attila Pók (Oxford: Oxford University Press, 2011), 19.
3. Donald J. Olsen, *The City as a Work of Art: London, Paris, Vienna* (New Haven: Yale University Press, 1986), 295–96.
4. See numerous examples on popular interest in historical works: Peter Burke, "Lay History: Official and Unofficial Representations, 1800–1914," in *The Oxford History of Historical Writing, vol. 4: 1800–1945*, ed. Stuart Macintyre, Juan Maiguashca, and Attila Pók (Oxford: Oxford University Press, 2011), 115–32.
5. Baár, *Historians and Nationalism*, 224.
6. For Northern European examples, see Kristi Kukk, "Stubborn Histories: Overcoming Pagan Brutality Narrative in Estonian 19th-Century National-Romantic Historiography in the Nordic and Baltic Context," *Scandinavian Journal of History* 38, no. 2 (2013): 135–53.
7. Thomas Carlyle, *On Heroes, Hero-worship, and the Heroic in History: Six Lectures* (London: James Fraser, 1841).
8. Burke, "Lay History," 126–27.
9. Thomas Nipperdey, "Nationalidee und Nationaldenkmal in Deutschland im 19. Jahrhundert," *Historische Zeitschrift* 206, no. 3 (June 1968): 529–85.
10. Charlotte Tacke, *Denkmal im sozialen Raum: Nationale Symbole in Deutschland und Frankreich im 19. Jahrhundert* (Göttingen: Vandoeck & Ruprecht, 1995).
11. George L. Mosse, *The Nationalization of the Masses: Political Symbolism and Mass Movements in Germany from the Napoleonic Wars through the Third Reich* (New York: New American Library, 1975), 8.
12. Rudy Koshar, *From Monuments to Traces: Artifacts of German Memory, 1870–1990* (Berkeley: University of California Press, 2000), 19.

13. Hans A. Pohlsander, *National Monuments and Nationalism in 19th Century Germany*, New German-American Studies, vol. 31 (Oxford: Peter Lang, 2008), 103–27.

14. Fritz Abshoff, *Deutschlands Ruhm und Stolz: Unsere hervorragendsten vaterländischen Denkmäler in Wort und Bild* (Berlin: Universum, n. d.).

15. Pohlsander, *National Monuments*, 129–230.

16. On the transformation of modern cities in Europe see: Andrew Lees and Lynn Hollen Lees, *Cities and the Making of Modern Europe, 1750–1914* (Cambridge: Cambridge University Press, 2007). On Vienna, the city being the model for Hungarian cities, see the classic work of Carl E. Schorske: *Fin-de-Siècle Vienna: Politics and Culture* (New York: Vintage Books, 1981).

17. Olsen, *The City as a Work of Art*, 296–297.

18. James M. Brophy, *Popular Culture and the Public Sphere in the Rhineland, 1800–1850* (Cambridge: Cambridge University Press, 2010).

19. Thorsten Gudewitz, "Performing the Nation: The Schiller Centenary Celebrations of 1859 and the Media," *European Review of History* 15, no. 6 (2008): 587–601.

20. Maria Bucur and Nancy M. Wingfield, eds., *Staging the Past: The Politics of Commemoration in Habsburg Central Europe, 1848 to the Present* (West Lafayette, IN: Purdue University Press, 2001).

21. Daniel L. Unowsky, *The Pomp and Politics of Patriotism: Imperial Celebrations in Habsburg Austria, 1848–1916* (West Lafayette, IN: Purdue University Press, 2005), 147.

22. Flóris Rómer, "A történeti érzék keltése a közönségnél, ünnepi menetek, színpadi előadások, nemzeti képek, történeti kiállítások és muzeumok által," *Századok* 19, no. 8 (1885): 130.

23. Árpád von Klimó, *Nation, Konfession, Geschichte: Zur nationalen Geschichtskultur Ungarns im europäischen Kontext (1860–1948)* (Munich: Oldenbourg, 2003), 92–130.

24. Péter Hanák, "Die Parallelaktion von 1898: Fünfzig Jahre ungarische Revolution und fünfzig Jahre Regierungsjubiläum Franz Josephs," in *Der Garten und der Werkstatt: Ein kulturgeschichtlicher Vergleich Wien und Budapest um 1900* (Vienna: Böhlau, 1992), 102–7.

25. Bálint Varga, "A barbár múlt és a nemzeti dicsőség," *Történelmi Szemle* 57, no. 2 (2015): 319–332.

26. János Tatay, "A Haza Tudósaihoz," *Tudományos Gyűjtemény* 15, no. 3 (1831): 126–27;

27. Ferenc Vadas, "Programtervezetek a millennium megünneplésére (1893)," *Ars Hungarica* 24, no. 1 (1996): 4–8.

28. Károly P. Szathmáry, ed. *Az 1881. évi szeptember hó 24-ére hirdetett országgyűlés képviselőházának naplója*, 17 vols. (Budapest: Pesti Könyvnyoma, 1881–1884), 7: 24.

29. Benedek Göndöcs, *Pusztaszer és az évezredes ünnepély* (Budapest: a szerző kiadása, 1883).

30. "A millenarium az Akadémiában: A Történelmi Bizottság jelentése," *Századok* 17, no. 2 (1883): 185–215.

31. Tivadar Pauler to Ágoston Trefort, 25 February 1884. MNL OL, K 26, 1895-22.II-1422/1884, box 333, 2–4.

32. The petition of Bereg County: Ödön Tájnel to Gábor Baross, 11 April 1889. MNL OL, K 26, 1895-22.II-1911/889, box 333, 2–3. The other petitions: ibid., 4–140.

33. Sándor Endrődi, ed., *Az 1887. szeptember hó 26-ára hirdetett országgyűlés képviselőházának naplója*, 27 vols. (Budapest: Pesti Könyvnyoma, 1892), 18:379–381.

34. "1892. évi II. törvényczikk az 1895. évben Budapesten tartandó országos nemzeti kiállításról," http://1000ev.hu/index.php?a=3&param=6452 (accessed 25 April 2011).

35. "1893. évi III. törvénycikk az országos nemzeti kiállitás költségeinek fedezéséről," http://1000ev.hu/index.php?a=3&param=6486 (accessed 25 April 2011).

36. Katalin Sinkó, "Árpád kontra Szent István," *Janus* 6, no. 1 (Winter 1989): 42–52.

37. Gábor Klaniczay, "The Myth of Scythian Origin and the Cult of Attila in the Nineteenth Century," in *Multiple Antiquities—Multiple Modernities: Ancient Histories in Nineteenth*

Century European Cultures, ed. Gábor Klaniczay, Michael Werner, and Ottó Gecser (Frankfurt: Campus, 2011), 185–212.

38. Alice Freifeld, *Nationalism and the Crowd in Liberal Hungary, 1848–1914* (Washington, DC: Woodrow Wilson Center Press, 2000), 184 and 242; Sándor Őze and Norbert Spannenberger, "Zur Reinterpretation der mittelalterlichen Staatsgründung in der ungarischen Geschichtsschreibung des 19. und 20. Jahrhunderts," *Jahrbücher für Geschichte und Kultur Südosteuropas* 2 (2000): 61–77; Sinkó, "Árpád kontra Szent István," pictures 18 and 19 in the appendix.

39. András Gerő, *Modern Hungarian Society in the Making: The Unfinished Experience* (Budapest: Central European University Press, 1995), 204.

40. János Borbély, "Heinrich Hentzi Magyarországon: 'Sárkányölő Szent Györgytől' a 'vaskísértetig'," *Aetas* 21, no. 4 (2006): 88–113; Michael Laurence Miller, "A Monumental Debate in Budapest: The Hentzi Statue and the Limits of Austro-Hungarian Reconciliation, 1852–1918," *Austrian History Yearbook* 40 (2009): 215–37.

41. These memorials included those erected in honor of several significant national poets (Sándor Petőfi, János Arany, etc.), the enthusiastic supporter of Magyar national integration Palatine Archduke Joseph, and the liberal politicians Ferenc Deák, József Eötvös and István Széchenyi. See Endre Liber, *Budapest szobrai és emléktáblái* (Budapest: n. p., 1934), 451–56.

42. Ibid., 223–24.

43. "Ministerelnök előterjesztése, az államalapítás ezredik évfordulójának megünneplése tárgyában," in *Az 1892. február hó 18-ára hirdetett országgyűlés képviselőházának irományai* (Budapest: Pesti Könyvnyomda, 1894), 16: 28–30.

44. The City Park is connected to the downtown by the Andrássy Avenue, a modern boulevard built in neo-Renaissance style in the 1870s. The end of this avenue, called Heroes' Square from 1932, hosts the central millennial monument. In 1896 this monument was still in planning stage and was only completed in 1906. The eclectic monument was designed by the architect Albert Schikadenz and carved by sculptor György Zala. In the center of the monument stand Prince Árpád and the other six Magyar chieftains. They encircle a 36-meter-high column, on which Archangel Gabriel is set, bearing in his right hand the Holy Crown of Hungary and in his left the apostolic cross. Gabriel symbolized divine providence in Hungarian history, as according to a legend, God sent him to the then pagan Stephen to convert his Magyars to the Christian faith. A semicircle portico provides the background to Árpád and Gabriel. Originally, Hungarian monarchs, ranging from St. Stephen to Francis Joseph, were placed among the columns. On two sides of the square the Hall of Arts and the Museum of Fine Arts were built (the latter was completed in 1906), representing the advanced culture of the country. This entire setting was connected to the downtown by an underground railway. The underground railway was the most modern technology of the age; only London and New York built underground railways before Budapest. Preceding Vienna, Berlin, and Paris, the underground railway was an achievement that displayed Hungarian modernity and obviously boosted national pride. Gerő, *Modern Hungarian Society*, 208–12; Katalin, Sinkó "A millenniumi emlékmű mint kultuszhely," *Medvetánc* 7, no. 2 (1987): 29–50.

45. László Kőváry, *A millennium lefolyásának története és a millenáris emlékalkotások* (Budapest: Athenaeum, 1897), 261–63.

46. John Hunyadi (or Corvinus) (c. 1406–1456) was governor of Hungary and commander of Hungarian military campaigns against the rising Ottoman Empire. His son Matthias (1443–490) became king in 1458 and his reign was considered the last glorious chapter in Hungarian history before the Ottoman conquest.

47. Katalin Sinkó, "'A História a mi erős várunk': A millenniumi kiállítás mint Gesamtkunswerk," in *A historizmus művészete Magyarországon: Művészettörténeti tanulmányok*, ed. Anna Zádor (Budapest: Magyar Tudományos Akadémia Művészettörténeti Kutató Intézet, 1993), 136–141.

48. Freifeld, *Nationalism and the Crowd*, 271.

49. Zoltán Bálint, *Die Architektur der Millenniumsausstellung* (Vienna: Kunstverlag Anton Schroll, 1897), 36 and appendix 26; Béla Czobor, *Egyházi emlékek a történelmi kiállításon* (Budapest: Pesti Könyvnyomda, 1896); Béla Czobor and Imre Szalay, eds., *Magyarország történeti emlékei az 1896. évi országos kiállításon* (Budapest: Gerlach Márton, 1903); *A történelmi főcsoport hivatalos katalogusa* (Budapest: Történelmi Főcsoport Igazgatósága, 1896).

50. Kőváry, *A millennium lefolyásának története*, 64–69, 266–312.

51. Ibid., 69–78.

52. Ibid., 92–123; Haslinger, *Hundert Jahre Nachbarschaft*, 34–44.

53. Kőváry, *A millennium lefolyásának története*, 57–123 and 207–82.

54. Ibid., 315.

55. Joep Leerssen, *When Was Romantic Nationalism? The Onset, the Long Tail, the Banal* (Antwerp: NISE, 2014), 5.

56. Ágnes R. Várkonyi, *Thaly Kálmán és történetírása* (Budapest: Akadémiai Kiadó, 1961).

57. Ibid., 253.

58. Endrődi, *Az 1887. szeptember hó 26-ára hirdetett országgyűlés*, 27: 351–54.

59. Kálmán Thaly, *Az ezredévi országos hét emlékoszlop története* (Pozsony: Wigand F. K., 1898), 7–9, 15–18.

60. Béla Lukács to Kálmán Thaly, 21 June 1893. MNL OL, P1747, box 1, 86.

61. The Liberty Memorial in Arad was dedicated to the 1848 revolution. Its location was highly symbolic, as the leading commanders of the Hungarian revolutionary army were executed at Arad castle in 1849. Margit Feischmidt, "Lehorgonyzott mítoszok: Kőbe vésett sztereotípiák? A lokalizáció jelentősége az aradi vértanúk emlékműve és a millenniumi emlékoszlopok kapcsán," in *Mindennapi előítéletek: Társadalmi távolságok és etnikai sztereotípiák*, ed. Boglárka Bakó, Richárd Papp, and László Szarka (Budapest: Balassi, 2006), 370–91.

62. Kálmán Thaly, "Az ezredéves emlékünnep," *Egyetértés*, 1 June 1890.

63. Esztergom was the seat of St. Stephen and its archbishop has been the head of the Hungarian Catholic Church. Ungvár, according to the *Gesta Hungarorum*, was occupied by the Magyars and Árpád was elected prince there. The Felek Hill is a scenic location, nonetheless, it has little historical relevance. The Budvár Hill, according to a forged eighteenth century-chronicle, which even Thaly considered fake, had been the seat of ancient Szeklers, who were allegedly the offspring of Attila's Huns. In spite of the obvious inaccuracy of this chronicle, the nineteenth-century Szekler public often referred to it as a proof of their aboriginal Hun-Magyar descendancy. On the myth of Budvár see: Gusztáv Mihály Hermann, *Az eltérített múlt: Oklevél- és krónikahamisítványok a székelyek történetében* (Csíkszereda: Pro-Print, 2007).

64. Endrődi, *Az 1887. szeptember hó 26-ára hirdetett országgyűlés*, 27:353. At this point, Károly Pulszky, a liberal member of the Parliament and an art historian having a broad European perspective, denounced Thaly's initiative as banal and unimaginative. Ibid., 27: 354.

65. "A bizottsági tárgyalás," *Pesti Napló*, 1 February 1894.

66. "Magyarország ezeréves fennállásának megünneplésére vonatkozó ministerelnöki előterjesztés tárgyalására kiküldött bizottság jelentése," in *Az 1892. február hó 18-ára hirdetett országgyűlés képviselőházának irományai* (Budapest: Pesti Könyvnyomda, 1894), 17: 362–63.

67. "1896. évi VIII. törvénycikk a honalapitás ezredik évfordulójának megörökitésére alkotandó müvekről," http://1000ev.hu/index.php?a=3&param=6625 (accessed 25 April 2011).
68. Thaly, *Az ezredévi*, 14.
69. The petition of Udvarhely County: Lajos Jung Cseke to Béla Lukács, 14 April 1894. MNL OL, K 26, 1895-22.I.A.623, box 333. 30–33. The copy of the petition was sent to Thaly, too: Memo of Udvarhely County to Kálmán Thaly, 6 April 1894, MNL OL, P1747, box 2, 101; Thaly, *Az ezredévi*, 14.
70. Thaly, *Az ezredévi*, 11–12.
71. Ibid., 11.
72. Ibid., 12.
73. Ibid., 11.
74. Ibid., 12.
75. Ibid.
76. Csaba Csapodi, *Az Anonymus-kérdés története* (Budapest: Magvető, 1978).
77. Thaly, *Az ezredévi*, 7.

Part II

CITIES

❧

The millennial monuments were built on the margins of cities; thus, first and foremost town-dwellers encountered them and they were utilized by urban societies. These urban societies and local politics were as diverse as the country in general. Nonetheless, Hungarian cities shared two important features. First, during the second half of the nineteenth century, their population and economic and political weight increased drastically. Second, the utilization of the urban space changed during the same time span: alongside modern urban planning, symbolic aspects gained priority for local governments.

Until 1848, cities were politically completely marginal, as the traditional framework of Hungarian politics below the national level was the county. The free royal cities (*szabad királyi város*) were present at the Diet practically symbolically: they were entitled to delegate their representatives but altogether had one vote only (counties had two each). Towns (*mezőváros*) were politically even less significant, as they were not entitled to send delegates to the Diet at all. The size of the urban population was rather tiny, too: in the late eighteenth century a mere 5% of Hungarians lived in settlements with more than ten thousand inhabitants.[1]

The marginal political role of the cities was changed by the demographic and economic growth of the second half of the nineteenth century. Cities emerged as the arena of mass politics, hubs of industry, banking, education, and transportation.

In 1910, 24% of Hungarians lived in cities with more than ten thousand inhabitants. Budapest (which came into being in 1873 by merging Pest, Buda, and Óbuda) turned from a provincial town into a metropolis of European size and rank. Although the provincial cities of Hungary could not compete in size and importance with the large cities of the Austrian half of the Empire (such as Trieste, Brno, or Lwów), a number of modern and well-developed cities emerged in Hungary, too (Pressburg, Kassa, Kolozsvár, Arad, Temesvár). The urban population boomed in the Great Plain particularly, although the infrastructure of these cities lagged somewhat behind.[2]

Analyzing the urban functions of Hungarian settlements according to the 1910 data, historical geographers Pál Beluszky and Róbert Győri established a fivefold pattern of hierarchy. Budapest, the only metropolis in Hungary, occupied the first hierarchy level. It was followed by eleven regional centers, which provided urban services for several counties. Among the investigated cities, Pressburg and Brassó fall into this category, occupying its very first and last rank. Pressburg belongs to the most developed sub-group of this category ("regional center with full-fledged urban functions"), while the position of Brassó is contested ("regional center with partial urban functions"). The next hierarchy level is that of the county seats. The fifty towns of this hierarchy level were central to a county only. Nitra has been classified in the most developed sub-category of this hierarchy level ("county seat with full-fledged urban functions"). The fourth level is the middle town (sixty-five settlements). Lacking the administrative function of a county seat, these settlements provided urban services to their immediate environment. Munkács was ranked at the top of this category ("middle town with full-fledged urban functions"). The lowest rank, that of the small towns, was represented by 203 settlements, which were legally often villages. Győri and Beluszky did not cover Croatia-Slavonia (with the exception of Zagreb). As Semlin was not a county seat but had a population and infrastructure similar to Nitra and Munkács, it would most probably rank as a "middle town with full-fledged urban functions."[3]

The reforms of the 1870s replaced the complex feudal system of urban privileges with a modern administration. Two types of city were created (Budapest was granted special status). The city with municipal rights (*törvényhatósági jogú város*, in this study Pressburg, Szeged, Semlin) was in legal terms equal to a county. The city assembly elected the mayor and the city officers. The central governmental will was represented by a lord lieutenant, appointed by the government. The second category was the corporate town (*rendezett tanácsú város*, in this study Nitra, Munkács, Brassó). Despite the fact that corporate towns were subordinated to the counties, they maintained a significant autonomy. At the end of the dualist period, there were 24 cities with municipal rights in Hungary and 4 in Croatia and approximately 115 corporate towns in Hungary and a dozen in Croatia (the exact number of corporate towns varied).[4]

Local politics was definitely less ideological than national politics. Importing a Prussian electoral system, 50% of the members of the municipal assemblies were not elected but the highest taxpayers were automatically granted a seat (they were called *virilista*). The other half was elected on a narrow franchise. The municipal government was therefore in the hands of the middle classes. Candidates in municipal assemblies were rarely backed by a party but rather relied on their professional, religious, or family network.

The tasks of the cities and towns were varied. They engaged in education and cultural policy, as they ran schools, theaters, museums, and libraries. They regulated the usage of urban space, too: they decided about infrastructure projects and the names of streets. The municipal assemblies were also competent in symbolic politics: through formal and informal channels they could decide about monuments and festivities, and in a broader sense they regulated the utilization of urban space.

Town-dwellers used the urban space in various forms; the traditions of these practices often went back centuries. Religious feasts were often celebrated on the streets (Catholic processions and patronal festivals are the most obvious examples). In Pressburg a spring carnival was held annually, while in Brassó the Saxon and Romanian youth held a festive march each year. Prominent guests were often paid homage by torchlight procession; in contrast, unpopular people were "honored" by caterwauling. Due to the emergence of mass politics, more modern practices of using the public space appeared, too: the mobilization of the electorate, protests, and strikes on the streets became more and more common, particularly in the large cities. These practices were usually located in the most central parts of the cities, which were in most cases dominated by historical ecclesiastical and civic buildings, churches and town halls often being their landmarks.[5]

As the role of the cities in politics and the economy and the urban population steadily grew, national activists began to believe that cities influenced the countryside; therefore, the urban population's national integration seemed a crucial task. A good example is Gusztáv Beksics, a lawyer and member of Parliament, who was a leading ideologist of the Hungarian state doctrine and author of several studies on governmental policies related to national integration. In his study *Magyarization, Regarding Our Cities in Particular*, Beksics claimed that by stabilizing the Magyar national identity in Hungarian cities, the entire "national question" could be solved: "In order to Magyarize, to assimilate all our nationalities into the Magyar race, only the cities shall be Magyarized. ... A dozen great and Magyar cities will maintain the Magyar nation more solidly in the next thousand years than the counties and the *aviticitas* did during the first millennia."[6] Beksics urged the government to accelerate national integration in cities. The erection of large monuments was believed by many of Beksics' contemporaries to be a suitable tool to support the expansion and crystallization of a Magyar national identity among the urban population of Hungary.

Notes

1. György Kövér, "Inactive Transformation: Social History of Hungary from the Reform Era to World War I," in *Social History of Hungary from the Reform Era to the End of the*

Twentieth Century, ed. Gábor Gyáni, György Kövér, and Tibor Valuch (Boulder, CO: Social Science Monographs, 2004), 68.

2. Ibid., 65–71.

3. Pál Beluszky and Róbert Győri, *The Hungarian Urban Network in the Beginning of the 20th Century* (Pécs: Centre for Regional Studies of the Hungarian Academy of Sciences, 2005).

4. Corporate towns differed from the cities with municipal rights on two issues. First, the corporate towns could deal with local matters only, while the cities with municipal rights were entitled to engage in national politics. Second, cities with municipal rights were entitled to handle first- and second-instance procedures, while corporate towns were restricted to first-instance procedures only. István Kajtár, *Magyar városi önkormányzatok (1848–1918)* (Budapest: Akadémiai Kiadó, 1992).

5. For a comprehensive investigation of the small and medium-sized towns in Austria-Hungary see: Hannes Stekl and Hans Heiss, "Klein- und mittelstädtische Lebenswelten," in Soziale Strukturen, ed. Ulrike Harmat, vol. 9/1 of *Die Habsburgermonarchie 1848–1918*, ed. Helmut Rumpler and Peter Urbanitsch (Vienna: Verlag der Österreichischen Akademie der Wissenschaften, 2010), 1: 561–619.

6. Gusztáv Beksics, *Magyarosodás és magyarosítás: Különös tekintettek városainkra* (Budapest: Athenaeum, 1883), 56 and 61. Until its abolishment in 1848, the *aviticitas* was a privilege of gentrymen, which ensured clan ownership over property. Here, together with the county, it is a metaphor of the gentry in general.

Chapter 3

PRESSBURG AND THEBEN

Figure 3.1. Pressburg on the eve of World War I. Courtesy of the National Széchényi Library, Budapest.

Pressburg, Hungary's western gateway on the Danube, has a rich history dating back to the Middle Ages. After the Ottoman conquest of Central Hungary in the sixteenth century, it bore some capital functions, hosting the Hungarian Diet, some national authorities, and the royal coronations. From 1783, it gradually lost these functions to Buda and Pest; finally, in 1848, the Parliament moved to Pest and Pressburg become a mere regional center. The decline in terms of administrative functions was compensated by an industrial boom witnessed from the 1880s, which made Pressburg one of the largest industrial hubs and the fourth largest city in Hungary by the end of the century. As a city with municipal rights, Pressburg was the most important city in Western Hungary in terms of economy, transport, administration, population, and culture. In 1900, there were three banks and forty-eight factories employing more than twenty workers, the city was the center for Pressburg County and various regional authorities, and it hosted the Royal College with faculties of law and philosophy, a Lutheran theological college, and five secondary schools. Pressburg had the most developed urban functions in Hungary proper after the capital Budapest in 1910.[1]

The city lay on the left bank of the Danube. Its medieval and early modern downtown was home to many historical buildings, including the St. Martin Cathedral, in which eleven Hungarian kings were crowned in the period between 1563 and 1830, and the building that hosted the Hungarian Diet until 1848 (today the library of the University of Bratislava). Above the downtown were the ruins of the castle, whose origins went back to the early Middle Ages. The St. Stephen Crown was kept in the castle after the Ottoman conquest of Buda and the National Archives were also located there in the eighteenth century. Outside the downtown, around the castle one could find the former Jewish ghetto, which was incorporated into Pressburg only in 1851. It was the least developed district of the city until 1913, when it burned down and was replaced by more modern buildings. Around the downtown, several residential and industrial outskirts emerged, giving the city a modern character.[2]

"We Are Only Preßburgers"

Pressburg's population, approximately sixty thousand inhabitants in the late nineteenth century, was predominantly Catholic, but there was a Lutheran and a mostly Orthodox Jewish community as well (see Table 13.1 in the Appendix). The dominant population and culture of Pressburg was German (see Table 13.2 in the Appendix). In 1837, G. R. Gleig, a Scottish traveler, noted about Pressburg:

> You might, both from the structure of the buildings, and the dress and manners of the inhabitants, easily fall into the error of supposing that it [Pressburg] belonged to Austria. ... He who goes to Pressburg without venturing further, need not flatter himself that he has made any, even the slightest acquaintance with the manners and usages of the Hungarians. The town is not a Hungarian, but a German town; the people are Germans, the language is German, and the style of living is German. It is true, that the historical associations connected with the place are all as thoroughly Hungarian as are those which greet you at Ofen [Pest] or at Graan [Esztergom]; but the living men and women seem to have striven, and striven

successfully, to lay aside all the peculiarities which could, by possibility, connect them with the tales of other days.[3]

The well-off Pressburg middle class spoke German, and supported mostly German schools, associations, and cultural institutions. Pressburg had frequent contact with Vienna, therefore German culture flowed unhindered from the imperial capital and flourished in the city. The theater played Schiller's *The Robbers* three years after its premiere in Germany, and Lessing's *Nathan the Wise* two years after.[4] The first choral society of Hungary was established in the city in 1846, and performed the most current German songs.[5]

There were several conditions that could have encouraged the emergence of German nationalism: the proximity to the German-speaking provinces of the Habsburg Monarchy, strong connections to Vienna and Germany, an educated and well-off middle class, an extensive schooling system, and a large number of associations. However, a German national movement did not rise in the city until the interwar period. Solidarity with Germany or the German speakers of either Austria or Hungary was completely absent. Instead, the majority of the German-speaking population insisted on its non-national identity well into the late nineteenth century. This pattern of identity was based on everyday multilingualism, the high prestige of German culture, and multiple loyalties to the city itself, the entire country, and the royal family. "The Preßburger loves his king, loves his homeland, is proud of his nationality, which are provided by the history, the constitution and the freedoms of his homeland," claimed the local doctor Paul Kolbány in 1811.[6] This nationality, however, was often conceptualized as a distinct "Preßburger nation" in the framework of *Hungarus* patriotism, in contrast to modern, ethnic nations. According to a telling anecdote, Francis Joseph once asked a delegation from Pressburg about their national affiliation and the answer was: "We are only Preßburgers."[7] Magyar national activists complained repeatedly about Pressburgers being indifferent to (Magyar) national affairs.[8]

While the concept of a modern German nation remained alien to the Pressburgers, the local identity could be easily harmonized with the idea of Magyar nationalism. The idea of a modern Magyar nation could have been interpreted as an advanced version of the traditional Pressburger-*Hungarus* loyalty. The liberal and modern concept of the Magyar nation included loyalty to the country, the myth of the eternal constitutional liberty of the Magyars, and the glorious history of Hungary; all of these elements seemed progressive and attractive to the Pressburgers.[9]

The painter József Könyöki (who Magyarized his original German name Ellenbogen in 1869), teacher of arts in the Realschule and head of the arts collection of the municipal museum, provides an apt example of this multilayered identity:

The German spirit and German activities soon made Pressburg a fortified and important place. ... The patriotism of the population of Pressburg cannot be exceeded by any other town of the country. They exercise the deepest love of king and fatherland, they were never afraid to sacrifice their goods or lives to keep their often threatened patriotic rights, and even though the majority of them belong to the German people by their language, most citizens of the city also speak Magyar well and care for it with the same love as the German language.[10]

This overlapping and multilayered identity can be demonstrated by a handful of local actors and institutions. The two most important dailies in the city were *Preßburger Zeitung*, a paper that articulated its Hungarian patriotism several times, and *Westungarischer Grenzbote*, an antisemitic daily supporting the liberal opposition that sought the complete independence of Hungary from Austria.[11] This latter proudly advertised itself as a paper banned in Austria (presumably for its open rejection of the Compromise) and supported Magyar liberalism and the national idea unconditionally.

The local Savings Bank (*Sparcasse*) proudly enumerated donations for "demands of the city and the nation," which included contributions to local achievements (several monuments, renovation of the city hall, support for schools and local artists) and the construction of the Magyar national theater and memorials in Budapest. The bank even supported the reconstruction of the flooded and completely destroyed city of Szeged, which was in competition with Pressburg to host the third Hungarian university. The Savings Bank was a founding member of the Pressburg Beautification Association, the Voluntary Firemen, and the Culture Association. It goes without saying that the Savings Bank supported only local and (Magyar) national goals and did not donate to any German or Slovak nationalist endeavors.[12]

The Pressburg associations also carried the typical identity of the city: loyalty to Hungary, strong local elements, and the absence of any exclusive national identity. Until the 1880s, middle class associations used German only. By the end of the century they turned to bilingualism, usually using German for everyday practice, but both languages for representation. When going abroad, the Pressburg associations stressed their Hungarian loyalty and used Hungarian symbols. Any modern German national idea was absent; none of the Pressburg associations included the term German in their name, nor did they share solidarity with the associations of the Cisleithanian part of the monarchy or Germany.[13] A form of national conflict emerged only once during the entire period: Magyar members left one of the freemason lodges to establish a purely Magyar lodge, but instead of damaging relations between the two groups, within two years they had decided to build a new club house together.[14]

From time to time, the Pressburger identity was attacked by local Magyar national activists, who perceived the very presence of German culture and language as a threat. Pressburgers defended their interests in mostly cultural matters, the most important of these being the issue of the theater. The German theater in Pressburg had very rich traditions, while Magyar ensembles performed in the *Vormärz* only during the rare Diet seasons for the overwhelmingly Magyar-speaking political class.[15] From the 1860s, Magyar ensembles were present in the city again, but they played in the less prestigious spring season only, reserving the elegant winter season exclusively for German performances. The new theater building was inaugurated in 1884 by a Magyar play by the Budapest opera and bore only a Magyar inscription, but this did not change the language of the ordinary performances.[16] Between 1899 and 1902, both seasons hosted plays in German and Magyar, but the Magyar plays were attended by far smaller audiences. This caused the local Magyar national activists to demand exclusively Magyar plays in the winter season, aiming to force the German-speaking Pressburgers to attend the theater in the state language.[17] Magyar national activists even accused the *Preßburger Zeitung* of being "unpatriotic" when the newspaper supported German theater plays in the winter season. However, the city assembly opted to return to German in the winter season and Magyar in the spring season; the Pressburger identity won over nationalist expectations.[18]

In political terms, the Pressburger identity meant solid support of pro-Compromise liberalism. The Liberal Party dominated both electoral districts of the city. Occasionally one of the mandates was won by a politician with a liberal agenda but supporting the moderate, i.e. pro-Compromise opposition in Parliament.[19] Catholic associations and from 1896 the Catholic press (the paper *Preßburger Tagblatt*) were present in the city; still, political Catholicism did not gain a foothold among the electorate, despite the fact that its overwhelming majority belonged to the Roman Catholic Church. Concomitantly, *Preßburger Tagblatt*'s agenda was far less antagonistic to liberal values than the hardcore Catholic press (such as in Nitra). The weak position of political Catholicism in the city stood in sharp contrast to Pressburg County, whose rural and small-town environments became a stronghold of the Catholic People's Party.[20]

The other political ideology that was present among the city's population but did not influence municipal politics was social democracy. As a booming industrial city, Pressburg had a large working class. Given the proximity of the city to Vienna and the Bohemian lands, social democracy gained a foothold in Pressburg quite early. In 1869, the Vorwärts Workers' Educational Association was founded. This association, similar to the middle class clubs, operated mostly in German, in the language of the majority of blue collar workers. Yet it frequently stressed its cosmopolitan character and was open to Magyar and Slovak-language activities too. A separate Slovak and Magyar section came into being within the association but they still used the same building (the so-called Arbeiterheim) and the workers' charity organization remained united.[21] The workers' identity was influenced by multiple factors. An international and democratic agenda was promoted by the workers' leaders, who were often immigrants to the city from the Bohemian and Alpine lands. In addition to these values, the genuine Pressburger workers seem to have been "closer to the Pressburger bourgeois world view," as local pride and multilingualism were attractive components of this identity, as Eleonóra Babejová states.[22] Still, the initiative to establish a separate Slovak socialist party (to be discussed below) and the very engagement of the HSDP in national issues, suggests that national identification was not an unknown and automatically refuted concept among the workers of Pressburg.

"It is Predictable that Pressburg will Bear a True Magyar Character in a Couple of Decades"

The first attempt to bring modern nationalism to Pressburg came from the Slovak national movement during the *Vormärz*. The Lutheran Lyceum, the most well-known Lutheran gymnasium and theological college in Hungary, hosted these endeavors. In 1803, Hungary's first chair of Slavic language was established at the Lyceum, teaching the so-called Kralice Czech, the almost-holy language of the Slovak and Czech-speaking Protestants. The chair was occupied by Juraj Palkovič, who was assisted by the key figure of the emerging Slovak nationalism, Ľudovít Štúr.[23] Students of Palkovič founded the main Slovak cultural institution of the age, the Czecho-Slav Association (Společnost česko-slovanská, 1827–37). The subscription data in the 1836 yearbook of the association shows well the important place Pressburg occupied in the Slovak national movement: 40% of all Hungarian subscribers were from the city.[24] Pressburg, in addition, hosted the first Slovak newspaper, the *Slovenjske národňje novini* (1845–48), edited by Štúr.

Yet the importance of the city in the Slovak national movement strikingly declined from the mid 1840s. Štúr was dismissed from the Lyceum in 1843; he could not pay the deposit for his *Slovenjske národňje novini* in 1848 and had to suspend publication, and the chair of Slavic language was dissolved and never reopened after Palkovič's death in 1850. The importance of Pressburg in general decreased as the seat of the Hungarian Parliament moved to Pest in 1848, and the neo-absolutist era of the 1850s repressed all kinds of liberal and nationalist political activity. In the 1860s, the Slovak national movement had to move to the Tatras and basically lost the city.[25] The last fragments of the Slovak institutions ceased to exist in the 1870s. With the exception of some insignificant student associations in the 1880s, they were not replaced until the early twentieth century.[26]

As a result, not only was the Slovak national movement absent in Pressburg, but a Slovak-speaking middle class was missing between the 1880s and 1900s. Slovaks were seen as almost exotic: the figure of the Slovak wireman and tinker appeared at carnivals among the "ridiculous strangers" in the company of the Chinese, the Moor, the Jew, and the Turk.[27] Several governmental reports testify to the absence of Slovak national activists in Pressburg; these documents explain the lack of Slovak nationalism by the absence of a Slovak-speaking middle class.[28] Consequently, the Slovak national elite, then located in the remote and unimportant towns of the Tatras, was unable to disseminate its ideas in Pressburg, as Slovak newspapers were rarely read in the city.[29] The Slovak National Party did not even try to run a candidate in the parliamentary elections in 1901, when it decided to end its passive policy.[30]

While the few Slovak national activists were often persecuted by the Hungarian authorities, their relation to the German-speaking Pressburgers was more ambiguous, as the cases of Vendelin Kutlík and Michal Mudroň show. The former, a son-in-law of Michal Miloslav Hodža (one of the most important Slovak national leaders of the period), encouraged Slovak students to form an underground nationalist association in the early 1880s. The latter worked as a lawyer and became well known for defending Jozef Miloslav Hurban, the leader of the failed Slovak national uprising against the Hungarian revolution in 1848, when sued for a press article with Slovak nationalist claims. Mudroň also published a reply to Béla Grünwald's infamous pamphlet *The Upper Land*.[31] Although both Kutlík and Mudroň were Slovak national activists, and thus both of them were labeled "pan-Slav agitators," their position in local society differed significantly. While Mudroň was a respected member of Pressburg's middle class, Kutlík was basically excluded from the local "high society." The difference lay in their individual identities: Mudroň, besides being a Slovak nationalist, was eager to accept a local identity, and indeed held himself to be a good and loyal Hungarian, but Kutlík saw himself exclusively as a Slovak. Mudroň's multilayered identity, including Slovak national sentiments, was tolerated but Kutlík's exclusive Slovakness was incompatible with the values of the Pressburg middle class, and he therefore found himself on the very edge of the city's society.[32]

While the middle class Slovak nationalism completely failed, a Slovak social democratic movement emerged in the early 1900s. In 1904, the socialist paper *Robotnícke noviny* was published, and in the following year a separate Slovak section was founded within the Vorwärts Association. There was even an attempt to organize a Pressburg-based Slovak Social Democratic Party, independent from the HSDP. This party in fact came into being in 1905 but a year later became affiliated with the HSDP.[33]

As German nationalism did not emerge and the Slovak national movement had failed by the 1850s, the Magyar remained the only effective national elite group to influence Pressburgers. Local Magyar nationalism emerged in the

1870s with the appearance of a Magyar-speaking middle class in the city. The local Magyar national activists were mostly newcomers to the city; among them one could find state, county, and municipal officials, teachers, journalists, and lawyers. The city's Magyar middle class was dependent on the state much more than their German-speaking counterparts, who sustained themselves mainly through their private businesses.[34] The differences between the German-speaking autochthonous Pressburgers and the immigrant Magyars remained palpable under the surface during the entire period.[35]

The Magyar-speaking middle class gained more and more space in municipal politics and in several spheres under governmental control. To challenge the position of German in the city, Magyar was introduced in several spheres. The municipal administration used both German and Magyar until the exclusive introduction of Magyar in 1885, although German speeches at the magistracy and the assembly were allowed throughout the period.[36] Following a brief period of partly Magyar education in the late *Vormärz*, the Pressburg schools gradually changed their language of instruction from German to Magyar between the 1860s and 1880s. After some years of bilingual education, the Academy of Law was the first school to introduce purely Magyar education in 1861, to be followed by the Lutheran Lyceum in the 1860s, the Roman Catholic gymnasium in the 1880s, and lastly by the Realschule in 1893.[37] The schools founded in the dualist period educated exclusively in Magyar from the very beginning. These included the state Teachers' Training College, the Commercial Academy, the Upper Grammar School for Girls, and the Catholic Middle School for Girls.[38] Starting from the 1880s, elementary schools also adopted Magyar as their language of instruction. In 1877, only one elementary school taught in Magyar and six in German and Magyar, but in eighteen schools German remained the sole language of instruction, with Magyar only being taught as a subject.[39] Within ten years, by 1887, there were hardly any purely German schools left in the city, as most instructed pupils bilingually from the third grade. A Magyar observer was pleased by this "even more rejoicing [process], as it makes the Magyardom of Pressburg also spread."[40] From the 1890s, the Catholic schools (which made up approximately half of the elementary education of the city) developed their own method of teaching Magyar, causing a rapid increase in pupils speaking the state language.[41]

Magyar also spread in the sphere of associations. Until the 1880s, the only bilingual association was the Casino, the meeting hub of the aristocracy and the highest society of the city. The social composition of the Casino, in this case the presence of Magyar nobility, gives an obvious explanation for its bilingual character.[42]

From the late 1870s, Magyar national associations began to emerge in the city. These associations, including the most important Toldy Association, carried the idea of the modern Magyar nation and were devoted to spreading this concept among the population of the city.[43] The Toldy Association was established in 1874; in the following decades more or less the entire elite of the city joined it, particularly the civil servants, who comprised a third of the total membership. Between 1875 and 1878, when Kálmán Thaly lived in Pressburg, he actively engaged with the Toldy Association: he was a member of its board and delivered public lectures.[44] The aggressive national rhetoric of the Toldy Association[45] is, however, only one side of the story. For the city elite, it became almost a must to gain membership of this club, despite the fact that many German speakers among the members were less enthusiastic about any sort of national idea. Some members acted against the official goals of the association, as in the case of the language of the theater. Although the Toldy Association was one of the most active protagonists of the introduction of Magyar into the winter theater season, the city assembly's decision to favor the German ensemble was supported by many Toldy Association members.[46] To interpret the participation of the German-speaking middle class in the Toldy Association as pure opportunism, however, would be a misleading oversimplification. Participation in the Toldy Association was probably seen by the less nationally enthusiastic German-speaking members as a sign of patriotism, a tool for demonstrating loyalty to the country and respect for Magyar culture which, however, did not necessarily prevent the cultivation of German language and culture. Indeed, one of the early member lists also included Michal Mudroň: he certainly entered the Toldy Association to demonstrate his loyalty to the Kingdom of Hungary.[47]

The advance of the Magyar language was far slower in other domains of cultural life, being under significantly less governmental pressure than education. The theater continued to play mostly in German and the local press was also dominated by German papers. A Magyar paper was published first in 1873; during the millennial year the only Magyar daily in the city was *Nyugatmagyarországi Híradó*, a paper vehemently supporting Magyar national ideas.

Despite failures such as the theater, the Magyar language achieved remarkable advances in fin-de-siècle Pressburg. As demonstrated in Table 13.2, censuses recorded a booming number of Magyar speakers. In the 1880s, observers saw the city's character as bilingual, foreshadowing complete Magyarization within a few decades. "It is predictable that Pressburg will bear a true Magyar character in couple of decades," claimed a traveler in 1883.[48]

The increase in the number of Magyar speakers was in direct connection with population growth. For a few decades after losing its capital functions, the city was declining but industrialization and economic growth in the 1880s caused its population to increase rapidly. The economic boom attracted a large number of people; approximately 80% of the population increase was a result of immigration.[49] Lacking a large German-speaking hinterland, the majority of newcomers to Pressburg were Magyar and Slovak speakers.[50]

The boom in the Magyar-speaking population was due not only to immigration, but also to linguistic Magyarization of the German- and Slovak-speaking population. This expansion correlated with certain social markers. The small Calvinist community, accommodating the nationwide trend, became predominantly Magyar-speaking by the end of the century (55% in 1880 vs. 79% in 1900). Members of the two large Christian communities, the Roman Catholics and the Lutherans, were quite open to adopting the state language; in 1880 17% and 13% and in 1900 30% and 22%, respectively, declared Magyar as their native tongue. The most rapid change took place in local Jewry. While in 1880 only 14% of Jews declared themselves as Magyar native speakers, in 1900 39% marked the state language as their mother tongue.[51]

Magyar speakers were overrepresented among large estate owners, officials (including transportation and communication), and free professions. German speakers were more likely to be found among the small and middle-sized estate owners, artisans, industrial white collar workers, shopkeepers, money lenders, and conveyers. Slovak speakers were overrepresented among industrial and agricultural blue collar workers, underrepresented in commerce and handicrafts, and were almost absent in higher governmental jobs and the free professions.[52]

In strong correlation with the professional structure, languages were used unevenly in the districts. German and Magyar speakers lived in all districts in more or less equal numbers, the former group slightly overrepresented in the less prestigious parts, while the latter in the more elegant quarters. Slovak speakers were underrepresented in the city center, but reached a higher proportion in the outskirts. Jews mostly lived in the former ghetto near the castle, but their wealthy representatives tended to move into more elegant districts.[53]

During the dualist period, the local languages market was significantly restructured. In 1880, the German language had the highest prestige in Pressburg, far higher than the state language, Magyar. According to the census, only 51% of the Pressburg population spoke a second language. Knowledge of a second language was needed least by the dominant German speakers: only 38% of them spoke at least one language beyond German. The two smaller groups, the Slovak and Magyar speakers, clearly needed more linguistic skills to find their way in German-speaking Pressburg, thus 69% and 82% respectively spoke a second language. The gender aspect of the linguistic composition is also remarkable: German speakers with Magyar as a second language were more likely to be men, while women spoke either German only or German and Slovak. Similarly, native Magyar speakers who knew German were usually men, while Magyar-speaking women preferred either Slovak or no other language. The case of native Slovak speakers is different: among them, German was more familiar to women, and Magyar or no other language for men.[54]

This means that in 1880 the German-speaking milieu of Pressburg was large enough for its members to get on in life without learning Magyar or Slovak, while the Slovak and Magyar speakers had to adjust and learn the dominant language of the city, German. A quarter of the native German speakers (men) knew Magyar, presumably the better educated ones. German-speaking women, if they knew another language, preferred Slovak, as they were more likely to meet Slovak speakers as housemaids or vendors of agricultural goods at the markets. Native Slovak-speaking women, if they knew another language, therefore preferred German to communicate with their mostly German-speaking employers or customers. Slovaks knowing Magyar as a second language were rare and were mostly men. The dominant position of the German language is also shown by the high number of Magyar speakers among both genders who were able to speak German. However, the low number of native Slovak speakers acquainted with the German language demonstrates that in certain areas German was not required. It was probably the large number of day laborers who could afford not to learn the dominant language of the city.

Within two decades, a serious change took place. The multilingual population increased from 51% to 59%. This trend spread unevenly; while the proportion of monolingual German speakers decreased (from 62% to 57%), that of Slovak speakers increased slightly (from 31% to 34%), and the number of Magyar speakers without a second language grew significantly (from 18% to 27%). Still, German continued to be the most prestigious language of the city and native Slovak speakers still preferred it to Magyar: 66% of all Slovak speakers knew at least one other language, but only 27% declared also speaking Magyar. Magyar speakers still knew German more frequently than vice versa (64% to 36%). The German-speaking community was thus still large enough to allow its members to live without speaking other languages. The expansion of education and the introduction of Magyar either as the language of instruction or as a mandatory subject in schools definitely contributed to the increasing knowledge of Magyar among native German speakers. Therefore, German monolingualism must have been restricted to the less educated and the elderly. At the same time, the increase in monolingual Magyar speakers indicates that the Magyar milieu of Pressburg was slowly but surely expanding.[55]

Speaking Magyar was more likely among people having a job connected to the government; non-Magyar speakers among employees of the post, railway, civil administration, justice, and academic institutions knew Magyar in high numbers. Although declaring knowledge of Magyar can by no means be equated with Magyar national identity, it can be presumed that the Magyar national integration project was successful mostly with middle class males, as education, army service, and jobs dependent on the government influenced them at the highest rate.

An Orthodox Bastion in a Modern City

The process of Magyar national integration was heavily backed by Jewish communities throughout the modern cities of Hungary. However, this was only partly the case in Pressburg. Although Jews of the city contributed remarkably to the increase in Magyar native speakers in the censuses, they did not take part in the process of Magyar national integration to the same extent as their fellows in Budapest, Szeged, or Nagyvárad. The Pressburg Jewry was quite slow in regard to social progress until the turn of the century. The 1900 census shows local Jewish society lagging behind in modernization. Fifty percent of all male Jews earned their living in traditional petty commerce, but their presence in free professions did not significantly exceed the city average.[56] Jewish modernization seems to have begun to increase by the prewar years, as the 1910 census shows a boom in modern professions among the Pressburg Jews.[57]

The background of slow modernization lay in the Orthodox tradition of Pressburg Jewry.[58] The Jewish community, one of the largest and oldest in Hungary, gained international importance through its famous ultra-conservative rabbi Chatam Sofer (Moses Schreiber, 1763–1839, rabbi in Pressburg 1807–39). His activity and legacy influenced the Jewry of the city well beyond his death, as his son and then grandson inherited his position.[59] The traditional mentality of the Sofer rabbinical dynasty drove the vast majority of Pressburg Israelites into the Orthodox camp during the 1868 schism (in that year, reacting to the emancipation law, the Hungarian Jewry divided into three bodies: the reform Judaism or so-called Neologs, the Orthodox, and a third party in between, the Status Quo).[60]

Despite Chatam Sofer condemning any novelty, integration and modernization were inevitable in the second half of the nineteenth century. Due to governmental pressure, Orthodox primary and middle schools began to instruct all lay subjects in Magyar in the 1880s and 1890s and had to adapt the curriculum to meet national standards.[61] The yeshiva, however, was able to maintain its own rules. This school, founded by Chatam Sofer, had a large impact on the entire Orthodox Jewry of Hungary, having sometimes as many as four hundred students. As a bastion of Orthodoxy, it instructed pupils in Yiddish and Hebrew. The curriculum—theoretically—included only theological subjects in order to isolate pupils from the Christian world. In order to prevent any lay temptation, yeshiva students were forbidden to read any non-religious texts, though this practice was sanctioned only by Chatam Sofer. His successors had to tolerate forbidden reading; following the 1867 introduction of Jewish emancipation, maintaining the complete separation of yeshiva students from the lay world seemed anachronistic. A further step toward the destruction of the intellectual ghetto of the yeshiva was an 1884 law that required rabbis either to complete middle school or to pass the first four grades of a gymnasium, therefore yeshiva students had to enroll in lay education and were thus required to learn Magyar at a high level. By the end of the century, Magyar had become a mandatory subject even in the yeshiva.[62]

However, participation in lay education was not enough to ensure Magyar national identity among the students of the yeshiva. As an answer to the emerging demands concerning national self-identification, significant numbers of Orthodox Jewish intellectuals in Pressburg, students of the yeshiva in particular, turned to Zionism on the eve of World War I. Mizrahi, an Orthodox Zionist movement founded in 1902 in Vilnius, found followers in the city. Their support for Orthodox Zionism was so significant that the first world congress of the Mizrahi was held in Pressburg in 1904.[63]

While some Orthodox Jewish intellectuals joined Zionism in the early years of the twentieth century, participation in Magyar nationalism was chosen by a large number of Jews, particularly Neologs. Tensions between liberal and Orthodox-minded members of the Jewish community can be traced back as far as the 1820s.[64] Some liberal members of the community established a private elementary school offering secular subjects too. This school openly encouraged pupils to study further in gymnasiums, earning the bitter criticism of Chatam Sofer. The desire for modernization was expressed not only by the structure of the school, but also by the language of instruction. Magyar was taught in a pioneering way from the 1840s, and only the lack of proper teachers prevented the school from introducing complete Magyar education in the 1860s. Magyar finally became the only language of instruction between 1885 and 1892, with the exception of theological subjects; students were also required to speak Magyar during breaks. Benő Berger's study of the school's history proudly claimed that it was the first local institution to undermine the spirit of the *heder* (an old-fashioned elementary school teaching religious subjects only) and, in a broader sense, the traditional Jewish way of life.[65] The promoters of this school founded the Neolog community in 1872. It soon became consciously Magyar-speaking and presumably also took the modern Magyar national identity. They harshly criticized their Orthodox counterparts, accusing Orthodoxy not only of being counterproductive but also of lacking patriotism.[66]

The Second Capital and the Bastion on the Borderland: Reading the City

During the nineteenth century, two main narratives were produced about Pressburg: a local German interpretation and a Magyar national interpretation. The former narrative was produced by local, mostly German-speaking intellectuals. This interpretation put the city at the center, though it always considered the Hungarian context as well, stressing Pressburg's importance and loyalty in Hungarian history. Emphasis was put on the important events and institutions of Hungarian history related to Pressburg. These included the coronation of Hungarian kings from 1563 until 1830 in the city's St. Martin Church and the Hungarian Diet having its sessions in the city from the sixteenth century until 1848. Two periods of the Diet's activity were highlighted: on the one hand, the 1741 session, when the Hungarian estates offered their "life and blood" (*Vitam et sanguinem*) to Queen Maria Theresa and thus saved the Habsburg Monarchy from a total collapse in the War of the Austrian Succession; on the other hand, the liberal achievements of the *Vormärz*. Loyalty to the monarch, particularly to the Habsburg family, was a cornerstone of this city-centered narrative. In this interpretation it was the eighteenth century, particularly the reign of Maria Theresa, that was seen as the golden age of the city. A travel guide summarized this narrative: "After Buda had fallen into the hands of the Ottomans, in 1536 Ferdinand I made Pressburg the capital of the lands of St. Stephen's Crown, and it remained so until the times of Joseph II; and from then until the year 1848 the meetings of the Diet were held here, and these epochs are still remembered well by the generation of today."[67]

The other feature to make the German-speaking Pressburgers proud was the economic and cultural performance of their city, particularly its factories, high literacy rate, and important schools. Thus, Pressburgers proudly called their city the second capital of Hungary even after 1848, the year when Pressburg ceased to hold any of the functions of a capital.

While the local interpretation put the city at the center, a Magyar national narrative also emerged, which rather emphasized the nation. A contemporary pamphlet claimed in the style of the times:

> Can the meritorious citizens of the city not look back at an almost 1900-year-long history, rich in fights and peaceful events? ... No wild waves were able to hollow out and undermine its existence founded upon a rock castle, and a millennium-old power [Hungary] may show its living message to the city. Pozsony appears everywhere by its respect and intelligent influence on the golden pages of Hungarian history; almost all notable events found their starting point here. Just think of the epoch-making work of the raising of awareness of national self-confidence, the constitutional rebirth of the 1830s and 1840s, the efforts for national independence, the emergence of the manly self-consciousness—we always find there all the notable persons of Pozsony, shoulder to shoulder. ... How the faithful citizens of the city made sacrifices, how they suffered for the liberty and honor of the homeland, the chronicles of the city may show thousands of examples.[68]

The Magyar reading of the city's past thus connected Pressburg with the national history, referring to national activists of the *Vormärz* Diets (Lajos

Kossuth, István Széchenyi, Ferenc Deák). The first Magyar daily, published in the city in 1780, was also highlighted.[69] The Magyar vision included the city's position on the border with Austria and its role as a bastion of Magyar national culture. Pressburg was referred to as a desert in Magyar national culture where the Magyar national associations formed the only oasis; indeed, the city was seen as being threatened by the proximity of Vienna and German culture.[70] The construction of the railway between Pressburg and Vienna particularly alarmed the Magyar national activists, as they perceived the direct rail connection as a tool to import even more German culture to the city, thus degrading it to a mere suburb of the imperial capital.[71]

Comparing the two narratives, however, radical differences cannot be observed; both interpretations stressed the links and loyalty of the city to Hungary and its profound role in Hungarian history. The Magyar national narrative more strongly emphasized the border function, and thus saw Pressburg as a bastion of Magyardom, stressing particularly the contribution of the city to the progress of the nation in the *Vormärz*. The traditional vision of the city focused rather on the royal connection and German high culture, interpreting the eighteenth century as its climax. Nevertheless, these narratives were mutually compatible and merged without any severe contradictions.[72]

An important example of overlaps is shown by the shared interpretation of the 1848 revolution, making the local public proud of Pressburg's contributions to the liberal political and military achievements. These contributions included hosting the last feudal Diet in 1847/48, the new, liberal constitution of the country inaugurated by this Diet, and then the numerous volunteers in the Hungarian army fighting Jozef Miloslav Hurban's Slovak insurrectionist army. Particular attention was dedicated to the Pressburg-born martyrs, including the prime minister, Lajos Batthyány, the officers, Ludwig Aulich, János Jeszenák, László Mednyánszky, and the local Lutheran priest, Paul Rázga, all of them executed in 1849. As several other locals were persecuted and sentenced to prison, practically all layers of Pressburg society were represented among the victims of the repression following the defeat of the Hungarian revolution.[73]

The argumentation concerning the third Hungarian university is another remarkable example of the overlaps between the two readings of the city. Hungary maintained an insufficient number of universities, having only two complete institutions of higher education in Budapest and Kolozsvár and several minor colleges, which were not able to provide enough well-trained professionals for the booming economy, education, and public administration. The issue of establishing a new university was discussed from the 1880s onwards, but for financial reasons it was delayed until 1912. The potential cities, including Pressburg, Szeged, Debrecen, and Kassa, tried to convince the public and the government to favor them over the other candidates by issuing pamphlets and memorandums. The official communiqué of Pressburg to the Hungarian Parliament, signed by the mayor, argued for locating the new university in the city by emphasizing its high culture, rich cultural heritage, large hinterland, and even the short-lived college established by King Matthias Corvinus in the fifteenth century. The argumentation did not stress the role of the planned university in the increase of Magyar national identity in the city, but rejected the accusation of the rival Szeged of being unpatriotic and supporting "German *Burschenschafts* and Slovak *maticas* [i.e. German and Slovak nationalist clubs]."[74]

A similar argument was delivered by Lajos Wagner, a multilingual teacher, himself an immigrant to the city, born in Banská Bystrica. Wagner, probably due to his multilingual background (he taught Magyar, German, Slovak, and Serbian in various schools) was remarkably tolerant of the non-Magyar speakers of Pressburg; he considered them loyal citizens of the country in need of further patriotic education. The establishment of a university, argued Wagner, would be a tool in strengthening the loyalty of these citizens, as it showed the benevolence of the Hungarian government toward the city.[75]

While the national aspect did not form a decisive part of the city's official argumentation, it certainly played a central role in the arguments of local Magyar national activists. Born in the central Hungarian and purely Magyar-speaking city of Debrecen, Gábor Pávai Vajna, doctor at the Pressburg hospital, was such a national activist. He was a well-known figure for his endeavors to Magyarize the theater and the schools of Pressburg. He also lobbied for the Pressburg university. He echoed the practical arguments of the official memorandum, stressing the historical and cultural importance of the city, but his main argument was for the role of a university in the course of Pressburg's Magyarization. He claimed that the only way to consolidate the Hungarian state doctrine and to complete the Magyarization of the city and northwestern Hungary was to establish a university in Pressburg, which could serve as a stronghold of Magyar culture against Vienna:

> Shall Pozsony, such an important part of the body of the state, not expect from the nation to receive the stamp of the national character, by pursuing a self-conscious policy here on the border, to establish a great university that would propagate to everyone arriving the land of Hungary from across the Lajta [Leitha, the border river between Hungary and Austria, a symbol of the border] that the land where he stands is Magyar?[76]

He furthermore cited the example of Strasbourg, where the German government had consciously established a university to strengthen the German nation in the recently acquired Alsace. In order to fulfill the Magyarizing mission of the university, Pávai Vajna even proposed electing city counselors and a mayor who spoke only Magyar, making Magyar performances dominate the theater, and firing all the school teachers who did not have enough knowledge to instruct in the state language.[77]

The same line of argument was employed by György Schulpe, a local expert on social policy. In order to justify the establishment of a Pressburg university, he referred to the city's rich heritage and its practical advantages, but his final argument was again the decisive role that a college would play in strengthening Magyardom on the Austrian border and against the "pan-Slav" (i.e. the Slovak national) threat.[78]

The endeavors of the city's elite proved to be successful, as the government decided to establish a university in the city in 1912, named after the late Queen Elisabeth. One of the reasons to locate the university in Pressburg was clearly its intended role in the final Magyarization of the city. To what extent this task could have been fulfilled was never determined, due to World War I and the transfer of the city to Czechoslovakia in 1919.

The impetus for a third reading of the city, a Slovak national one, was present but was not properly elaborated. A Slovak reading of the city's past had to cope with certain difficulties. Although the city was probably inhabited during the Moravian period, sources did not ascribe a major role to it. Pressburg's overwhelmingly German-speaking population prevented its connection to the Slovak national past. What gave Pressburg some Slovak relevance was the activity of the Slovak national elite in the *Vormärz* and its substantial Slovak-speaking minority. In 1845, Štúr referred to Pressburg as one of the "Slovak central towns" but the city lost this position in the Slovak national imagination in parallel with the disappearance of Slovak nationalist activity.[79] Lacking a local Slovak-speaking middle class, the Slovak reception of the city was produced by Slovak and Czech intellectuals outside the city. Pressburg was thus interpreted as a multilingual city lying on the border of Slovak territory but not belonging to it in an organic way.[80] The failure to construct a true Slovak character had a long-lasting impact, as the capital function of the city was contested even during the interwar period.[81]

Compared to other Hungarian cities, the memory landscape of Pressburg was definitely rich. The St. Martin Cathedral and the castle boosted local and national pride; the Gothic town hall on the main square (hosting the municipal museum) represented the solid bourgeois identity.

The transformation of the urban space started in the late 1870s. Streets received new names from 1879, representing well the different layers of the city's identity. These names included important figures of Hungarian history, often without any connection to the city itself (like national poets, kings, and politicians), several people who had an important role in the history of the city (mayors, local artists), and some members of the Habsburg family. The multiple layers of local identity were also shown by the fact that the important figures of the *Vormärz* period, as well as the 1848/49 revolution and the dualist era, were honored by having streets named after them. It goes without saying that national heroes of Germany were completely absent from Pressburg street names.[82]

Changing street names was an easy and cheap task but did not fulfill all the demands of the city elites. In accordance with the "statuomania" of the century, new public monuments were erected throughout the city. The first such monument, dedicated to the Pressburg-born musician Johann Nepomuk Hummel, was inaugurated in 1887 on the promenade (now Hvezdioslav Square) with the contribution of the city and its citizens. This monument represented the multilingual, non-national identity of Pressburg, as the bilingual celebration and the remarks on German culture and Hungarian loyalty in the *Festschrift* clearly display.[83] A similar non-national monument dedicated to Franz Liszt (born in the west Hungarian village of Raiding and having his first success in Pressburg) was planned in 1890, but due to a lack of proper financial sources this monument remained on paper only.[84] A monument demonstrating a clearly Magyar national agenda, however, was not yet planned.

The Past Glory and the Porta Hungarica: Reading the Castle

In the vicinity of Pressburg, the Castle of Theben gained the greatest relevance in the course of inventing national identities. Occupying a high hill above the Danube at the confluence of the Morava river, the castle was located exactly on the Austro-Hungarian border. It is clearly visible from the river and also from the nearby Marchfeld field in Austria. Accounts of outsider travelers and guidebooks often explained the beauty of the Theben castle but the sources did not indicate either that Pressburgers genuinely linked it to their city or that they would have visited it frequently. It rather seems that before the castle was endowed with national relevance and before modern practices of leisure (such as excursions) became popular, Theben and Pressburg had lived side by side.

The castle had a long history. In the ninth century it was a major fortress, and perhaps the capital of Moravia, too, particularly under Duke Rastislav (846–869/70). Later it lost its military significance and it was finally demolished by Napoleon's army in 1809. Since then, Theben has been simply a romantic ruin above the Danube.[85]

Theben held the greatest importance for Slovak nationalism. As the works of Slovak enlightened scholars concerning Moravia exercised more and more influence, Theben gradually became one of the most important locations for the emerging Slovak national movement. The romantic Slovak national intellectuals in particular portrayed Theben as the capital of the Moravians. The castle appeared several times in the influential romantic epics of Ján Hollý (*Svatopluk*, 1833; *Cirillo-Methodiada*, 1835; *Sláv*, 1839), and in the most powerful poetic articulation of the pan-Slav idea, Jan Kollár's *Slávy dcera* (1824). In Kollár's poem, Theben appears as a major element of the Slav national landscape, together with the Danube and the Lomnický and Křivan peaks in the High Tatras. As the Moravian period was seen as the Slovak golden age, the ruined Theben castle was the perfect symbol of past glory and at the same time also expressed the future resurrection of the nation.[86] This process could not be stopped even by such influential scholars as Pavel Josef Šafařík, who rejected the idea of Theben having been the ancient Moravian capital, arguing instead for Velehrad, a village in the modern Austrian crownland Moravia, as the seat of Rastislav.[87]

Once the belletrists had constructed the romantic *topos* of the past golden age, embodied by the ruins of the Castle of Theben, Slovak national activists started to use it for national purposes. The construction of the Theben myth correlated with the Pressburg-centered period of Slovak nationalism, enabling and encouraging national activists to carry out political activities in the castle, within walking distance of the city center. The first and most important of these events was an excursion by Ľudovít Štúr and his students of the Lutheran Lyceum in 1836. In the course of this excursion, the participants sang Slovak national songs and poems and finally re-baptized themselves choosing ancient Slavic forenames. This excursion clearly copied Christian traditions; walking to a holy place and performing religious acts there are necessary parts of Christian pilgrimages.[88]

Štúr's national pilgrimage provoked a negative reaction in the city. Rumor had it that "pan-Slav" students sacrificed a pig to the ninth-century Moravian ruler Svatopluk, setting fire to the animal using burning pictures of Miklós Wesselényi and István Széchenyi (leading figures of the Hungarian national-liberal movement), and called for the Magyar nation to perish. Štúr's excursion was interpreted as an attack on the emerging Hungarian liberalism and the Magyar nation itself; indeed, the story of the animal sacrifice deprived the trip of its Christian character. As a consequence of these allegations, students of the Catholic gymnasium provoked a fight with the students of the Lutheran Lyceum.[89] The very change of identity patterns in this conflict is remarkable: the students' denominational difference was suddenly embedded into the national framework, identifying Lutheran as Slovak and Catholic as Magyar, despite the students of both schools learning Latin and speaking German, Magyar, or Slovak as their mother tongue. The fight did not discourage Lutheran Slovak students, who regularly conducted similar excursions in the following years.[90]

Yet the importance of Theben started to decline from the 1860s. As the Slovak national movement moved to the Tatras, the number of Slovak national activists able to organize any performance in Theben decreased significantly. References to the castle in the Slovak national press became sporadic. The festivities commemorating the 1000th anniversary of Cyril and Methodius were mostly held in Nitra, Turčiansky Svätý Martin, Baňská Bystrica, and Velehrad in Moravia; there is no evidence of such celebrations in Theben.[91]

While Theben became a standard reference in Slovak national literature in the mid nineteenth century, it remained quite unimportant in other national imaginations. Due to its border location, Theben was usually referred to as Porta Hungarica, the Gate of Hungary.[92] The prominently visible castle caught the attention of travelers, prompting several descriptions of the ruins.[93] The border function along the main route to Vienna and the picturesque ruins made Theben quite well known, but it lacked importance for the Magyar national imagination. Indeed, until the mid-nineteenth century, the Moravian origins of the castle were also accepted by Magyar authors.[94] The Moravian concept came to be challenged from the mid nineteenth century as national narratives started to diverge. The Moravian past was consciously downplayed by Magyar historians of the second half of the century, so they were happy to buy the arguments of Šafařík identifying Rastislav's capital with Velehrad in order to dismantle the pre-Magyar importance of Theben.[95] This narrative was also popularized in the Magyar media and in government-supported Slovak papers with the apparent goal of undermining the distribution of the Slovak national past.[96]

Until the very millennial year, no Magyar national monument marked the presence of the modern Magyar nation either in the city or in the vicinity. The millennial year provided a great occasion to address this "shortcoming."

Notes

1. The ranks of particular locations in the urban hierarchy can be found in Beluszky and Győri, *The Hungarian Urban Network*, 100–24. For the number of factories, see *Magyar statisztikai közlemények* 2 (1904): 966–1010. The administrative functions are listed in József Jekelfalussy, ed., *A Magyar Korona Országainak Helységnévtára 1900* (Budapest: Pesti Könyvnyomda-Részvénytársaság, 1900). These references apply to the other investigated cities.
2. Ödön Vutkovich, "Pozsony," in *Magyarország vármegyéi és városai: Pozsony vármegye, Pozsony sz. kir. város, Nagyszombat, Bazin, Modor, és Szentgyörgy r. t. városok*, ed. Samu Borovszky (Budapest: Apollo, n. d.), 131–68.
3. G. R. Gleig, *Germany, Bohemia and Hungary: Visited in 1837* (London: John W. Parker, 1839), 2: 390–92. The same observation was made in 1852 by Charles Loring Brace, *Hungary in 1851; with an Experience of the Austrian Police* (New York: Charles Scribner, 1852), 22.
4. Raimund Friedrich Kaindl, *Geschichte der Deutschen in den Karpathenländern* (Gotha: Friedrich Andreas Perthes, 1911), 3: 312.
5. Uzor Kuppis, *Jelentés a Pozsonyi Dalárda huszonöt évi művészeti tevékenységéről 1857–1882* (Pozsony: Stampfel, Eder és társai, 1882).

6. Josef Tancer, *Im Schatten Wiens: Zur deutschsprachigen Presse und Literatur im Pressburg des 18. Jahrhunderts* (Bremen: Lumière, 2008), 29.

7. J. J. Skalský, "Vývin mesta Bratislavy po stránke národnostnej, administratívnej a politickej," in *Zlatá kniha mesta Bratislavy* (Bratislava: Čechoslovakia, 1928), 18.

8. *A pozsonyi Toldy-Kör harmincéves története* (Pozsony: Wigand F. K., 1905), 11; Eleonóra Babejová, *Fin-de-Siècle Pressburg: Conflict & Cultural Coexistence in Bratislava 1897–1914* (Boulder, CO: East European Monographs, 2003), 85–91.

9. Elena Mannová, "Associations in Bratislava in the Nineteenth Century: Middle Class Identity or Identities in a Multiethnic City?" in *Civil Society, Associations and Urban Places: Class, Nation and Culture in Nineteenth-Century Europe*, ed. Graeme Morton, Boudien de Vries, and R. J. Morris (Aldershot: Ashgate, 2006), 80.

10. József Könyöki, *Kleiner Wegweiser Pressburg's und seiner Umgebung mit einer Karte von Pressburg* (Pressburg: Angermayer, 1873), 1–3.

11. Károly Angermayer, *A Preßburger Zeitung Magyarország legrégebbi hirlapja története: Geschichte der Preßburger Zeitung* (Pozsony: Angermayer Károly, 1896), 10 and 23; Mária Rózsa, "Pozsony a német nyelvű helyi sajtóban (1850–1920)," in *Fejezetek Pozsony történetéből magyar és szlovák szemmel*, ed. Gábor Czoch (Pozsony: Kalligram, 2005), 420–36.

12. Johannes Jónás, *Rückblick auf die fünfzigjährige Thätigkeit der Preßburger ersten Sparcassa in den Jahren 1842–1891* (Pressburg: Stampfel, Eder, 1892), 36–38.

13. Elena Mannová, "Identitätsbildung der Deutschen in Pressburg/Bratislava im 19. Jahrhundert," *Halbasien: Zeitschrift für deutsche Literatur und Kultur Südosteuropas* 5, no. 2 (1995): 60–76.

14. Elena Mannová, "Die Entstehung einer neuen Hauptstadt und der Wandel der Vereinsöffentlichkeit: Pressburg 1900–1939," in *Stadt und Öffentlichkeit in Ostmitteleuropa 1900–1939*, ed. Andreas R. Hofmann and Anna Veronika Wendland (Stuttgart: Franz Steiner, 2002), 188.

15. Károly Benyovszky, *A pozsonyi magyar szinészet története 1867-ig* (Bratislava–Pozsony: Steiner Zsigmond, 1928); Tamás Szekcső, "Sz. Kir. Pozsony városának és környékének helyrajzi és statisztikai ismertetése," in *Pozsony és környéke* (Pozsony: Wigand Károly Frigyes, 1865), 101; Milena Cesnaková-Michalcová, *Geschichte des deutschsprachigen Theaters in der Slowakei* (Cologne: Böhlau, 1997), 211–28.

16. Károly Samarjay, *A pozsonyi régi és új színház: Töredékek Pozsony multja és jelenéből* (Pozsony: Wigand F. K., 1886).

17. Gábor Pávai Vajna, *A pozsonyi színügyi kérdésről* (Pozsony: Wigand F. K., 1901).

18. Cesnaková-Michalcová, *Geschichte des deutschsprachigen Theaters*, 158–63.

19. Adalbert Toth, *Parteien und Reichstagswahlen in Ungarn 1848 bis 1892* (Munich: R. Oldenbourg, 1973), 94 and 157.

20. Dániel Szabó, "A Néppárt az 1896. évi országgyűlési választásokon," *Századok* 112, no. 4 (1978): 756.

21. Pieter C. van Duin, *Central European Crossroads: Social Democracy and National Revolution in Bratislava (Pressburg), 1867–1921* (New York: Berghahn Books, 2009), 90–97.

22. Babejová, *Fin-de-Siècle Pressburg*, 152.

23. Peter Brock, *The Slovak National Awakening: An Essay in the Intellectual History of East Central Europe* (Toronto: University of Toronto Press, 1976), 17.

24. *Plody zboru Učencû Řeči Českoslowanské Prešporského* (Prešporok: Landerer, 1836), introduction without page numbers. Out of the total 286 subscriptions, there were 172 in Hungary; in Pressburg, 41 subscriptions were by private persons and 30 by bookshops. Pressburg was followed by Prešov, with only 11 subscriptions.

25. Babejová, *Fin-de-Siècle Pressburg*, 185–88. While the 1836 *Plody* yearbook was subscribed to mostly in Pressburg, the 1864 *Lipa* literary yearbook had only 11 local subscribers out of 528. See *Lipa* 3 (1864): 395–406.

26. Konštantin Čulen, *Slovenské študentské tragédie* (Bratislava: Slovenska Liga, 1935).

27. Elena Mannová, "Vereinsbälle der Preßburger Bürger im 19. Jahrhundert," in *Städtisches Alltagsleben in Mitteleuropa vom Mittelalter bis zum Ende des 19. Jahrhunderts: Die Referate des internationelen Symposions in Časta–Píla vom 11.–14. September 1995*, ed. Viliam Čičaj and Othmar Pickl (Bratislava: Academic Electronic Press, 1998), 253.

28. József Zichy to Gyula Szapáry, 1890, SNA, 46, 2–11–1450/90; István Kutsera to Gyula Szalovszky, 10 September 1895, ŠOAB, 1052, 1896–262–35/1896–91 eln./1895; István Kutsera to Gyula Szalovszky, 9 June 1897, ŠOAB, 1052, 264–2/1897–18/1897 eln.

29. Vince Nádor to Gyula Andrássy, 21 May 1907, MNL OL, K 149, 1907–2–315, 51; István Kutsera to Dénes Vay, 17 January 1899, ŠOAB, 1052, 305–1/1899–3/1899 eln.

30. Milan Podrimavský, "Slovenská národná strana vo volebnej aktivite r. 1901," *Historický Časopis* 26, no. 3 (1978): 409–36.

31. Mihály Mudroň, *A Felvidék: Felelet Grünwald Béla hasonnevű politikai tanulmányára* (Pozsony: Stampfel, 1878).

32. Babejová, *Fin-de-Siècle Pressburg*, 95–98.

33. van Duin, *Central European Crossroads*, 91, 96, and 139.

34. For instance, according to the 1900 census, 1021 artisans declared German, 281 Magyar, and 255 Slovak as their mother tongue, while 808 public servants declared Magyar, 237 German, and a mere 25 Slovak. MNL OL, XXXII–23–h, census 1900, box 167, folio Pressburg, table 41.

35. *A Toldy-Kör a pozsonyi egyetemért* (Pozsony: Angermayer Károly, 1908), 9.

36. Babejová, *Fin-de-Siècle Pressburg*, 38 and 59–60.

37. *Annual Report of the Pressburg Lutheran Lyceum*, 1840/41, 1853/54, 1857/58, and 1864/65; Endre Bozóky and Károly Antolik, *A pozsonyi állami főreáliskola története 1850–1893 és az intézet jelenlegi* állapota (Pozsony: Eder István, 1895), 59–60 and 70; Tivadar Ortvay, *Száz év egy hazai főiskola életéből: A pozsonyi Kir. Akadémiának 1784-től 1884-ig való fennállása alkalmából* (Budapest: Magyar Kir. Egyetemi Könyvnyomda, 1884), 222–28; Bertalan Schönvitzky, *A pozsonyi kir. kath. főgymnasium története: Hazánk ezeréves fennállásának emlékére* (Pozsony: Eder István, 1896), 358–67.

38. *Annual Report of the Pressburg Commercial Academy*, 1885/86; *Annual Report of the Pressburg State Female Teachers' Training College*, 1873/74; *Annual Report of the Pressburg State Upper Grammar School for Girls*, 1894/95; *Annual Report of the Pressburg Ursuline Middle School for Girls*, 1893/94.

39. József Róth, *A pozsonymegyei tankerület valamint külön Pozsony szab. kir. városa népoktatásának 1877. évi állapota (tekintettel a városi iskolák történeti fejlődésére)* (Pozsony: Nirschy Ferenc könyvnyomdája, 1878), 50–60.

40. Mór Pisztóry, *Pozsony: Közgazdasági, közművelődési és közegészségügyi állapotok ismertetése. Különlenyomat a Nemzetgazdasági Szemle 1887. évi XI. évfolyamának 5. 6. és 7. füzetéből* (Budapest: Athenaeum, 1887), 59.

41. In the 1895/96 school year, only 33.8% of non-Magyar-speaking pupils knew Magyar, but in 1900/1901 the same figure was 89.5%. See *Annual Report of the Pressburg Roman Catholic Elementary Schools*, 1895/96: 12–13, and 1900/1901: 5 and 13–15. Such a boom is hard to believe; it is likely that the method of measuring the knowledge of Magyar was changed. However, there is no reason to doubt the trend toward increasing knowledge of the state language.

42. Karl Samarjay, *Das 50-jährige Jubiläum der Preßburger Casino am 1. Juli 1887* (N.p., n.d.); Károly Samarjay, *Vázlatok a pozsonyi társas körök a Toldy-kör, Casino és Magyar Kör ügyében*

(Pozsony: Wigand F. K., 1885); Elena Mannová, "Elitné spolky v Bratislave v 19. a 20. storočí," in *Diferenciácia mestského spoločenstva v každodennom živote*, ed. Zuzana Beňušková and Peter Salner (Bratislava: Ústav etnológie SAV, 1999), 52–69.

43. Babejová, *Fin-de-Siècle Pressburg*, 64–65.
44. R. Várkonyi, *Thaly Kálmán*, 185.
45. Endre Masznyik, *A "Pozsonyi Toldy-Kör" hivatásáról: Különlenyomat a "Nyugatmagyarországi Hiradó" 253. számából* (Pozsony: Wigand F. K., 1905); Babejová, *Fin-de-Siècle Pressburg*, 65–73.
46. Babejová, *Fin-de-Siècle Pressburg*, 65–74; Mannová, "Associations in Bratislava," 83.
47. Babejová, *Fin-de-Siècle Pressburg*, 97.
48. Rudolf Bergner, *Eine Fahrt duch's Land der Rastelbinder: Bilder und Skizzen aus Nordungarn* (Leipzig: S. L. Morgenstern, 1883), 3–4.
49. Monika Glettler, "Ethnische Vielfalt in Pressburg und Budapest um 1910," *Ungarn Jahrbuch* 16 (1988): 50–53. According to the 1900 census, 57% of Pressburg's population was born outside the city.
50. According to the 1890 census, 29,404 inhabitants of Pressburg were born outside of the city, out of which 7874 were from the Austrian half of the Empire. Precise data on the national/linguistic proportion of these "Austrians" is not available, but it is presumable that they were mostly German and Czech speakers. *Magyar statisztikai közlemények* 1 (1893): 18–19.
51. MNL OL, XXXII–23–h, census 1880, box 524, folio Pressburg, table XVI, and 1900, box 283, folio Pressburg, table 47–48/d.
52. MNL OL, XXXII–23–h, census 1900, box 167, folio Pressburg, table 41.
53. Babejová, *Fin-de-Siècle Pressburg*, 34–37; Vladimír Horváth, "Preßburger Bürger in der inneren Stadt (1740–1916)," in *Städtisches Alltagsleben in Mitteleuropa vom Mittelalter bis zum Ende des 19. Jahrhunderts: Die Referate des internationalen Symposions in* Časta-Píla *vom 11.–14. September 1995*, ed. Viliam Čičaj and Othmar Pickl (Bratislava: Academic Electronic Press, 1998), 225–30.
54. MNL OL, XXXII–23–h, census 1880, box 531, folio Pressburg, table XIII.
55. MNL OL, XXXII–23–h, census 1880, box 531, folio Pressburg, table XIII, and 1900, box 283, folio Pressburg, tables 47/a and 47–48/c.
56. MNL OL, XXXII–23–h, census 1900, box 283, folio Pressburg, tables 47 and 48/c.
57. The calculations are based on the percentages of occupation group no. 3 (civil and church service and free professions, thus covering most of the *Bildungsbürgertum*) in relation to the complete Jewish population of the respective towns. All the cities compared to Pressburg were famous for their modern, mostly Neolog, Jewry. See *Magyar statisztikai közlemények* 56 (1915): 380–81 and 384–85.
58. Karl Benyovszky and Josef Grünsfeld, *Preßburger Ghettobilder* (Bratislava-Pressburg: Sigmund Steiner, 1932); Sigmund Mayer, *Die Wiener Juden: Kommerz, Kultur, Politik 1700–1900* (Vienna: K. Löwit, 1917), 3–203.
59. Jacob Katz, "Towards a Biography of the Hatam Sofer," in idem., *Divine Law in Human Hands: Case Studies in Halakhic Flexibility* (Jerusalem: Magnes Press, Hebrew University, 1998), 403–43.
60. David Groß, "Äusserer Verlauf der Geschichte der Juden," in *Die Juden und die Judengemeinde Bratislava in Vergangenheit und Gegenwart: Ein Sammelwerk*, ed. Hugo Gold (Brünn: Jüdischer Buchverlag, 1932), 3–10. A later source estimated an Orthodox community of 900–1000 members, the Neolog 60–70 at the schism. See Josef Grünsfeld, "Geschichte der orth. israelitischen Kultusgemeinde," in *Die Juden und die Judengemeinde Bratislava in Vergangenheit und Gegenwart: Ein Sammelwerk*, ed. Hugo Gold (Brünn: Jüdischer Buchverlag, 1932), 109.

61. "A pozsonyi Talmud-tórával egyesitett orth. izraelita elemi fiuiskola keletkezésének és fejlődésének története," in *A magyar-zsidó felekezet elemi és polgári iskoláinak monográfiája*, ed. Jónás Barna and Fülöp Csukási (Budapest: Corvina, 1896), 1: 414–28; "Die Schulen der orth. israelitischen Gemeinde," in *Die Juden und die Judengemeinde Bratislava in Vergangenheit und Gegenwart: Ein Sammelwerk*, ed. Hugo Gold (Brünn: Jüdischer Buchverlag, 1932), 121–25.

62. Samuel Bettelheim, "Geschichte der Preßburger Jeschiba," in *Die Juden und die Judengemeinde Bratislava in Vergangenheit und Gegenwart: Ein Sammelwerk*, ed. Hugo Gold (Brünn: Jüdischer Buchverlag, 1932), 61–67; Josef Grünsfeld, "Neue Geschichte der Jeschiba," in *Die Juden und die Judengemeinde Bratislava in Vergangenheit und Gegenwart: Ein Sammelwerk*, ed. Hugo Gold (Brünn: Jüdischer Buchverlag, 1932), 67–69; Shaul Stampfer, "Hungarian Yeshivot, Lithuanian Yeshivot and Joseph Ben-David," *Jewish History* 11, no. 1 (Spring 1997): 131–41.

63. David Groß, "Zionistisches Leben in Bratislava," in *Die Juden und die Judengemeinde Bratislava in Vergangenheit und Gegenwart: Ein Sammelwerk*, ed. Hugo Gold (Brünn: Jüdischer Buchverlag, 1932), 141–46; Solomon Hornik, "Misrachi in Pressburg und in der Slowakei," in *Die Juden und die Judengemeinde Bratislava in Vergangenheit und Gegenwart: Ein Sammelwerk*, ed. Hugo Gold (Brünn: Jüdischer Buchverlag, 1932), 147–50; Ehud Luz, *Parallels Meet: Religion and Nationalism in the Early Zionist Movement (1882–1904)* (Philadelphia: Jewish Publication Society, 1988), 249–54.

64. Benő Berger, "A pozsonyi kong. izr. hitközség fiuiskolájának monográfiája," in *A magyar-zsidó felekezet elemi és polgári iskoláinak monográfiája*, ed. Jónás Barna and Fülöp Csukási (Budapest: Corvina, 1896), 1: 331–33.

65. Ibid., 1: 331–52. Cf. Heinrich Buxbaum, *Geschichte der israel. öffentlichen Gemeinde-Primär-Hauptschule, und des Hermann Todesco'schen Stiftungsgebäudes in Pressburg: Von ihrem Entstehen bis auf den heutigen Tag (1820–1884)* (Pressburg: Selbstverlag des Verfassers, 1884), 22 and 38.

66. Carsten Wilke, "Orthodoxy's Stronghold: The Educational Policies of the Pressburg Yeshiva and Their Bearing on the Hungarian Jewish Schism" (paper presented at the conference Schism, Sectarianism and Jewish Denominationalism: Hungarian Jewry in a Comparative Perspective, Budapest, 14 October 2009).

67. Alexander F. Heksch, *Neuester Führer durch Pressburg und Umgebungen* (Pressburg: Selbstverlag des Verfassers, 1880), 20–21.

68. György Schulpe, *Pozsony és a harmadik egyetem: Értekező felhívás* (Pozsony: Drodtleff Rezső, 1893), 13.

69. See the festive speech of Sándor Vutkovich, "A millennium megünneplése Pozsonyban," *Nyugatmagyarországi Hiradó*, 12 May 1896.

70. Babejová, *Fin-de-Siècle Pressburg*, 65–68, 155–58, and 170–78.

71. Felix Jeschke, "Dracula on Rails: The *Preßburgerbahn* between Imperial Space and National Body, 1867–1935," *Central Europe* 10, no. 1 (May 2012): 1–17.

72. Alexander F. Heksch, *Die Donau von ihrem Ursprung bis an die Mündung: Eine Schilderung von Land und Leuten des Donaugebietes* (Vienna: A. Hartleben, 1881), 411–25; A. Imendörffer, W. Gerlai, and J. Sziklay, *Nach und durch Ungarn: Von Wien nach Budapest* (Zürich: Orell Füssli, n.d.), 32–33; Tivadar Ortvay, "Pressburg und das Preßburger Comitat," in *Die Österreichisch-Ungarische Monarchie in Wort und Bild: Ungarn V/1* (Vienna: Verlag der kaiserlich-königlichen Hof- und Staatsdruckerei, 1898), 192–97; István Rakovszky, "Adatok Pozsony történetéből," in *Pozsony és környéke* (Pozsony: Wigand Károly Frigyes, 1865), 1–73.

73. Emil Kumlik, *Adalékok a pozsonyi országgyűlések történetéhez (1825–1848)* (Pozsony: Stampfel Hugó, 1908); Emil Kumlik, *Pozsony und der Freiheitskampf 1848/49* (Pozsony:

Karl Stampfel, 1905); Emil Kumlik, *A szabadságharc pozsonyi vértanui* (Pozsony: Stampfel Károly, 1905).

74. *Pozsony Sz. Kir. Város Törvényhatóságának a Magyar Országgyűlés Képviselőházához intézett emlékirata a Pozsonyban fölállítandó egyetem tárgyában* (Pozsony: Angermayer Károly, 1880).

75. Lajos Wagner, *A pozsonyi m. kir. állami tudomány-egyetem tervezete* (Pozsony: Stampfel Károly, 1900), 48–49. It is remarkable that Wagner's arguments almost completely coincided with the municipal pamphlet, as he stressed the cultural performance of the city much more than the national advantages.

76. Gábor Pávai Vajna, *Pozsony és a harmadik egyetem* (Pozsony: Stampfel Károly, 1884), 6.

77. Gábor Pávai Vajna, *Hol állítsuk fel a harmadik egyetemet?* (Pozsony: Wigand F. K., 1887).

78. Schulpe, *Pozsony és a harmadik egyetem*. György Schulpe was also an immigrant to the city, as he was born in Banat.

79. The other "Slovak central cities" were Pest, Banská Štiavnica, Banska Bystrica, and Liptovský Svätý Mikuláš. It is interesting that Turčiansky Svätý Martin, the town that was the unofficial capital of the Slovak national movement from the 1860s until 1918, was not on this list. It is even more remarkable that a year later Štúr failed to include Pressburg on the list of the centers of the Slovak national book trade. Demmel, *"Egész Szlovákia elfért,"* 57.

80. Karel Kálal, *Na krásném Slovensku* (Praha: Jos. R. Vilímek, n. d.), 57–58; Lubor Niederle, *Národopisná mapa uherských slováků na základě sčítání lidu z roku 1900* (Praha: Národopisná Společnost Českoslovanske, 1903); *Ottův slovník naučný: Illustrovaná encyklopaedie obecných vědemostí* (Praha: J. Otto, 1888–1909), s.v. "Prešpurk"; Ľudevít V. Rízner, *Krátky Zemepis so zvláštnym ohľadom na Kráľ'ovstvo Uhorské: Pre III., IV., a V. triedu slov. ľudových škôl* (Uh. Skalice: Jozef Škarnicl, 1876), 8; Maxmilian Weinberger, *Vzpomínky z cest* (Brno: Papežská Knihtiskárna Benediktinů Rajhradských, 1899), 79–86.

81. Ľubomír Lipták, "Nehlavné hlavné mesto?" *OS* 4, no. 8 (2000): 3–7.

82. Tivadar Ortvay, *Pozsony város utcái és terei: A város története utca- és térnevekben* (Pozsony: Wigand F. K., 1905).

83. Johann Batka and Emerich Wodiáner, *Zur Enthüllung des Hummel-Denkmals 16. October 1887. Joh. Nep. Hummel: Biographische Skizze. Geschichte des Denkmals und Rechnungsausweis* (Pressburg: Denkmal-Comité, 1887).

84. Elena Mannová, "Von Maria Theresia zum schönen Náci: Kollektive Gedächtnisse und Denkmalkultur in Bratislava," in *Die Besetzung des öffentlichen Raumes: Politische Plätze, Denkmäler und Straßennamen im europäischen Vergleich*, ed. Rudolf Jaworski and Peter Stachel (Berlin: Frank & Timme, 2007), 206.

85. Gabriela Kiliánová, *Identität und Gedächtnis in der Slowakei: Die Burg Devín als Erinnerungsort* (Frankfurt am Main: Peter Lang, 2012), 23–24.

86. Ibid., 30–40.

87. Pawel Josef Šafařjk, *Slowanské starožitnosti* (Praha: Jana Spurný, 1837), 831.

88. Vladimír Matula, *Devín, milý Devín: Národná slávnosť štúrovcov na Devíne 1836. História a tradícia* (Martin: Matica slovenská, 2008). Štúr, for instance, became Velislav.

89. Schönvitzky, *A pozsonyi kir. kath. főgymnasium*, 321–22.

90. Sámuel Markusovszky, *A pozsonyi ág. hitv. evang. Lyceum története kapcsolatban a pozsonyi ág. hitv. evang. egyház multjával* (Pozsony: Wigand F. K., 1896), 461; "Výlet na Devín," *Sokol: Časopis pre zábavu a poučenie*, 15 June and 30 June 1853.

91. Kiliánová, *Identität und Gedächtnis*, 43–44; Joseh M. Kirschbaum, "The Role of the Cyrilo-Methodian Tradition in Slovak National and Political Life," *Slovak Studies* 3 (1963): 165; Matula, *Devín, milý Devín*, 72–87.

92. Theben as a symbol of the western gate of Hungary became particularly well known due to the introductory poem of Endre Ady's *Új versek* (New Poems), entitled *Góg és Magóg fia vagyok én* (I Am the Son of Góg and Magóg): "May I now break through at Dévény / With the new songs of a new age?" Dévény in this context is a symbol of the border between the modern West and an underdeveloped Hungary. As *Új versek* is treated as the start of modern Magyar literature, it is still taught in every Hungarian school.

93. "Dévény várromjai," *Az ország tükre* 2, no. 22 (1863): 255; "Dévényi vár romjai," *Vasárnapi Ujság*, 13 July 1856; A. J. Gross-Hoffinger, *Die Donau vom Ursprung bis in das schwarze Meer: Ein Handbuch för Donaureisende von Ulm, Linz, Wien, Pesth, Galatz über das schwarze Meer nach Constantinopel* (Breslau: Eduard Trewendt, 1846), 198–99; Alexander F. Heksch, *Illustrirter Führer durch Pressburg und seine Umgebungen* (Vienna-Pressburg: C. Stampel, 1884), 80–82; Imendörffer et al., *Nach und durch Ungarn*, 8–9 and 36–37; Paget, *Hungary and Transylvania*, 1: 17–19. As early as 1831, a German traveler reported that Theben was a place already described by many authors. Adalbert Joseph Krickel, *Wanderung von Wien über Pressburg und Tyrnau in die Bergstädte Schemnitz, Kremnitz und Neusohl, und von da in die Turoß und das Waagthal* (Vienna: M. Ehr Adolph, 1831), 15.

94. István Sándor, "Szvatoplugról 's Divin Váráról," *Sokféle* 6 (1799): 19–24; "Theben," *Taschenbuch für die vaterländische Geschichte* 9 (1828): 359–60; Szekcső, "Sz. Kir. Pozsony városának," 108; Paul von Ballus, *Presburg und seine Umgebungen* (Presburg: Andreas Schwaiger und I. Landes, 1823), 239–41; Adolf Emmanuel Pernold, *Magyarország' Távcső-földképe: Első Osztály magában foglalván Pozsonyt a' környékeivel* (Bécs: szerző saját kiadása, 1839), 18; J. C. v. Thiele, *Das Königreich Ungarn: Ein topographisch-historisch-statistisches Kundgemälde. Das ganze dieses Landes in mehr denn 12,400 Artikeln umfassend* (Kaschau: Thiele'schen Erben, 1833), 1: 28.

95. Arnold Ipolyi, "Fehérhegységi utiképek: Második rész. Lefelé Szakolczától Dévényig," *Vasárnapi Ujsag*, 13 May 1860; *A Pallas nagy lexikona: Az összes ismeretek enciklopédiája* (Budapest: Pallas Irodalmi és Nyomdai Részvénytársaság, 1893–1904), s.v. "Dévény."

96. György Valentényi, "Dévény vára," *Nyugatmagyarországi Hiradó*, 18 October 1896; "Rumy hradu devínského," *Vlast' a Svet*, 28 October 1887.

Chapter 4

NITRA

❦

Figure 4.1. Nitra in 1887. Reprinted from *Vasárnapi Újság* 34, no. 36 (1887).

By the end of the nineteenth century, Nitra was a corporate town of average importance in northwestern Hungary. Around the millennial year,
it had a population of about fifteen thousand and, as a county seat with full-
fledged urban functions, was ranked twenty-sixth in the Hungarian urban
hierarchy. Its urban functions were mostly connected to administration and
culture. It was the most important town in and seat of Nitra County, and
hosted a Catholic bishopric and an infantry regiment. The town was also an
important cultural center in the region: Nitra County's only gymnasium (run
by the Piarist Order) and theater (supported by the municipality) were there

and it hosted a Catholic seminary and an adjoining library. Nitra's economy was less remarkable: traditional industries and lower plant size were common (only five industrial companies employed more than twenty workers in 1900), and it also lacked a well-established railway connection to other parts of the country, being served only by a side line.[1]

Fin-de-siècle Nitra was divided into three major districts. The townscape was ruled by the castle on the hill that had been the bishopric seat since the Middle Ages. The bishopric cathedral, palace, and the seminaries dominated this district, which was inhabited by clerics only. The castle hill was dominated by historic buildings: the cathedral dates back to the eleventh century and the other buildings were built mainly in Baroque style in the eighteenth century. In contrast, the downtown underwent a dramatic modernization in the second half of the nineteenth century: its muddy streets were paved, and its village-like small houses were replaced by modern, two-story buildings. This district hosted the county and the municipal administrations, the theater, the barracks, and a modern hospital. The gymnasium, built in the eighteenth century, was also located in the downtown.[2] Párovce, the former Jewish ghetto near the downtown, was incorporated into the town in 1886. This ghetto used to be infamous for its bad living conditions, small houses, chaotic streets, and lack of modern hygienic fixtures, which were gradually mended by the end of the nineteenth century in the course of modernization.[3]

In contrast to its average significance in fin-de-siècle Hungary, a millennium earlier the town had served as a major center of Moravia and early Slav Christianity, and gained therefore high importance in the modern Slovak national imagination. Despite this justification, the Slovak national elite failed to exercise a deep influence on the town's population, even though most of them spoke Slovak. The lack of Slovak nation-builders opened the way for Magyar national integration. Nevertheless, the Catholic Church and the conservative local bishops posed a major challenge to any national integration project. The millennial monument consequently challenged both Slovak national integration and the anti-liberal, nationally indifferent Catholic clergy.

Magyar Liberals vs. Catholics

The population of Nitra was divided into two large groups of denominations, Catholics and Jews (see Table 13.3 in the Appendix). In the mid-nineteenth century, the town's Christians spoke predominantly Slovak and the Jews German, and it was rare to hear Magyar.[4] The identity of Nitra was shaped mostly by the Catholic Church, whose local representatives were particularly indifferent to national matters. Both Nitra bishops in the period, Imre Palugyay (1838–58) and Ágoston Roskoványi (1859–92), contributed to the development of the diocese by building and supporting schools, publishing theological works, and promoting better organization in Catholic society, but political activity and national agitation were absent from their agendas.[5] The other important identifying element of the Nitra clergy was royalist loyalty. In Nitra's only secondary school, the Piarist gymnasium, Catholic and dynastic festivities were held more frequently than at other schools in Hungary, but Magyar national holidays were celebrated only occasionally. A Magyar national celebration commemorating 1848 became a standard program of the school year only in 1898, significantly lagging behind national standards.[6]

Embedded in a liberal and progressive framework, Magyar national ideas were rather unattractive to the Catholic clergy. The 1894/95 liberal ecclesiastical legislation particularly provoked Catholic ire and was not forgotten for many years. Even in 1896, when national sentiments were running high, in the nearby Prievidza district nineteen Catholic priests left a Magyar national association because it supported liberal newspapers.[7] Magyar nationalism started to exercise some influence on the Catholic clergy by the appointment of Imre Bende as bishop of Nitra. Bende was born in 1824 in the south Hungarian town of Baja; he became priest in Novi Sad where he actively engaged in local politics, which was dominated by Serbian liberal nationalists under the leadership of Svetozar Miletić. Bende became a member of the municipal assembly and in 1881 was elected to the Hungarian Parliament, where he joined the governing Liberal Party. Bende successfully combined Catholicism with Magyar national integration: in Novi Sad, he promoted Magyar instead of German as the language of instruction in Catholic primary schools and successfully lobbied for the foundation of a state-sponsored Catholic gymnasium educating in Magyar only. His efforts resulted in his appointment to bishop of Banská Bystrica in 1886, followed by a transfer to Nitra in 1893.[8] In his inauguration speech in Nitra, he called upon the audience to fulfill both religious and patriotic duties.[9] However, Bende seems to belong to the minority in the Nitra diocese: as the Catholic People's Party was founded, Nitra County emerged as its natural stronghold and was supported by a vast number of clergyman and Catholic voters.[10] In the town itself, the mayor and parliamentary deputy remained supporters of the Liberal Party but several Catholic candidates were elected to the municipal assembly in 1896.[11]

The Catholic clergy was definitely in a position to have a great impact on the Catholics, who made up approximately three-quarters of the town's population. Being the seat of the diocese, the town hosted several canons, monks, and other priests, who, together with the teachers of the Piarist gymnasium, made up a large part of the local intelligentsia. The school system was almost completely run by the Catholic Church. Several Catholic associations were active and the town's urban space was also dominated by the Church. The ideas of the Church were easily disseminated among the Catholic believers of the town, particularly after 1892, when the weekly *Nyitramegyei Szemle* was established.

The mostly Slovak-speaking Catholics were not confronted by Slovak national ideas at all. Due to the Catholic character of the town, the presence of Slovak national activism was closely interrelated with the denominational splits within Slovak nationalism. In the late eighteenth century, several Nitra priests participated in the first Slovak national academic association, the Trnava-based Slovak Learned Society (Slovenské učené tovarišstvo), a circle of intellectuals dominated by the Catholic clergy.[12] During the *Vormärz*, however, the Lutheran wing took the leadership in Slovak nationalism, which led to the almost complete absence of Nitra-based intellectuals, as shown in subscription lists for the *Vormärz* literary yearbooks. Out of 286 subscribers to the 1836 *Plody*, no one from Nitra is present, and the 1842 edition of Miloslav Hurban's yearbook, *Nitra*, attracted only a single local lawyer out of 434 subscribers.[13] As the relevance of the Lutheran-Catholic contestation within the Slovak national movement decreased, the 1860s witnessed some development in Slovak national positions in the town. In 1864, sixteen Nitra priests and a teacher at the Catholic gymnasium subscribed to the *Lipa* yearbook.[14] Even though these seventeen subscribers outnumbered those of Pressburg (only eleven), a Slovak society conscious of its Slovakness in Nitra was still a dream. Indeed, the total lack of secular subscribers showed a remarkable weakness of Slovak national activity in the town.

Slovak national activism was thus limited to the Catholic institutions, which meant quite a fragile framework for any national project. Even though Bishop Roskoványi and several canons and school teachers joined the St. Adalbert (Vojtech) Association (Spolok Sv. Adalberta [Vojtecha], a Slovak-speaking Catholic circle based in Trnava), this society can be seen as a Catholic rather than a national group.[15] The Slovak nation-builders in Nitra did not have the luck that their fellows in the Banská Bystrica diocese enjoyed during the 1850s and 1860s. While the Banská Bystrica bishop of that period, Štefan Moyzes (1850–69), was himself a leading Slovak national activist (he was the first chairman of the Matica slovenská),[16] the Nitra bishops were indifferent not only to the Magyar, but also to Slovak nationalism. In fact, Slovak national activism was completely absent in Nitra between the 1870s and 1918. The Slovak national elite, based in the Tatra towns, was therefore neither in a position to have any impact on the Slovak speakers of Nitra nor to influence the utilization of the town's urban space.[17]

The absence of Slovak national activism gave way to Magyar national politics. The local Magyar liberal elite found the Catholic identity and the low proportion of Magyar speakers indeed uncomfortable and worked hard to integrate the population of Nitra into the modern Magyar nation. Local Magyar national activists were true representatives of the liberal, progressive vision of Magyar nationalism that was promoted by the government. Similar to their Pressburg counterparts, they were mostly dependent on the government as clerks in the municipal or county administration. Nitra became the seat of several associations backed by the government to promote the idea of liberal Magyar nationalism. The most important among them was the Upper Hungarian Cultural Association (Felsőmagyarországi Közművelődési Egylet, FMKE).[18] The FMKE and other prestigious institutions, such as the local Casino, were dominated by civil servants, lawyers, and other middle class representatives of the Magyar national integration project. Magyar national ideas were transmitted through the activity of associations and the weekly *Nyitramegyei Közlöny*.

While the Catholic Church was reluctant to accept Magyar liberal nationalism, local Jews showed a remarkable willingness to participate in Magyar national integration, even though they were Orthodox (in 1908, a small Neolog community was established but the majority of Nitra Jews remained Orthodox). In contrast to Pressburg's Orthodox Jewry, which held reservations about Magyar national integration, the Nitra Orthodox changed their loyalty rapidly. The elite of the Nitra Jewry seemed to be enthusiastic supporters of liberal and progressive Magyar nationalism. Jewish leaders confirmed their Magyar national loyalty on many occasions. Several founding members of the FMKE were Jews, and the Jewish elementary school had a so-called FMKE Day, a full-day Magyar national celebration each year. The first solid Magyar weekly, the liberal-nationalist *Nyitramegyei Közlöny*, was also established by a Jewish lawyer in 1881. Furthermore, Jews played a decisive role in the modernization of the town as founders of the local savings bank and members of the municipal assembly and municipal administration.[19]

The Jews of Nitra seem to confirm Victor Karady's theory about the "unwritten social contract" between the liberal gentry and Hungarian Jews. According to Karady, the liberal Magyar gentry sought

> ethnic allies for the realization of its program of nation building and modernization. Jews proved to be reliable allies. In return, the liberal nobility (the future ruling class), extended protection against manifestations of violent anti-Semitism and offered a plan for a tolerant, secularized modern political constitutionality which, besides free exercise of religion, guaranteed Jews almost all freedom of occupational and economic mobility.[20]

Despite the clear Jewish support for liberal Magyar nationalism, denominational cleavage did not disappear. Social, economic, even spatial differences in Jewish and Christian society continued to dominate in Nitra throughout the period. In the first wave of Jewish immigration in the eighteenth century, Jews were not allowed to settle in Nitra proper, but inhabited the Párovce suburb. During the dualist period, the well-off Jews moved to the downtown but the majority of local Jewry continued to live in Párovce. Jews earned their living mostly from small trade and banking, while rarely in agriculture or handicrafts, which left them subject to accusations of exploiting Christians.[21] Jews and Christians were separated in education too. Jewish children were sent to the local Jewish elementary school, attended only by Jews. At the higher levels of education, a certain amalgamation was inevitable, but denominational differences persisted. The trade section of the municipal Trade and Commerce Middle School was attended by Catholic artisan students, while the commercial section was dominated by Jewish pupils.[22] Local associations showed divisions too, particularly in the denomination-based welfare system.[23] Balls and other social events were also often attended by members of one denomination only.[24] The journal *Neutraer Zeitung-Nyitrai Hirlap* was edited by Jewish journalists and represented a liberal Jewish perspective.

The poor conditions of Párovce, the "strange" Jewish customs, and the economic differences between the Christian and Jewish communities evoked considerable antisemitism among the Catholic population of the town. Local antisemitism was, however, not strong enough to provoke pogroms, or to give the parliamentary seat to an antisemitic politician, even during the early 1880s, when Hungarian antisemitism reached its zenith and several anti-Jewish riots took place in Nitra County.[25]

The absence of Slovak nationalism in Nitra meant that the population of the town was not confronted by national contest. By the last decade of the nineteenth century, the main political cleavage was Catholicism vs. liberalism. The political and religious cleavages formed three blocks in the local society: liberal Christians, Catholics, and Jews.

"The Town Today Has a Definitely Magyar Character"

As the Catholic clergy was rather indifferent to national questions, Nitra's Jewish elite supported Magyar national integration, Slovak national activists were absent, the Magyar national protagonists found favorable conditions. The most visible achievement of the Magyar national integration was the complete Magyarization of the school system. Although the Catholic clergy was reluctant to disseminate Magyar national ideas, Magyar was introduced as the main language of instruction in all schools. The Piarist gymnasium instructed in Latin until 1844, and following the Hungarian Diet's decision to introduce Magyar as the administrative language of Hungary, the school started to teach both in Magyar and in Latin. During the 1850s, instruction was offered in German and "Slav" (probably using *bernolákovčina*, the language standard introduced by the Catholic priest Anton Bernolák in 1787). From 1860, Magyar became the main language, German was taught as a mandatory subject, and

"Slav" as an elective subject until 1868/69 when the instruction of the latter was abolished, resulting in the school teaching only in Magyar and offering German as a second language.[26]

A similar process took place in the town's elementary schools. In 1840, in the Catholic elementary school, Latin, Magyar, and "Slav" were used, but they were replaced by Slav and German in the neo-absolutist period. From 1860, Magyar became the main language of instruction, complemented by optional German and "Slav" courses. From 1878/79, "Slav" courses were completely abolished and elective German courses were offered only to girls until 1894/95, when the last German classes ceased to exist, making the Catholic schools completely monolingual (Magyar).[27] New schools, including a Municipal Trade School and a Catholic Middle School for Girls, were founded as solely Magyar institutions.[28] The Jewish Elementary School followed this pattern with a minor delay; Magyar was introduced as the main language of instruction in 1881.[29]

Magyar became the language of other institutions too. Theatrical plays were occasionally performed in German and Magyar until 1883, when a theater was built to host Magyar ensembles only.[30] The local media market also witnessed the advance of Magyar: occasional Magyar papers were published from the 1870s, followed by several well-established papers between the 1880s and World War I. At the same time, German-Magyar bilingual papers were also published, but their originally overwhelming use of German was replaced by Magyar. Due to a lack of sources, there is no evidence of the evolution of language usage in associations, churches, and the municipal administration, but presumably all of them became officially monolingual in Magyar by the last quarter of the nineteenth century. By the end of the nineteenth century, Magyar had become the only language spoken in cafes, restaurants, and other institutions of "better society," although some decades earlier even the local gentry had used Slovak.[31]

The extensive introduction of Magyar in public institutions, particularly schools, led to remarkable results, as shown in Table 13.4 in the Appendix. In 1880, Magyar speakers constituted the smallest group of Nitra's population, outnumbered by Slovak speakers and mostly German-speaking Jews. In 1890, Magyar speakers emerged as the second largest group; a decade later they were in first place, and finally, in 1910, the absolute majority of the town declared Magyar as its mother tongue, satisfying the demands of contemporary Magyar observers. The success of this process was strengthened further by the fact that the "new Magyars" were mostly not the product of immigration to the town, since Nitra's industry did not attract a large population. The rocketing increase in Magyar speakers was rather the result of the change in mother tongue admitted in the official census. In 1900, 78% of native Magyar speakers declared themselves multilingual. This suggests a high number of Magyar speakers who either took up Magyar instead of their original Slovak or German, or were socialized in a bilingual environment. The Magyarization of Jews was particularly remarkable: in the same year, 48% of Jews declared Magyar as their mother tongue, but bilingualism (knowing German) was common.[32]

These figures caused Magyar national activists to celebrate the advance of the state language and the presumed expansion of the Magyar national identity as well. As a contemporary analyst remarked:

> The town today has a definitely Magyar character, even though it is still inhabited by a large number of foreign speakers. They, however, follow the general trend, as the cultural institutions in the direct service of civilization are Magyars only, so amalgamate into the Magyar intelligentsia without resistance.[33]

Despite the efficient statistical Magyarization and the exclusive position of Magyar in cultural and administrative institutions, a deep Magyar national identity remained rather elusive. The fragile national identity of the Nitra population lasted well into the interwar period. The incorporation of the town into Czechoslovakia in 1918 suddenly changed the patterns of linguistic behavior, as the first Czechoslovak census, carried out in 1921, found 71% Slovak-speaking and a mere 11% Magyar-speaking inhabitants. This means that in just eleven years the proportion of declared mother tongues had turned completely upside down.[34] The Czechoslovak authorities had to realize that local children lacked any kind of national identity, so they had to be educated to become "good" Czechoslovaks.[35] Slovak national historiography interpreted these details as the liberation of the suppressed, denationalized, and Magyarized Slovaks. However, the depth of the change of identities should not be overestimated. A typical opinion, articulated by a Hungarian and then Czechoslovak civil servant, stated that:

> In the evenings we keep on dancing *csárdás* on the Zobor hill. And what has actually happened? Not a big deal at all. In the past we used to speak Slovak in the kitchen but Magyar in the office. Now it is upside down. We are *povedaling* [talking] in Slovak in the office and in Magyar at home, that is all.[36]

By the late nineteenth century, the national identity of the Nitra masses must have been even more indefinite. As national affiliation did not form the primary marker of social identification, the Christian–Jewish and the Catholic–liberal split represented the most relevant points in collective identity. It is not surprising, therefore, that the town's Magyar national elite welcomed the millennial monument with enthusiasm. A large monument was certainly needed to fix Magyar national identity, as the Catholic Church dominated not only the town's identity but its urban space as well.

The Lasting Impact of Moravia: Reading the Town

Three different readings of Nitra emerged: a Catholic, a national Slovak, and finally a national Magyar one. The Catholic reading, in accordance with the policy of the diocese, was indifferent to national questions. The works published by Catholic authors dealt in depth with the past of the Church institutions, including the diocese, monasteries, churches, and schools. These topics allowed them to avoid contradictory Magyar and Slovak narratives and the issue of the Jewish presence in the town. A complete Catholic narrative of the town never emerged, as the analysis of the particular Catholic past seemed to have satisfied the demands of the clergy.[37]

The Catholic past of the town was also used by Slovak national activists. From the eighteenth century, it was well known that Nitra had been the seat of several Moravian rulers and a diocese.[38] It was presumed that the Slavic apostles, Cyril and Methodius, had been active in the town, although no written evidence proved this.[39] Nitra soon became a place of outstanding importance in the Slovak historiography and symbolic geography. The early Slovak national historical narrative already credited Nitra as the most important town in Slovak history.[40] Three overlapping myths were constructed: the town was praised as the mother of Slovak towns, the cradle of Slovak Christianity, and the seat of St. Methodius.[41] Nitra, just like Theben, became a symbol of the lost glory of the Slovak nation.[42] The town's glorious Moravian past was recalled in many poems and literary and scientific works, including the well-known poem and song *Milá Nitra* (Dear Nitra). It is a telling fact that Hurban, a Lutheran minister, published his literary yearbook under the title *Nitra*, referring to a town lacking any Protestant population but central to a Catholic diocese.

As detailed sources describing Nitra in the Moravian period were not available, an account of the town in the early Middle Ages could not be written. Instead, the history of Moravia replaced a town-centered narrative. By the late nineteenth century, the key person in imagining the Moravian past was František Víťazoslav Sasinek, Catholic priest and self-trained historian. Sasinek's narrative was radically anti-Magyar: he tried to deprive Árpád of his Magyar character by claiming that his people had been "Slavic Turks" and Khazars, and pointed to the Muslim tribes of Pechenegs and Cumanians as the forefathers of the Magyars.[43] He also rejected the idea that Árpád had conquered the "Slovak land," claiming that it had belonged to some Czech and then Polish princes and only became part of Hungary as late as 1025, following the death of Polish monarch Bolesław the Valiant. After 1025, the "Slovak territories" were ruled by a Slovak prince in Nitra, appointed by the Hungarian king. Sasinek credited this polity with a Slovak character and thought it to have been based on the former Moravian state.[44] Furthermore, he supposed strong connections between the Nitra diocese and the archbishop of Prague during the entire tenth and eleventh centuries, which meant that Sasinek believed in the undisturbed cultural contuinity of Moravian Christianity even after the fall of Moravia.[45] As the principality ceased to exist in the twelfth century, Nitra's following period lost its central role for Sasinek. Sasinek's footsteps were cautiously followed by Jozef Kompánek, a Catholic priest in the village of Ostratice, who in his youth attended schools and later worked in Nitra. Kompánek also referred to Czech and Polish rule in Nitra after the Moravian period; consequently, it was argued that Nitra became part of the Kingdom of Hungary as late as 1025.[46] However, Kompánek refrained from more delicate issues; his work is more of a factographic collection than a Slovak national account.

The Slovak reading of the glorious Moravian Nitra did not hinder Magyar historians from interpreting the town's history in Magyar terms. Until the 1850s, Magyar intellectuals, who were still cherishing a *Hungarus* identity, regarded Nitra's glowing Moravian past with a certain pride.[47] As the national narratives diverged more and more, beginning in the 1860s, this reading of Nitra declined, to be replaced by a more ethnic-centered Magyar interpretation. The new Magyar national narrative downplayed the importance of the Slavs, treating the Moravians as a backward, barbarian, superficially Christian, cowardly, and violent people. The existence of the Moravian state was seen as an "incident" thanks to the talented but dishonest and Machiavellian ruler Svatopluk. In general, Slavs were not regarded as a people advanced enough to establish a solid polity, so they fell under the burden of the Magyar conquest. Nitra was clearly an important place in these events, since the *Gesta Hungarorum* provided a detailed account. According to its unidentified author (who is traditionally called Anonymus), the Magyar army defeated the Moravians of Nitra in a long battle. Following this battle, the Moravian prince, a certain Zobor, was executed on the nearby hill, which was named after him.[48] This story was retold in many academic works until increasing doubts finally discredited the *Gesta Hungarorum* at the end of the nineteenth century.[49]

As the credibility of Anonymus came to be questioned, the details of Nitra's conquest could not be explained by the scholarship. Nonetheless, this did not affect the core of the Magyar reading. In the Magyar narrative, Nitra continued to be seen as a major Moravian town, conquered and then ruled by the Magyar tribes throughout the tenth century, smoothly integrated into the Kingdom of Hungary.[50] Sasinek's interpretation of the Czech and Polish conquest of the town and its later autonomous status was completely rejected by Magyar historians. Unlike the Slovak national narrative, the Nitra principality did not receive major attention in the Magyar historiography, since it was regarded as a mere administrative institution within the Kingdom of Hungary without any Slovak character. Magyar historians were also sure that the Moravian diocese ceased to exist after the Magyar attack and was re-established as late as the early twelfth century by the Hungarian King Coloman I the Book-Lover, as an achievement of Hungarian rule, with no connection to the former Slav state.[51]

The fact that the reliability of Anonymus was contested did not prevent popular literature from referring to the great Magyar victory and the execution of Moravian leader Zobor. Indeed, popular literature and local geography textbooks for elementary schools offered this story until the very end of Austria-Hungary.[52] The glorious battle and its consequences were often retold in the town and formed well-known local myths.[53]

Magyar historians interpreted the town's Slav past as finished, not only in terms of leadership, but also in terms of population. Magyar scholarship held the town and its vicinity to be mostly Magyar speaking until the late seventeenth century. The Magyar-speaking period of the town was terminated by the great internal migration following the liberation of central Hungary from Ottoman rule, which attracted people from north Hungary to the southern parts. As a consequence, large Magyar-speaking masses moved to the south, to be replaced by Slovak-speaking peasants. Magyar historians argued for the emergence of Slovak speakers in Nitra as late as the eighteenth century.[54]

This imagined former ethnic character of northern Hungary was to be restored by both the Hungarian government and the local administration. Due to its schools, the fact that it was the seat of a diocese, that it housed a seminary, theater, and the headquarters of the FMKE association, and its location near the Magyar-Slovak language border, the local Magyar national elite regarded Nitra as a crucial point in the (re-)Magyarization of Upper Hungary. This caused Nitra to aspire to the status of the natural center of Upper Hungary.[55]

Given the modest resources of the town, however, these high aspirations got stuck at an early phase and were not written into the townscape. Liberal and Magyar nationalist ideas were represented by governmental buildings and the theater, while some streets bore names of Magyar national heroes. There is no evidence of large-scale public national celebrations and no national monuments were built until the millennial year. This means that the town was incapable of achieving a breakthrough in national integration on a symbolic level.[56]

While the urban space was occupied by the secular Magyar elite only to a small extent, the Catholic Church continued to dominate the town's representative space. The castle hill and its episcopal church naturally ruled the plain city center. According to all travel guides, the cathedral and the surrounding ecclesiastical quarter were the most beautiful and historically most interesting buildings in the town.[57] Church buildings (such as the gymnasium) were also of outstanding importance in the city center. The Catholic presence was further strengthened by the streets that were named after important bishops and saints of local importance.

Besides the castle hill, the other landmark of the town was the nearby Zobor Hill, which naturally dominates the landscape around the town and is visible from all of its streets. It was this hill where, according to the *Gesta Hungarorum*, the Moravian leader Zobor was executed by the conquering Magyars; furthermore, several monks were believed to have lived in the caves of the hill. These myths were popular and well known among locals. The hill was not used for any political purpose until 1896, but its numerous restaurants and bars and its pleasant environment meant it served as a local leisure destination.[58]

By the end of the nineteenth century, Magyar national integration in Nitra and in northern Hungary was still quite fragile. The local Magyar national elite did not possess the required resources to achieve a breakthrough in Magyar national integration, though Nitra was perceived as a crucial point in this process. As the local liberal elite was not in a position to challenge the Catholic domination of the town, the millennial monument seemed to be an excellent tool for this job on a symbolic level.

Notes

1. János Sziklay, "Nyitra," in *Magyarország vármegyéi és városai: Nyitravármegye*, ed. Samu Borovszky and János Sziklay (Budapest: Apollo, 1898), 28–33.
2. Ibid., 28–33.
3. József Szinnyei, "Nyitra negyvenhat év előtt és most," *Nyitramegyei Közlöny*, 22 August 1886.
4. Thiele, *Das Königreich Ungarn*, 1: 58; Elek Fényes, *Magyarország geographiai szótára, mellyben minden város, falu és puszta, betürendben körülményesen leiratik* (Pest: Kozma Vazul, 1851), 1: 154; József Kelecsény and Imre Vahot, "Nyitra jelen állapota," in *Nyitra és környéke képes albuma* (Pest: Vahot Imre, 1854), 15.
5. István Cserenyey, *Palugyay Imre püspök és a nyitrai irgalmas nővérek emlékezete* (Nyitra: Risnyovszky János, 1911); Stefan Vragaš, "Augustin Roškovány Bischof von Nitra (1807–1892): Sein Leben und Werk," *Slovak Studies* 19 (1979): 167–75.
6. *Annual Report of the Roman Catholic Gymnasium in Nyitra*, 1877/78–1917/1918, passim.
7. "A '*Vágvölgyi Lap*' és a Fmke," *Nyitramegyei Szemle*, 12 January 1896.
8. *Emlékkönyv: Fennállásának tizedik évfordulója alkalmából kiadta a Nyitrai nagyobb papnevelőintézet magyar egyházirodalmi iskolája* (Nyitra: Huszár István, 1899), 263–79; "Két püspök," *Vasárnapi Ujság*, 26 December 1886.
9. Alajos Jeszenszky, ed., *Bende Imre püspök beszédei: Ötven éves áldozárságának emlékére* (Nyitra: Huszár István, 1897), 59.
10. Gereben Nagy, *Album: Nyitramegye nagy férfiainak fény és árnyképei* (Nyitra: Kapsz és Kramár, 1904).
11. "A nyitrai képviselő-testületi tagok választása," *Nyitramegyei közlöny*, 12 January 1896; Ferenc Fodor, "A magyarországi országgyűlési képviselőválasztási kerületek térképei 1861–1915-ig," Országgyűlési Könyvtár, http://www.ogyk.hu/e–konyvt/mpgy/valasztasiterkep/ (accessed 25 May 2012); Szabó, "A Néppárt 1895–1914," map VI in the appendix; Toth, *Parteien und Reichstagswahlen*, 156. It fact, Nitra County was infamous in the

entire country for an outstanding level of electoral manipulation carried out by the liberal government. See Kálmán Mikszáth, "Nyitra," in *Isten hóna alatt*, ed. Csaba Gy. Kiss and Karol Wlachovsky (Miskolc: Felsőmagyarország, 2003), 143–47; *Nyitramegyei közállapotok* (Nyitra: n. p., 1885); Gusztáv Tarnóczy, *A nyitrai választás* (Budapest: Márkus Samu, 1895).

12. Jozef Ambruš, "Slovenské národné obrodenie v Nitre," in *Nitra*, ed. Juraj Fojtík (Bratislava: Obzor, 1977), 69–79; Michal Eliáš, "Pobočka stánok Slovenského učeného tovarišstva v Nitre," in *Kapitoly z dejín Nitry: Sborník štúdií k 1100. výročiu príchodu Cyrila a Metóda*, ed. Alexander Csanda (Bratislava: Slovenské Pedagogické Nakladateľstvo, 1963), 68–80.

13. *Plody zboru Učencú*, unpaginated introduction; Miloslaw Jos. Hurban, ed., *Nitra: Dar dcerám a synüm Slowenska, Morawy, Čech a Slezka obětowaný* (Prešporok: Antonjn Šmid, 1842), 1: 297–309.

14. *Lipa* 3 (1864): 395–406.

15. For the list of Nitra members of the Spolok Sv. Adalberta, see Hadrián Radváni, "Nitra a Spolok sv. Vojtecha," in *Nitra v slovenských dejinách*, ed. Richard Marsina (Martin: Matica slovenska, 2002), 293–300.

16. Svetozár Hurban Vajanský, *Storočná pamiatka narodenia Štefana Moysesa, biskupa banskobystrického: Jeho veličenstva skutočného tajného radcu, doktora filosofie, predsedu Matice Slovenskej 1797–1897* (Turčiansky Sv. Martin: Kníhkupecko–nakladateľský spolok, 1897).

17. Géza Rédeky to Vilmos Thuróczy, 31 December 1896, ŠOAN, 11, 1896–1–22. res/1895.

18. Joachim von Puttkamer, "Die EMKE in Siebenbürgen und die FEMKE in Oberungarn: Die Tätigkeiten zweier ungarischer Schutzvereine in ihrem nationalen Umfeld," in *Schutzvereine in Ostmitteleuropa: Vereinswesen, Sprachenkonflikte und Dynamiken nationaler Mobilisierung 1860–1939*, ed. Peter Haslinger (Marburg: Herder-Institut, 2009), 158–69.

19. Lipót Erdélyi, ed., *Emléklap a nyitrai izr. hitközségi népiskola új épületének felavatása alkalmából* (Nyitra: Iritzer, 1898); Náthán Grünfeld, "Nyitra és vidéke," in *Magyar zsidók a millenniumon: Művelődéstörténeti tanulmány*, ed. Hermán Zichy and Gy. M. Derestye (Budapest: Miljković Dragutin, 1896), 91–108; Gusztáv Libertiny, *Nyitravármegye népoktatásügye 1895-ben: Nyitravármegye közigazgatási bizottsága elé terjesztett tanfelügyelői jelentés* (Nyitra: Neugebauer Nándor, 1896), 3–12.

20. Victor Karady, *The Jews of Europe in the Modern Era: A Socio-historical Outline* (Budapest: Central European University Press, 2004), 170.

21. Kelecsény and Vahot, "Nyitra jelen állapota," 16–17; Petra Rybářová, *Antisemitizmus v Uhorsku v 80. rokoch 19. storočia* (Bratislava: Pro Historia, 2010), 108–10.

22. *Annual Report of the Municipal Trade and Commercial Apprentice School in Nyitra*, 1885/86–1917/18.

23. György Lőrinczy, "Nyitravármegye társadalma," in *Magyarország vármegyéi és városai: Nyitravármegye*, ed. Samu Borovszky and János Sziklay (Budapest: Apollo, 1898), 221.

24. "Izraelita bál," *Nyitramegyei Szemle*, 5 January 1896.

25. József Szinnyei, "Nyitra negyvenhat év előtt és most," *Nyitramegyei Közlöny*, 22 August 1886; Rybářová, *Antisemitizmus v Uhorsku*, 110–16.

26. Imre Csősz, *A kegyes-tanító-rend nyitrai gymnasiumának történeti vázlata* (Nyitra: Neugebauer E., 1876), 93–148.

27. Sándor Jabukovich, "A nyitrai róm. kath. elemi fiúiskola multja és jelene," in *A nyitrai városi róm. kath. elemi fiú- és leányiskolák értesítője az 1896–97. tanévről* (Nyitra: Huszár István nyomdája, 1897), 3–163.

28. *Annual Report of the Municipal Trade and Commercial Apprentice School in Nitra*, 1884/85; *Annual Report of the Roman Catholic Middle School for Girls in Nitra*, 1895/96.

29. *Annual Report of the Jewish Elementary School in Nitra*, 1908/09, 14.

30. Cesnaková-Michalcová, *Geschichte des deutschsprachigen Theaters*, 131–32 and 262–65.

31. József Kőrösy, *A Felvidék eltótosodása: Nemzetiségi tanulmányok. Pozsony és Nyitra megyék külön lenyomata* (Budapest: Grill Károly, 1898), 23.

32. MNL OL, XXXII–23–h, census 1900, box 283, folio Nitra, tables 47/a, 47–48/c, and 47–48/d. The 1880 data are unfortunately incomplete, as the numbers do not include Párovce, then an independent village. The 1900 data refer to the complete town, now including the ghetto as well. Therefore, the exact dynamics of the process cannot be established, though it is highly likely that the complete data would not change the argument.

33. Sziklay, "Nyitra," 33.

34. *Sčítánie ľudu v Republike československej zo dňa 15. februára 1921* (Praha: Státni uřad statistický, 1925), 2/3: 328–29.

35. Owen V. Johnson, *Slovakia 1918–1938: Education and the Making of a Nation* (Boulder, CO: East European Monographs, 1985), 106–7; Ida Zubácka, *Nitra za prvej Československej republiky* (Nitra: Univerzita Konštantina, 1997), 25–29.

36. Rezső Peéry, "Pista bátyám és a nemzetiségi kérdés," in *A magyar esszé antológiája*, ed. Mátyás Domokos (Budapest: Osiris, 2006), 2: 139–41.

37. Imre Csősz, *A kegyes-tanító-rend nyitrai gymnasiumának*; Imre Csősz, *A kegyes-tanító-rendiek Nyitrán: Magyar műveltségörténelmi rajz* (Nyitra: Siegler M., 1879); Sándor Horvát, ed., *Okmánytár a piaristák Sz. László királyról czímzett nyitrai kollegiumának történetéhez 1698–1849* (Nyitra: Huszár István, 1896); János Tóth, *Adatok a nyitrai papnevelde történetéhez* (Nyitra: Huszár István, 1905); József Vagner, *Adatok a nyitrai székes-káptalan történetéhez* (Nyitra: Huszár István, 1896); József Vagner, *Adatok a Nyitra-városi plebániák történetéhez* (Nyitra: Huszár István, 1902).

38. However, the exact position of the town relative to the other Moravian political centers and the place of the bishopric within the Catholic hierarchy, particularly its relation to the archbishops of Passau and Salzburg, was unclear.

39. Šafařjk, *Slowanské starožitnosti*, 793–832.

40. Ibid., 793–96.

41. Juraj Zajonc, "Prečo je Nitra staroslávne mesto," in *Mýty naše Slovenské*, ed. Eduard Krekovič, Elena Mannová, and Eva Krekovičová (Bratislava: Academic Electronic Press, 2005), 134–49.

42. Kálal, *Na krásném Slovensku*, 54–55.

43. Fr[antišek] V[íťazoslav] Sasinek, *Arpád a Uhorsku* (Turč. Sv. Martin: Kníhtlačiarsko účastinárský spolok, 1885).

44. Fr[antišek] V[íťazoslav] Sasinek, *Dejepis slovákov* (Ružomberok: Karol Salva, 1895), 21–49; Fr[antišek] V[íťazoslav] Sasinek, *Slováci v Uhorsku* (Turčiansky Sv. Martin: Kníhtlačiarsko-účastinárský spolok, 1902), 4–26.

45. Fr[antišek] V[íťazoslav] Sasinek, "Biskupstvo v Nitre," *Tovaryšstvo* 1 (1893): 119–22.

46. Jozef Kompánek, *Nitra: Nástin dejepisný, miestopisný a vzdelanostný* (Ružomberok: Karol Salva, 1895), 9–25; Alexander Lombardini, "Zoborské opátstvo," *Tovaryšstvo* 2 (1895): 115–24.

47. "Das Schloss Neutra," *Taschenbuch für die vaterländische Geschichte* 3 (1822): 191–210; János Hunfalvy, *Magyarország és Erdély eredeti képekben* (Darmstadt: Lange Gusztáv György, 1864), I/II: 132; Alajos Mednyánszky, "Nyitravár- és város története," in *Nyitra és környéke képes albuma* (Pest: Vahot Imre, 1854), 2–3.

48. *Gesta Hungarorum*, 35–37.

49. Mihály Horváth, *Magyarország történelme* (Pest: Heckenast Gusztáv, 1871), 1: 49; László Szalay, *Magyarország története* (Lipcse: Geibel Károly, 1852), 1: 14.

50. Lajos Dedek Crescens, "Nyitravármegye története," in *Magyarország vármegyéi és városai: Nyitravármegye*, ed. Samu Borovszky and János Sziklay (Budapest: Apollo, 1898), 477–82.
51. Ibid., 485–86 and 530–32.
52. Elek Bielicky, *Nyitra vármegye földrajza: A Nyitra vármegyei népiskolák III-ik osztálya számára segédkönyvül* (Nyitra: Huszár István, 1908), 19–20; János Györffy and Arnold Zellinger, *Földrajzi előismeretek: Nyitravármegye rövid földrajza. Vezérkönyv a nyitravármegyei római kath. népiskolák III. osztályú tanítói számára* (Budapest: Szent István Társulat, 1913), 58; Alexander F. Heksch, *Illustrirter Führer durch Ungarn und seine Nebenländer (Siebenbürgen, Croatien, Slavonien und Fiume)* (Vienna: A. Hartleben, 1882), 20; László Petrovics, *Zobor vezér: Költői elbeszélés* (Budapest: szerző kiadása, 1884); Károly Thuróczy, *Nyitra megye: Felolvastatott a Magyar Tudományos Akadémia II. osztályának 1895. évi deczember hó 9-én tartott ülésében* (Budapest: Magyar Tudományos Akadémia, 1896), 3.
53. József Szinnyei, "Nyitra negyvenhat év előtt és most," *Nyitramegyei Közlöny*, 22 August 1886.
54. Pál Balogh, *A népfajok Magyarországon* (Budapest: M. Kir. Vallás- és Közoktatásügyi Ministerium, 1902), 396–414; Tivadar Botka, "Nyitrai emlékek," *Századok* 7, no. 9 (November 1873): 642–45; Dedek Crescens, "Nyitravármegye története," 510; Vilmos Fraknói, "Előszó," in *Magyarország vármegyéi és városai: Nyitravármegye*, ed. Samu Borovszky and János Sziklay (Budapest: Apollo, 1898), XIV; Kőrösy, *A Felvidék eltótosodása*, 22–23; János Sziklay, "Nyitravármegye lakossága," in *Magyarország vármegyéi és városai: Nyitravármegye*, ed. Samu Borovszky and János Sziklay (Budapest: Apollo, 1898), 172–75; Thuróczy, *Nyitra megye*, 12–13.
55. This reading of Upper Hungary (Felvidék) included mostly today's western and middle Slovakia. The much larger and clearly far more important and developed Pressburg was regarded as a city facing west due to its intensive Viennese relations. The activity of the FMKE covered ten counties (Nitra, Trenčín, Orava, Turiec, Zvolen, Liptov, Tekov, Hont, Nógrád, and Spiš). In these ten counties, only Banská Štiavnica outnumbered Nitra in population. However, due to its peripheral location and lack of railway, it was gradually decaying and losing its medieval and early modern glory.
56. *Nyitra rend. tan. város utczái-, és házszámainak és külterületeinek jegyzéke* (Nyitra: Huszár István, 1890).
57. Heksch, *Illustrirter Führer durch Ungarn*, 20–21; Adolf Schmidl, *Reisehandbuch durch das Königreich Ungarn mit den Nebenländern und Dalmatien, nach Serbien, Bukarest und Constantinopel* (Vienna: Carl Gerold, 1835), 112; Thiele, *Das Königreich Ungarn*, 1: 58–59.
58. Kelecsény and Vahot, "Nyitra jelen állapota", 13–14.

Chapter 5

MUNKÁCS

Figure 5.1. The main street of Munkács in 1865. Reprinted from *Ország Tükre* 4, no. 215 (1865).

By the end of the nineteenth century, Munkács, a corporate town on the swampy banks of the river Latorca, was a "middle town with full-fledged urban functions" on the least developed northeastern periphery of Hungary. Although Munkács was not a county seat (nearby Beregszász hosted the seat of Bereg County), it gave home to district authorities and two infantry regiments stationed in the town. Munkács also served its hinterland with economic, financial, transportation, and education services. In the millennial year, Munkács was home to a state gymnasium and two banks, and it was well connected to other parts of Hungary via the Budapest–Lwów railway line. Still, the urban infrastructure of Munkács was underdeveloped and its buildings were in poor condition until the last years of the nineteenth century. In 1882, a local observer claimed that lots of houses resembled tumble-down cottages covered by straw and in 1870 only seventeen houses had two stories. Only some governmental buildings, churches, and a few private buildings corresponded to the standards of the age.[1]

A definite modernization process started during the 1900s. Modern features of urban infrastructure, such as asphalt cover of the streets and electric illumination, were introduced. Within a few years, a modern shopping center, a bank, a courthouse, a Roman Catholic church, and some private houses were built in the center of the town. National authorities, including the border police and the Ministry of Agriculture, opened offices in the town. A large tobacco factory employing around three hundred workers started production in 1898. On the eve of World War I, Munkács was a far more modern town than two decades before.[2] Still, in 1910, it was ranked only sixty-sixth in the Hungarian urban hierarchy, forty places behind Nitra, despite hosting a population of the same size.

While Munkácsers were certainly proud of the advancement of their town, they regarded an ancient building as the most valuable artifact. This building was the castle, dating back to the Middle Ages and playing an immensely important role in Hungarian history. The castle found itself outside the town but within walking distance. Until 1896, however, the town-dwellers could not use the castle, as it served as a prison and was thus practically cut off from the town. Nonetheless, it was the castle that was used by local Magyar national activists to ascribe national importance to their town. Despite the actual limited significance of Munkács, the local Magyar elite was able to portray the town and the surrounding Bereg County as the quintessence of Hungary and to convey this well to the Hungarian public.

National Integration of the Christian Society

The population of Munkács, slightly fewer than fifteen thousand at the end of the century, was heterogeneous in terms of both religion and language. Four religious groups were present: the Roman and Greek Catholics, the Calvinists, and the mostly Hasidic Orthodox Jews (see Table 13.5 in the Appendix). Three languages were spoken in Munkács: Magyar, Rusyn, and Yiddish (see Table 13.6 in the Appendix). Magyar speakers were mostly Calvinists or Roman

Catholics, the Rusyn speakers belonged to the Greek Catholic Church, while Yiddish was spoken by the Hasidic Jewry.

Despite the large Rusyn-speaking population of Munkács, a Slavic national project did not emerge in any form. The key factor was the behavior of the local Rusyn-speaking elite. As no Rusyn-speaking lay middle class existed in Munkács, the only Rusyn-speaking elite group was the Greek Catholic clergy. The Greek Catholic clergy lacked both financial resources and proper personnel for any political project. The parish was so poor that in the eighteenth century the priest fled from the awkward conditions of the parsonage and his low salary, and the congregation was unable to replace him for years. The financial conditions did not improve in the following decades either, as only the donations of the parish's patron, the Schönborn-Buchheim family, ensured the salary of the priest and the construction of a stone church in 1859.[3] As the Greek Catholic bishop moved his seat and the seminary from Munkács to the more urbanized and central Ungvár in 1780, the town ceased to host enough Greek Catholic clergymen to launch any large-scale social movement.[4]

Yet, it was neither the poor financial conditions nor the insufficient number of clergymen that proved to be decisive, but the local market of national ideas. Hungarian Greek Catholics had no connection to either Galician Ukrainian or Russian national activists.[5] Ukrainian and Russian attempts to imagine Hungarian Rusyns as members of the Ukrainian or Russian nation were not communicated by anyone in Munkács. Therefore, just like the other Greek Catholic clergymen in northeastern Hungary, the Munkács priests opted for Magyar national integration. A telling piece of evidence of this choice was delivered by a Greek Catholic priest, who removed the motto "Peace on this house," written originally in "Russian," from the parsonage in order to declare his Magyar loyalty.[6]

Local Greek Catholics were not influenced by political Catholicism either. Bishop Gyula Firczák (1836–1912, bishop in Ungvár 1892–1912) was himself a liberal member of the Hungarian Parliament in the early 1880s.[7] Even though Firczák's social activities largely coincided with the program of political Catholicism, he flirted with the Catholic People's Party for a short period only and then sought cooperation with the liberal government.[8]

The absence of national competitors and political Catholicism opened the way to Magyar national integration. Unlike other cities analyzed in this study, the most prestigious, well-off, and influential group of Munkács was the genuinely Magyar-speaking middle class, including the local gentry. The local middle class was eager to accept the liberal and modern ideas of Magyar nationalism, which seemed to bring progress to both the town and the entire country. A typical representative of this group was lawyer and scholar Tivadar Lehoczky. Born in 1830, young Lehoczky volunteered for the Hungarian revolutionary army in 1848. He studied law in Kassa and settled down in Munkács to be the manager of the Schönborn estate. As an amateur archeologist, he led excavations in the region and as a self-trained historian and ethnographer, he published important studies on the history of Munkács and Bereg County in the factographic style of the age. His works earned him national fame and he was appointed as a member of the National Committee of Monuments and several societies for history and ethnography. He owned a large archeological collection, which could have been the basis of a local museum but the town council would not contribute to the costs of such an establishment.[9] Lehoczky was a respected member of Munkács society; his works mirror his liberal, progressive, and Magyar national vision.

Liberal nationalism was thus the default political ideology in Munkács. While northeastern Hungary was well known for its sympathy toward the Party of Independence, Munkács routinely elected members of the Liberal Party to Parliament. The dominance of the Liberal Party in Munkács was ensured by the heavy influence of the Schönborn family, owners of the largest estate in the area. The Schönborns were typical representatives of the supranational Habsburg aristocracy, loyal to the emperor and not to single nations. Although the family did not live in the town, it significantly influenced local politics, and the town's parliamentary delegate was often the manager of the Schönborn estate.[10]

As a result, lacking major competitors, possessing local resources, and being supported by the government, the Magyar national elite had a relatively easy task in integrating the Christian population of Munkács into the Magyar nation. Local institutions were monolingual Magyar; they included the town's administration, the local press emerging from the 1880s, theatrical performances held either in a hotel or in the town's own theater (completed in 1899), and all the local associations.[11] Magyar also became the sole language of education from the 1860s. Until then, the municipal elementary school had instructed in Rusyn, German, and Magyar.[12] The middle school and the school of trade and commerce also taught exclusively in Magyar.[13] The gymnasium instructed in Magyar as well, although literary Russian was taught for the Greek Catholic students.[14]

The Magyar monopoly in the local market for national ideas, the overlap between Magyar national integration and modernity, and the exclusively Magyar language of local institutions made the Magyar project largely successful. At the same time, this success was dependent on the social and denominational status of the target population.

The largest Christian community was the Greek Catholics, making up approximately a quarter of the town's entire population. Traditionally, the Greek Catholics spoke Rusyn and occupied the lowest social rank. Among state or municipal employees in higher positions, there were no Rusyn speakers[15] and hardly any Greek Catholics were to be found among the members of the town assembly, and if they were, they probably declared themselves as Magyar speakers.[16] In 1900, half of Rusyn-speaking males earned their living as day laborers and workers, a mere eleven had their own field, and only eighteen ran their own shop or workshop. Even in 1927, eight years after the introduction of Czechoslovak rule promoting Rusyn as an administrative language, shops were advertised with Rusyn slogans, but neither shopkeepers nor the middle class customers knew the language. Rusyn was seen as the tongue of "poor, primitive and absolutely backward" peasants only.[17]

During the nineteenth century, Greek Catholics in Munkács were subject to rapid linguistic Magyarization. In 1880, 40% of Greek Catholic believers declared Magyar as their native language, outnumbered by the 59% of Rusyn speakers. In twenty years, this ratio reversed and Magyar was declared as a native language by 57% of Greek Catholics, with Rusyn chosen by only 42%. The detailed data clearly show that linguistic Magyarization was determined by social status, as the wealthier and better educated Greek Catholics tended to declare themselves as Magyar speakers in far higher numbers than members of the lower classes.[18] Rusyn-speaking peasants also adopted the customs of their Magyar-speaking neighbors and were on the way to complete integration into Magyar society.[19]

The Roman Catholics (approximately one-fifth of the entire town) were either German or Magyar speakers until the mid nineteenth century, but as early as 1880 four-fifths of them declared Magyar as their native language.[20] In 1900, a mere 234 Roman Catholics declared German as their mother tongue.[21] The small Lutheran community, lacking their own church, was also channeled into the Magyar national integration project by their Calvinist brethren, turning their native language from Magyar and German into Magyar exclusively by the turn of the century.[22] Language change did not affect Calvinists (about a tenth of the entire population), who had always spoken Magyar. Members of these three denominations dominated the city's middle class and controlled the local government.

As an outcome of the genuinely large number of Magyar speakers and the linguistic assimilation of some Greek Catholics, the position of Magyar was uncontested in Munkács. The Christian society of the town was structured by religious and social differences. Local associations were founded partly on a religious and partly on a social basis.[23] The urban space of the town was structured by social divisions: the promenade was separated into parts for the upper and lower classes and neighborhoods were also structured by social position and not language or denomination.[24] The Christian society of Munkács was on the way to forming a modern, single society based on Magyar national ideas, overcoming denominational barriers.[25]

Resisting Modernity: The Hasidic Jewry of Munkács

While Jews formed a minority in the other locations analyzed in this study, the demographic data were quite different in Munkács. Before the eighteenth century, Jews appeared in northeastern Hungary only sporadically. In 1711, the huge estates of the exiled Francis II Rákóczy around Munkács were confiscated and the new owner, the Schönborn-Buchheim family from the Holy Roman Empire, invited a number of Jews from Galicia to develop commerce and provide other services. In the following decades, the Jewish population increased steadily. In 1786 there were only thirty-six Jewish taxpayers in the town, in 1851 the Jewish community encompassed 651 members, and due to further immigration the proportion of Jews reached approximately 45% of the town's population by the end of the nineteenth century, making the Jewish community of Munkács the largest in all of northeastern Hungary. Some sources hint that many Jewish immigrants did not register with the authorities, likely making Jews the absolute majority group in the town.[26]

The influx of Galician, mainly Hasidic Jews into northeastern Hungary profoundly changed the social, economic, and ethnic character of the region in the second part of the nineteenth century. Commerce became dominated by Jews; as early as 1860, all the retailers in Munkács were Jews, with the exception of a single Christian merchant.[27] Jews were also to be found among artisans, innkeepers, and even peasants, i.e. in jobs related to the economy but not requiring higher education.

Their strict Hasidism, however, prevented the Munkács Jews from becoming part of a modern *Wirtschaftsbürgertum*. Munkács was famous for being the most conservative congregation among the Hasidic Jewry of northeastern Hungary. A telling story concerned Joachim Schreiber (Hayyim Sofer), a distinguished student of Chatam Sofer, who became a respected leader of Hungarian Orthodoxy. Schreiber was an Orthodox hardliner: he forbade any contact with Neolog Jews, including fulfilling such basic duties as visiting the sick in hospital or mourning for the dead. Still, he was not conservative enough for the Munkács Jews, where he served as a rabbi during the 1870s. Following accusations of modernity (which included an argument against wearing the traditional Hasidic garb), he had to leave his seat to become the Orthodox rabbi of Budapest. After his dismissal he was followed by the Shapira family, a dynasty of Hasidic *rebbes* of supra-regional fame for its nothing-to-change mentality.[28]

The ultra-conservative mentality of the Hasidic Jews meant that they lived in isolation from the Christians, insisted on speaking Yiddish, a language incomprehensible to Christians, wore strange clothes and hairstyles, and ran their own social and welfare institutions. They also largely ignored the

Christian society's efforts to move toward modernity and national integration.[29] Politics was also a field unappealing for the Munkács Jews: modern
Jewish politics, as it emerged among the Hasidim in Galicia,[30] was unknown
in the town.

As the agenda of the modernizing Hungarian government and that of its
local agent, the Christian middle class, were not compatible with the values of
Hasidism, the emergence of conflicts between the Munkács Jews and the civil
authorities was predictable. One such conflict concerned civil marriage, as
rebbes tried to prevent congregation members from registering marriages with
the authorities (mandatory since 1894), making the number of officially un-
married couples exceptionally high. Another conflict was due to the so-called
eruv hazerot. This practice meant that a wire fence around the Jewish quarter
was built before the Sabbath in order to enclose all the Jewish houses in a large
courtyard. Since according to the Talmud a single courtyard was a private
domain, this practice made carrying goods within this courtyard permitted.
Civil authorities, however, were not open to such practices, and saw this as a
remnant of the dark Middle Ages that is not compatible with a modern town.
The town council demanded several times that Jews give up *eruv hazerot*, but
without success.[31]

The issue causing local authorities the most trouble was education. First,
Jewish pupils did not attend elementary school on Saturdays. Second, Hasidism
insisted on the primacy of the *heder*, which practically meant that Jewish boys
were sent to the *heder* early in the morning before the compulsory elementary
school and they continued their Talmudic studies in the afternoon.[32] As a result, Jewish boys lacked both time and energy to focus on secular subjects, including the Magyar language, so their performance was definitely poorer than
that of the Christian pupils, and even that of the Jewish girls, who were not
obliged to attend the *heder*.[33] The *heder*s themselves were located in poor, small,
and unhealthy houses. The overcrowded, Yiddish-speaking schools teaching
the most conservative, anti-liberal, and anti-national agenda thus prevented
sufficient secular education and were condemned by the town council and
the local public.[34] However, limited efforts were made to change the situation.
The municipal elementary school moved its Saturday classes to Wednesday in
1877, and thus the issue of the Sabbath was resolved.[35] In the higher schools,
however, the central government forbade such measures.[36] Teachers of the municipal elementary school filed for the replacement of the poor *heder*s by the
construction of a large, modern, healthy Talmudic school several times, but
the town did not fulfill this demand, probably for financial reasons.[37]

The prevalence of ultra-conservative customs, poor living conditions,
the rejection of modern, progressive, and national ideas, and the prestige of
the *rebbe* (irrational and mystic in the eyes of contemporaries) all contributed to definite hostility toward Jews. The local public condemned Jewish

customs as barbaric, uncivilized, and immoral, and accused Jews of exploit-ing Christians.[38] Pogroms were nevertheless not committed and neither the Antisemitic Party nor the Catholic People's Party ran a candidate for a parlia-mentary mandate.[39]

While the majority of Munkács Jews followed the strict regulations of the Hasidic *rebbes* and chose a voluntary separation from the Christian society, a minority tried to adopt modernity without giving up their Jewish faith. As early as 1844, six Munkács Jews attended the local gymnasium.[40] The number of Jewish pupils in this school increased during the 1870s and then the 1890s in particular, but it never reached the ratio of the local Jewish population, making Jews underrepresented in the highest form of education available in the town.[41] Although the attempts of this modern minority did not lead to the formation of a Neolog congregation (both synagogues remained Hasidic), a demand for reforms was raised. Bernát Weisz, owner of a local brewery and a member of the municipal and county assembly, furnishes an example. He was a "pioneer of religious reforms, because his patriotic pride did not allow him to be neutral towards the issue of turning the Jews living in Munkács, mostly immigrants from Galicia and filled with the most slavish retrogression, into Magyars as soon as possible in the interests of Magyar culture and Hungarian Jewry," as claimed in a festive album celebrating the Jewish contribution to modern Hungary.[42]

The Christian public of Munkács largely supported the reform-minded Jewry, as agents in turning Jews toward modernity and Magyar national inte-gration.[43] Religious reform and national identity were thus associated. For con-temporaries, it was clear that Hasidic Jews would never be open to modernity and nationalism without serious religious reforms, so the municipal admin-istration and the Christian public offered their help to the reform movement within the congregation. Reform-minded Jews, like the above-cited Bernát Weisz, were respected members of the town, holding a number of prestigious positions, such as in the municipal and county assembly or on the board of the Casino, the club of the local elite.[44]

Indeed, in 1896 half of the members on the board of the craft association and the reading club were Jews.[45] The sources do not tell us whether these Jews were reform-minded or conservative; if the latter was the case, it would suggest participation of Hasidim in a modern institution. To be sure, Jews in Munkács were able to participate in the less prestigious areas of the public sphere and the more progressive and wealthy members of the congregation had access to even higher positions.

Despite all the above, the reform-minded Jews were not able to challenge the ultra-conservative party. The Hasidic majority kept on ignoring the de-mands of both the reform-minded Jews and the local Christian public. In 1893, the ultra-conservative members were able to appoint the son of the late *rebbe* Solomon Shapira to inherit his father's seat, even though he did not speak a word of Magyar, having been raised in Galicia. The new *rebbe*, the aggressive rejection of the critics raised by the reform-minded, and in particular the apparent ignorance of the demands of the Magyar public, led to a scandal in the town and were harshly condemned by *Egyenlőség*, the flagship of the Hungarian Neolog press.[46]

"The Country of Munkacs was the Cradle of the Magyars:" Reading the Town and the Castle

As the only modern elite group in the town was the Magyar, the only powerful narrative of the town was produced by Magyar intellectuals. To interpret the town in Magyar national terms was not at all difficult. The *Gesta Hungarorum* already claimed that the castle of Munkács was the first place to be conquered by the Magyars and it was named after the "greatest toil in the land they had chosen for themselves."[47] Based on Anonymus' report, the story of Munkács' conquest and naming became a mandatory element of the romantic Hungarian scholarship at both the national and local levels.[48] Tivadar Lehoczky cited these well-known words, too, despite the fact that he questioned the reliability of the *Gesta Hungarorum*.[49] Whether critical historians doubted the accuracy of the *Gesta Hungarorum* or not, nineteenth-century Magyar public opinion disregarded sophisticated academic arguments and held Munkács castle as an outstanding place in early Magyar history.[50] The myth of Munkács found its way into foreign literature, too: François Sulpice Beudant, a French mineralogist undertaking a voyage in Hungary in 1818, credited "the country of Munkacs" as "the cradle of the Magyars."[51]

The importance of the Munkács castle was further strengthened by its early modern history. The main heroine of the age was Ilona Zrínyi, the wife of the rebel prince, Imre Thököly, and mother of Francis II Rákóczi. Between 1685 and 1688, Zrínyi defended the well-fortified castle against the Habsburg army. She earned fame in Europe for both herself and the castle, since as a woman she fought without her arrested husband, while taking care of her young daughter and son Francis.[52] The castle later served as a stronghold in both Rákóczi's uprising and the 1848/49 war. As the *kuruc* insurrections became a cornerstone of the Magyar national imagination of the past, particularly in the Protestant tradition, Ilona Zrínyi, Imre Thököly, and Francis II Rákóczi became national heroes. After 1849, the tradition of the *kuruc* rebellions and the 1848 revolution merged and the cult of the Rákóczi family steadily increased.[53]

The exact place of Munkács in the *Gesta Hungarorum* and in the series of anti-Habsburg wars made the castle a key location in the Magyar national historical imagination. The successful dissemination of the story of the conquest and the *kuruc* age definitely made Munkács well known to the Magyar audience, as the passionate words of János Balogh, a soldier serving in the town, show:

> All Hungarian children have heard during their school age such elevating stories [of the Munkács castle] that they all yearn to see the place of these events and almost regret that only a single Munkács castle exists in this homeland or that they could not at least be born in Munkács.[54]

Indeed, as the castle served as an infamous prison during most of the eighteenth and nineteenth centuries, its ancient Magyar glory was juxtaposed with the "repressive" Habsburg regime.[55]

These historical events took place in the castle of Munkács and not in the town itself; indeed, the town did not play a significant role in them. Yet the local Magyar national elite connected the myth and history of the castle to the town and it was able to portray the town of Munkács as heir to these important events.

The great importance of Munkács was further strengthened by the Magyar reading of the surrounding Bereg County, which held the region as the quintessence of Hungary. This reading was supported by historical, ethnographic, and geographical arguments. First, the *Gesta Hungarorum* claimed that Árpád's Magyars crossed the northeastern Carpathians before they ascended to Munkács. Thus, the Veretsky Pass, a mountain pass northeast of Munkács that connected Hungary to Galicia, was believed to be the route by which the Magyar tribes entered the Carpathians. Consequently, Bereg became the first possession in the new Magyar homeland.[56] The county's participation in the anti-Habsburg wars was portrayed as a stubborn demand for liberty and Hungarian independence. The county also mirrored the multiethnic character of the country in the way Magyar national activists liked to see it. Rusyn speakers were portrayed as completely "patriotic," as they participated in several *kuruc* uprisings, and the lack of local nation-building aspirations confirmed their loyalty to Hungary. The geography of the county supported the reading of the county as "small Hungary" too. The territory of the county included mountains, lowlands, and the "most Magyar" river, the Tisza, so all the major elements of the Hungarian landscape were to be found there. This all meant that the Magyar national master narrative and the local reading of both Munkács town and Bereg County completely coincided; the Magyar nation, Munkács, and Bereg went through the same events in the past (conquest, uprisings, seeking liberty), the county condensed Hungarian geography, and its non-Magyar speakers had always been loyal to the nation.[57]

Besides the Magyar, there was a definite potential for narrating Munkács in a Slavic national historical narrative. Slavs were reported by Anonymus as having accompanied the conquering Magyars; the town had been ruled by the Galician Ruthenian Prince Fedur Koriatovych in the fourteenth century, and the Greek Catholic monastery hosted the diocese for more than a century and continued to play an important role. The town also had a substantial Rusyn-speaking population. Nevertheless, Ukrainian and Russian national protagonists did not read Munkács in their terms, mainly due to the peripheral location of the town. Local Greek Catholic intellectuals, being aware of their Rusyn origin but participating in Magyar national integration, accepted the Magyar reading of Munkács and understood themselves as heirs to the Slavic allies of Árpád.

Munkács was, however, not in a position to represent this narrative in the urban space. The town's own financial resources were very limited. The only completed representative project was the renaming of the town's important streets in 1895 and 1907.[58] Occasionally, national festivities were also held to commemorate important figures in Hungarian history. However, these celebrations were mostly held in schools for the pupils and adults did not participate.[59]

Other, more spectacular plans were announced but never completed. First, a local initiative was published in 1884 to place the mortal remains of the Rákóczi family in the castle, to thus replace the prison in the castle with a national shrine.[60] (Imre Thököly, Ilona Zrínyi, and Francis II Rákóczi died in exile in the Ottoman Empire and were buried there.) From 1889, local initiatives were framed in the concept of the millennium. As shown in Chapter 2, Bereg County initiated a nationwide millennial celebration, which was warmly welcomed in the local press, as for a "town so deeply involved in the conquest and the festivities," active participation in the celebrations seemed essential.[61] A year later, the county established a millennial committee, including the mayor and the notable local historian, Tivadar Lehoczky.[62] How deeply the millennial ideas were present even before the festive year is shown by a request of the local Greek Catholic parish. The congregation decided to celebrate the millennial year by renovating its church. Its request referred to the belief that the Greek Catholics' forefathers "conquered this homeland together [with Árpád], whose memory had been kept well in the vivid tradition and in the most ancient historians' writings." Since then, the Rusyn speakers had always been the most faithful to Hungary, which had sometimes been a significant burden on them. Hence, the Greek Catholic parish did not have any resources to finance the renovation, and the town was therefore asked to support and finance the idea.[63]

The town did not have enough resources to support the Greek Catholic demand. In fact, it did not have resources to finance any of its many millennial ideas. Instead, the town tried to win governmental support, justified by its well-known historical role, for local ideas. When Kálmán Thaly visited Munkács in 1893, the council members proposed to him a grandiose plan:

they offered their town as a host for a decisive part of the national millennial celebrations, referring to the town's unsurpassed historical importance, and in particular its role in the conquest. Yet the town was not in a condition to become a proper host. Therefore, the assembly initiated a comprehensive urban development plan, including the building of a new town hall, a theater, electric street lighting, a sewage system, and a new avenue named after Árpád to connect the downtown and the railway station. This plan would have turned Munkács into by far the most modern city, not only in the region but probably in the entire country. Lacking local resources, the aldermen demanded that the government cover the costs of this project.[64]

Other ideas emerged in the sphere of symbolic politics. In 1893, Bereg County demanded the conversion of the Munkács castle into an Upper Hungarian national museum because of its exceptional importance in the *kuruc* uprisings.[65] Count Jenő Zichy, a well-known scholar and national activist, initiated the erection of a monument to Árpád in the town; this idea was warmly welcomed by the Munkács public. Although Zichy did not have any personal relation to Munkács (his family estates lay mostly in Western Hungary), he acknowledged the town's relevance to the history of the Magyar conquest and its function in distributing the Magyar national idea to Rusyn speakers, so he proclaimed Munkács to be the most appropriate place in the country for a memorial commemorating the conquest.[66]

However, all these projects counted on governmental support: to remove the prison, to bring the remains of the Rákóczis to Hungary, to build a national museum and a large monument all fell within the competence of the government, which, until the millennial ardor, disregarded symbolic politics and focused on more practical issues. Neither did the government accept the demand of financial aid for infrastructure development, as the sole historical justification seemed an unsatisfying argument. The town's initiative to host the nationwide celebrations was disregarded too.

Still, due to these intensive campaigns, Magyar national activists in Munkács believed that Hungary owed some symbolic recognition for the town's glorious contribution to Hungarian history. After so many failed projects, the millennial monument was finally able to fill the imagined gap between the importance of the town and the recognition of the nation.

Notes

1. Tivadar Lehoczky, *Beregvármegye monographiája* (Ungvár: Pollacsek Miksa, 1881), 3: 444.
2. Tivadar Lehoczky, *Munkács város uj monografiája* (Munkács: Grünstein Mór, 1907), 239–59 and 322–27.
3. Tivadar Lehoczky, *A beregmegyei görögszertartású katholikus lelkészsége története a XIX. század végéig* (Munkács: Grünstein Mór, 1904), 128–36.

4. Antal Hodinka, *A munkácsi görög-katholikus püspökség története* (Budapest: Magyar Tudományos Akadémia, 1909), 768–71.

5. Paul Robert Magocsi, *The Shaping of a National Identity: Subcarpathian Rus', 1848–1948* (Cambridge, MA: Harvard University Press, 1978), 42–75.

6. Lehoczky, *A beregmegyei görögszertartású*, 134–35. Whether Russian in this context meant literary Russian, church Slavonic, or a local vernacular cannot be determined.

7. István Marosi, "Firczák Gyula (1836–1912) munkácsi püspök élete és munkásságának súlypontjai," *Acta Beregsasiensis* 9, no. 2 (2010): 80.

8. Mária Mayer, *The Rusyns of Hungary: Political and Social Developments 1860–1910* (Boulder, CO: East European Monographs, 1997), 103–23.

9. "Lehoczky Tivadar," *Archeologiai értesítő* 35 (1915): 366–67.

10. András Cieger, "A Bereg megyei politikai elit a dualizmus időszakában," *Szabolcs-Szatmár-Beregi Levéltári Évkönyv* 12 (1997): 213–81.

11. Lehoczky, *Beregvármegye monographiája*, 3: 508–11; Lehoczky, *Munkács város*, 294–300 and 320–22; Cesnaková-Michalcová, *Geschichte des deutschsprachigen Theaters*, 260–61.

12. *Annual Report of the State Elementary School in Munkács*, 1883/84, 3–6 and 17–19. The language of instruction of the Greek Catholic elementary school cannot be established but presumably it was Magyar too.

13. *Annual Report of the State Middle School for Girls in Munkács*, 1882/83; *Annual Report of the State Trade and Commercial Apprentice School in Munkács*, 1885/86.

14. *Annual Report of the State Gymnasium in Munkács*, 1868–1914. The textbook of Russian language makes it clear that standard Russian was taught as the literary version of the local Rusyn dialect: Eumén Szabó, ed., *Orosz nyelvtan és olvasókönyv: A magyarországi oroszok irodalmi nyelvének tanulásához* (Ungvár: Kelet Könyvnyomda, 1890).

15. MNL OL, XXXII–23–h, census 1900, box 167, folio Munkács, table 41.

16. Cyrill Medvigy, *Munkács geográfiája* (Budapest: Globus, 1917), 34.

17. Eugen Holly, *Im Lande der Kabbalisten, der Religionskämpfe und des Hungers: Quer durch Karpatorussland* (Pressburg: Grenzbote, 1927), 9.

18. MNL OL, XXXII–23–h, census 1880, box 524, folio Munkács, table XVI; and 1900, box 288, folio Munkács, tables 47/a, 47–48/c, and 47–48/d.

19. Lehoczky, *Beregvármegye monographiája*, 2: 199.

20. MNL OL, XXXII–23–h, census 1880, box 524, folio Munkács, table XVI.

21. MNL OL, XXXII–23–h, census 1900, box 288, folio Munkács, table 47–48/d.

22. MNL OL, XXXII–23–h, census 1880, box 524, folio Munkács, table XVI; and 1900, box 288, folio Munkács, table 47–48/d.

23. Lehoczky, *Munkács város*, 320–22.

24. Medvigy, *Munkács geográfiája*, 18 and 33.

25. József Tabódy, *Munkács múltja és jelene Magyarország történetében* (Pest: Winter, 1860), 107–8.

26. Lehoczky, *Munkács város*, 209–35; Tabódy, *Munkács múltja*, 105.

27. Medvigy, *Munkács geográfiája*, 33; Tabódy, *Munkács múltja*, 105.

28. Allan L. Nadler, "The War on Modernity of R. Hayyim Elazar Shapira of Munkacz," *Modern Judaism* 14 (1994): 233–64.

29. Livia Rothkirchen, "Deep-Rooted yet Alien: Some Aspects of the History of the Jews in Subcarpathian Ruthenia," *Yad Vashem Studies* 12 (1977): 151.

30. Joshua Shanes, *Diaspora Nationalism and Jewish Identity in Habsburg Galicia* (Cambridge: Cambridge University Press, 2012).

31. Lehoczky, *Munkács város*, 234.

32. Yeshayahu A. Jelinek, *The Carpathian Diaspora: The Jews of Subcarpathian Rus' and Mukachevo, 1848–1948* (Boulder, CO: East European Monographs, 2007), 83–89; Aron Moskovits, *Jewish Education in Hungary (1848–1948)* (New York: Bloch, 1964), 76.

33. According to the 1890 census, the literacy rate of Jews (ca. 50%) definitely lagged behind that of Protestants and Roman Catholics. Only the Greek Catholic believers were less literate. MNL OL, XXXII–23–h, census 1890, box 434, folio Munkács.

34. *Annual Report of the State Elementary School in Munkács*, 1885/86, 24.

35. *Annual Report of the State Elementary School in Munkács*, 1883/84, 7.

36. *Annual Report of the State Middle School for Girls in Munkács*, 1895/96, 4; "Kérelem a középiskolai tanulók szombati írás és rajzolás alól való felmentés ügyében: A szombat a középiskolákban," *Magyar-Zsidó Szemle* 3, no. 10 (1886): 682–83. In the Western Hungarian town of Pápa, Jewish children attended the local gymnasium on Saturdays but they were exempted from writing, drawing, and taking tests. Presumably the same policy was followed in Munkács. See Jacob Katz, *With My Own Eyes: The Autobiography of an Historian* (Hanover, NH: Brandeis University Press, 1995), 23.

37. *Annual Report of the State Elementary School in Munkács*, 1885/86, 19–26; 1886/87, 8; and 1887/88, 10–11.

38. Miklós Bartha, *Kazár földön* (Kolozsvár: Ellenzék, 1901); Lehoczky, *Beregvármegye monographiája*, 2: 91; Lehoczky, *Munkács város*, 235.

39. Judit Kubinszky, *Politikai antiszemitizmus Magyarországon 1875–1900* (Budapest: Kossuth, 1976), 127–28 and 205–8; Szabó, "A Néppárt az 1896. évi országgyűlési választásokon," 756.

40. "Informatio De Adolescentibus privati Instituti Munkácsiensis per exmisos e. R. M. Gymnasio Unghvariensi examinatores pro utroque Semestri Semestraliter Munkácsini 1843/44 examinatis," in *Informationes generales de Gymnasiali literarii districtus Cassoviensis juventute pro 2-do semestri anni scholastici 1843–4. praestitae*, 159–61, OSZK K, Fol. Lat. 3471.

41. The exact number of local Jews cannot be determined, as the school reports do not provide detailed statistics. The proportion of Jews in the school varied between 20% and 30% from the 1870s to World War I. *Annual Report of the State Gymnasium in Munkács*, 1868–1914.

42. Hermán Zichy and Gy. M. Derestye, eds., *Magyar zsidók a millenniumon: Művelődéstörténeti tanulmány* (Budapest: Miljković Dragutin, 1896), 239–40.

43. Medvigy, *Munkács geográfiája*, 33–34.

44. "A munkácsi 'Társaskör' 56-ik évi rendes közgyülése," *Munkács*, 2 February 1896.

45. "Ipartársulati közgyülés," *Munkács*, 16 February 1896; "A munkácsi ipartestület," *Munkács és vidéke*, 23 February 1896; "A munkácsi polgári olvasókör," *Munkács és vidéke*, 23 February 1896.

46. Miksa Szabolcsi, "Akikért szégyelnünk kell magunkat," *Egyenlőség*, 24 July 1896. The discontent was only further strengthened by the unclear book-keeping and scandalous personal conflicts of the congregation. "A rabbi kérdés," *Munkács*, 14 June 1896; "Izr. hitközség Munkács," *Munkács*, 2 August 1896; "Rendkívüli izr. hitközségi közgyűlés," *Munkács*, 2 August 1896.

47. *Gesta Hungarorum*, 12. *Munka* in Magyar means work or toil.

48. József Balajthy, *Munkács. Azaz: Munkács várának és városának topographiai, geographiai, históriai és statistikai leírása* (Debreczen: Tóth Lajos, 1836), 15–16; Johann Christian von Engel, *Geschichte des Ungrischen Reichs* (Vienna: Camesinasche Buchhandlung, 1813–14), 1: 69; Horváth, *Magyarország történelme*, 1: 40; Szalay, *Magyarország története*, 1: 12; Tabódy, *Munkács múltja*, 5–7.

49. Lehoczky, *Beregvármegye monographiája*, 3: 512. See also János Balogh, *Munkács-vár története* (Munkács: szerző kiadása, 1890), 12–20.

50. Balajthy, *Munkács*, 68; Balogh, *Munkács-vár*, 3.

51. F. S. Beudant, *Travels in Hungary in 1818* (London: Richard Phillips, 1823), 108.

52. Aladár Kuncz, *Thököly a francia irodalomban* (Budapest: Fritz Ármin, 1914).

53. Katalin Mária Kincses, "Minden különös ceremonia nélkül: A Rákóczi-kultusz és a fejedelem hamvainak hazahozatala," in idem., *Kultusz és hagyomány: Tanulmányok a Rákóczi-szabadságharc 300. évfordulóján* (Budapest: Argumentum, 2003), 132–77.

54. Balogh, *Munkács-vár*, 3. The concept of Munkács and Bereg County as the first place of the Magyar conquest and an outstanding location of the fights for Magyar independence became so much the necessary elements of any local reading that the Beregszász-born writer Lajos Pálóczi Horváth started his autobiographical novel (written several decades after the collapse of historic Hungary) by introducing this myth. Lajos Pálóczi Horváth, *Álompákász: Egy dzsentri gyermekkora* (Budapest: Magvető, 1986), 11–12.

55. Take for instance the poem *A munkácsi várban* (In the Munkács Castle) by Sándor Petőfi, the most influential romantic poet. "Petőfi Sándor összes költeményei," Magyar Elektronikus Könyvtár, http://mek.oszk.hu/01000/01006/html/vs184704.htm (accessed 25 May 2012).

56. For this reason, the town's vicinity served as a model for Árpád Feszty to paint his monumental panorama, a major attraction of the Millennial Exhibition. This fact was well known in Munkács and locals understood it as further proof of their town's glowing past connected to the conquest. See Béla Popovics, *Munkács kultúrtörténete a korabeli sajtó tükrében* (Munkács: Kárpátaljai Magyar Cserkészszövetség, 2005), 51–58.

57. See, for instance, the speech of Sándor Lónyay, Lord Lieutenant of Bereg County at the festive meeting of the county on 12 May 1896: minutes of the assembly of Bereg County, 12 May 1896, 71–73, DAZO, 890, 1–28.

58. Lehoczky, *Munkács város*, 256.

59. An exception was the mourning festivity of István Széchenyi in 1860. Tabódy, *Munkács múltja*, 107.

60. Popovics, *Munkács kultúrtörténete*, 140–41.

61. "Az ezredéves ünnepély," *Munkács*, 16 July 1889.

62. "A honfoglalás," *Munkács*, 4 February 1890.

63. "A g. k. hitközség tanács kérvénye," *Munkács*, 26 April 1892.

64. "A millennium ügye," *Munkács*, 14 May 1893.

65. Excerpt from the minutes of the assembly of Bereg County, 9 and 10 October 1893, DAZO, 10, 5–91.

66. Gábor Bay, ed., *A munkácsi Árpád-szobor regénye* (Munkács: Munkácsi Árpád-szobor bizottság, 1942), 4.

Chapter 6

BRASSÓ

Figure 6.1. The main square of Brassó in 1902. Courtesy of the National Széchényi Library, Budapest.

B rassó, a corporate town in the southeast corner of Hungary, has been an important economic and cultural hub in Transylvania since the Middle Ages. In the eighteenth century, it was the largest and wealthiest town in Transylvania. Due to the dynamic development of Kolozsvár, Brassó lost this position, but in 1910 it was still ranked twelfth in the Hungarian urban hierarchy (ranked second in Transylvania) as a regional center with partial urban functions. The town was home to four secondary schools, and around the millennial year four dailies were published. Beyond being the seat of Brassó County, regional administrative functions and higher education were not located in the town.

For many centuries, Brassó had the most advanced economy in Transylvania. In the early modern period, Brassó was a commercial and manufacturing hub but it had lost this position by the mid nineteenth century due to the emergence of a capitalist economy. From 1851, steamers were able to float the Danube, connecting the Black Sea with Central Europe, thus offering unbeatably cheap shipping compared to land transportation. The 1872 abolition of the guild system and the 1873 economic crisis ruined the traditional Saxon manufacturing system, and finally the Austro-Hungarian–Romanian customs war (1886–91) destroyed entire industries in the town. Brassó's economy had recovered by the turn of the century, as a number of modern factories were established to replace the older manufacturers, run mostly by Saxon entrepreneurs.[1] In 1900, twenty-eight factories employing more than twenty workers and two banks were located there, making Brassó the second most important Transylvanian economic center after Kolozsvár.

The town was divided into four districts: the downtown and three suburbs—Altstadt in the north, Bolonya in the east, and Şchei in the west. Although the town's structure derives from the Middle Ages, most houses were built in the eighteenth century, since in 1689 the Habsburg army set fire to the downtown.

The Lutheran church, downtown's most prominent building and an elaborate example of Gothic style, received its epitaph Black at this time. Although the fire ruined most of the town, it retained an elaborate historic character. Beside the Black Church, another characteristic building was the town hall on the market square that was built in 1420 and restructured in the 1770s in Baroque style. The downtown was defended by an elaborated system of walls, parts of which were replaced by a modern boulevard following the Viennese model in the late nineteenth century.[2] Other parts of the walls, including bastions and gates, were kept, further endorsing the historic nature of the town. The most characteristic of the town's outskirts was Şchei, where the Orthodox (mostly Romanian) merchants had their houses, business facilities, church, and school. The Bolonya district, between the downtown and the railway station, had a more industrial character: it hosted modern factories and grew rapidly in the discussed period. The Altstadt neighborhood was rather a sleepy outskirt.

One Town, Three Societies

The nuanced education, culture, and local media were the outcomes of Brassó's heterogeneity: its inhabitants fell roughly in equal numbers into three large religions and languages (see Tables 13.7 and 13.8 in the Appendix).

Language and religion largely determined each other: Romanians and Orthodox believers were practically identical, all Saxons belonged to the Lutheran Church, whereas Magyar speakers were split among the Roman Catholic Church and Protestantism. "Kronstadt is an essentially Saxon town," observed an English traveler in 1860, and even though the composition of the population did not prove his argument completely, he was certainly right.[3] Until the age of Joseph II, Brassó was a Saxon town *per definitionem*, as only members of the *natio Saxonica* were allowed to buy houses in the city center, and thus gain civic rights.[4] Despite the fact that Joseph II and then the liberal laws of 1848 abolished this privilege, by the end of the nineteenth century the town was still under Saxon dominance in terms of political influence, economy, and culture. The administrative language of the town remained German throughout the Hungarian period, with almost all municipal employees declaring German as their mother tongue. The leading positions in the town, particularly in political life, were controlled almost exclusively by Saxons: all mayors and most aldermen and parliamentary deputies were Saxons. These positions were filled mostly by people who played an important role in the life of the Lutheran Church as elders at the same time.[5] A majority of the local intelligentsia, factory owners, and artisans were also Saxons, owning most of the houses in the city center.[6] The only domain that Saxons did not control was trade with Romania, a major factor in the town's economy, which became dominated by Orthodox (Romanian) merchants.[7]

The Saxon society ran a comprehensive and well-functioning system of institutions, including associations, banks, and newspapers, such as the German Casino (founded in 1789), the Kronstadt Male Choral Society representing the middle class (Kronstädter Männergesangverein, 1859), the Kronstadt German Choral Society (Kronstädter Deutsche Liederkranz, 1885) for Saxons of lower social status, the Kronstadt General Savings Bank (Kronstadter Allgemeiner Sparkasse, founded in 1835 as the first modern bank in Transylvania),[8] and the influential daily *Kronstädter Zeitung* (established in 1849; its predecessor *Siebenbürger Wochenblatt* was first published in 1837).[9] The Lutheran Church established a comprehensive German schooling system, including elementary and middle schools, and the famous gymnasium, founded by the church reformer Johannes Honterus (1498–1549) in the sixteenth century.[10] Some associations, such as the Philharmonic Society, the Town Beautification Association, and the Volunteer Firemen were not directly tied to Saxon society, but were largely dominated by Saxons in the leading positions and had German as an official language.[11]

A Transylvanian Saxon identity developed from the Middle Ages and it remained persistent well after the abolition of the feudal *nationes* of Transylvania. Core elements of this identity were membership in the Lutheran Church, memory of the feudal *natio Saxonica*, and German culture and language (both the vernacular and the literary form). The presence of German culture among Transylvanian Saxons indicated membership in the German nation.[12] Until the 1890s, this membership was understood not in a political sense but only in a cultural sense, as promoted by the Saxon People's Party, and in particular by its older leaders, the so-called "Blacks." This identity meant an unsurpassable barrier for Magyar national integration, which could hardly accommodate the Saxon identity with the Magyar national concept.

Indeed, during the early 1890s Brassó became the headquarters of the young German nationalist Saxon politicians, the "Greens," who promoted German nationalism and cooperation with Romanian national politics and harshly condemned the older "Blacks." In a couple of years, the two streams rejoined to form a united Saxon party again. Yet, around the millennial year, *Kronstädter Zeitung* was edited by Green Saxons.[13]

The large Romanian-speaking Orthodox community formed a well-integrated, modern society too, based on a solid economic background. Established in 1830, the Romanian Merchant Company controlled long-distance trade mainly between Brassó and Romania, but also with the Balkans.[14] The flagship of the Romanian national financial system, the Albina Bank, opened its Brassó branch in 1880.[15] This economic background explains the high number of Romanian intellectuals living in Brassó. The 1900 census established that ten out of twenty-six lawyers and twenty-three out of seventy-four secondary school teachers in the county were Romanians, ensuring a particularly high proportion of Romanians among the free professions compared to other Hungarian counties.[16]

These intellectuals used the economic resources wisely. The first Transylvanian Romanian newspaper, *Gazeta de Transilvania*, was established in the town in 1838, only one year after the first German paper. *Gazeta de Transilvania* continued to be one of the most important Romanian dailies throughout the entire period.[17] Several associations were established, some of them very early, including the Romanian Casino (1835), the Romanian Female Association (1850), and the Romanian Singing and Sport Association (1863).[18] An important factor in producing Romanian culture was the Ciurcu publishing house, established in 1880. This firm published an enormous quantity of literature, dedicated to the intelligentsia, schools, and the wider public.[19] The wealth and willingness to promote culture attracted a number of Romanian intellectuals to Brassó, including Gheorghe Barițiu (teacher and later the first editor of *Gazeta de Transilvania*), Andrei Mureșianu (national poet, author of the current anthem of Romania), and, later, Gheorghe Dima (composer).[20] Four of the six board members of the Romanian Theater Association lived in the town in 1908 and the main Romanian national cultural institution, the ASTRA, had its second largest branch in Brassó, with 110 members.[21]

Beginning in the 1850s, a full-scale elementary and secondary school system was set up within the framework of the Romanian Orthodox Church.[22]

The flagship of this system, the Romanian Orthodox gymnasium, was an institution of outstanding importance and high quality. This school was the first modern Romanian institution of secondary-level education, established in the town in 1838 as an initiative of Orthodox businessmen to train merchants. It employed several famous teachers and honored them with the highest salaries by far in the entire Romanian Orthodox Church.[23] This gymnasium attracted Romanian-speaking pupils from all over Transylvania and Hungary, and even from Romania.[24] The national importance of the school was acknowledged with generous contributions from numerous private donors and with an annual subsidy from the Romanian government. This subsidy was considered illegal by the Hungarian government, which soon realized the danger of a rival state influencing education within the borders of Hungary. However, in spite of the ban on foreign aid, the Orthodox gymnasium relied on this resource for many years and thus was able to dodge direct control by the Hungarian Ministry of Religion and Culture.[25] The Brassó Romanians maintained vivid economic, cultural, and religious contacts with Moldova and Wallachia. Romanian merchants earned their fortunes through the trade between Transylvania and Romania and members of the upper class of Romania often spent their holidays in Brassó.[26]

The tiny Romanian-speaking Greek Catholic community became well integrated into Romanian national society. Gheorghe Barițiu and Mureșianu brothers Andrei and Iacob graduated from the Greek Catholic gymnasium in Blaj but this did not prevent them from becoming teachers at the Orthodox high school in Brassó.[27] Barițiu also served as the first editor of *Gazeta de Transilvania,* a paper financed by Orthodox merchants.[28]

Beyond Greek Catholics, the other group targeted by the mostly Orthodox Romanian national activists was the Greek-speaking Orthodox population. Since they had settled in Brassó in the thirteenth century, the Orthodox inhabitants had spoken a variety of southeastern European languages, including Greek, Romanian, and several Balkan Vlach and Slav dialects. By the second half of the nineteenth century, most of them had taken up Romanian and only a tiny minority kept Greek; Slav dialects had disappeared earlier.[29] Following denominational lines, the Romanian national activists also targeted the Greek-speaking Orthodox, but their transformation into modern Romanians was a long and difficult process.

The Orthodox merchant elite of the town was bilingual until the crystallization of national identities. As Greek was considered more prestigious, the wealthy Orthodox merchants tended to portray themselves as Greeks regardless of their linguistic or ethnic backgrounds. The emergence of modern national identities started in the 1780s, when a serious conflict emerged between a "Greek" and a "Romanian" party for control of the wealthy Holy Trinity Church and its school in the city center. This conflict derived from a rivalry between interest groups organized along social and economic cleavages (originally the Greek party included Romanian speakers and vice versa); nevertheless, it soon took on a national character and poisoned relations between the Greek- and Romanian-speaking Orthodox. The quarrel over the church lasted for a century and led to the separation of Greek speakers from the Romanian-speaking Orthodox. Romanian-speaking merchants established their own merchant company in 1830 and two separate reading clubs were founded. The language of the Holy Trinity Church and its school continued to be Greek, as the judicial process over the church was finally won by the Greek party.[30]

However, Greece was a country too small, poor, and far away to support any national integration project in Hungary. The overlaps between the Romanian- and Greek-speaking Orthodox did not disappear, as their cultural, religious, and economic practices largely coincided. As a consequence, the idea of a separate Greek society in Brassó failed. Even though the language of the Holy Trinity Church and its school continued to be Greek, the number of Greek speakers decreased dramatically, impoverishing their institutions. In 1892, the Xeropotamou Monastery of Mount Athos was unwilling to send a new priest to the Holy Trinity Church, alluding to its poor condition, and in 1908 the Greek school ceased to exist due to the lack of students.[31] By the end of the nineteenth century, most of the Greek speakers in Brassó seem to have acquired a modern Romanian identity; the appeal of Orthodoxy definitely proved to be greater than that of Magyar national integration.[32]

All of the above suggests the complete victory of the Romanian national integration project: the transformation of the Romanian speakers and Orthodox into a modern national Romanian society overcoming denominational barriers seemed complete by the end of the nineteenth century. Contemporaries held the Brassó Romanians to be the most modern, urbanized, and nationalized group within the entire Romanian-speaking society of Hungary.[33]

While both the Saxon and Romanian societies were well organized, the making of a modern Magyar society lagged behind. The Magyar national activists principally targeted the whole population of the town, but they had to recognize the unfavorable conditions and the advance of their competitors. Magyar integrative attempts were therefore restricted to groups ignored by both the Saxon and the Romanian elites: the Magyar speakers, the German-speaking Roman Catholics, and the Jews.

Promoters of a modern Magyar national society faced serious challenges due to a shortfall of Magyar middle class in Brassó. Compared to the Saxon or even the Romanian elite, the Magyar national elite of Brassó was small, weak, poor, and lacked prestige. According to the 1900 census, the number of Magyar males who owned houses or land was significantly smaller than that of Romanian or German speakers[34] and the majority of Magyars worked in domestic service (maids), agriculture, or small industry.[35] Although the number and influence of the Magyar national activists increased steadily due to the support of national authorities, they did not gain dominance in either the political or economic life of the town. At most, Magyar institutions and activists could compete with Romanians for second rank in the local hierarchy. The number of Magyar companies overtook that of Romanians during the 1880s but Romanian representatives outnumbered Magyars in the municipal assembly even in the 1890s. Needless to say, Saxon companies and municipal representatives largely exceeded both parties.[36]

Magyar institutions were established decades later than Saxons and Romanians and proved to be fragile well until the end of the nineteenth century. The first solid Magyar paper, *Nemere* was established in 1871, following some earlier and unsuccessful attempts.[37] The Magyar non-governmental institutions lacked resources; in 1882 the Magyar associations were on the edge of ceasing to exist altogether.[38] In 1892 the Magyar Civic Association had to suspend its public lectures due to lack of interest.[39] While the Saxon Lutheran Church completely financed its own schools, the Magyar Realschule was run by the government and the Roman Catholic gymnasium had to be transferred to the Transylvanian Catholic diocese since the local Catholic parish had insufficient resources.[40]

Despite all the failures discussed, Magyar national integration made some important achievements. The Magyar-speaking Lutherans were able to secede from the Saxon Lutheran Church and form an independent parish in 1883.[41] The Calvinist parish, whose members were predominantly Magyars, managed to build its own church in 1892, despite the alleged hostility of the town administration.[42] During the 1870s and 1890s, several state-sponsored elementary and middle schools and a Realschule were established, which operated only in Magyar by default. The Catholic gymnasium became German-Magyar bilingual following the Compromise, and then exclusively Magyar in the early 1880s, while the originally trilingual (German, Latin, and Magyar) downtown elementary school first dropped Latin, then introduced Magyar as the main language of instruction in the 1870s. By the end of the century, state elementary schools attracted most pupils in the town and government-run schools also had decisive positions in the middle and high school market.[43] By 1910, Magyar inhabitants outnumbered German speakers in the most prestigious part of the city, the downtown (4380 vs. 4169).[44] The 1900 census showed a Magyar majority in a handful of intellectual professions, mostly those related to the state (9 Magyar lawyers vs. 7 Germans; 27 Magyar gymnasium teachers vs. 23 Germans). In free professions less dependent on the state, Germans were still dominant (for instance, 15 Magyar doctors vs. 26 Germans).[45]

Magyar national activists were lucky enough to find out that German-speaking Roman Catholics and Jews did not fit into the Saxon identity based on its feudal heritage and strong Lutheran component. A modern German national platform disregarding confessional boundaries was thus not formed.

Due to the centralized character of the Catholic Church and particularly the Magyar dominance in the Transylvanian Catholic diocese, German Catholics in Brassó could not have as much autonomy as the Lutheran Saxons did. German Catholics had to share their institutions, including the school system, with their Magyar brethren, which led to the gradual Magyarization of these bodies. Magyar became the dominant language of the Catholic parish and schools during the 1870s and early 1880s. In 1900, 71% of German Catholics declared knowledge of Magyar.[46] By the end of the nineteenth century, German Catholics seemed to be on the way to Magyar national integration. The festive millennial annual report of the Catholic gymnasium claimed that the ratio of Magyar speakers boomed in the 1870s and 1880s in the school because many non-Magyar-speaking fathers decided to claim their sons as native Magyar speakers at enrollment as an accomplishment of the "constitutional character of dualism," i.e. the Hungarian state doctrine.[47] Catholic Germans even joined a Magyar–Romanian alliance to challenge the exclusive Saxon political positions in the 1870s.[48]

A similar process occurred in the case of the Brassó Jews. In the early years of dualism, they spoke predominantly German (72% declared German as their mother tongue in 1880) and Jewish pupils were sent partly to state-run, partly to Lutheran Saxon elementary schools.[49] In the following decades local Jews consciously orientated themselves toward Magyar national integration; the official language of the Neolog community became Magyar in 1885;[50] by the turn of the century Jewish pupils were sent to state elementary schools only; and in 1900 the language proportion became quite the opposite to the 1880 pattern: 75% of the Brassó Jewry declared Magyar as their mother tongue.[51] The engine of this process was Ignác Weisz, the chairman of the Neolog community. In 1882, he made an early attempt to organize a Magyar party and echoed the most liberal and Magyar national agenda of Hungarian Neology.[52]

The competing integration processes had a deep impact on the everyday life of Brassó, dividing the town into three distinct pillars. Following the terminology of Dutch historical social research, the term pillar is used here as

> a subsystem in society that links political power, social organization and individual behavior and which is aimed to promote, in competition as well as in cooperation with other social and political groups, goals inspired by a common ideology shared by its members for whom the pillar and its ideology is the main locus of social identification.[53]

Unlike the other towns in this book, the population of Brassó was divided by vertical lines which overshadowed the relevance of denomination and class. The three pillars of the Saxons, the Romanians, and the Magyars managed to integrate their primary target groups efficiently and attracted secondary targets as well (the Greek-speaking Orthodox and the Romanian-speaking Greek

Catholics were absorbed by the Romanian pillar, Jews were mostly integrated into the Magyar pillar, and German-speaking Roman Catholics were on the way to integration into the Magyar pillar). The pillar structure pervaded Brassó society entirely, as is demonstrated by marriages, spatial structure, schools, associations, economic and financial institutions, and political parties.

The marriage statistics demonstrate well how the pillar structure influenced everyday life in Brassó. According to the 1887 data, pillar-based endogamy was the dominant marriage pattern. The most segregated pillar was the Romanian: 71 marriages were registered that involved at least one Orthodox party, out of which 69 were between Orthodox partners and only 2 were between an Orthodox partner and a spouse of another denomination. In the same year, 115 Saxon Lutherans were married, out of whom only 11 chose a spouse of a different denomination, while 52 Lutheran marriages were concluded between Saxon partners. Given the multireligious nature of the Magyar pillar, inter-denominational marriage was far more frequent among Magyars: there were 8 Calvinist, 1 Magyar Lutheran, and 37 Roman Catholic weddings, while 17 Calvinists, 8 Magyar Lutherans, and 27 Roman Catholics chose spouses of a different denomination.[54]

The spatial structure of the town suggests the same pattern of segregation. Until the Josephinian liberalization of house ownership, Saxons lived in the downtown and in Altstadt, the Orthodox in Şchei, and Bolonya was inhabited mostly by Magyars. Since then, a slow mingling process had been taking place. Nonetheless, by the late nineteenth century, Şchei was still clearly Orthodox and Romanian: the most significant Romanian institutions were located there, including St. Nicholas Church, the elementary and secondary schools, and the bulk of Romanian business.[55] Only the handful of streets next to the downtown gate were inhabited by some Saxons and Magyars. Altstadt was still mostly a Saxon quarter with a few Romanian neighborhoods. The downtown, once a pure Saxon district, attracted a great number of Magyars and Romanians, but was still dominated by Saxons.[56] Bolonya became the most heterogeneous due to its industrial zone. It was populated mostly by Magyars, particularly by railway workers, though some Saxons lived in the area as well.[57]

The pillar structure influenced the local education market also, especially the language of instruction and the pattern of school attendance. The Lutheran Church ran a comprehensive educational system, including elementary schools in all of the quarters with a substantial Saxon population, and a prestigious gymnasium in the center of the town. These schools operated in German throughout the period. Saxon children rarely attended schools other than their own Lutheran ones.[58] The Orthodox Church also maintained elementary schools and a gymnasium with a commercial section, which instructed in Romanian. They were attended almost exclusively by Orthodox Romanians (with the exception of a few Greek Catholics); Orthodox pupils went to other denominational or state schools mostly in the districts that were far from an Orthodox school.[59] Magyar pupils almost exclusively went to Magyar schools, run mostly by the government and the Catholic Church.[60]

Associations and other cultural institutions also showed remarkable differences compared to the other locations of this study. The structures of the local choral societies can serve as a good example. The two Saxon societies, the Kronstadt Male Choral Society and the Kronstadt German Choral Society, sang predominantly German songs. In their early years, the Romanian Choral and Sport Association and the Brassó Magyar Choral Association performed some German songs as well, as Romanian and Magyar compositions were not yet available in sufficient numbers. In the following decades, Romanian and Magyar musical culture developed enough to change the repertoires. Even though a certain level of cooperation among these four associations could be witnessed in the form of common concerts and personnel, the primary reason for their existence was national, clearly overshadowing social or denominational factors. National events gave reasons to stage festive concerts: the Romanian society, for instance, performed a concert to commemorate the 400th anniversary of the death of the Moldovan Prince Stephen the Great and sang for Charles I of Romania at the royal castle of Sinaia in 1904.[61]

Although the economy of the town does not entirely correspond to the pillar system (no Magyar bank came into being), contemporaries interpreted the structure of the local industries in terms of the pillar structure.[62]

Local politics was also determined by the pillars. Ideological differences gained relevance within pillars only, such as the contest of the Black and Green Saxon orientations. The Saxon dominance was challenged only in the 1870s by a joint Romanian-Magyar-Catholic German party, although this attempt soon failed.[63] In theory, social democracy could have challenged the pillar-based politics. As a major industrial center, Brassó was home to a large number of workers, among whom social democracy gained a foothold during the 1890s. The First of May was celebrated first in 1890; in the same year, some Brassó workers were present at the founding congress of the HSDP in Budapest. First of May celebrations took place in some of the following years too, and workers discussed social issues.[64] Nonetheless, the presence of the social democrats was hardly tangible around the millennial year; neither the local papers nor the governmental reports discussed their activities.

The pillar structure influenced language use and mother tongue declarations in censuses. Linguistic assimilation took place only in the case of Jews and German-speaking Catholics. In 1880, 72% of local Jews declared their mother tongue as German; as a result of their conscious orientation toward Magyar nationalism, two decades later this percentage was reversed and 75% gave Magyar as their mother tongue.[65] Members of the other groups mostly insisted on preserving their mother tongues. Consequently, the change in the percentages among the language groups was primarily determined by the economic development of the town.

The economic decay of the town hit the Saxons most seriously. Following demolition of the artisan industry, a number of Saxons emigrated out of Brassó and could not be replaced, as the size of the Saxon hinterland was limited. The German-speaking population increased only by 24% between 1850 and 1910.[66] As a result, by the end of the century Saxons had become numerically the smallest group in the town, alarming the Saxon public and also foreshadowing political and economic threats.[67] The 48% increase in the number of Romanians in the same period proved to be enough to ensure them second place among the town's linguistic groups. The winner in the demographic change was the Magyar society, increasing by a dramatic 649% between 1850 and 1910.[68] The main source of this increase was immigration, as Magyar-speaking Szeklers were attracted by the new Brassó factories to work as day laborers. Maids employed by wealthier families were almost without exception Szekler girls; several sources claim that they had a crucial role in teaching Magyar to the children of non-Magyar-speaking families.[69] Immigration led to a rapid increase in Magyar speakers in Brassó, making the tiny Magyar-speaking population of 1850 the largest linguistic group by the turn of the century.

Language statistics suggest again that the most segregated pillar was the Romanian one. In 1880, 88%, and in 1900, 74% of the Romanian-speaking population was monolingual. Gender played a crucial role in linguistic behavior: while 36% of Romanian men knew a second language, only 16% of women did so. The position of the Magyar language was surprisingly advantageous; in 1900, 87% of Romanians who knew at least one second language spoke Magyar, regardless of their gender.[70] Magyar as a native language was only declared by a mere 164 Orthodox in 1880 and by 215 in 1900, which clearly means that a decisive factor in Magyar national integration, linguistic Magyarization, did not have any impact on the Romanian pillar of Brassó.[71]

Monolingualism was also a characteristic feature of the Magyar pillar. In 1880, 72%, and two decades later 67% of Magyar speakers were monolingual. Magyar-speaking women in particular lacked a second language, mainly due to the immigration of uneducated Szekler maids.[72]

In contrast to the monolingual Romanian and Magyar pillars, Saxons knew a second tongue in outstandingly high numbers. According to the 1900 census, 70% of Saxons spoke Magyar as a second language (males being slightly overrepresented).[73] This number was the outcome of the fact that almost all Saxon children attended school, where Magyar was taught as a second language from elementary school onwards. Sources highlight that the high number of Saxons knowing Magyar was also due to their Szekler maids and clients. For the Szekler girls it was common to go to Brassó to serve, and the peasants of the nearby Szekler counties often visited the town to buy goods from the Saxon manufacturers, therefore merchants had to learn their language to run the businesses.[74] To know Magyar was seen as a practical issue that did not influence native language and identity.[75]

The pillar structure thus pervaded Brassó society entirely. Although sources agree that the distance between the pillars (including spatial segregation) decreased during the dualist period, it is clear that separation prevailed and continued to dominate the town's society.[76]

The Magic Mountain: Reading the Town and the Hill

The pillarized society enabled the emergence of three different readings of the town. The Saxon interpretation of the town was produced within the larger framework of the Saxon reading of Transylvania. According to this interpretation, Brassó was an almost exclusively Saxon town, founded and later developed by the German-speaking colonists in an empty space. The Saxon authors argued for the foundation of Brassó in the thirteenth century by the Teutonic Knights, who were invited by the Hungarian king, Andrew II, to defend the eastern borders from barbaric Cumanians. The region around the town was seen as a territory lacking any population; the knights persuaded colonists to move there from Germany and thus they secured and civilized the province.[77] The Saxon narrative emphasized Brassó as part of the privileged Royal Land and thus downplayed its relations to the other provinces of Hungary and Transylvania. The Magyars and Romanians had played, according to the Saxon authors, a secondary, almost negligible role in the Saxon town of Brassó. The population of the town was reported to have been composed mostly of Saxons; ancestors of the Romanians were claimed to have arrived a century later as day laborers for the construction of the Black Church downtown, and the Magyars were also portrayed as immigrant workers. In particular, the town was seen as the most eastern point of Western civilization, embodied by the largest Gothic church in southeastern Europe, the Black Church.[78]

The Saxon intellectuals were in an easy position, as several factors supported their reading of a Saxon Brassó. On the territory of the town there was no evidence of any older settlement than that of the German-speaking colonists of the thirteenth century, therefore no Roman continuity was claimed, even by Romanian authors. Power in the nineteenth century meant state-controlled, hard, and legal power; in Brassó only Saxons executed this kind of power. As the municipality was controlled by Saxons from the thirteenth century until the interwar period, the Romanians and Magyars were easy victims of this state-oriented view. Utilizing their political power, the Saxons established the most remarkable cultural and economic achievements of the town, such as the foundation of the flourishing Balkan and Levantine trade and the Reformation and establishment of the famous Lutheran schools.[79]

A typical articulation of this narrative can be found in a travel guide to Brassó published in 1898; the author, Joseph Schuller, interpreted the large number of Magyar speakers as an illusion, as many of them were temporary immigrants to the town, therefore the percentage of German speakers among the "real" (permanent) population of Brassó must have been higher. In Schuller's historical account, the only actors were the Saxons. He ignored even the foundation of the neighborhood of Şchei. His description of the condition of the town almost completely disregarded monuments that had Romanian or Magyar relevance.[80]

Magyars and Romanians were also completely ignored in the representative volume *The Saxon Burzenland*, also published in 1898. This book was written to celebrate the 400th anniversary of the birth of Johannes Honterus. A native of Brassó, Honterus studied in Vienna and Cracow and became the leading Transylvanian Saxon humanist intellectual, theologian, publisher, and cartographer of the sixteenth century. His activity in Brassó was crucial in the conversion of Saxons to Lutheran Protestantism. The 1898 festivity that was dedicated to his memory thus provided a good excuse to limit the scope solely to Saxons.[81]

While Saxon political, economic, and cultural dominance made a Saxon-oriented reading of the town an easy task, Magyar intellectuals faced a more complicated challenge. In the first pieces of Magyar regional literature that addressed a wide audience, the Transylvanian Saxon towns were either not covered[82] or were not credited with a Magyar character.[83] The foundations of a Magyar reading of Brassó were constructed by the influential scholar Balázs Orbán in the 1870s. Orbán rejected the Saxon interpretation of Brassó on several points. He claimed that the Brassó district had definitely belonged to Hungary and that it had been inhabited by Magyars and Szeklers before the Saxon colonization. Therefore, the achievements of Western civilization were not imported only by the Saxons, but were a joint effort by the locals. He also argued that the town had had a substantial Magyar population from the very beginning, but the "aggressive, tyrannizing" Saxons had forced them to adopt the German language, Germanize their names, and convert to Lutheranism instead of their preferred Calvinism in the sixteenth century. This process left only the lowest classes speaking Magyar. Orbán also stressed Brassó's strong connection to the almost completely Magyar-speaking neighboring province of the Szekler Land. A typical argument, for instance, emphasized that Brassó had been under the jurisdiction of the Szekler governor until 1542, when it had become part of the Royal Land. The very incorporation of the Brassó region into his book devoted to the Szeklers was already a way to downplay Brassó's Saxon character and portray it as a province attached to the Szekler

Land. The coverage of Brassó in a book about the Szeklers was explained by the proximity, the strong historical connections, and the large Szekler population of the region.[84] Orbán's arguments were ambiguous enough not to be used unconditionally by other Magyar authors; the later Magyar reading accepted the Saxon accounts about the thirteenth-century German foundation and did not claim a substantial Magyar population until the late nineteenth century. The Magyar character of the town was provided by giving modern governmental buildings the same importance as historical structures.[85]

While Magyar intellectuals faced serious problems with the construction of a Magyar reading of Brassó, Romanians were in an easier position, as their presence and cultural and economic achievements were clearer than those of the Magyars. Lacking any evidence of Dacian-Roman-Romanian continuity in the region of Brassó, Romanian authors agreed that the first inhabitants of the Şchei district had arrived from the Balkans in the fourteenth century as workers on the Black Church.[86] As Brassó lacked Roman origins and the historical sources did not allow it to be interpreted as a main location in Romanian history, the town was narrated as a place of Romanian modernity. All the descriptions focused on its advanced cultural and economic life, the large number of Romanian intelligentsia, and stressed its importance in Romanian national integration. The Romanian narrative emphasized the flourishing economic relations between Brassó and Wallachia and the financial support of St. Nicholas Church provided by the Moldovan princes, thus the town emerged as a central place in the Romanian space, connecting the Transylvanian and Old Kingdom Romanians.[87] The Romanian reading of the town emphasized the Romanian character; while the suburb of Şchei was portrayed as having almost exclusively Romanian-speaking inhabitants, the ethno-linguistic structure of the other parts of the town was either ignored or portrayed as a mixed population.[88]

Unlike Pressburg, where the Pressburger and the Magyar national readings of the city mostly coincided, or the case of Munkács, where the local and Magyar national narratives were completely identical, the three interpretations of Brassó did not overlap, but excluded each other. The Saxon interpretation ignored all other players and narrated the town in exclusively Saxon terms. The Romanian reading acknowledged the Saxon dominance but gave Brassó the credit of being a center of Romanian modernity in the Romanian space. Magyar intellectuals made serious efforts to find the place of Magyars in the town's past. The local Saxon and Romanian historical interpretations did not fit into the Magyar master narrative; the thirteenth-century foundation of Brassó contradicted the Magyar conquest and Saxon autonomy and the Moldovan and Wallachian connections opposed the idea of a unitary Hungarian state.

The historical and spatial narratives were incompatible not only with each other, but also with the present experiences, particularly the interpretation of the 1848 revolution and the 1867 Compromise. A majority of Saxon and Romanian politicians took the side of the Habsburgs in 1848, so the revolutionary Magyar army had to conquer Brassó in March 1849. Therefore, Saxon and Romanian intellectuals, unlike the enthusiastic and proud pro-revolutionary Pressburgers, interpreted the 1848 events mostly in negative terms and connected the revolution only to the Magyar nation instead of narrating them as achievements of Hungary as a whole, thus excluding themselves from the most integrative contemporary experience of the Magyar society.[89] The negative interpretation of the 1848 events earned them bitter criticism and accusations of disloyalty and treason by Magyar authors.[90] Similarly, the interpretations of the 1867 Compromise were also strikingly divergent; while the governing Liberal Party celebrated it as the restoration of the liberal constitution of 1848, Saxon and Romanian politicians understood it as the opening act of a "violent Magyarization policy," as the "eternal" Saxon autonomy and the advantageous status of the Romanians introduced in the 1860s were both abolished.

These competing historical and spatial narratives were well distributed through the autonomy of the denominational schools. In the Lutheran gymnasium, instruction in the history and geography of Hungary was introduced in the mid 1870s only, a decade after Transylvania became part of Hungary. Transylvania remained a major object of geography and history instruction, even though the subject was officially the geography and history of Hungary. The textbooks used in this school, including a volume written by Saxon bishop and historian Georg Daniel Teutsch, presented the Saxon historical and spatial narrative.[91] Magyar high schools taught the Magyar master narrative, focused on the whole country, and downplayed any regional identity. Although the textbooks used in the Romanian Orthodox gymnasium were mostly translations of Magyar books, it can be supposed that the Romanian teachers encouraged their students to accept the narrative of the textbooks only on the surface and to believe in fact the Romanian interpretation of the past and space.[92]

The contest of Brassó's interpretations was well represented on the streets of the town. Despite the emergence of the Romanian and Magyar communities, Saxons continued to dominate the public space of Brassó. The most important buildings in the center, such as the Black Church, the old town hall, and the Lutheran gymnasium all showed the Saxon dominance. The most prestigious institutions were either directly Saxon (Black Church, Lutheran gymnasium) or officially neutral in ethnic terms but dominated by Saxons (municipal administration, the Beautification Association, etc.).[93]

During the second half of the nineteenth century, representative Romanian buildings were built closer and closer to the center, claiming a Romanian demand for a greater voice in town matters. The most famous Romanian building, the ancient St. Nicholas Church, was located in the peripheral Şchei; its location represented the secondary role of Romanians. In 1856, the Orthodox gymnasium was built facing the Catherine Gate but still outside of the center. Finally, in 1895, an Orthodox church was erected in the main square, although it was hidden in an inner courtyard.[94] The most important Romanian institutions, like the Romanian Casino or the branch of the Albina Bank, also had their offices in the city center.[95] Despite the fact that the main square was still more Saxon in character, the symbolic and real distance the Romanians covered in a few decades was remarkable.

The local Magyars were hardly in a position to challenge the Saxon appearance of the town, making both local and Budapest-based Magyar national protagonists dissatisfied.[96] The tiny Magyar Protestant churches and Magyar associations were not able to compete with the glory of the Black Church or the Saxon institutions. The Magyar presence in Brassó was represented rather by modern governmental buildings praising the liberal and progressive Hungarian state. Most of these buildings were erected on Rudolfring, a modern boulevard at the edge of the city center, which replaced old town walls following the Viennese model.[97] The demolition of the old town walls and their replacement by a modern boulevard was not only a practical matter, but also served symbolic goals. In the eyes of Magyar commentators, the spirit of the feudal, privileged Saxon town was superseded by the modernity of liberal Hungary.

The streets of Brassó did not have any national or ethnic character, as they kept their old names, mostly referring to their functions;[98] neither were public monuments erected until 1896.[99] The most spectacular events on the streets of the town were the traditional marches of the Saxon and Romanian youths. Despite copying older traditions (the Saxon march, for instance, commemorated the Reformation and Johannes Honterus), both rituals included national elements. Both marches attracted large crowds and were among the most alluring events in the town. Lacking such traditions, the local Magyars had to invent a festivity. The 1848 revolution was commemorated for the first time in 1885. Yet this festivity did not take place in the urban space; it was always held in a club. Nevertheless, the Magyar 1848 commemoration managed to captivate most Magyar associations and the pupils of Magyar-speaking middle and high schools; youths of the Saxon or Romanian schools never participated.[100]

While the town itself was definitely empty in terms of monuments, the same cannot be said for Cenk Hill above the downtown, where the millennial memorial was planned to be built. The hill dominates Brassó: the peak is visible from all parts of the city center and the nearby suburbs, and it functioned as a landmark of the town. Dozens of travel guides and itineraries reported enthusiastically about the wonderful panorama from the peak and the refreshing walks along the serpentine paths on the hillside. The hill was used by locals and tourists for leisure and entertainment and it also inspired local literary works. Art historian Hans Wühr called it the Magic Mountain of local poets and painters.[101]

Beyond tourism, the hill was also used for ideological purposes. In 1712, a Catholic chapel was constructed with a donation from a town senator, but it was damaged by a lightning strike in 1737. After the failure of the Hungarian revolution in 1848/49, the town council erected a pyramid decorated with a lion in honor of the victorious Russian and Austrian armies. Of course, this first modern monument of the town outraged the Magyar public. Due to some damage caused by lightning, it collapsed in 1870 and the town council did not wish to provoke the government and the local Magyars by repairing it.[102]

At the end of the nineteenth century, Brassó still had a traditional Saxon character. At the same time, the emergence of Magyars and Romanians was more and more visible, even though the Magyar pillar was definitely in need of governmental support. The millennial year thus provided a great opportunity to provide this support by symbolic means.

Notes

1. Maja Phillippi, "Die Anfänge der industriellen Entwicklung in Kronstadt (1872–1900)," *Forschungen zur Volks- und Landeskunde* 36, no. 1 (1993): 66–77.

2. Anca Maria Zamfir, "Un posibil model vienez pentru Brașovul celei de-a doua jumătăți a secolului al XIX–lea," *Cumidava* 22–24 (1998–2000): 321–60.

3. Charles Boner, *Transylvania: Its Products and Its People* (London: Longmans, Green, Reader, and Dyer, 1865), 260.

4. This privilege was called *Konzivilität*. See Angelika Schaser, *Josephinische Reformen und soziale Wandel in Siebenbürgen: Die Bedeutung des Konzivilitätsreskriptes für Hermannstadt* (Stuttgart: Franz Steiner, 1989), 40.

5. Friedrich Sindel, "Die Vermögensverhältnisse der Kirchengemeinden," in *Das sächsische Burzenland* (Kronstadt: Honterusdruckerei Joh. Gött's Sohn, 1898), 274; Andreas Schöck, "Brassó, Brașov, Kronstadt: Beiträge zur Stadtentwicklung, Bevölkerungs- und Berufsgruppenstruktur" (PhD diss., Freie Universität Berlin, 1995), 169.

6. Friedrich Lexen, *Zur wirtschaftlichen Entwicklung Kronstadts in den letzten 50 Jahren* (Kronstadt: Separatdruck aus Nr. 78, 79, 80 und 81 der *Kronstädter Zeitung*, n. d.), 6–12; August Jekelius, *Der Grund- und Hausbesitz im Burzenland* (Kronstadt, n. p., 1904), 4–8.

7. Ambrus Miskolczy, *A brassói román levantei kereskedőpolgárság kelet-nyugati közvetítő szerepe (1780–1860)* (Budapest: Magyar Tudományos Akadémia, 1987).

8. Gábor Egry, "Nemzet és gazdaság: A Brassói Általános Takarékpénztár társadalmi-gazdasági szerepfelfogása (1835–1914)," *Pro Minoritate* (Spring 2003): 59–68.

9. Heinrich Polonyi, "Das 'Deutsche Kasino' in Kronstadt: Zur Geschichte des 'Kronstädter Lese- und Geselligkeitsvereins' kurz 'Deutsches Kasino' genannt," *Siebenbürgisch-sächsischer Hauskalender* 16 (1971): 97–99; *Die 50jährige Tätigkeit des Kronstädter Männer-Gesangvereins 1859 bis 1909* (Kronstadt: Johann Gött's Sohn, 1909), 2–5; Wolfgang Sand, *Kronstadt: Das Musikleben einer multiethnischen Stadt bis zum Ende des Habsburgerreiches* (Kludenbach: Gehann-Musik-Verlag, 2004), 234.

10. Julius Groß, *Geschichte des evangelischen Gymnasiums A. B. in Kronstadt: Festschrift zur Honterusfeier* (Kronstadt: Honterusdruckerei J. Gött's Sohn, 1898).

11. "A 'Szépitő Egyesület'," *Brassói Lapok*, 30 May 1896; Karl Ludwig Schuster, ed., *Leben und Wirken der Kronstädter Freiwilligen Feuerwehr im ersten Vierteljahrhundert 1874–1899: Festgabe zum 25-jährigen Jubiläum des Vereines* (Kronstadt: Schlandt, 1899), 41–43; Kurt Phillippi, "Kurze Geschichte der 'Kronstädter Philharmonischen Gesellschaft' (1878–1944)," *Zeitschrift für Siebenbürgische Landeskunde* 5, no. 2 (1982): 144–85.

12. Harald Roth, "Autostereotype als Identifikationsmuster: Zum Selbstbild der Siebenbürger Sachsen," in *Das Bild des Anderen in Siebenbürgen: Stereotype in einer multiethnischen Region*, ed. Konrad Gündisch, Wolfgang Höpken, and Michael Markel (Cologne: Böhlau, 1998), 179–91; Harald Roth, "Von der Nation zum Volk der Nation: Ethnische Identitäten im Siebenbürgen des 18. und 19. Jahrhunderts," in *Ethnische und soziale Konflikte im Neuzeitlichen Osteuropa: Festschrift für Heinz-Dietrich Löwe zum 60. Geburtstag*, ed. Ralph Tuchtentagen and Christoph Gassenschmidt (Hamburg: Dr. Kovač, 2004), 233–45; Krista Zach, "'Wir wohnten auf dem Königsboden...' Identitätsbildung bei den Siebenbürger Sachsen im historischen Wandel," in *Minderheitenfragen in Südosteuropa: Beiträge der internationalen Konferenz: The Minority Question in Historical Perspective 1900–1990. Inter University Center, Dubrovnik, 8.–14. April 1991*, ed. Gerhard Seewann (Munich: Oldenbourg, 1992), 115–37.

13. Oscar Wittstock, *Grün oder Schwarz? Eine Beleuchtung der gegenwärtigen politischen Verhältnisse der Siebenbürger Sachsen* (Hermannstadt: G. U. Seraphim, 1896); Carl Göllner, "Abwehr von Magyarisierungsversuchen 1877–1900," in *Die Siebenbürger Sachsen in den Jahren 1848–1918*, ed. Carl Göllner (Cologne/Vienna: Böhlau Verlag, 1988), 170–205.

14. N. G. V. Gologan, *Cercetări privitoare la trecutul comerțului românesc din Brașov* (Bucharest: Lupta, 1928), 44–55; Miskolczy, *A brassói román levantei kereskedőpolgárság*, 60–132; Phillippi, "Die Anfänge der industriellen Entwicklung," 72.

15. Veritas [pseud.], *A magyarországi románok egyházi, iskolai, közművelődési, közgazdasági intézményeinek és mozgalmainak ismertetése* (Budapest: Uránia, 1908), 397–98. Gábor Egry called my attention to the relatively small size of the Albina branch. This suggests that Romanian business relied on capital of other banks as well, but does not challenge the exclusive subsidy policy of donating to Romanian national and Orthodox religious goals.

16. *Magyar statisztikai közlemények* 16 (1906): 192–93 and 234–35.

17. Ioan Lumperdean, *Romanian Economic Journalism in Transylvania in the First Half of the Nineteenth Century* (Cluj-Napoca: Romanian Cultural Institute, 2005), 44–53.

18. Mircea Băltescu, "Contribuții la istoricul 'Reuniunii Femeilor Române' din Brașov," *Cumidava* 1 (1967): 191–211; Ion Colan, *Casina Română din Brașov (1835–1935)* (Brașov: Institutul de Arte Grafice "ASTRA," 1935), 29–32; Sand, *Kronstadt*, 200–201.

19. Ion Colan, "După cincizeci de ani: Librăria Ciurcu din Brașov," *Țara Bârsei* 2, no. 6 (1930): 547–50.

20. Sand, *Kronstadt*, 210–12.

21. Veritas, *A magyarországi románok*, 220–22 and 328.

22. Ovidiu Savu, "Situația învătâmântului românesc din Brașov la jumătatea secolului al XIX-lea," *Țara Bârsei* 5, no. 5 (2006): 63–84.

23. Paul Brusanowski, *Învățământul confesional ortodox din Transilvania între anii 1848–1918: Între exigențele statului centralizat și principiile autonomiei bisericești* (Cluj-Napoca: Presa Universitară Clujeană, 2005), 562–63.

24. Andreiŭ Bârseanu, *Istoria Șcólelor Centrale Române Gr. Or. din Brașov* (Brașov: Ciurcu, 1902); Onosofir Ghibu, *Viața și organizația bisericească și școlară in Transilvania și Ungaria* (Bucharest: Nicolae Stroilă, 1915), 184–92; Arsène Vlaicu, *Monographie de l'École Supérieure de Commerce Gréco-Orientale Roumaine de Brassó* (Brassó: Ciurcu, 1913). Some

famous teachers: Andrei Bârseanu (ethnologist, chairman of the ASTRA association), Virgil Onițiu (writer, publicist), in the 1930s Emil Cioran (philosopher). Some famous students: Lucian Blaga (philosopher and poet), Sextil Pușcariu (philologist), Octavian Goga (poet), Ioan Lupaș (historian), Ioan Bogdan (philologist), Alexandru Lapedatu (historian).

25. Zoltán Szász, "A brassói román iskolák ügye a századvég nemzetiségi politikájában," *Történelmi Szemle* 19, no. 1 (1976): 35–63; Simion Toma, *Monografia Colegiului Național "Andrei Șaguna"* (Brașov: Cocordia, 2000), 39–40.

26. Ernst Anton Quitzmann, *Reisebriefe aus Ungarn, dem Banat, Siebenbürgen, den Donaufürstenthümern, der Europäischen Türkei und Griechenland* (Stuttgart: J. B. Müller's Verlagsbuchhandlung, 1850), 239.

27. Savu, "Situația învătământului românesc," 64–66.

28. Remus Zăstroiu, "Einige Beobachtungen hinsichtlich des sozialen und beruflichen Status' des rumänischen Journalisten im 19. Jahrhundert," in *Deutschsprachige Öffentlichkeit und Presse in Mittelost- und Südeuropa (1848–1948)*, ed. Andrei Ciorbea-Hoișie, Ion Lihaciu, and Alexander Rubel (Iași: Editura Universității "Al. I. Cuza," 2008), 78.

29. E. A. Bielz, *Handbuch der Landeskunde Siebenbürgens eine physikalisch-statistisch-topographische Beschreibung dieses Landes* (Hermannstadt: S. Filtsch, 1857), 143; Balázs Orbán, *A Székelyföld leírása: Történelmi, régészeti, természetrajzi s népismereti szempontból* (Budapest: Tettey Nándor, 1868–1873), 6: 266–73.

30. Bartolomeu Baiulescu, *Monografia comunei bisericesci gr. ort. române a Sfintei Adormiri din Cetatea Brașovului cu acte și dovezi* (Brașov: Ciurcu, 1898); Nicolaus Strevoiu, *Aktenmässiger Sachverhalt des Kirchenstreites der gr.-or. Bürger rumänischer Nationalität gegen die gr.-or. Bürger griechischer Zunge wegen der Dreifaltigkeitskirche in der innern Stadt Kronstadt* (Kronstadt: J. Gött & Sohn, 1881); Miskolczy, *A brassói román levantei kereskedőpolgárság,* 43–59.

31. Richard Clogg, "The Greek Merchant Companies in Transylvania," in *Minderheiten, Regionalbewusstsein und Zentralismus in Ostmitteleuropa,* ed. Heinz-Dietrich Löwe, Günther H. Tontsch, and Stefan Troebst (Cologne: Böhlau, 2000), 165.

32. An attempt by the Hungarian government to separate the Greek speakers from the Romanian-speaking Orthodox happened in the 1880s. The Ministry of Religion and Education decided to establish a commercial school specializing in Balkan trade. The government intended to upgrade the Greek school in Brassó, which would definitely have raised its prestige and financial opportunities. The Greek parish, however, rejected the proposal and insisted on its complete control over the school. The school's independence was thus ensured but the price was high, as due to lack of students it only functioned until 1908. Ferencz Koós, *Tanfelügyelői visszaemlékezések* (Brassó, 1903), AH, Stenner collection, 5676/4.

33. Ioan I. Lăpĕdatu, *Probleme sociale și economice: Ajută-te și Dumnedĕu te va ajuta* (Brașov: A. Mureșianu, 1904), 28–30; Barna Ábrahám, "Urbanizáció, urbanitás az erdélyi románoknál a dualizmus korában," in *Erdélyi várostörténeti tanulmányok,* ed. Judit Pál and János Fleisz (Csíkszereda: Pro Print, 2001), 224–53.

34. The exact figures are as follows. Ratio of males possessing a house: 460 out of 5857 Magyars (7.8%), 528 out of 4936 Germans (10.7%), 1141 out of 5291 Romanians (21.6%). Ratio of males possessing land: 130 out of 5857 Magyars (2.2%), 234 out of 4936 Germans (4.7%), and 329 out of 5291 Romanians (6.2%). MNL OL, XXXII–23–h, census 1900, box 292, folio Brassó, table 47–48/a.

35. MNL OL, XXXII–23–h, census 1900, box 167, folio Brassó, table 41.

36. Lexen, *Zur wirtschaftlichen Entwicklung,* 9–10; Schöck, "Brassó, Brașov, Kronstadt," 166–73.

37. Orbán, *A Székelyföld,* 6: 304–6.

38. Ignácz Weiss, *Az Erdélyi Magyar Közművelődési Egylet és a brassói magyarság: Hirlapi czik-kek* (Brassó: Alexi, 1885), 19–32.

39. Ferencz Nagy, *A brassói magyar polgári kör története az 1873. évtől, az 1893. év végéig* (Brassó: Alexi, 1894), 28.

40. *Annual Report of the Roman Catholic Gymnasium in Brassó*, 1895/96, 18–22.

41. Károly Nikodemusz, *A brassói magyar ág. h. ev. egyházmegye megalakulásának története* (Kolozsvár: Concordia, n. d.).

42. Eduard Morres, "Die kleinen Kirchen," in *Kronstadt*, vol. 3 of *Das Burzenland*, ed. Erich Jekelius (Kronstadt: Burzenländer Sächs. Museum, 1928), 162; János Molnár, *A brassói magyarság és ev. ref. egyház története* (Brassó: Brassói Ev. Ref. Egyházkebli Tanács, 1887).

43. *Annual Report of the State Elementary Schools in Brassó*, 1895/96, 14–17.

44. *Magyar statisztikai közlemények* 42 (1912): 618.

45. *Magyar statisztikai közlemények* 16 (1906): 192–93, 234–35, and 244–45.

46. MNL OL, XXXII–23–h, census 1900, box 292, folio Brassó, table 47–48c.

47. *Annual Report of the Roman Catholic Gymnasium in Brassó*, 1895/96, 53.

48. Stephanie Danneberg, "Die Verbrüderungsbewegung und Partei 'Nemere': Ein besonderer Moment im politischen Leben Kronstadts der 1870er Jahre," *Forschungen für Volks- und Landeskunde* 54 (2011): 107–20.

49. MNL OL, XXXII–23–h, census 1880, box 524, folio Brassó, table XVI. Whether this German meant Yiddish or standard German remains unclear.

50. Carmen Manațe, Sami Fiul, and Viorica Oprea, *Comunitatea evreilor din Brașov: Secolele XIX–XX* (Brașov: Transilvania Expres, 2007), 40.

51. In 1900 there were 101 Jewish children aged between 6 and 10. In the school year 1900/1901, 116 Jewish pupils attended state elementary schools in classes 1–4. Even though the attendance at other elementary schools of the same year is not available, it can be presumed that there were only isolated cases of Jews being enrolled in denominational elementary schools, therefore the Jews of Brassó and its vicinity were almost completely in favor of state education. MNL OL, XXXII–23–h, census 1900, box 292, folio Brassó, table 47–48c, and 47–48/d, and *Annual Report of the State Elementary Schools in Brassó*, 1900/1901, 18–23.

52. Ignácz Weisz, *A zsidók és a nemzetiségek* (Brassó: Brassó Könyvnyomda, 1894); Péter Ujvári, ed., *Magyar Zsidó Lexikon* (Budapest: Magyar Zsidó Lexikon, 1929), s.v. "Weiss Ignácz."

53. E. H. Bax, "Modernization and Cleavage in Dutch Society: A Study of Long Term Economic and Social Change" (PhD diss., University of Groningen, 1988), 104 as quoted in Paul Dekker and Peter Ester, "Depillarization, Dedenominalization, and De-Ideologization: Empirical Trends in Dutch Society 1958–1992," *Review of Religious Research* 37, no. 4 (June 1996): 327–28. The application of the Dutch pillar system in the Transylvanian context was first suggested by Gábor Gyáni, though his concept was built rather on intuition than a deep analysis of Transylvanian social history. See Gábor Gyáni, "A középosztály és a polgárság múltja különös tekintettel a dualizmus kori Erdélyre," in *Erdélyi várostörténeti tanulmányok*, ed. Judit Pál and János Fleisz (Csíkszereda: Pro Print, 2001), 164–69.

54. Eduard Gusbeth, *Die Bewegung der Bevölkerung im Kronstädter Komitat in den Jahren 1876–1887* (Kronstadt: Albrecht & Zillich, 1888), 33. Before the introduction of civil marriage in 1894, Jewish–Christian marriages were not possible.

55. Sterie Stinghe, *Die Schkejer oder Trokanen in Kronstadt* (Leipzig: Johann Ambrosius Barth, 1900).

56. Jekelius, *Der Grund- und Hausbesitz*.

57. Schöck, "Brassó, Brașov, Kronstadt," 58–74.

58. Hansgeorg Kyllien, "Die ethnische und konfessionelle Zusammensetzung der Schülerschaft am Kronstädter deutschen Gymnasium von 1856/57 bis 1946/47," *Zeitschrift für Siebenbürgische Landeskunde* 29, no. 1 (2006): 37–43.

59. In the school year 1912/13, 588 pupils attended the Orthodox Romanian elementary school, out of which only a single student was a Greek Catholic Romanian. In the same year, the Lutheran elementary school was attended by 9 Orthodox pupils and the state elementary schools by 183 Orthodox pupils. Real competition took place only in the overwhelmingly Orthodox and Romanian-speaking Șchei district; there the state elementary school was able to attract 49 Orthodox pupils among its 215 students. The other state elementary schools were in an easier position, as the Romanian Orthodox school was quite far from them, therefore reasons of pure convenience also supported the state schools.

60. *Annual Report of the Roman Catholic Elementary School in Downtown of Brassó*, 1901/1902, 17–18; *Annual Report of the Roman Catholic Gymnasium in Brassó*, 1895/96, 104–5.

61. Sand, *Kronstadt*.

62. Jekelius, *Der Grund- und Hausbesitz*; Lexen, *Zur wirtschaftlichen Entwicklung*.

63. Orbán, *A Székelyföld*, 6: 273 and 6: 303–4; Danneberg, "Die Verbrüderungsbewegung."

64. Augustin Deac, *Mișcarea muncitorească din Transilvania 1890–1895* (Bucharest: Editura Științifică, 1962).

65. MNL OL, XXXII–23–h, census 1880, box 524, folio Brassó, table XVI; and 1900, box 292, folio Brassó, tables 47–48c and 47–48/d. Whether German meant Yiddish or standard German remains unclear.

66. Schöck, "Brassó, Brașov, Kronstadt," 97.

67. Jekelius, *Der Grund- und Hausbesitz*; Lexen, *Zur wirtschaftlichen Entwicklung*.

68. Schöck, "Brassó, Brașov, Kronstadt," 97.

69. Boner, *Transylvania*, 249–50; Réthi Lajos, "A székely leányok Brassóban: Életkép," *Vasárnapi Ujság*, 1 March 1874.

70. MNL OL, XXXII–23–h, census 1900, box 292, folio Brassó, table 47–48c.

71. MNL OL, XXXII–23–h, census 1880, box 524, folio Brassó, table XVI; and 1900, box 292, folio Brassó, tables 47–48c and 47–48/d.

72 Ibid.

73. Ibid.

74. Árokalyi [pseud.], "Reminiscentiák 1837ről," *Nemzeti Társalkodó*, 14 March 1839; Boner, *Transylvania*, 249–50.

75. Joachim von Puttkamer, "Mehrsprachigkeit und Sprachenzwang in Oberungarn und Siebenbürgen 1867–1914: Eine statistische Untersuchung," *Zeitschrift für Siebenbürgische Landeskunde* 26, no. 1 (2003): 16.

76. Jekelius, *Der Grund- und Hausbesitz*, 6–7; Schöck, "Brassó, Brașov, Kronstadt," 102–7.

77. Julius Groß, "Aus der Geschichte des Burzenlandes," in *Das sächsische Burzenland* (Kronstadt: Honterusdruckerei, Joh. Gött's Sohn, 1898), 1–70; Friedrich Philippi, *Aus Kronstadt's Vergangenheit und Gegenwart: Begleitwort zum Plan von Kronstadt* (Kronstadt: Gött, 1874), 15; Friedrich Philippi, *Die deutschen Ritter im Burzenlande: Ein Beitrag zur Geschichte Siebenbürgens* (Kronstadt: Johann Gött, 1861), 7–10; Josef Schuller, *Kronstadt: Neuer illustrierter Führer durch die Stadt und deren Umgebung* (Kronstadt: Heinrich Zeidner, 1898), 43–44.

78. Lucas Joseph Marienburg, *Geographie des Großfürstenthums Siebenbürgen* (Hermannstadt: Martin Hochmeister, 1813), 2: 327–49; Philippi, *Aus Kronstadt's Vergangenheit und Gegenwart*; Cristian Cercel, "Transylvanian Saxon Symbolic Geographies," *Civilisations* 60, no. 2 (2012): 89–91.

79. It is telling that the huge source collection published by the municipality included almost only German and Latin sources. See *Quellen zur Geschichte der Stadt Brassó: Chroniker*

und Tagebücher. 7 vols. (Kronstadt: Heinrich Zeidner, 1896–1915). At the same time, a large number of sources on the town's Romanian past were also published by Romanian authors.

80. Schuller, *Kronstadt.*

81. *Das sächsische Burzenland* (Kronstadt: Honterusdruckerei, Joh. Gött's Sohn, 1898). Burzenland is the German name for the Brassó region.

82. Ferencz Kubinyi and Imre Vahot, eds., *Magyarország és Erdély képekben* (Pest: Emich Gusztáv, 1853–1854).

83. Árokalyi [pseud.], "Reminiscentiák 1837ről," *Nemzeti Társalkodó,* 7, 14, and 21 March 1839; Hunfalvy, *Magyarország és Erdély,* 2: 83–93; László Kőváry, "Barczaság," in *Erdély képekben,* ed. Károly Szathmári Pap (Kolosvár: Kir. Lyceum, 1842), 55–62.

84. Orbán, *A Székelyföld,* 6: 2–5, 259–66, and 281–83.

85. *A Pallas nagy lexikona: Az összes ismeretek enciklopédiája,* s.vv. "Barcaság" and "Brassó"; Dezső Radnóti, ed., *Erdélyi kalauz: Utmutató Magyarország erdélyi részében* (Kolozsvár: Erdélyi Kárpát-Egyesület, 1901), 354–61; Oszkár Reich Milton, *Erdély térképmellékletek-kel és képekkel* (Budapest: Eggenberger, 1910), 97–101. Both of these travel guides claimed that the most beautiful building in the town was the courthouse (built in 1902).

86. Silvestru Moldovan, *Țara nóstră: Descrierea părților Ardélului dela Mureș spre médă-di și valea Mureșului* (Sibiu: Tipografia archidiecesană, 1894), 185; Sterie Stinghe, ed., *Istoriïa bésérece ï Șchéilor Brașovuli ï (manuscript dela Radu Témpé)* (Brașov: Ciurcu, 1899), 1.

87. C. Diachonovich, ed., *Enciclopedia română* (Sibiu: Krafft, 1898–1900), s.v. "Brașov." N. Iorga, *Brașovul și romînii: Scrisorïṣi lămurirï* (Bucureștï: I. V. Socecu, 1905); Moldovan, *Țara nóstră,* 180–211.

88. Ión Dariu, *Geografia comitatuluï "Brasso": Precedată de elementele întroductive în geografia universală pentru șcólele poporale, anul al III-lea de șcólă* (Brassó: Ciurcu, 1901), 34–39; Diachonovich, *Enciclopedia română,* s.v. "Brașov"; Moldovan, *Țara nóstră,* 196.

89. Joseph Schuller's travel guide framed the 1848 events as the "war of liberty of the Magyars" ("Freiheitskampf der Madjaren," Schuller, *Kronstadt,* 51). Needless to say, this formulation would have been impossible for any Pressburg author. Georgie Barițiu, *Parti alese din Istori'a Transilvaniei: Pe doue sute de ani din urma* (Sibiu: W. Krafft, 1890), 2: 1–622; Georg Daniel Teutsch, *Geschichte der Siebenbürger Sachsen für das sächsische Volk,* 2nd ed. (Leipzig: G. Hirzel, 1874), 2: 415–17.

90. György Gracza, *Az 1848–49-iki magyar szabadságharcz története* (Budapest: Lampel, 1895); Mihály Horváth, *Magyarország függetlenségi harczának története 1848 és 1849-ben* (Genf: Puky Miklós, 1865); Orbán, *A Székelyföld,* 6: 230–39. It is noteworthy that the accusation was not the only voice of Magyar intellectuals. László Kőváry, for instance, interpreted the 1848 events in Transylvania as a common achievement of Magyars, Saxons, and Romanians and he accused the Habsburg government and some "trouble-makers" of manipulating the non-Magyar peoples against the revolution. See László Kőváry, *Erdély története 1848–49-ben* (Pest: Emich, 1861).

91. *Annual Report of the Saxon Lutheran Gymnasium in Brassó,* 1868–96.

92. Joachim von Puttkamer, *Schulalltag und nationale Integration in Ungarn: Slowaken, Rumänen und Siebenbürger Sachsen in der Auseinandersetzung mit der ungarischen Staatsidee 1867–1914* (Munich: Oldenbourg, 2003), 362–63.

93. Philippi, *Aus Kronstadt's Vergangenheit und Gegenwart.*

94. Baiulescu, *Monografia comunei bisericesci.*

95. *Adressenbuch der Stadt Kronstadt* 58 (1896): 35; Colan, *Casina Română din Brașov,* 84.

96. János Samassa, ed., *Bartha Miklós összegyüjtött munkái* (Budapest: Benkő Gyula, 1908–12), 2: 167–73; Weiss, *Az Erdélyi Magyar Közművelődési Egylet,* 19–32 and 42–61.

97. Zamfir, "Un posibil model vienez."

98. Only five streets bore the name of a person: Honterus Court, Hirscher, and Michael Weiss streets were named after important Saxon figures of the town, the Rudolfring after Crown Prince Rudolf, and the square at the Orthodox gymnasium after Archbishop Andrei Şaguna, who had founded the school. Later the Market Square was named after Francis Joseph. See *Das neue Straßen und Häuser–Schema der Stadt Kronstadt* (Kronstadt: Johann Gött & Sohn Heinrich, 1890); Christof Hannak, "Die alten Kronstädter Gassennamen," in *Kronstadt: Eine siebenbürgische Stadtgeschichte*, ed. Harald Roth (Munich: Universitas, 1999), 268–85.

99. Balázs Orbán noted the absence of modern monuments; interestingly enough, he did not miss any Magyar national monument, but urged the erection of a Honterus memorial. Orbán, *A Székelyföld*, 6: 327.

100. Ferenc Koós, *Az 1848 márczius 15-iki ünnepély hét éves története Brassóban* (Brassó: Közművelődés, 1892).

101. Hans Wühr, "Die Zinne und die Kronstädter Maler," *Klingsor* 3, no. 4 (April 1926): 128.

102. Orbán, *A Székelyföld*, 6: 348–49.

Chapter 7

THE MAGYAR INLAND

Pannonhalma and Pusztaszer

Figure 7.1. The Pannonhalma Archabbey. Courtesy of the National Széchényi Library, Budapest.

Both the Pannonhalma and Pusztaszer millennial monuments were erected outside of urban spaces; the former was located at the archabbey of an insignificant village in west Hungary, while the latter was built practically in the middle of the Hungarian Great Plain (*puszta*), far from any inhabited place. The absence of an urban environment, however, did not prevent the construction of both places as core locations in the Magyar national imagination, leading them to be chosen to host millennial monuments.

The Cradle of Western Civilization in Hungary: Reading the Monastery

The Benedictine Archabbey of Pannonhalma was founded in 996 by Géza, the last pagan prince of the Magyars, as a sign of a new policy toward Christianity. Géza's son, St. Stephen, the first Christian Hungarian monarch, confirmed his father's donations to the abbey and exempted it from the Hungarian Roman Catholic Church by subordinating it directly to the pope. The abbey, being the first Benedictine monastery in Hungary, kept its central position in the history of Hungarian Christianity. The monastery flourished particularly in the Middle Ages and after the re-conquest of Hungary from the Ottoman Empire. Though Joseph II dissolved the Benedictine Order in 1786, and the abbey thus ceased to exist for some fifteen years, it was re-established in 1802 and enjoyed great prosperity again.

The monastery is situated on the St. Martin hilltop above the small town of Győrszentmárton (today Pannonhalma) in Győr County. It consists of a Gothic basilica (built in the early thirteenth century), cloisters (fifteenth century), a Baroque refectory (eighteenth century), and a grandiose library (early nineteenth century). The monastery belonged to the historically most relevant and most sophisticated buildings in Hungary.

Benedictine monks were able to write a comprehensive narrative of their monastery and to locate it in the course of Hungarian history. This reading holds the monastery as a holy place in the history of Hungary, as the frequently used Latin term, *Mons sacer Pannoniae* (Sacred Hill of Pannonia), showed. The first move toward granting Pannonhalma a holy character was the assumption that one of the most popular saints of the Middle Ages, St. Martin of Tours, was born there. Although it was uncertain whether Savaria, the place where Martin had been born, was identical with the modern town of Szombathely or Pannonhalma, the monks clearly argued for the latter.[1]

Though lacking any Christian character, the Magyar conquest was also seen as an important event in the early history of Pannonhalma. According to the *Gesta Hungarorum*, Árpád and his army encamped next to the hill of Pannonhalma and then, "having ascended the mountain and seen the beauty of the land of Pannonia, they became exceedingly happy."[2] The region was so beautiful and rich in natural resources that Árpád's own tribe was believed to have settled there. The *Gesta Hungarorum* confirmed the beauty of the landscape, providing later interpreters with one more argument to claim Pannonhalma's inevitable Magyar national character.[3]

Both St. Martin of Tours and the Magyar conquest served as preludes to the "proper" history of Pannonhalma, which started with the foundation of the monastery in 996. The foundation of the monastery and the Christian monarchy of Hungary thus coincided. Indeed, the crown of Stephen was brought from Rome to Hungary by the first abbot of Pannonhalma, Astrik, and the first known official document of the new state was St. Stephen's letter of donation to the monastery. Moreover, in local mythology, the hills of Pannonhalma were identified with the hills of the sinister of the Hungarian coats of arms.[4]

The narrative of the Benedictine Order stated that since the foundation of the monastery the Benedictines played an important role in the history of Hungary. They explicitly used the well-known Catholic argument that only Christianization had saved the pagan Magyars from the emerging Holy Roman and Byzantine empires. In the Benedictine reading it was the Pannonhalma monastery that had started the process of Christianization and remained its engine in the decisive eleventh century. The Benedictines, as the only Western-minded intellectuals in the earliest history of Christian Hungary, founded the first schools and trained the first priests and bishops and the entire literate stratum of the country. It was the Benedictine Order that disseminated Christian morals among the pagan Magyars, making an unsurpassed contribution to the rescue of the Magyar nation. The Benedictines contributed to the development of the country not only by their spiritual values, but also by the propagation of agriculture, trades, industries, and medicine, as their earliest documents proved. After the consolidation of Christian Hungary, the Benedictines supported the governmental administration by being entrusted with notarial functions. A number of kings visited the monks; indeed, St. Ladislaus I (1077–95) even issued some important decrees in Pannonhalma. The abbey helped in forging Hungarian foreign policy also, as it hosted the negotiations between Hungarian King Coloman I and Godfrey of Bouillon, whose army passed through Hungary during the First Crusade. Hungarian monarchs and aristocrats confirmed the national importance of the monastery by frequent donations, as the Benedictine authors often recalled in their historical accounts.[5]

While Pannonhalma was portrayed as an important engine in building the new Christian, civilized society in the early history of Hungary, it also shared the sufferings of the country, first in the Mongol attack in 1241/42 and later during the Ottoman conquest in the sixteenth and seventeenth centuries. The monastery itself fell under Ottoman rule between 1593 and 1597. The history of the Hungarian Benedictine Order reached its nadir in 1786 when Joseph II dissolved it. Benedictine historiography interpreted these events as the parallel suffering of Pannonhalma and the Hungarian nation at the hands of foreign invaders and "tyrannical" absolutism. The resurrection of Pannonhalma from foreign invaders and the "unconstitutional tyranny" of Joseph II were equated with the rebirth of the nation. Immediately after the death of Joseph II, the

Hungarian Diet demanded the re-establishment of the Benedictine Order because of its national importance, a fact often cited by Benedictine authors.[6]

The first period of national contributions, terminated by foreign invasions, was continued from the eighteenth century. Benedictine monks played an important role in the Hungarian enlightenment and then in the evolution of national sciences and the modern Magyar language. Some of them even rose to become professors at the University of Budapest or members of the Hungarian Academy of Sciences, among them the physicist Ányos Jedlik, the archeologist Flóris Rómer, and the linguist Gergely Czuczor.[7] From the early nineteenth century, the Order took over a complete network of gymnasiums throughout western Hungary. All these features were often recalled by Benedictine intellectuals to support the concept of the exceptional importance of the Order in the cultural history of Hungary.[8]

To summarize the Benedictine narrative: like the local reading of Munkács, the Benedictine Order saw Pannonhalma as a quintessential element of Hungarian Christianity and civilization for having imported Christian morals and cultural goods into the country, for having contributed to the national culture, and for the beauty of the landscape around the monastery. This Benedictine narrative held that the history of the monastery and Hungary were completely intertwined. In the words of Kolos Vaszary, Abbot of Pannonhalma, later Archbishop of Esztergom and head of the Hungarian Catholic Church:

> [Pannonhalma] is an enshrined place, which is a memorial to our millennium-old national existence, has taken part faithfully in the short days of joy and long years of sorrow of our nation, has been the cradle of Christianity in our homeland, has been the first allotment of the ennobling sciences in our country, which saw from its hills Árpád when he was looking around at the gorgeous landscape of the beautiful homeland, which welcomed the homeland-founder Stephen.[9]

This powerful interpretation demonstrates well that the Benedictine Order was able to combine its Catholic faith and loyalty with the goals of Magyar national integration. The Benedictines have been traditionally less conservative and more likely to be open to modern ideas, well displayed by the numerous Benedictine scholars employing the most recent academic methods. Benedictine participation in the making of a modern Magyar national culture was so powerful that their Magyar national identity was beyond doubt. The conservative, nationally rather indifferent Catholic People's Party did not find followers in Pannonhalma, even though the 1894/95 church legislation must have provoked the Benedictine monks as well.[10]

The representation of the archabbey's national importance started as early as 1824, when Izidor Guzmics, a Benedictine monk and early proponent of the Magyar language and culture, coined the very word Pannonhalma (literally meaning the Hill of Pannonia) to replace the original Szent Márton-hegy (St. Martin Hill).[11] The term soon became popular as the emerging Magyar master narrative completely absorbed the plausible Benedictine reading of Pannonhalma.[12]

Until the millennial celebrations, the monastery was not used for explicit national purposes. The building was seen as a national monument *per se*, and as Pannonhalma was far from any urban centers, further national usage was neither needed nor possible. Yet the approaching millennium inspired both the Order and the surrounding Győr County to develop this shrine further. In 1894, Győr County decided to erect a monument commemorating the millennium, although neither an exact location nor the form was defined.[13] At the same time, the Order also decided to build its own monument in the monastery, dedicated to Abbot Astrik.[14] Although none of these monuments was completed by 1896, the idea of affirming the monastery's national importance by erecting a memorial was already present by the millennial year.

The Cradle of the Eternal Constitution and Liberty: Reading the Ruins

The ruins of medieval Szer abbey lay somewhere outside Szeged in Csongrád County in the middle of the Hungarian *puszta*, quite far from any inhabited place. The medieval monastery and the nearby village did not survive the Ottoman conquest, hence the name Puszta-Szer. In the eighteenth and early nineteenth centuries, the ruins were inhabited by bandits who escaped governmental control, earning the place a bad reputation.[15] Nineteenth-century Pusztaszer was divided between two owners. The southern part, including the ruins of the monastery, belonged to the estate of the Pallavicini family, a prominent family of the Hungarian aristocracy. The northern part was owned by the city of Kecskemét. Both owners used the territory as pastureland.

The discovery of the *Gesta Hungarorum* launched a process that turned Pusztaszer from dangerous grazing ground to a national shrine: according to the chronicle, the victorious Magyar tribes held their first assembly there in the recently conquered homeland.[16] As this event was seen as the starting point of the Hungarian constitution, a fundamental myth of Hungarian political culture dating back to the early modern period, Pusztaszer emerged as the symbol of the "eternal liberty" of the Hungarian nation. As early as 1799, it was referred to as the "famous Pusztaszer" and in 1817 it was called the place that was "held the most famed not only in the county but also in the entire homeland."[17] In 1830 the celebrated romantic poet Mihály Vörösmarty wrote a poem entitled "Pusztaszer" praising the place as the cradle of 900-year-old Hungarian liberty. Historians played a decisive role in the production of this

Figure 7.2. The ruins of the Pusztaszer Abbey in 1883. Reprinted from *Vasárnapi Ujság* 30, no. 1 (1883).

narrative: until the critical turn of Hungarian historical scholarship, all the standard works included the enactment of the Hungarian constitution at Pusztaszer.[18] Critical scholarship finally questioned the very existence of the Pusztaszer assembly in the late nineteenth century, referring to the lack of any other source but the *Gesta Hungarorum*.[19] However, this doubt did not influence the greater public, which was eager to see the beginnings of Hungarian constitutionalism at a concrete location.

Another myth relevant for Pusztaszer was that of the *puszta* and its genuine Magyar inhabitants. Beginning in the early nineteenth century, the concept of the *puszta* as the most Magyar landscape was constructed (obviously in contrast to the Austrian Alps). The grassland and its people keeping livestock were endowed with ahistorical qualities: the landscape and the way of farming resembled Eastern Europe and the way of life of ancient Magyars before the conquest; the unlimited space of the *puszta* was also seen as a parallel to the liberty of the nation; and the homogeneous Magyar-speaking population of the *puszta* was regarded as ideal, in contrast to the mountainous and multilingual peripheries. The core of the *puszta* is situated somewhere around Debrecen (precise borders were obviously not established) but the grassland between Kecskemét and Szeged was also known for its pastoral traditions. The *puszta* and the shepherds as the most Magyar landscape and people became a well-known concept for a large audience, and enabled a wide variety of people to identify themselves with the Magyar nation.[20]

The first attempt to materialize the myth of Pusztaszer emerged in the 1860s. The main initiator of this process was the city of Kecskemét, which partly owned the field of Pusztaszer (but not the ruined monastery) and also the field of Alpár, where, according to the *Gesta Hungarorum*, a decisive battle between the Magyars and a certain prince Salan had taken place. These two fields made the elite of Kecskemét read their city as the true heir of the Magyar conquest and therefore the Hungarian constitution. The municipal assembly of Kecskemét coined the idea of a national monument that would commemorate the Magyar conquest and the foundation of the constitution, ideally financed by the Hungarian government. To gather precise information about the proper location of the future monument, a commission, led by the municipal archivist János Hornyik, was sent to explore the area. The commission found seven small hills that were identified as memorials built by the seven Magyar tribes to commemorate the constitutional assembly following the conquest. Furthermore, the commission was convinced that the medieval abbey was also founded exactly at Pusztaszer to memorialize the glorious constitutional assembly, an argument going back to the assumption of István Katona, an influential, erudite historian of the late eighteenth and early nineteenth century. The fact that there were at least a dozen hills around the ruins of the abbey and the lack of any evidence connecting a pagan assembly and a

Christian monastery did not really disturb the Kecskemét commission. Based on this "evidence," the city renamed one of the hills, formerly bearing some banal name, as Árpád Hill and proposed the construction of a national monument financed by the government and private donations.[21]

The timing of this proposal was not accidental. The year 1861 was marked by the February Patent, the second reform attempt by the Viennese government to return some autonomy to Hungary after the failure of the neo-absolutist regime of the 1850s. The Hungarian Parliament was again convened, and the future legal status of Hungary was uncertain and dependent on the ongoing negotiations between Vienna and the Hungarian liberals. Under these circumstances, the concept of an eternal Hungarian constitution served as an important argument for the autonomy of Hungary; the materialization of this idea was therefore definitely of high political relevance. However, the dissolution of the Hungarian Parliament and all the municipal assemblies prevented the realization of Kecskemét's proposal for a Pusztaszer monument.

Although the push for a yet-to-materialize monument at Pusztaszer did not stop in the following decades, Kecskemét lost its position as the initiator and main heir of the conquest and the constitutional assembly. In 1868, the title "Abbot of Pusztaszer" was created, to be occupied by Benedek Göndöcs, priest of nearby Újkigyós and an active protagonist of Magyar national integration.[22] In 1882 Göndöcs, then priest and parliamentary representative of the nearby town of Gyula, initiated archeological excavations to find scientific proof for the constitutional assembly. The excavation was led by the renowned archeologist Flóris Rómer. Although the excavation had to be stopped at an early stage for financial reasons, Rómer was able to uncover extensive ruins of the medieval abbey. Several papers reported on the excavations, so the findings became well known to the larger public. Both Rómer and Göndöcs were convinced that the monastery had been built to commemorate the Pusztaszer assembly; the excavated ruins confirmed the idea that the major force in preserving the nation was the constitution dating back to the Pusztaszer assembly. Göndöcs, as a member of the Hungarian Parliament, officially proposed that, preparing for the approaching millennial year, the government should continue the excavations, renovate the abbey, build a monument and a memorial park around the ruins, and open the millennial year in Pusztaszer.[23] To cover the high costs of the construction, Göndöcs demanded 2000 florins from the national budget's fund for preservation of monuments; this sum was around 45% of the fund's total budget.[24]

Yet, the grandiose plans were never implemented, as the government did not agree to spend almost half of the budget for monuments on Pusztaszer. Perceiving Göndöcs' intensive lobbying and the emergence of Pusztaszer as the symbol of an eternal Hungarian constitutionalism, the Magyar public became convinced that this "holy place" should be turned into a national shrine by erecting a monument. Taking into account the importance of the place, the Hungarian public was also strongly convinced that it was the government's responsibility to build the memorial. The millennial year finally provided the opportunity to carry out this idea.

Notes

1. Mór Czinár, "Győr vármegyei Sabáriáról," *Magyar Akadémiai Értesítő* 19, no. 6 (1859): 515–26; József Dankó, *Győrmegyei Sabaria vagyis Pannonhalmi Szent-Márton toursi Sz. Mártonnak születéshelye: Történeti tanulmány* (Esztergom: Horák Egyed, 1868).
2. *Gesta Hungarorum*, 50.
3. Mór Czinár, "Sacer Mons Pannoniae aevo vetere et cunabula benedictina monasterii S. Martini super eo siti," *Status personalis, officialis et localis religiosorum antiquissimi, celeberrimi, regii, nullius dioeceseos, sedi apostolicae immediate subiecti Archi-coenobii Sancti Martini in Sacro Monte Pannoniae ordinis S. Benedictini congregationes cassinensis alias S. Iustinae de Padua* (1846): 12.
4. Ipoly Fehér, "Pannonhalma," in *Győr megye és város egyetemes leírása*, ed. Ipoly Fehér (Budapest: Franklin-Társulat, 1874), 660.
5. László Erdélyi, ed., *A pannonhalmi főapátság története: Első korszak. A megalapítás és terjeszkedés kora 996–1243*, vol. 1 of *A Pannonhalmi Szent-Benedek-Rend története* (Budapest: Stephaneum, 1902); Norbert Francsics, "Das Raaber Comitat," in *Die Österreichisch-Ungarische Monarchie in Wort und Bild: Ungarn IV.* (Vienna: Verlag der kaiserlich-königlichen Hof- und Staatsdruckerei, 1898), 469–72; Ciprián Halbik, "Adatok Pannonhalma múltjához," *A pannonhalmi Sz. Benedekrend névtára 1880-ik évre* (1880): IX–XVIII; Ciprián Halbik, *Pannonhalma a milleniumon: Ünnepi beszéd* (Budapest: Hunyady Mátyás Intézet, 1896); *Pannonhalma a multban és napjainkban* (Ungvár: Székely és Illés, 1913), 5–8; Viktor Récsey, *Győr és Pannonhalma nevezetességei* (Budapest: Hornánszky Viktor, 1897), 19–21; Kolos Vaszary, "Pannonhalma helytörténete," in *Győr megye és város egyetemes leírása*, ed. Ipoly Fehér (Budapest: Franklin-Társulat, 1874), 580–90.
6. Récsey, *Győr és Pannonhalma*, 27; Pongrácz Sörös, *A pannonhalmi főapátság története: Hatodik korszak. A rend új kora, új munkaköre. 1802-től napjainkig*, vol. 6, bk. A of *A Pannonhalmi Szent-Benedek-Rend története* (Budapest: Stephaneum, 1916), 8–14; Vaszary, "Pannonhalma helytörténete," 601.
7. Irén Zoltvány and Antal Klemm, "A magyarországi benczés irodalom," in *A pannonhalmi főapátság története: Hatodik korszak. A rend új kora, új munkaköre. 1802-től napjainkig*, vol. 6, bk. B of *A Pannonhalmi Szent-Benedek-Rend története* (Budapest: Stephaneum, 1916), 134–889.
8. Sörös, *A pannonhalmi főapátság története*, 59–133.
9. Vaszary, "Pannonhalma helytörténete," 580.
10. Despite the Catholic People's Party's intensive campaign within the Catholic Church, the archabbey's documents fail to discuss the issue.
11. Irén L. Zoltvány, *Guzmics Izidor életrajza* (Budapest: Franklin-Társulat, 1884), 190.
12. Fényes, *Magyarország geographiai szótára*, 4: 107–108; Hunfalvy, *Magyarország és Erdély*, I/2: 35–42; *Pannonhalma a multban és napjainkban*.
13. *Győrvármegye törvényhatósági bizottságának Pannonhalmán az országos ezredéves emlékmű alapkövének letétele alkalmával 1896. évi augusztus hó 26-án tartott ünnepélyes közgyűléséről felvett jegyzőkönyv* (Győr: Gross testvérek, 1896), 6.

14. PFL I.1.g. Minutes of the Archabbey Convent, 23 April 1895, 79–82.
15. József Katona, "A Kecskeméti Pusztákról," *Tudományos Gyűjtemény* 7, no. 4 (1823): 50–58.
16. *Gesta Hungarorum*, 40.
17. Katalin Vályi and István Zombori, *Ópusztaszer*, ed. László Blazovich (Budapest: Száz magyar falu könyvesháza, 2000), 55.
18. Horváth, *Magyarország történelme*, 1: 52–53; Szalay, *Magyarország' története*, 1: 16.
19. Samu Borovszky, *A honfoglalás története: A művelt közönség számára* (Budapest: Franklin-Társulat, 1894), 71; Henrik Marczali, "A vezérek kora és a királyság megalapitása," in *A magyar nemzet története*, ed. Sándor Szilágyi (Budapest: Athenaeum, 1895), 1: 133. For an early critique of the Pusztaszer myth, see Imre Révész, "Pusztaszer," *Sárospataki füzetek: Protestáns tudományos folyórat* 10 (1866): 97–115.
20. Réka Albert, "A nemzet tájképe: Történeti-antropológiai elemzés," in *Nemzeti látószögek a 19. századi Magyarországon: 19. századi magyar nemzetépítő diskurzusok*, eds. Réka Albert, Gábor Czoch, and Péter Erdősi (Budapest: Atelier, 2010), 179–211.
21. János Hornyik, *Pusztaszer, a honalapító magyar nemzet első törvényhozási közgyűlése színhelyének története* (Kecskemét: Gallia Fülöp, 1865).
22. *Dalfüzér nagyságos és főtisztelendő Göndöcs Benedek Ujkigyósi lelkésznek Zeer monostori apáttá lett örvendetes kineveztetése alkalmára szerkesztve* (N.p.: Első magyar egyesületi könyvnyomda, 1869); József Szinnyei, *Magyar írók élete és munkái* (Budapest: Hornyánszky Viktor, 1891–1914), s.v. "Göndöcs Benedek."
23. Benedek Göndöcs, *Pusztaszer és az évezredes ünnepély* (Budapest: szerző kiadása, 1883).
24. Benedek Göndöcs to Kálmán Thaly, 13 April 1894, MNL OL, P 1747, box 5, 2213.

Chapter 8

SEMLIN

Figure 8.1. The main street of Semlin. Courtesy of the National Széchényi Library, Budapest.

By the end of the nineteenth century, Semlin was a city with municipal rights of medium importance in Croatia-Slavonia at the confluence of the Sava and the Danube on the southern periphery of the Habsburg Empire. Semlin had belonged to the Habsburg Empire only since 1717, when the Austrian–Ottoman war terminated Ottoman rule. Since 1739, when Belgrade was reconquered by the Ottoman Empire, Semlin had been the most important Habsburg town on the Danube frontier. In 1749 it received the rank of free military community (*freie Militär-Kommunität*) within the Slavonian Military Frontier, which exempted its inhabitants from military service, guaranteed certain autonomy, and enabled the development of manufacturing and commerce.[1]

Modern Semlin's society and economy were determined by its position on the Serbian border. The town was home to borderland and customs authorities and served as a hub of transport and Oriental trade. The state-run secondary school thus educated in two sections: a gymnasium and a commercial school. Commerce outnumbered industry: only five factories employed more than twenty people in 1900. Beyond the institutions related to the border, district authorities were also present in the town (but no county offices were located in Semlin, as the seat of Srem County was in the more central Vukovar).

Lying on the southern shore of the Danube, Semlin became an attractive town during the mid nineteenth century. In 1837 Semlin gave the impression of "a poor, mean, deserted-looking town"[2] and according to another observer in 1843, it "resembles more a Turkish than a Hungarian town."[3] In contrast, two decades later the town made a far more pleasant impression. The English geologist David Thomas Ansted noted that "[the] town is tolerably large and not badly paved, and as in the most recent published accounts of the place mention is expressly made of its miserable condition in these respects, there is no doubt it must have undergone great and rapid improvement of late years."[4]

On the so-called Gypsy Hill (Zigeunerberg) above the downtown lay the ruins of the castle. This castle was an important point in the southern defense system of medieval Hungary but only a few ruins remained by the nineteenth century. Belgrade, on the other side of the Sava, is a few kilometers to the west. Due to the hilly landscape, the two cities were partly visible to each other. The best panorama of Belgrade could be enjoyed from the hill where the ruins were situated.

National Integration in a Heterogeneous Borderland Society

Semlin, as a frontier town, had a population that was highly heterogeneous by Habsburg standards. When reconquered from the Ottomans, the town and the province lay in ruins, and the population either fled or did not survive the extensive wars lasting from 1683 to 1718. The town's consolidation started in the mid eighteenth century by extensive immigration. The first immigrants were Roman Catholic German-speaking artisans from the Holy Roman Empire. The Orthodox population arrived from two sources. On the one hand, Habsburg-subject Serbian-speaking families, mostly obliged to military service, settled in the town. On the other hand, Orthodox Ottoman subjects and some Jews moved to Semlin to engage in trade between the Balkans and the Habsburg Empire. The population growth was accelerated by the immigrants fleeing from Belgrade to the Habsburg Empire in 1737.[5]

The various sources of immigration turned Semlin into a highly heterogeneous town. The diverse backgrounds of the immigrants to Semlin were displayed well in the 1761–63 data on baptism. During these three years, 175 children were baptized. Out of these, 25 had a father born in the town, 26 in the vicinity, 10 in Srem County, 4 in other parts of Croatia, 4 in Hungary proper, 34 in Serbia, 16 in Bulgaria, 38 in Wallachia, 13 in Macedonia and Greece, 2 in Herzegovina, and 3 in Albania.[6] A traveler in 1791 reported that Semlin's population was "Serbian and German, Jewish, Armenian, Greek and other mishmash people."[7] The heterogeneous character of Semlin prevailed during the long nineteenth century (see Tables 13.9 and 13.10 in the Appendix). Due to the extensive commercial activity and the town's border position, there was a high level of multilingualism in the town. Catholics used both German and "Illyrian" (Croatian), while the Orthodox employed Greek and Slav vernaculars in schools, churches, and commercial and administrative correspondence.[8]

Ethnic relations in the eighteenth century were mostly influenced by place of origin, social status, and religion. Early in the eighteenth century, conflicts were recorded between Catholic German-speaking artisans and Orthodox, mostly Serbian-speaking soldiers. The background of these conflicts lay in the different mentalities of the two groups, as their socialization took place in the Holy Roman and Ottoman Empires, respectively, thus they had radically different experiences of norms, social co-existence, cultural practices, and so on. A later account explained that the German speakers "possessed all the culture they were used to in their former homeland, but the immigrants from Turkey were sons of nature, raw and violent, who yielded to organized conditions with great difficulty."[9] Parallel guilds were formed in a number of industries, one for the mostly German-speaking Catholics and another for the Serbian-speaking Orthodox. The Serbian-speaking craftsmen often failed to learn German, in contrast to the Greek-speaking merchants.[10] Spatial segregation between Catholic German and Orthodox Serbs appeared early on. In addition to the heterogeneous downtown, two suburbs were founded: Gornja varoš was established by the Orthodox in 1787, and in 1818 Catholic German-speaking peasants settled in another suburb, Franzenstal.[11]

Conflict emerged among the Greek and Serbian-speaking Orthodox, too. The emerging parties, similar to the Greek–Romanian conflict in Brassó, were based on kinship, place of origin, and business networks, and were conceptualized within a proto-national framework. Just like their Transylvanian counterparts, the parties in Semlin aimed to influence the language of the Orthodox parish and the school. While the parties in Brassó were unable to reach a compromise and the two communities established parallel institutions, the parties in Semlin signed an agreement in 1784. This compromise declared that twelve members of the church board were delegated by the Serbian community and the other six by the Greek community. The language of the church service became Serbian, but every other Sunday a Greek service was also held. While the church service was thus shared, the Orthodox primary school instructed only in Serbian.[12] Greek education prevailed in the town, as Greek merchants established their own school. This school served commercial interests by providing practical business training and it even attracted a number of German-speaking students until its closure in 1876.[13]

Given its diverse population and borderland position, Semlin came to be targeted by several national integration projects. The large number of Orthodox inhabitants and the proximity to Serbian national centers both in Hungary (Karlovci and Novi Sad) and in Serbia made Serbian national integration the most visible in the town. Local merchants had strong economic contacts with the Ottoman Empire's Belgrade Pashalik and provided significant support to the First Serbian Uprising (1804–1813).[14] However, until 1848 nationalist ideas had limited influence in the town. Public space in the Military Frontier was restricted, the town lacked higher education and church institutions, and the number of intelligentsia was rather low. These circumstances weakened the potential of national ideas, including that of Illyrianism.[15]

The events of 15 March 1848 brought national ideas directly into the town. The town's Serbian-speaking public initially welcomed the revolution in Pest for its liberal demands; for some days Hungarian (red, white, and green) rosettes were worn and flags flown. But news spread about the incorporation of the town into an integrated Hungary, an idea that was absolutely unacceptable to the Serbian elite of the Military Frontier. On 25 March, Hungarian rosettes and flags were replaced by Illyrian colors (red, white, and blue). The town sent a delegation to Vienna to demand the prevention of the incorporation of the Military Frontier into Hungary. At the same time, a large delegation represented the town's Serbs at the Serbian national congress in Karlovci. The town refused to send its deputy to the Hungarian Parliament and rejected its sovereignty; instead, the Croatian Parliament was accepted as the only legal authority. Meanwhile, Semlin emerged as one of the centers of the Serbian uprising. For a period of time, Stevan Šupljikac, the first voivode (civil and military commander), and Patriarch Josif Rajačić had their seats in the town. The local Serbs offered a large sum, 60,000 florins, to the Serbian military units fighting the Hungarian army. Agents of the Principality of Serbia frequently traveled through and stopped for negotiations.[16]

From 1849, efforts at Serbian national integration became more tangible. The town became a major center of Serbian cultural production. A number of Serbian intellectuals, exercising an impact far beyond Semlin, either were born or lived in the town. These include the language reformer Vuk Karadžić, the author, politician, and chairman of Matica srpska, Jovan Subotić, and Stefan Marković, founding member of the Society of Serbian Letters and holder of several ministerial posts in Serbia.[17] In the 1850s, Danilo Medaković, the well-known historian and owner of a printing house, published more than forty books in Semlin, including the oeuvre of Dositej Obradović, an influential protagonist of Serbian national culture and pioneer of modern Serbian literature. In the following decades, other printing houses were established, which published hundreds of Serbian books. Several Serbian newspapers were published too, including the radical nationalist *Graničar*, whose editor was sent to prison several times for attacking both the Hungarian and the Croatian governments.[18] A Serbian library was established in 1825, followed by the foundation of a Serbian reading club in 1860.[19] Serbian theatrical performances, in particular by the Novi Sad-based Serbian National Theater, were also held frequently.[20] Several Serbian associations came into being, including a church choir, a choral society for artisans and another for peasants, and the Sokol sport club.[21] The local financial system also had a national background, as the Savings Bank (Zemunska štedionica) did not hide its Serbian national aspirations.[22]

The extensive network of the Orthodox Church and Serbian associations enabled the wide dissemination of a modern Serbian national identity. The Serbian Radical Party, the most outspoken representative of Serbian nationalism, received considerable support among the electors of the town. The other Serbian party having a pure Serbian (i.e. not Yugoslav) agenda, the Serbian Independent Party, was also popular with the Serbian electorate of Semlin.[23] The same tendency continued in the interwar years, as the National Radical Party, made up of the former radical parties of Serbia proper, Hungary, and Croatia, continued to receive the highest support and dominated local and regional political life.[24]

Serbian society also attracted the handful of Greek-speaking Orthodox of the town. This process was similar to that of the Greek integration into the Romanian pillar in Brassó. After settling the conflict of the language of the congregation, the Orthodox population, regardless of its language, successfully integrated into the local Serbian society. In 1848, two out of the four leaders of the Serbian national council of the Semlin region (*odbor*) had "Greek" origins; indeed, the chairman, Petar Spirta, belonged to one of the most famous "Greek" families of the town.[25] During the 1880s, the town's mayor, Panajot Morphy, was an Orthodox Serb with Greek origins.[26]

Semlin was targeted by Croatian national integration as well, in particular following the incorporation of the town into civil Croatia in 1881. Replacing German, the official language of the town's administration became Croatian in 1872 and the town's only secondary school, the state-sponsored Realschule and commercial school, also instructed in Croatian from its foundation in 1858. Starting in the 1890s, several Croatian institutions came into being. A Croatian choral society was founded in 1895, comprised mostly of the town's intellectuals and middle class. The performances of this choral association were criticized by local Serbian and Viennese German papers, who accused it of disloyalty to the dynasty and exclusive Croatian nationalism. Furthermore, another Croatian choral association with an even more openly nationalist program, recruiting its members mostly from the petty bourgeoisie, was established in 1907.[27] A Croatian sport club was founded in 1905, while the People's Bank (Semliner Volksparkasse/Zemunska pučka štedionica) was established in 1888 with capital invested by local Catholic and Jewish investors, aiming to compete with the Serbian bank.[28]

The German-speaking population was not targeted by any nationalist project until the interwar period. In the *Vormärz*, the mostly German-speaking officials of the local and military administration defined themselves by imperial loyalty. Only the town's Orthodox population participated actively in the turbulent events of 1848 and 1849, as the mostly German-speaking Catholics faced the sometimes dramatic incidents with a certain apathy. In the following decades German national activism did not increase significantly, with German national activists being present in the region only incidentally. As a result, the approximately 100,000 German speakers of Slavonia were not attracted by the concept of a modern German nation even on the eve of World War I. Instead, they preserved their predominantly local, Catholic, and imperial loyalties.[29]

The local media affirms the national indifference of Semliner Germans: even though several German newspapers were published in the town, none of them represented German national ideas. When the main publisher, Ignaz Soppron, died in 1894, even Serbian newspapers praised his tolerance and respect for Serbian national interests.[30] Nor did German national associations emerge. The Male Choral Society (Semliner Männergesangverein), which recruited its membership mostly from the middle class of the downtown, was a typical case. This association operated officially in German, although there were a number of Croatian speakers among its members. However, a Croatian choral society was founded in 1895, and Croatian-speaking members left the "common" association, thus pushing the German speakers toward segregation.[31]

It is also telling that there was no German attempt to increase German influence in local political matters. Instead of running their own candidates, the German speakers of Franzenstal were split between the Croatian and the Serbian parties. The Franzenstal district supported a local Serbian candidate during the 1890s, when the National Party (the governing party promoting a Hungarian–Croatian alliance and refraining from further extension of Croatian autonomy) imposed outsiders to represent the town in the Croatian Parliament.[32]

The few Magyar speakers of the town also found themselves on the edge of national integration. According to the Hungarian-Croatian Compromise, the Hungarian government was not in possession of sufficient means to disseminate Magyar national identity to the population of Croatia-Slavonia. Local Magyar speakers were mostly employees of the Hungarian State Railways, a company directed from Budapest and under strict governmental control. A Magyar elementary school established in 1894 was also run by the Hungarian State Railways.[33] Although sources do not reveal the depth of Magyar national identity in Semlin, due to the governmental control over railway employees it was probably present.

Semlin Jewry found itself between traditional Jewish identity, Zionism, and the national identity offered by the dominant elite, in this case Croatian. Unlike many other towns in the region, Zionism emerged very early in Semlin. This was due to the famous Judah ben Solomon Hai Alkalai, a pioneer of modern Zionism, who served as the rabbi of Semlin for decades during the mid nineteenth century. He published numerous books and pamphlets aimed at establishing a Jewish settlement and polity in Palestine and was also an advocate of the modern Hebrew language. Although his publications were mostly read in the major centers of European Jewry, he promoted his ideas among his local brethren as well. In 1868, twenty-four Semlin Jews established a local branch of the Alliance Israélite Universelle, a pan-European Jewish organization founded partly due to Alkalai's intellectual impact.[34] Yet definitive Zionist ideas appeared in the town only on the eve of the Great War, when a Jewish reading club was founded in 1910 and a Theodor Herzl Association came into being in 1911. In fact, Zionism enjoyed considerable support first in the interwar period, as some Jewish protagonists of Croatian national integration were disappointed by the integrative potential of the new Yugoslav state.[35]

The competing national integration processes and the heterogeneous, religiously diverse population would suggest a description of Semlin's society as a strict pillar system, as observed in the case of Brassó. The spatial arrangement of the town contributed to social separation. In particular, the Franzenstal suburb was monolithic, inhabited by 90% Roman Catholic Germans in 1910. Less explicit was the majority of Orthodox Serbs in the suburb of Gornja varoš, where they constituted 55% of the population. Linguistic skills also suggest the relevance of vertical splits: in Franzenstal 38% of Germans knew Croatian as a second language, while among the Serbian Orthodox of Gornja varoš a mere 14% spoke German, even though the district hosted a large German-speaking minority.[36] Local choral societies suggest the dominance of vertical cleavages similar to the pillar system in Brassó; competing Croatian and Serbian sport and cultural associations were founded and even Jewish organizations appeared on the eve of World War I. This process also made German associations more closed, as several Croatian and Jewish members left them for their own clubs.

Nevertheless, several other relevant factors call into question whether Semlin can be described as a pillar-structured society. The city center, unlike the outskirts, was home to people representing all the classes, languages, and denominations present in the town. The largest group, Orthodox Serbs, constituted 44%, followed by 31% Roman Catholic Germans, 17% Roman Catholic

Croats, 9% mostly Roman Catholic Magyars, and 6% German-speaking Jews. Additionally, the census recorded approximately one hundred Spanish (Ladino)-speaking Jews, and some other minor groups as well. Consequently, inhabitants of the city center had more advanced language skills compared to their counterparts from the outskirts. Croatian was spoken by 72% of Roman Catholic Germans and German was known by 56% of Roman Catholic Croats and 37% of Orthodox Serbs.[37]

Several institutions worked in favor of integration, too. The Catholic Church integrated Germans and Croatians, as separate national churches were not established, but sermons were held in both languages. The choral societies mentioned above, even though representing different linguistic and social groups, frequently performed joint concerts, which was less common in the strict pillar society of Brassó. Another contrast to Brassó is the local system of higher education, monopolized by the Croatian Realschule and having a large impact on integration. Although one of the local banks explicitly supported Serbian national goals, the other bank was established as a common Croatian-German-Jewish enterprise.

Local political life was determined by a more complex set of preferences than solely national blocks. No serious national clashes were recorded during the dualist period. For instance, the mayor and parliamentary representative of the town in the period 1887 to 1892, Panajot Morphy, coming from a mixed Serbian and Greek-speaking Orthodox background, was most vehemently attacked by Sima Pajić, editor of the radical Serbian *Novo Vreme*. Pajić accused Morphy of corruption and violation of the town's interests; national and ideological questions were not raised.[38] In a pamphlet explaining his activities as a member of the Croatian Parliament, Morphy replied to these accusations. He also focused on practical issues, refraining from applying nationalist argumentation.[39] The major Croatian party striving for exclusive Croatian nationalism, the Party of State Right, never became popular with Semlin's Croats. Despite the solid support of the Serbian radicals, in a pragmatic way, Semlin routinely sent a member of the National Party to the Croatian Sabor. Fridolin Kosovac, the mayor of the town between 1893 and 1907, was also a well-known representative of the National Party.[40]

Local pragmatism is shown by a controversy in 1895. In June that year, the influential Serbian merchant Georg Spirta published an article in the *Pester Lloyd*, a traditional liberal paper read by Budapest business elites. Spirta juxtaposed Semlin's past importance in Oriental trade with the present conditions, and he accused the Croatian government of discriminating against Semlin and favoring other towns. Spirta firmly believed that due to the geographic location of Semlin, the town's economy depended on governmental policy, such as the railway lines, the customs regimes, and state-run warehousing. He also flirted with the idea that if the town belonged directly to Hungary, the Hungarian government would certainly grant the help Semlin needed and thus turn it into a commercial hub similar to Fiume or Trieste (the two major international ports on the Habsburg Adriatic).[41] This initiative was radical but by no means an isolated action. Shortly before, Semlin businessmen had lobbied for establishing facilities in relation to the livestock imports from Serbia into the Austro-Hungarian Monarchy (which were already directed through the town). Yet, the Hungarian Ministry of Agriculture, which was in charge of the issue, did not give a definite answer to this demand and Semliners feared to be discriminated against and not treated like citizens in Hungary proper. In early May 1895, 180 Semlin burghers signed the petition which demanded the Zagreb government to better represent Semlin's interests.[42] Spirta's article about joining Hungary was published a month later and was heavily discussed in the town. Both local papers, the nationally indifferent *Semliner Wochenblatt* and the Serbian nationalist *Novo vreme* shared Spirta's concerns and credited him as a respected burgher of the city. The former even sympathized with Spirta's idea while the Serbian journal clearly refuted it.[43] At the end, after a four hour discussion, the town assembly rejected the initiative and solemnly declared loyalty to Croatia while urging the Zagreb government to represent the town's interests.[44] Thus, the matter was dropped but local businessmen still counted on governmental help: while the livestock facility was still demanded, a bit later a recently founded weekly, the *Semliner Zeitung*, advocated the idea that the government should establish a tobacco factory in the town.[45] Since the Croatian government had a limited say in economic matters, Semlin had a genuine interest to maintain a cordial relationship with Budapest, where the important decisions on economic policy were made.[46] Fear of Semlin's separation from Croatia was then also used as an argument by the Croatian opposition when labeling the government economically incompetent.[47]

The even demographic evolution of the linguistic groups, the local political arena, and the overlapping institutions thus show a twofold picture, where both integrative and diverging factors were present. This puts Semlin somewhere between the strict pillar-shaped society of Brassó and that of the other three urban case studies, which were structured by class, ideological, and denominational cleavages.

Reading a Borderland Town

The most comprehensive reading of Semlin was developed by Serbian national activists. Serbs were reported as the indigenous people living in Semlin, already composing a large population during the Middle Ages, in contrast to immigrant German speakers and Jews.[48] The town's contribution to the war against the Hungarian army in 1848 and its subsequent imperial loyalty was also highlighted.[49] Thus, it is no wonder that the influential Belgrade scholar and politician Stojan Novaković listed Semlin among the future cities of Yugoslavia in his utopian vision of the South Slav state-to-be.[50]

Despite the fact that the town belonged to Croatia, its peripheral position, along with the lack of a large Croatian-speaking and Catholic population and relevant historic events in Croatian history, hindered a detailed Croatian national reading. Croatian authors argued for the sovereignty of the Croatian crown over Slavonia until the thirteenth century.[51] However, these arguments, like their Magyar counterparts, rarely referred to Semlin itself. Neither was an argument made for the genuine Croatian character of the town; its possession by the Croatian nation was reinforced by its legal position within Croatia-Slavonia.[52]

At the same time, Magyar and Croatian intellectuals fought a bitter battle to demonstrate Croatia's subjection to Hungary on the one hand, and the equality of the two parties on the other. One chapter of this conflict concerned Slavonia in particular. Magyar authors argued for Slavonia as a genuine part of Hungary, and thus outside the sovereignty of the Croatian crown, beginning with the Croatian coronation of Hungary's St. Ladislaus I in 1091.[53] Nevertheless, arguments from both sides were based mostly on diplomatic sources issued by monarchs, which rarely reflected local conditions. Lacking a major Magyar-speaking population and belonging to Croatia-Slavonia, a comprehensive Magyar national reading of Semlin was never produced. The only event concerning the town that could be highlighted in a Magyar national reading was the death of warlord and Hungarian governor John Hunyadi. In 1456, Hunyadi liberated Belgrade from an Ottoman siege but died from plague immediately after the victory. Some authors placed this event in the Semlin castle[54] and local tradition confirmed this.[55]

Neither did a German national reading emerge. Although the town had a substantial German-speaking population, there was no motivation to imagine Semlin as a German place. The monograph by Ignaz Soppron, the only comprehensive German account of the history of the town, did not place Semlin in any wider national narrative, but remained a detailed interpretation of the local experience.[56]

National narratives were hardly embodied in the urban space of Semlin by the end of the nineteenth century. Until the millennial year, only street names represented the different layers of Semlin identities. These street names represented dynastic loyalty (Joseph II), members of the Serbian national pantheon occasionally having some local reference (Dositej Obradović, Dimitrije Davidović, Josif Rajačić), and heroes who fought the Ottoman Empire (Eugene of Savoy, John Hunyadi). Károly (Dragutin) Khuen-Héderváry, *banus* between 1883 and 1903, also received the honor of lending his name to a central street.[57]

Anniversaries were also held, including the regular celebration of Francis Joseph's 1848 accession to the throne. Such celebrations would have been impossible in Hungary proper, where the 1848 event was seen as illegitimate and the 1867 coronation was commemorated instead. Local Serbian intellectuals routinely participated in national festivities in Belgrade as well. The 1896 visit of Prince Nicholas I of Montenegro to Belgrade, aimed at setting up a Montenegrin-Serbian alliance in the hope of integrating all Serbs into a single state, was attended by thousands of Hungarian Serbs, including citizens of Semlin, and their travel was actively supported by Serbian authorities.[58] A year later, teachers at the Semlin Realgymnasium collectively participated in the reburial of Vuk Karadžić, also held in Belgrade.[59] As no public monument was erected on the streets of Semlin until the millennial year, no memory regime had yet materialized.

Notes

1. Lazar Ćelap, *Zemunski vojni komunitet* (Beograd: Izdavačka Ustanova Naučno Delo, 1967).
2. Gleig, *Germany, Bohemia and Hungary*, 3: 273.
3. J. G. Kohl, *Austria: Vienna, Prague, Hungary, Bohemia, and the Danube; Galicia, Styria, Moravia, Bukovina and the Military Frontier* (London: Chapman and Hall, 1843), 261.
4. D. T. Ansted, *A Short Trip in Hungary and Transylvania in the Spring of 1862* (London: Wm. H. Allen & Co., 1862), 171.
5. Later, the periods of revolt and war in the Balkans provoked the flight of Ottoman subjects to the town, such as the immigration of Greek-speaking Orthodox following the failure of the Orlov revolt in the Peloponnese in 1770 and Serbian speakers and Jews after the First Serbian Uprising (1804–13). Political developments in the Balkans not only pushed the population into Semlin, but also drew it back. After Greece became independent in 1829, a number of Greek-speaking families left Semlin for Greece, causing the Greek-speaking community of the town to disappear by the end of the century. Ignaz Soppron, *Monographie von Semlin und Umgebung: Zumeist nach handschriftlichen Quellen* (Semlin: Selbstverlage des Verfassers, 1890), 316–18, 470, and 558.
6. Soppron, *Monographie von Semlin*, 271.
7. G[róf] T[eleki] D[omonkos], *Egynéhány hazai utazások' le–irása Tót és Horváthországoknak rövid esmertetésével egygyütt* (Vienna: n. p., 1791), 135.
8. Soppron, *Monographie von Semlin*, 293–301, 472; Friedrich Wilhelm von Taube, *Historische und geographische Beschreibung des Königreiches Slavonien und des Herzogthumes Syrmien, sowol nach ihrer natürlichen Beschaffenheit, als auch nach ihrer itzigen Verfassung und neuen Einrichtung in kirchlichen, bürgerlichen und militarischen Dingen*, 3 vols. (Leipzig: n. p., 1777–1778), 1: 59–63.
9. Soppron, *Monographie von Semlin*, 249–50.
10. Ibid., 471–73.
11. Nikolaus Hefner, Franz Egger, and Josef Braschel, *Franztal 1816–1944* (Salzburg: Verein der Franztaler Ortsgemeinschaft, 1984); Nikola Ilić, *Zemunska Gornja Varoš* (Zemun: Mostart, 2000).
12. Soppron, *Monographie von Semlin*, 425–26 and 538; Ćelap, *Zemunski vojni komunitet*, 62–63.
13. Soppron, *Monographie von Semlin*, 543–46; Ćelap, *Zemunski vojni komunitet*, 89–90.

14. Gordana Korać, "Zemun i Zemunci u Prvom srpskom ustanku," *Godišnjak Grada Beograda* 55–56 (2008–2009): 129–205.

15. Soppron, *Monographie von Semlin*, 558.

16. Lazar Ćelap, *Zemun u srpskom pokretu 1848–1849* (Novi Sad: Matica Srpska, 1960); József Thim, *A magyarországi 1848–49-iki szerb fölkelés története* (Budapest: Magyar Történelmi Társulat, 1930–1940), passim.

17. Isidor Stojčić, ed., *Znameniti zemunski Srbi u 19. veku* (Zemun: Isidor Stojčić, 1913).

18. Vasilije Dj. Krestić, *Istorija srpske štampe u Ugarskoj 1791–1914* (Novi Sad: Matica Srpska, 1980); Ilija Nikolić, *Zemunska bibliografija: Knjige, listovi i časopisi štampani u Zemuni* (Zemun: Narodna biblioteka Jovan Popović, 1976).

19. Miodrag A. Dabižić and Stevan S. Radovanović, *Zemunska biblioteka 1825–1975* (Zemun: Matična Biblioteka Jovan Popović, 1975).

20. Alojz Ujes, *Zemunska pozorja: Iz pozorišne istorije Zemuna* (Zemun: Festival Monodrame i Pantomine Zemun, 2007).

21. Branko Najhold, *Hronika Zemuna 1871–1918* (Zemun: Trag, 1994), 231–36 and 269–78.

22. Ibid., 348–49.

23. Ibid., 54–55.

24. Ivo Banac, *The National Question in Yugoslavia: Origins, History, Politics* (Ithaca: Cornell University Press, 1984), 157; Branko Najhold, *Hronika Zemuna 1918–1941* (Zemun: Trag, 1991), 30.

25. Ioannis A. Papadrianos, "Die Spirtas: Eine Familie klissuriotischer Auswanderer in der jugoslawischen Stadt Zemun während des 18. und 19. Jahrhunderts," *Balkan Studies* 16, no. 1 (1975): 116–25; Thim, *A magyarországi 1848–49-iki szerb fölkelés*, 1: 96 and 2: 44–45.

26. Najhold, *Hronika Zemuna 1871–1918*, 11.

27. Vlatko Rukavina, *Hrvati stvaraoci u Zemunu* (Zemun: Hrvatska matica iseljenika, 1999), 112–17.

28. Najhold, *Hronika Zemuna 1871–1918*, 274 and 350.

29. Michael Lehmann, "Die katholischen Donauschwaben in Kroatien und Slawonien (1867–1918)," in *Die katholischen Donauschwaben in der Doppelmonarchie 1867–1918: Im Zeichen des Liberalismus*, ed. Michael Lehmann (Stuttgart: Buch und Kunst Kepplerhaus, 1977), 426–96; Valentin Oberkersch, *Die Deutschen in Syrmien, Slawonien und Kroatien bis zum Ende des Ersten Weltkrieges: Ein Beitrag zur Geschichte der Donauschwaben* (Stuttgart: Selbstverlag, 1972).

30. Najhold, *Hronika Zemuna 1871–1918*, 213.

31. Ibid., 241.

32. Oberkersch, *Die Deutschen in Syrmien*, 90–91.

33. Najhold, *Hronika Zemuna 1871–1918*, 183.

34. *Encyclopedia Judaica* (Jerusalem: Encyclopedia Judaica, 1971), s.v. "Alkalai, Judah ben Solomon Hai." Among the Jews in this sphere of influence was the grandfather of Theodor Herzl, who lived in Semlin, and also Herzl's father, who later left the town for Budapest. The young Herzl was surely inspired by the famous rabbi of his ancestors' town.

35. Danilo Fogel, *The Jewish Community in Zemun: Chronicle (1739–1945)* (Zemun: Jewish Community in Zemun, 2007), 92–115.

36. HDA, 367, box 24, vol. 34, census 1900, table 9, folio Zemun.

37. Ibid.

38. Sima Pajić, *Ein wahrheitsgetreues Bild des Herrn Panajot Morphy, Bürgermeister, Landtags- und Reichstagsabgeordneten, Besitzers des königl. Serb. Takova-Ordens, etc., etc.* (Semlin: S. Pajić, 1891); *Panajot P. Morphy an die Wähler der Stadt Semlin* (Semlin: S. Pajić, 1892).

39. Panajot Morphy, *Rechenschaftsbericht des Landtagsabgeordneten Panajot P. Morphy an die Wählerschaft Semlins* (Semlin: Selbstverlag, 1892).

40. Nicholas J. Miller, *Between Nation and State: Serbian Politics in Croatia before the First World War* (Pittsburgh: University of Pittsburgh Press, 1997), 94–97; Najhold, *Hronika Zemuna 1871–1918*, 54–55.

41. "Für Errichtung von Lagerhäusern in Semlin," *Pester Lloyd*, 13 June 1895.

42. "Petition," *Semliner Wochenblatt*, 15 May 1895.

43. "Die Errichtung von Lagerhäuser in Semlin," *Semliner Wochenblatt*, 16 June 1895; "Za podizane skladishta," *Novo vreme*, 4 June 1895.

44. "Stadrat," *Semliner Wochenblatt*, 30 June 1895.

45. "Was Semlin mit Recht erhofft!" *Semliner Zeitung*, 12 January 1896; "Hilfe für Semlin!" *Semliner Zeitung*, 26 April 1896.

46. Kálmán Thaly also claimed that during his negotiations in Semlin in April 1895, Mayor Kosovac expressed his wish to join Hungary as a free city, similar to Fiume, as a response to the convenient railway connection that the Hungarian State Railways provided. Thaly, *Az ezredévi*, 32.

47. "Sitzung vom 19. November," *Agramer Zeitung*, 19 November 1895.

48. Stojčić, *Znaminiti zemunski Srbi*, 5–7.

49. Petar St. Marković, *Zemun: Od najstariji vremena pa do danas* (Zemun: Jovan Karamat, 1896), 117.

50. Bojan Aleksov, "One Hundred Years of Yugoslavia: The Vision of Stojan Novaković Revisited," *Nationalities Papers* 39, no. 6 (November 2011): 1002.

51. Vj[ekoslav] Klaić, *Slavonija od X. do XIII. stoljeća* (Zagreb: Dionička tiskare, 1882).

52. Vj[ekoslav] Klaić, *Opis zemalja u kojih obitavaju hrvati* (Zagreb: Dionička tiskare, 1881), 1: 179–82.

53. Sándor Halász, *Horvát-, Szlavon-, Dalmátországnak Magyarországhoz való viszonya a történelmi és közjogi alapon* (Pápa: Debreczeny Károly, 1885); Frigyes Pesty, *Die Entstehung Croatiens* (Budapest: Friedrich Kilian, 1882) and *Száz politikai és történeti levél Horvátországról* (Budapest: Akadémiai könyvkereskedés, 1885); József Podhradczky, *Szlavóniáról mint Magyarországnak alkotmányos részéről* (Buda: Gyurián és Bagó, 1837).

54. Antal Pór, *Hunyadi János: Élet- és korrajz* (Budapest: Szent István Társulat, 1873), 301–3; József Teleki, *Hunyadiak kora Magyarországon* (Pest: Emich Gusztáv, 1852–1857), 2: 442–46. Some other accounts placed Hunyadi's death in Belgrade.

55. Marković, *Zemun*, 43; Soppron, *Monographie von Semlin*, 152–53.

56. Ignaz Soppron dedicated his work to the whole population of the city, regardless of their ethnic or national identity. Soppron, *Monographie von Semlin*, v–viii.

57. *Popis kuća u gradu Zemunu sa novom numeracijom i nacrtom novih naziva ulica* (Zemun: Semliner Tagblatt, 1897).

58. "Szerb csendőrök a zimonyi hajón," *Budapesti Hirlap*, 30 June 1896; "A belgrádi ünnepségek," *Budapest Hirlap*, 1 July 1896.

59. *Annual Report of the Semlin State Realgymnasium and Upper School of Commerce*, 1897/98, 37; Najhold, *Hronika Zemuna 1871–1918*, 279–80.

Chapter 9

LOCAL CONDITIONS OF NATIONAL INTEGRATION

❦

Chapters 3–8 have guided us through the largely different milieus of the locations that became hosts to millennial monuments in 1896. These locations offered different conditions for national integration. This section organizes the constituents of these milieus into a threefold pattern, consisting of pre-national conditions, the question of emotional appeal (in particular that of the past), and finally the issue of modernity.

Factor 1: The Long Impact of Pre-national Conditions

Although nationalism is an essentially modern phenomenon, pre-modern and pre-national conditions had a significant impact on it. The key factor here is whether identity markers in the pre-national age defined themselves mutually and led to the crystallization of clear-cut groups or whether they rather created overlapping communities.

The case of Transylvanian Romanians offers one extreme. In this case, social status (mostly serfdom), denomination (either Orthodox or Greek Catholic), language (Romanian), and everyday cultural practices were closely associated. Before 1848 and the abolition of serfdom, an Orthodox person was usually a serf and spoke Romanian; a Romanian speaker usually belonged either to the Orthodox or the Greek Catholic Church and—with few exceptions—lived as a serf. Endogamy based on religion and social status ensured that most Romanian speakers fit into these patterns well.[1] Since these distinctive social characteristics coincided, clear-cut groups had emerged long before the idea of nationalism took root. Even though these groups did not have a national identity in the modern sense of the term, a certain ethnic awareness was definitely present. Although peasants were frequently apathetic toward the "national cause" and groups prag-matically cooperated occasionally,[2] in conflict situations, national activists could quite easily turn these groups into national communities (take for instance the bloody Hungarian-Romanian civil war in Transylvania in 1848/49). In other parts of the country, in western, central and northern Hungary in particular, such structural coincidences were far more sporadic. In present-day Slovakia, for instance, social status, denomination, language usage, and patterns of everyday culture largely overlapped. Thus, nobility, town-dwellers, and peasants spoke German, Magyar, or Slav vernaculars and denominational differences were not linked to these social features.[3] Social characteristics therefore did not define each other mutually, making the groups "us" and "them" ambiguous, overlap-ping, and situational. This setting provided a far more challenging task to na-tional protagonists who dreamed of clear-cut national groups. Similar patterns appeared in other parts of Central Europe, too. In Riga, previously established social, legal, and religious differences had a deep impact on the evolution of social groups into nationally conscious entities. In contrast, in Odessa social status had never correlated with other group characteristics; group belongings remained far more fluid and situational.[4] In the Bohemian and southern Alpine lands of Austria and in Upper Silesia (German Empire), overlaps of social char-acteristics effectively prevented national activists from evoking national loyalty.[5]

This meant that the population could most easily be integrated into modern nations in Brassó and in Semlin. In the former, ethnic cleavages were so strong that local society was divided by vertical national splits, resulting in three distinct pillars absorbing some minor groups as well. Such clear-cut pillars did not crystallize in Semlin, though national identity seemed to prevail among the Croats and Serbs by the late nineteenth century. In the other three urban locations, however, social characteristics overlapped far more. Social conflicts were rather defined by class and ideology than by the uncertain category of national belonging.

This difference had a decisive impact on both everyday life and local poli-tics. Everyday social contacts were deeply influenced by the nature of local splits, as the structure of choral societies demonstrates. Choral associations were organized by the national principle only in Brassó, and to a certain ex-tent in Semlin. In all the other locations choral societies were organized along social and denominational differences, leaving no space for the national prin-ciple. Another case is the market for local newspapers. In Pressburg, Nitra, and Munkács the market for newspapers was primarily defined by ideology, mak-ing language only a secondary issue (indeed, in Nitra several bilingual papers were published). At the same time, in Brassó it was the national principle that structured the market for the newspapers, while in Semlin both national and ideological affiliation played a role.

The nature of splits had a decisive impact on local politics also. Modern parties representing political ideologies were rather unusual at a local level at the end of the nineteenth century; the political sphere was determined by prestigious persons and denominational, personal, and economic networks. It was only in Brassó that local politics was predominantly influenced by national cleavages, as votes were determined by the pillar structure of local society. Ideological issues were overshadowed by national belonging and were present only within the pillars, as the controversy regarding Black and Green Saxon factions showed. In Semlin, Serbian and Croatian national parties were active, although the controversy seems to have been less than in the case of Brassó. In the other urban locations national conflicts were absent from local political life, leaving ideological and class issues to play the most prominent roles. In Pressburg, the local political arena was dominated by the liberals, challenged by Christian conservatives and social democrats. In Nitra, the antagonism of liberals and Catholics was the most important issue. In Munkács, the controversy of the pro-1867 liberals and the Party of Independence was palpable under the surface. Magyar national activists formed the hard core of the liberal party in all three towns. Nevertheless, the liberal party also included the nationally less engaged Jewish and German, Slovak, and Rusyn-speaking members of the middle classes. While the political arenas of Brassó and (to a certain extent) Semlin were playgrounds for already established national elites, in all the other locations the main enemy of Magyar national activism was national indifference.

Factor 2: Nationalism as Emotional Appeal

Early modern conditions made a deep impact on national integration processes, but this relation was far from being teleological. The second factor was already a modern condition: the emotional appeal of nationalism. As Liah Greenfeld argues, "[n]ational identity is, fundamentally, a matter of dignity. It gives people reasons to be proud."[6] Despite its profoundly modernist and forward-looking character, the nineteenth century was the age of historicism, which framed dignity and pride in historicized terms. To make a particular identity attractive, national activists had to offer a plausible past of glory and dignity.

Prince Árpád and the conquest became cornerstones of the Magyar national historical imagination: for modern Magyars, they provided fame, glory, and the justification of a Hungary dominated by Magyars. In a handful of locations, a direct historical connection to the conquest could be established, as at Nitra, Munkács, Pannonhalma, and Pusztaszer; the "evidence" was delivered by the *Gesta Hungarorum*. This "evidence" led local Magyar national activists to read the story of the conquest in local terms and to use it as proof of the importance of their particular location in the body of the nation. In Pressburg and Brassó, such direct links were not given; nonetheless, local Magyar intellectuals welcomed the millennial idea: the conquest was also seen by them as a necessary step in the formation of the Kingdom of Hungary. This meant that whether the conquest had a direct link to particular locations or not, local Magyar national activists interpreted it as an event of outstanding relevance, which enabled them to recognize themselves in the mirror of the millennium.

While the mirror completely reflected the Magyar historical imagination, it rarely did so for other elite groups. Exceptions to this rule were the Neolog Jewish and Rusyn-speaking intellectuals, who were able to recognize their ancestors on the winning side by arguing for their forefathers' direct participation in the conquest. In a popular book on the history of Hungarian Jewry, the Neolog rabbi of Budapest, Sámuel Kohn, emphasized the fact that the early Magyars were influenced by the Khazar tribe, which converted to Judaism in the ninth century. He claimed that the early Magyars followed the example of the Khazars, and some of them converted to Judaism (although he admitted the superficial character of this conversion). Therefore, Jews were seen as co-founders of Hungary and as having been inhabitants of the country as long as the "proper" Christian Magyars. Thus, Kohn claimed full membership for Jews in the medieval Hungarian nation, as Christian and Jewish Magyars shared the same fate.[7] The theory of Kohn was also shared by Orthodox Jews. Rusyn-speaking intellectuals understood the conquest as a common enterprise of the Magyars and the Slavs: according to the *Gesta Hungarorum*, some Slavs had joined Árpád's Magyars before the conquest. Therefore, they had every reason to read the celebrations as an articulation of their own identity. The German-speaking intellectuals in Pressburg did not find their ancestors in the story of the conquest, but they accepted the event as a major development in Hungarian history where there was also a place for their community. As the Magyar millennial idea was thus plausible and emotionally positive, it enabled a high level of self-identification and acceptance.

For any other national elite group, the millennial mirror showed either a meaningless or a devastating picture. Transylvanian Saxon, Serbian, and Croatian national history started with the Saxon colonization, and the formation of Serbian and Croatian statehoods in the Balkans, respectively. Hasidic Jews did not care about any secular history at all. For Christian socialists, the coronation of St. Stephen was the only meaningful beginning of the Hungarian history and not the pagan Árpád. Social democratic intellectuals framed the past in a way profoundly different from any liberal reading. For these groups, the conquest was meaningless. For the Slovak and Romanian national activists, the conquest was not only implausible but also humiliating, as it was believed to have terminated their ancient golden age.

On a local level, the monuments at Theben and Nitra must have been particularly painful for Slovak national activists, as both locations were fundamental places in the Moravian heritage. In Brassó, the millennial monument challenged Saxon superiority while in Semlin it questioned the autonomy of Croatia. Discontent with the Magyar national reading of the conquest meant condemning Magyar national identity and, in a broader sense, the rejection of Hungary as a united, liberal state dominated by the Magyar national elite.

Factor 3: The Perception of Modernity

Besides the early modern legacy and emotional attractiveness, the third factor to play a role in national integration was modernity. According to the modernist school of nationalism theory, modernity and the spread of nationalism were two sides of the same coin. Among the analyzed cities, Pressburg was by far the most modern, followed by Brassó, Nitra and Semlin, and finally Munkács. Consequently, following the modernist model, the population of Pressburg should have been the most and Munkács the least advanced in adopting national identity. However, this was far from being the case. In fact, national identity was the most important social characteristic for the vast majority in Brassó only. In the other locations, a certain segment of the population underwent a process of national integration (Magyars in Munkács, Serbs in Semlin). At the same time, the German speakers of Pressburg proved to be reluctant to take an exclusive national identity, despite being the most advanced in several indicators of modernity.

The modernist model itself is thus definitely not suitable to explain the spread of national identity. This statement, of course, is not a novelty any more. Scholarship has already emphasized that several territories with a solid state structure, a highly developed economy, and a dense communication network often resisted the nationalization projects offered by their elites and can be labeled as nationally indifferent. In regions like East Prussia, Alsace, the Rhineland, Upper Silesia, the Basque Land, Brittany, Belgium, and Wales, national indifference and the dominance of regional identities prevailed well beyond the early twentieth century.[8]

Instead of the exact achievements of modernity, its *perception* seems more important. Therefore, the major question is the following: which group of national protagonists was able to create the illusion that modernity, the vision of perpetual progress, cognitive and economic development, and the rule of rationality (as Ernest Gellner defined it), was to be achieved through a particular national integration project?

The two most extreme locations for the perception of modernity are Munkács and Brassó. In Munkács all local actors firmly believed that only Magyar national integration would bring the achievements of progress to the town, as shown by the request of the town in 1896 for a grandiose plan of urban development, to be financed solely by the Hungarian government, justified by the historic role and "national sacrifices" of the town. The idea of Magyar national integration thus coincided with the expectations of modernity, provided exclusively by the Magyar national center. The result of this coincidence was that the middle class in the town, regardless of religious and ethnic background, took Magyar national identity as the prerequisite for modernity, even though the town itself was far less developed than any other location analyzed in this study. Paradoxically, the underdevelopment of the town was an advantage for Magyar national integration, as local intellectuals did not have a chance of achieving modernity by relying on resources other than those provided by the government. The rejection of modernity also meant the refusal of Magyar national identity, as the case of Hasidim Jewry demonstrated.

At the same time, in Brassó modernity had three distinct forms, all of them directly related to a particular national integration project. The Saxon community's wide social, cultural, and economic network enabled an effective adaptation of such modern achievements as the Raiffeisen cooperative movement and almost universal literacy without any need to rely on the government and subsequently on Magyar national integration. Instead, the achievements of modernity were learned in Germany, where young Saxon intellectuals frequently received higher education; the superiority of Germany to Hungary in terms of modernity was beyond doubt. At the same time, the Romanian middle class of Brassó also organized modernity within its own social pillar. The development of Romanian schools, churches, and media and cultural institutions was mostly financed by local Romanian entrepreneurs and by support from Romania without Hungarian governmental involvement. The Magyar way of modernity, even though it would have more been lucrative than either that of the Transylvanian Romanians or that of Romania itself, was rejected.[9] The Brassó Magyars, like their counterparts in Munkács, had to rely on governmental support to compensate for their limited sources.

The pattern of modernity in Pressburg and Nitra lay somewhere in between these two extreme points. Pressburg was one of Hungary's most advanced cities; its middle class put emphasis on local achievements and proudly believed itself to be the master of progress for the entire country. At the same time, the progress of the city was always seen in a Hungarian framework. Indeed, both the Pressburger and the Magyar national elites enthusiastically supported the idea of establishing a university in the city as a state-sponsored coronation of local efforts and the ultimate tool of progress. Such a demand would have been unimaginable for the Saxon or Romanian intellectuals in Brassó. This ultimately meant that in Pressburg progress was seen as a twofold phenomenon, relying both on local and state-sponsored national achievements.

In Nitra, modernity was offered in two ways. For a long period, Magyar national liberals seemed to dominate the local market for progressive ideas, meaning that modernity and Magyar national integration went hand in hand. However, from the 1890s, Christian socialist ideas appeared in the Nitra diocese, offering a different route to modernity, maintaining and further deepening integration into Catholic universalism. Yet the split between liberals and Catholics was never as strict as the pillar system of the Transylvanian towns, as an increasing number of Catholics were able to combine Catholicism with national identity. Nevertheless, the competition between Catholicism and liberalism was tangible by the end of the nineteenth century, and the final victory of the latter did not seem as self-evident as it does today.

In Semlin, modernity was connected in a pragmatic way to governmental policies; the idea to join Hungary is an apt example of this thinking. The idea, however, soon failed; loyalty to Croatia proved stronger, although locals were dissatisfied with its pay-off.

In summary, the chance of any national integration depended on three factors. First, the sharper the former social cleavages were, the easier it was for clear-cut national groups to be formed. Second, the more plausible and emotionally more attractive the content (particularly a glorious past) offered by national protagonists, the greater the chance that their particular identity offer would succeed. Third, the more progressive a certain integration project seemed, the more it could attract the target population.

This meant that any national integration, including the Magyar one, had profoundly different chances in different locations. A resounding success for Magyar national integration was to be expected in the two "inland" locations. The key to this prospective success was the acceptance of the Magyar historical narrative by local intellectuals, both the Benedictine Order and the elites in the cities of the Great Plain. Complete success was also sought among the Christian population of Munkács, since for them Magyar national identity seemed both the most progressive and historically plausible option. Yet the hostility of Hasidim Jewry toward any kind of modernity caused the Magyar national attempts to fail among approximately half of the population. Although the structure of pre-national social splits was favorable for Magyar national activists in both Pressburg and Nitra, the high prestige of German culture and the influence of the Catholic Church limited national endeavors. In Brassó, Magyar national protagonists were able to offer an attractive integration project only to those groups that were not targeted by the competing Saxon and Romanian activists, whose offer of identity seemed emotionally and, in the Saxon case, even economically far more appealing. In Semlin, a town outside of Hungary proper, Magyar national integration was absurd, even though practical advantages were associated with Hungary.

It was in these profoundly diverse locations that Kálmán Thaly's uniform monuments were built. They provoked different local reactions, depending mostly on the local social patterns. The third part of this book will show how the millennial rituals worked and whether they fulfilled the genuine aim of Thaly and the Hungarian government.

Notes

1. Exceptions to these rules were confined to micro-regions: Romanian-speaking nobility lived in southwest Transylvania and Maramureş, while among Magyar-speaking Szeklers there were a few Orthodox.
2. Robert Nemes, "Obstacles to Nationalization on the Hungarian-Romanian Language Frontier," *Austrian History Yearbook* 43 (2012): 28–44.
3. József Demmel, *Pánszlávok a kastélyban: Justh József és a szlovák nyelvű magyar nemesség elfeledett története* (Pozsony: Kalligram, 2014).
4. Ulrike von Hirschhausen, *Die Grenzen der Gemeinsamkeit: Deutsche, Letten, Russen und Juden in Riga 1860–1914* (Göttingen: Vandenhoeck & Ruprecht, 2006).
5. James E. Bjork, *Neither German nor Pole: Catholicism and National Indifference in a Central European Borderland* (Ann Arbor: University of Michigan Press, 2008); Pieter M. Judson, *Guardians of the Nation: Activists on the Language Frontiers of Imperial Austria* (Cambridge, MA: Harvard University Press, 2006); Jeremy King, *Budweisers into Czechs and Germans: A Local History of Bohemian Politics 1848–1948* (Princeton: Princeton University Press, 2003).
6. Liah Greenfeld, *Nationalism: Five Roads to Modernity* (Cambridge, MA: Harvard University Press, 1992), 487.
7. Sámuel Kohn, *A zsidók története Magyarországon: A legrégebbi időktől a mohácsi vészig* (Budapest: Athenaeum, 1884), 12–46. A similar argument was made by contemporary Bohemian Jewish authors. See Hillel J. Kaval, "Texts and Contest: Myths of Origin and Myths of Belonging in Nineteenth-Century Bohemia," in *Jewish History and Jewish Memory: Essays in Honor of Yosef Hayim Yerushalmi*, ed. Elisheva Carlebach, John M. Efron, and David N. Myers (Hanover, NH: Brandeis University Press, 1998), 348–68. On historical narratives of fin-de-siècle Hungarian Jewry see: András Zima, "Cult or Spirit? Integration Strategies and History of Memory in Jewish Groups in Hungary at the turn of the 19th-20th century," *Acta Ethnographica Hungarica* 53, no. 2 (2008): 243–263.
8. Zahra, "Imagined Noncommunities," Daniel Mollenhauer, "Die Grenzen der Germanisierung: Identitätsentwürfe im Elsass um 1900," *Comparativ* 15, no. 2 (2005): 22–44; Kai Struve and Philipp Ther, eds., *Die Grenzen der Nationen: Identitätwandel in Oberschlesien in der Neuzeit* (Marburg: Herder-Institut, 2002).
9. The Hungarian government found itself in a paradoxical situation. The rise of literacy and the spread of culture were seen as pivotal by the progressive liberal state bureaucrats. At the same time, they realized that the emergence of Romanian culture prevented Magyar national integration. The effort to control this process remained rather unsuccessful, as the controversy over the finances of the Brassó Orthodox Gymnasium demonstrates well.

Part III

EVENTS

Chapter 10

PROLOGUE

The Many Faces of the Millennium

❧

Celebrating a Millennium-Old Past in Hungary

Between May and October 1896, Hungary celebrated its millennium-old past in a grandiose way. Schools and local authorities were ordered to hold festivities, and the government exerted pressure on church leaders to instruct congregations to celebrate too. These festivities reached the vast majority of Hungary's population and led to the most diverse reactions. An overview of these reactions is thus helpful to better understand the reception of the particular monuments erected in recognition of the millennium.

The festivities and the tangible achievements served the goal of representing the ideal unity of the nation. Yet conflicts persisted. In order to avoid the cheap political application of the millennial festivities, the veteran liberal politician Albert Apponyi proposed the suspension of petty political debates during the millennial year.[1] The proposal, copying the medieval institution of *Treuga Dei* (Truce of God), was accepted by the dominant Magyar liberal parties and their political papers delivered less vehement articles than usual. However, postponing internal conflicts by the liberals (mainly the question of the relation to Austria) did not silence other critics of the Hungarian state doctrine. Challenges and discontent emerged from three sides: the Christian socialist wing of the Catholic Church, the social democracy movement, and the various non-Magyar nationalists.

The majority of the Catholic clergy welcomed the festivities, as they provided an opportunity to emphasize the Catholic reading of Hungarian history.[2] The conscious merging of the cults of Árpád and St. Stephen significantly eased the reception of the millennium.[3] At the same time, a Christian socialist understanding of Hungarian history also provided a chance for representatives of political Catholicism to criticize the "archenemies," the liberal government, and the Jews, and to warn of liberalism as the main factor working against Catholic values in Hungary.[4] Indeed, a Catholic–Protestant rivalry surfaced; in Levoča the Catholic priest banned Catholic students from participating in the common millennial festival held in the Lutheran church. The students, however, followed school orders and took part in the celebration, earning the criticism of the Catholic press.[5] Nevertheless, the critical attitude of the Catholic Church was usually overshadowed by national sentiments.[6]

The two Protestant churches found themselves in a much more convenient situation. Árpád had been a central figure for the Protestant, in particular for the Calvinist, understanding of Hungarian history. Although the denominational policy of the liberal government was also condemned by the Protestants, they suffered less severe losses than the Catholic Church. With the exception of the Lutheran Slovak national activists, both the Hungarian Lutheran and Calvinist churches welcomed the idea of the millennial festivities.[7]

In a similar way, the standard Jewish reception of the millennium was positive. Several Jewish congregations used the millennial festivities to introduce Magyar instead of the previously used German as the language of service and prayers.[8] The acceptance of the millennial idea can be easily explained by the 1895 church legislation, which elevated Judaism to the same level as the Christian denominations, and by the theory of Kohn introduced in the previous chapter. This meant that the millennium was the perfect occasion for Neolog Jewry to demonstrate its gratitude and loyalty to Hungary and its Magyar national sentiments.[9]

The Orthodox Jewry was also positive about the millennium, although their emphasis definitely differed. While the Neolog press stressed the Jewish participation and contribution to the Magyar nation, the Orthodox papers focused rather on the denominational equality provided by the state and less on the national themes. Some articles, particularly in the *jüdisch-deutsch* (German written with Hebrew letters) press read mostly by the more traditional Orthodox, emphasized loyalty to the king far more than to the nation.[10]

Far more critical was the voice of the social democrats. The conquest itself was narrated as a positive event, as a necessary element in historical progress. The conquest and the foundation of the Kingdom of Hungary by St. Stephen were regarded as direct consequences of the absence of grazing lands in the East and pressure by the Catholic states. This narrative was based on historical materialism and lacked any high sentiments.[11] The millennial festivities were regarded by social democrats as fake celebrations solely for the upper classes. The splendid celebrations and the exhibition representing the present as the golden age of Hungary contrasted sharply with the poverty of the working class and peasants. The often-mentioned Hungarian constitutionalism was also a target of criticism, as the low voting franchise prevented an overwhelming majority of the workers from voting.[12] The socialist papers therefore mostly ignored the millennial festivities and encouraged their readers to celebrate 1 May instead, causing a large crowd to demonstrate for universal suffrage and better social conditions on the streets of Budapest.[13] Yet the potential for socialist agitation must have been rather limited, as besides this single demonstration no other relevant political act was recorded during the festivities.

As the Catholic Church was mostly able to internalize the millennial celebrations and social democracy was weak, the most serious critique of the millennium emerged among the non-Magyar national elites. As the festivities were seen as a powerful tool for influencing the historical consciousness of the masses, the non-Magyar national elites tried to prevent the dissemination of the Magyar master narrative by mobilizing their target population against the celebrations. At the same time, the millennium provided non-Magyar-speaking elites, who were open to Magyar national integration, with a good occasion to testify their loyalty.

The most comprehensive action of discontent by the non-Magyar national elites took place in April 1896, when Slovak, Romanian, and Serbian national activists held a conference and issued a declaration condemning the millennial idea. This declaration claimed that the memory of the Magyar conquest offended the descendants of the indigenous population and therefore it could not be commemorated by them. Furthermore, the millennial celebrations created the illusion that Hungary had always been a Magyar nation-state, so the festivities were a direct challenge to the very existence of the non-Magyar nations of Hungary.[14]

These arguments were published in the non-Magyar nationalist papers. An article in the Slovak *Národnie noviny* claims that the millennial festivities falsified history and celebrated the victory of the barbarians over the civilized Moravians. The festivities were as absurd as demanding that Jews celebrate the destruction of Jerusalem. In the view of *Národnie noviny*, the goal of the festivals was to educate Slovak-speaking children to be "Magyar Janissaries," i.e. Magyarized slaves. Therefore, the paper encouraged its readers to boycott the celebrations in schools and churches.[15] Romanian papers frequently highlighted negative incidents connected to the festivities. While Magyar papers often devoted a complete section to millennial news, proudly focusing on the achievements, Romanian periodicals regularly collected news in a special counter-millennial section, mostly featuring events painful for Magyar national activists such as counter-demonstrations and the burning of flags.[16] The emerging German nationalist wing of the Transylvanian Saxon politics harshly criticized the millennial festivities too. Even though the Slovak-Romanian-Serbian joint conference was not attended by Saxon representatives, its declaration was published in several papers.[17] A Ruthenian nationalist view emerged only in Galicia, where Ruthenian national leaders protested against the millennial celebrations, relying on a quite similar argumentation.[18] Croatian national activists, who promoted the complete independence of Croatia from Hungary, also rejected the millennial celebrations. According to them, Croats had nothing to do with the conquest of Árpád's Magyars, as by that time the Croatian state had already existed. Furthermore, they argued for solidarity with the "oppressed" and "forcefully Magyarized" non-Magyar peoples. Croatian nationalist papers therefore demanded a boycott of the millennial festivities and delivered detailed reports of any counter-demonstrations. Several protests against the millennium events were held in Croatian towns, although their intensity did not reach that of the student riots in the previous year.[19]

The Slovak, Romanian, and Serbian national activists tried to put their radical rejection on the European agenda, but beyond some marginal conferences and demonstrations this attempt remained unsuccessful.[20] Bucharest-based Nationalist associations organized some demonstrations in the Romanian capital. Nevertheless, as the Romanian government insisted on the alliance with Austria-Hungary, these demonstrations were officially supported only by the opposition and not the government. More serious demonstrations were held in Belgrade. The procession on 8 June in Budapest displayed the flag of medieval Serbia in order to represent the glory of Hungary by recalling the countries and provinces that had been at some point vassals of Hungary. This act was seen by the Serbian public as a violation of the sovereignty of Serbia, and as a response the Belgrade government officially protested to the Austro-Hungarian authorities. In early May, several mass rallies were held in Belgrade, protesting against the use of the medieval Serbian flag at the millennial procession, and the crowds, among them many students, burned Hungarian flags. The Belgrade protests outraged the Magyar public, although the official partnership between Austria-Hungary and Serbia continued.[21]

The radical rejection of the millennium was, however, far from being the only pattern among the non-Magyar national elites. *Slovenské noviny*, a Slovak paper sponsored by the government, provided a toolkit of pro-Hungarian concepts; a Slovak-Magyar brotherhood and common achievements characterized this understanding of the millennial festivities. The counter-millennial arguments of Slovak national activists were explicitly rejected by the editors of *Slovenské noviny*. The fact that the mainstream Magyar reading of the millennium, an outspoken ethnic interpretation, definitely challenged this moderate Slovak narrative was not taken into account; instead, moderate Magyar voices, such as the circulars of Catholic bishops, were highlighted.[22] Northeastern Hungary's Greek Catholic elite also welcomed the commemoration of the conquest.

The mainstream Saxon reaction was quite similar to this moderate Slovak position. Due to the 1890 compromise between the government and the Saxon People's Party, Saxon political leaders had to find a way to accept the millennium. The central paper of Saxon politics, the *Siebenbürgisch-Deutsches Tageblatt*, solved the problem by highlighting both St. Stephen and the Hungarian monarchs in defending Saxons and at the same time it stressed the Saxon contributions to Hungarian cultural achievements.[23]

While the Croatian nationalists condemned the millennium celebrations, the governing, pro-Hungarian conservative unionists argued for the importance of the Croatian-Hungarian alliance in preserving the Croatian state and nation, and therefore joined the side in favor of the festivities. As the unionists dominated the Croatian Parliament, it decided for Croatia's official participation in the Millennial Exhibition. More than eight thousand Croatian exhibitors were present at the exhibition; whether they agreed with the ideological setting of the event is unknown, but they definitely did not want to miss the opportunity to present their goods to a large audience. Thus, a separate section displayed Croatian history, culture, and economy, and Croatian flags were displayed along with the Hungarian, satisfying the unionists' demands for the symbolic equality of the two countries.[24]

Beyond discourse present in papers, people often had to take very personal choices regarding the celebrations. Bishops found themselves in a particularly delicate situation, as they had to comply with governmental pressure and with the demands of their believers. Saxon Lutheran bishop Friedrich Müller issued a millennial encyclical, combining Saxon history with Hungarian national history.[25] The Serbian Orthodox Church was divided under governmental pressure: the bishop of Werschetz supported the commemorations, but several priests delivered critique and discouraged their believers from participating in the festive events.[26] Both Romanian church leaders, Victor Mihali, the Greek Catholic metropolitan of Blaj, and Miron Romanul, Romanian Orthodox metropolitan of Hermannstadt, tried to balance their millennial encyclicals, which explained to church members the correct reception of the festivities. These circulars suggested discontent with the millennial celebrations as a festivity dictated by the government, although in order to avoid open conflict they ordered parishes and schools to hold a festive service and school celebration. Out of the two, the Orthodox discontent was less veiled and Romanul's circular even claimed that the celebrations represented only the Magyars. Romanul ordered a festive service, including prayers for the Romanian nation in Hungary and peace among peoples. At the same time, he forbade members, particularly priests of the Romanian Orthodox Church, to represent the congregation officially outside of this service. This circular outraged the Magyar press and the government and even though the metropolitan issued a declaration claiming his patriotic intentions, Magyar papers accused him of betrayal.[27]

Local officials, teachers, and priests developed various strategies to comply with the demands of the government and their own authorities. In northern Hungary, most festivities were held according to governmental wishes. The Lord Lieutenant of Spiš County could even proudly report that the millennium had provided a good chance to deliver Magyar speeches and poems in Slovak and German-speaking villages.[28] *Národnie noviny* reported only on three Lutheran churches and a single school that failed to hold millennial festivities. Only rarely did such incidents happen as that in Liptovský Svätý Mikuláš, where the Lutheran minister gave an "anti-Magyar" speech at a festival, Slovaks consciously did not illuminate their houses on the festive day, sang their national song *Hej, Slováci*, and shouted "Down with the Magyars."[29] Softer methods were used in other schools, where only superficial commemorations were held. For example, pupils at the Lutheran elementary school in Holíč did not know what they had commemorated, as their teacher failed to give them a detailed explanation of the millennium.[30]

Far more radical were the reactions in eastern and southern Hungary. Romanian members of county and municipal assemblies routinely boycotted the commemorations.[31] A number of schools and churches had no commemoration at all. The millennial celebrations in churches and schools that did not opt for a boycott were mostly attended only by a small audience. The content of these commemorations was often ambiguous; priests prayed for the Romanians only, and the imperial anthem "*Gott erhalte*" was sung instead of the Hungarian anthem, putting the very basis of Hungarian home rule within the monarchy in question. Sometimes Romanian flags were flown instead of Hungarian ones and commemorative trees were cut down in several villages. The press reported an abundance of petty incidents: in Lugoj, a lamb decorated with Romanian colors was the main prize at the town fair raffle; in the village of Kubin, the Romanian Orthodox priest named his dog Bánffy and forced students to remove the Hungarian rosette from their robes.[32] Even though in some Romanian towns and villages the festivities ran smoothly, the obvious Romanian discontent outraged the Magyar public.[33]

Similar incidents were reported in Serbian villages and towns. A comic anecdote comes from Budapest: the folklore section of the Millennial Exhibition in Budapest displayed rural environments of all the regions of Hungary, including the non-Magyar parts. In order to be as realistic as possible, peasants from the respective regions were hired to live in the exhibition area. The highlight of the section was a series of marriages where real couples wed, showing the wedding customs of the Hungarian countryside. However, it was so difficult to find a Serbian couple that the Serbian wedding almost had to be canceled. The organizers were finally able to find a Serbian couple just weeks before the closing of the exhibition, however the church marriage had to be canceled because the Orthodox archdeacon of Budapest refused to marry "traitors."[34] At the same time, the Serbs in Temesvár participated in the millennial festivities in a "patriotic" way (meaning being loyal), which was contrasted to the local Romanian boycott by Budapest papers.[35]

Despite all these incidents, the government and the Magyar press evaluated the millennial festivities as a great success. After all, millions of Hungarian citizens were reminded of the Hungarian state doctrine, and most of the celebrations ran according to the demands of the government.

The Local Millennial Festivities

In May 1896, large-scale millennial festivals were held in Pressburg, Nitra, Munkács, and Brassó. In the other locations, no festivities were held for various reasons. In Pannonhalma, a celebration in May seemed pointless, as the inauguration ceremony of the millennial memorial in August fulfilled the demands of the Benedictine monks. Neither was a celebration held in Pusztaszer, which was turned into a potential site of commemoration precisely by the erection of the millennial monument in June. As Semlin lay in Croatia-Slavonia, the Hungarian government did not have any say in local church and educational matters. Schools and churches therefore could not be ordered to celebrate the millennium and they had no reason to hold festivities voluntarily.

The organization of the local millennial festivities in May 1896 was in the hands of the local elites. The government ordered schools to hold festivities,[36] which were frequently accompanied by celebrations organized by local authorities, associations, and church congregations. Associations usually held their own festive gatherings inspired by the nationwide millennial celebrations.[37] The elevated spirit of the millennial festivities provided local elites with a good occasion to contribute to the millennium events in their own ways and to persuade local and national actors to help with fundraising. These local actors tried to internalize the millennial idea by stressing elements of the past relevant for them. As the exact execution of the festivities was largely a task of local actors, they could interpret the millennial idea according to their own preferences.

The celebrations ran most smoothly at the official level. The Pressburg city assembly commemorated the conquest at a festive meeting. The main speaker of the event, Sándor Vutkovich, a typical representative of liberal Magyar nationalism, highlighted the city's importance in the history of Hungary, mostly by stressing its contribution to Magyar national culture and at the same time emphasizing the Hungarian state doctrine. Mayor Gustav Dröxler instead delivered the traditional Pressburger narrative of the city in his speech, which focused less on the Magyar past but highlighted its loyalty to both the country and the monarch. Nevertheless, these two speeches were highly compatible with each other. Inspired by the millennium, the assembly offered a considerable sum of money to develop the Magyar theater in the city, the last segment of high culture where German language still dominated.[38] The other event, attracting mostly the elite of the city, was the Toldy Association's celebration, featuring the most famous actors of the Budapest National Theater. This occasion was used as a tool to develop Magyar theatrical performances too.[39]

In Nitra, speakers at the splendid festive meeting of the Nitra County assembly praised the Hungarian state doctrine and delivered addresses of a liberal-progressive vision. In order to demonstrate the millennial consensus, a representative of the Catholic People's Party also had the opportunity to deliver a moderate speech about Christian values in Hungarian history. However, even the millennial festivity proved inadequate to hide the conflicts between liberals and Catholics, as the festive banquet following the assembly meeting was boycotted by the majority of the Catholic clergy; only some representatives of the Piarist Order accepted the invitation.[40]

The celebration of Brassó County was boycotted too: almost all Romanian and several Green Saxon guests were absent. In the absence of the most vehement opponents of Magyar nationalism, the guests present tried to combine Magyar national idea with Saxon politics. In a bilingual festive speech, Deputy Lord Lieutenant Friedrich Jekel referred to both the history of Hungary and the county, particularly to the eminent role of the Saxons in the cultural achievements of the region. At the banquet, Lord Lieutenant Mihály Maurer also spoke about national and regional history, paying particular attention to the Saxons. Both speakers emphasized the duty of non-Magyars to participate in the celebrations, as the Hungarian state ensured the conditions for free development for each ethnic group. Furthermore, the Saxons had contributed to the culture of Hungary and had received rights and protection from the Hungarian kings, while the Romanians had witnessed quick development in the last decades, therefore both groups had reason to celebrate the Hungarian millennium, argued Maurer. In his toast, the dean of the Saxon Lutheran Church, Franz Herfuth, followed the same pattern and expressed appreciation for the liberal policy of Hungary, which contributed to the existence of the Saxon people.[41]

The Benedictine Order participated in the millennial festive meeting of Győr County. The main speaker at the event was Abbot Ipoly Fehér. In his speech, Fehér successfully combined a liberal vision, an ethnic Magyar reading, and the Catholic concept of Hungarian history.[42]

On a more popular level, the event attracting the largest audience was a series of church and school celebrations, held mostly on Sunday 10 May. Splendid and popular festivities were held in all schools, churches, and synagogues in Pressburg, Nitra, and Munkács. The details of the festive services in Pressburg are not known, but their sincere and high spirit seems beyond doubt. In almost all cases the language of these celebrations was Magyar.[43] The four secondary schools organized a common millennial commemoration. This event was attended by sixteen hundred students and the notables of the city; only some two hundred parents fitted into the hall, but the demand was much higher. The program of poems, songs, and speeches represented the Hungarian state doctrine, an ethnic reading of Hungarian history equating the country with the Magyar nation. One of the main speakers even praised the program of Magyarization, supported by arguments borrowed from social Darwinism. The audience, a majority of whom were either non-Magyar speakers or came from a non-Magyar-speaking background, learned the history of the Magyars as their own past. Local references were completely absent from the speeches and other performances.[44]

On the day of the school and church celebrations, the city was decorated with Hungarian flags, the official buildings and almost all central houses were illuminated, and people on the streets wore rosettes in the Hungarian tricolor. All the reports stressed the large number of participants, their voluntary and active participation, high spirits, and the festive costumes and frequent use of Hungarian symbols. According to the newspaper reports, the millennial festivities reached the majority of the city's population. Most homeowners volunteered to illuminate their houses and decorate them with Hungarian flags, shopkeepers beautified their shop windows with the Hungarian colors, and large crowds followed the public events, including the military orchestra's performance on the eve of the celebrations. No newspaper reported any appearance of discontent.[45]

On the same day, churches and schools celebrated the millennium in Nitra too. As in Pressburg, church and school celebrations, including the events in Catholic institutions, attracted a large audience and no sign of discontent or conflict was reported. The mass at the cathedral was celebrated by Bishop Imre Bende.[46] All schools organized splendid celebrations, in which both parents and representatives of the county and town administration took part. To demonstrate the supra-denominational character of the millennium, both the school and church festivals were attended by high-ranking guests of different religions. Students of the Catholic gymnasium learned about Árpád's Magyars as their forefathers, as a speech framed in the Hungarian state doctrine, lacking local references, was delivered to them. Pupils of the Catholic middle school for girls sewed a festive costume in "Magyar style" on their own, and their festive program had to be performed twice due to the high demand. The main speaker at the festivity of the Catholic elementary schools also took the Magyar ethnic discourse and highlighted the importance of some Catholic figures, including the medieval Hungarian monarchs St. Stephen and St. Ladislaus I. His audience, among them many Slovak-speaking students and parents, thus learned about the Magyar conquerors as their forefathers who fought Slavs based in

Nitra. In the Jewish elementary school, enthusiastic Magyar speeches were delivered to the Jewish children, a majority of whom wore Magyar national costume.[47] Fireworks, floodlights, a procession of the military and the youth, and public concerts also attracted a large audience (ten thousand people, according to the liberal, semi-official *Nyitramegyei Közlöny*).[48]

Sincerely enthusiastic celebrations also took place in Munkács in May 1896. The reports on the local celebrations showed wide voluntary participation. The main speaker at the local gymnasium followed the national standards to deliver a predictable speech on the virtues of the Magyar nation embedded in the framework of the Hungarian state doctrine.[49] The millennial festivities provided the Greek Catholic elite with a good opportunity to prove its loyalty to Hungary. The celebrations in Greek Catholic schools and parishes, featuring the archdeacon and the high-ranking monk of the local monastery, were held both in Rusyn and Magyar. One of the speakers, an archdeacon, claimed that Hungarian Rusyn speakers failed to learn the state language as a consequence of poor education and lack of governmental care, not disloyalty.[50]

Although the synagogues were decorated with Hungarian flags and the festive service was also quite impressive due to a special choir performance, the local Magyar press remained dissatisfied with the Jewish celebrations. Papers report only on the main prayer of the service; this text, written by the "central authorities," probably meaning the Orthodox Central Bureau in Budapest, proclaimed the eternal loyalty of Jews to Hungary. The reason for discontent was the language, as in Munkács not a word of Magyar was employed, but the whole service, speeches, and prayers were conducted in Hebrew and Yiddish. This fact raised the question of the true patriotism of local Jews in the eyes of Magyar commentators.[51] It seems that the Jewry of Munkács did everything to fulfill the demands of the government and the local Magyar public in so far as this cooperation did not conflict with their principles. Flags and songs did not challenge the religious practice of Hasidim Jewry, but a prayer in Magyar definitely did; for Hasidic Jews, the choice in such a conflict was beyond question.

While in Pressburg, Nitra, and Munkács all churches, synagogues, and schools celebrated the millennium, and their sincere devotion to the issue seems doubtless, the case of Brassó was remarkably different. "Proper" celebrations were held only in the Magyar institutions. Among the many churches of the town, only the Magyar parishes and Jewish congregations held festive millennial services. The Orthodox Jewish community celebrated the millennium in a splendid way, proving its loyalty to Hungary. The Orthodox rabbi even emphasized the necessity of Magyarizing the country.[52] The Magyar secondary schools (Realschule, Catholic gymnasium, Upper School of Commerce) organized a common festivity on 9 May 1896 in the Catholic church and then in a celebration hall. Besides patriotic songs and poems, festive speeches were delivered by the directors of the schools, referring to the glorious history of the country. Memorial trees were planted in the schoolyards and the Realschule also inaugurated a memorial plaque in its building. After the celebrations, the students made an excursion to the nearby Predeal Pass, the site of a battle in the 1848/49 Hungarian war of independence.[53] The Magyar elementary schools planted memorial trees, also accompanied by patriotic speeches, poems, and songs.[54] The director of the Upper School of Commerce acknowledged the results of the school celebrations in a report:

> The well-prepared and splendid celebration, in which all local civil, religious and military authorities, associations, parents and patrons of the public education participated, provided a suitable occasion to heat up the imagination and feelings of our pupils by looking at the vicissitudinous history of the fatherland.[55]

Similarly, although the town was rich in associations, only the Magyars held festivities.[56] The most popular among them was the festive procession held in the main square on 7 June, a day before the grandiose millennial march in Budapest. All the Magyar associations paraded in the downtown. The schedule of the festivity followed the usual pattern: patriotic songs, speeches, and poems were performed. According to *Brassói Lapok*, thousands of Magyars, among them many schoolchildren, participated in this celebration, occupying the town center for an entire day.[57] These festivities provided the first occasion in the history of the town to decorate streets predominantly with Hungarian flags and for the Magyars to symbolically conquer the center.[58] The exclusive Magyar participation in this festival is again remarkable: 8 June symbolized loyalty to Francis Joseph, still the most integrative force for Hungarian society. The fact that Saxons and Romanians did not participate in this event despite their sincere loyalty to the monarch showed the serious limits of the attempt to make Magyar national integration more attractive by placing it in a dynastic framework.

Saxon and Romanian associations held no millennial celebrations at all. Schools, however, could not afford the same omission, as even though they were run by church parishes, they were still under the control of the government. In order not to provoke the Hungarian authorities, the Saxon schools held a millennial celebration on 9 May in the Lutheran church in Șchei district. The director of the Unterrealschule delivered a speech about the role of the Saxons in Hungarian history with a hope for their existence in the future. He also expressed the loyalty of the Saxons to Hungary, which was the guarantee of their survival. Songs by the German poet Leopold Maximilian Moltke, along with poems by the Saxon poet Georg Friedrich Marienburg and the Magyar Mihály Vörösmarty (in German translation), were performed. The schools and the church were decorated with both the red, white, and green Hungarian flag and the red and blue Saxon flag.[59]

The festivities of the Saxon institutions confirm the delicate situation they had to face during the millennial festivities. By order of the Saxon Lutheran bishop and under governmental control, the schools and churches organized festivities, but none of the civil associations volunteered to celebrate the millennium. The school festivity was held in the peripheral Şchei Church and not in the central, prestigious Black Church. The buildings were decorated with both the Hungarian and Saxon colors, but the pupils themselves wore red and blue. Most of the poems performed were Saxon and the speaker emphasized the Saxon history of the town. Thus, the millennial school festivity was gradually transformed into a Saxon celebration, representing the historic legitimacy of the Saxon community in the town, but at the same time demonstrating loyalty to the state.

While the Saxon gymnasium turned the millennial celebration into a Saxon festivity, the Romanian gymnasium chose a different strategy. Details of this celebration are not known, since the annual report of the school mentioned the event only in a brief sentence, and *Gazeta Transilvaniei* did not report on it at all.[60] These omissions probably indicate that the celebration was a mere formality and an unimportant act, deliberately not transmitting the message intended by the Budapest government. Yet the millennial festivities made a definite impact on Romanian students, but in a different way than expected in Budapest. According to a report in *Brassói Lapok*, students of the local Romanian girls' school wore Romanian rosettes on the day of the millennial festivity and even forced some Magyar students to solemnly kiss the Romanian colors. The Hungarian rosette was used only to decorate a cat.[61] If this anecdote was true, it meant a clear sign that Romanian students understood the incompatibility of the millennial idea with the concept of Romanian national identity, which they were often taught in their schools.

City and county assemblies, most church congregations, and schools thus celebrated the millennium and in most cases managed to combine the Hungarian state doctrine with their own values. In contrast to these institutions, the government could hardly influence the local press, whose voice was far more diverse. *Preßburger Zeitung*, the representative of the traditional Pressburger identity, stressed mostly the liberal and modern character of the country, paying less attention to historical or national questions. The paper articulated the city's loyalty to both the country and the royal family several times, highlighting its own importance in the course of Hungarian history. Based on these contributions, it also had to refute the accusation of being unpatriotic by promoting German culture.[62] The millennium reminded the Christian socialist *Preßburger Tagblatt* of the Christian character of the country. The unity of the Austrian and Hungarian parts of the empire was also emphasized, and the editors wished Hungary to return to true Christianity (meaning the withdrawal of the 1894/95 religious legislation). It represented the overlapping layers of loyalty to the monarch, the Catholic Church, and the country itself without adopting modern nationalist elements.[63] *Westungarischer Grenzbote* confirmed the Hungarian state doctrine and clearly distanced itself from the Germans of Austria and Germany. At the same time, it marked the "too high" proportion of Jewish companies at the Millennial Exhibition and also warned of the increasing influence of Jewry in the second millennium of Hungary.[64] The paper of the liberal Magyar national activists, *Nyugatmagyarországi Hiradó*, interpreted the millennial festivities through the lens of the Hungarian state doctrine. Local references were not presented; instead it emphasized the eternal Hungarian constitution as a cornerstone of Hungarian modernity, but did not fail to remind non-Magyar-speaking Hungarians to remain faithful to the homeland.[65] The only serious criticism of the concept of the millennial festivities was delivered by the socialist weekly, *Westungarische Volkszeitung*. This paper accused the celebrations of being a fake event to direct the attention of the working class toward the festivities instead of their poor social conditions.[66] This critique, however, was rather rhetorical, as the paper did not discourage its readers from participating in the celebrations, and in fact no paper reported any organized boycott or discontent.

While the papers in Pressburg, with the exception of the socialist press, delivered narratives slightly different from each other, the conflict of the liberals and Catholics in Nitra was more visible. The Catholic *Nyitramegyei Szemle* combined the Magyar ethnic reading of history with the Catholic narrative, highlighting both the Magyar people and the faith of the Hungarians, which had preserved them over the last millennium.[67] It also accused the festive county assembly of being of low quality and lacking interest for the audience; only the speech of the Catholic representative was praised.[68] Reacting to these charges, the liberal *Nyitramegyei Közlöny* accused the clergy of being unpatriotic and destroying the morale of the festivities by its boycott, and in an offensive tone even demanded that the Catholic weekly and the bishop learn patriotism.[69] The liberal papers clearly narrated the millennial festivities in the framework of the Hungarian state doctrine. *Nyitramegyei Közlöny* claimed Magyar supremacy following a social Darwinist argument and demanded the complete linguistic Magyarization of the country in several articles.[70] Less aggressive rhetoric was employed by another liberal paper, the bilingual *Nyitrai Lapok (Neutra-Trenchiner Zeitung)*. Its editors also confirmed the Hungarian state doctrine, and ascribed the survival of other languages to Magyar generosity and love of liberty.[71] *Neutraer Zeitung-Nyitrai Hírlap*, edited by a prominent member of the Jewish community, found denominational tolerance one of the most important characteristics of Hungarian history.[72]

Even more diverse were the reactions of the papers in Brassó. German and Romanian papers failed to deliver a festive editorial about the millennium, and they mostly omitted reports on the local celebrations. The festivity of the

Lutheran schools was interpreted by the two Saxon political streams in a very different way: while the Green Saxon *Kronstädter Zeitung* reported that Saxon schools were forced to celebrate the millennium and emphasized the large number of pupils wearing the red and blue rosette,[73] the moderate and pro-government *Kronstädter Tageblatt* claimed that the Saxons participated in the festivity voluntarily, as they were loyal to Hungary.[74] The editorials in the issue following the largest millennial march in the downtown on 7 June differed even more. *Brassói Lapok* delivered an enthusiastic and detailed victory report on the process. *Kronstädter Zeitung* wrote about the forthcoming *Sachsentag* (meeting of the most important Saxon representatives) and reported on the festival only in a short and very critical article. *Kronstädter Tageblatt* published an editorial about the new members of the town's assembly and the Black-Green conflict, but ignored the festivity completely, while the *Gazeta Transilvaniei* complained about the administration of Hétfalu district and also omitted reports on the celebration.[75] The four papers were as different as if they were reporting about different cities.

The May festivities revealed the potential and limits of Magyar national integration and the various local interpretations of the Hungarian state doctrine. The millennial discourse could be combined with local political-historical concepts by most actors, in particular by the liberal middle classes. The conservative wing of the Catholic Church in Nitra, Hasidic Jews in Munkács, and some Saxons in Brassó tried to adjust to the millennial idea but their efforts remained only partly successful. Social democrats in Pressburg, and Romanians and the majority of Saxons in Brassó, however, completely rejected the millennial idea and elaborated various strategies to settle the conflict.

Notes

1. "Gróf Apponyi Albert beszéde," *Nemzeti Ujság*, 16 January 1896.
2. Take, for instance, József Cserei, *Szentbeszéd: Az ezredév alkalmával a tanuló ifjúságnak* (Temesvár: Uhrmann Henrik, 1896).
3. Sinkó, "Árpád kontra Szent István."
4. Two examples of the Catholic anti-Semitic discourse: "Zsidóvilág Szegeden," *Magyar Állam*, 16 May 1896; "A meggyalázott magyar címer," *Magyar Állam*, 17 May 1896.
5. "A lőcsei eset," *Magyar Állam*, 12 May 1896.
6. *Ezeréves Magyarország: XIII. Leó pápa és a magyar katholikus főpásztorok ünneplő szava papjaik- és hiveikhez a magyar honfoglalás ezredik évfordulója alkalmából* (Budapest: Szent-István-Társulat, 1896).
7. Juliane Brandt, "Die ungarischen Protestanten und das Millennium: Nationale und konfessionelle Identität bei Reformierten und Evangelischen im Spiegel der Tausendjahr–Feiern der Landnahme," *Jahrbücher für Geschichte und Kultur Südosteuropas* 1 (1999): 57–93.
8. *Pesti Hirlap*, 1 May 1896.

9. Anikó Prepuk, "A zsidóság a millenniumon," *Századvég* 17 (Summer 2000): 89–117.
10. "Das erste Jahrhundert des ungarischen Staates," *Allgemeine Jüdische Zeitung*, 1 May 1896; "Zur Millenniar-Feier," *Der ungarische Israelit*, 1 May 1896.
11. "A honfoglalás," in *Népszava naptár 1896. szökő évre a magyar munkásnép számára* (Budapest: Boruth E., 1896), 128–33.
12. "A magyarországi munkásokhoz," *Népszava*, 4 January 1896; "A millennium, a burzsoázia és a munkások," *Népszava*, 1 February 1896.
13. "Május elseje," *Pesti Hirlap*, 2 May 1896; "A vörös május," *Pesti Napló*, 2 May 1896.
14. "Verwahrung der Romänen, Serben und Slovaken bezüglich der Millenniumsfeier," *Siebenbürgisch-Deutsches Tageblatt*, 5 May 1896.
15. "Gesslerov klobúk," *Národnie noviny*, 8 April 1896. See other examples: Pavol Komora, "Milenárne oslavy v Uhorsku roku 1896 a ich vnímanie v slovenskom prostredí," *Historický Časopis* 44, no. 1 (1996): 3–16.
16. Petru Weber, "Das ungarische Millennium bei den Rumänen," in *Interethnische- und Zivilisationsbeziehungen im siebenbürgischen Raum: Historische Studien*, ed. Sorin Mitu and Florin Gogâltan (Cluj: Verein der Historiker aus Siebenbürgen und dem Banat, 1996), 256–71.
17. "Protest gegen die Millenniumsfeier," *Kronstädter Zeitung*, 2 May 1896.
18. "I my v Evropi: Protest halyts'kyh Rusyniv proty madiars'koho tysiacholitia," *Zhyte i slovo: Vistnyk literatury, polityky i nauky* 3, no. 1 (1896): 1–9.
19. *Horvát- és Szlavónország a Magyarország ezeréves fennállásának megünneplésére Budapesten 1896.-évben rendezett országos kiállításon* (Zágráb: Narodne Novine, 1896); Dénes Sokcsevits, "A magyar millennium a horvát közvélemény szemében," in *Croato-Hungarica: Uz 900 godina hrvatsko-mađarskih povijesnih veza*, ed. Milka Jauk-Pinhak, Csaba Gy. Kiss, and István Nyomárkay (Zagreb: Katedra za hungarologiju Filozofskoga fakulteta Sveučilišta u Zagrebu i Matica hrvatska, 2002), 437–46.
20. *La question des trois nationalités.*
21. "A meggyalázott millennium," *Pesti Napló*, 3 May 1896; "Elégtételt," *Pesti Napló*, 4 May 1896; "A belgrádi zászlóégetés," *Pesti Napló*, 6 May 1896.
22. "Zasvätenie millenniuma," *Slovenské noviny*, 4 January 1896.
23. "Zum Millennium," *Siebenbürgisch-Deutsches Tageblatt*, 2 May 1896.
24. Sokcsevits, "A magyar millennium," 446–48.
25. Petru Weber, "The Nationalities and the Millennium in Dualist Hungary," *Transylvanian Review* 6, no. 4 (1997): 103.
26. *Pesti Hírlap*, 10 April 1896.
27. Antonie Plămădealā, *Lupta împotriva deznaţionalizării Românilor din Transilvania în timpul dualismului austro-ungar în vremea lui Miron Romanul 1874–1898 după acte, documente şi corespondenţe inedite* (Sibiu: Typografiei Eparhiale, 1986), 150–80.
28. von Puttkamer, *Schulalltag und nationale Integraton*, 406.
29. *Pesti Hirlap*, 5 June 1896.
30. Timót Frideczky to Vilmos Thuróczy, 1 June 1896, ŠOAN, 11, 1896/1/186–16. eln. 1896.
31. Gábor G. Kemény, ed., *Iratok a nemzetiségi kérdés történetéhez Magyarországon a dualizmus korában* (Budapest: Tankönyvkiadó, 1952–1999), 2: 477–78.
32. *Pesti Hirlap*, 15 May, 23 May, and 5 June 1896.
33. Of the endless examples, take *Pesti Hirlap*, 23 and 26 April, 10 and 11 May 1896.
34. "Szerb esperes a millennium ellen," *Pesti Napló*, 16 September 1896.
35. *Pesti Napló*, 12 May 1896.
36. Lajos Sretvizer, *Ezer esztendő: A milleniumi ünnepségek anyaga a népiskolákban a Vallás és Közoktatásügyi M. Kir. Minister tervezete szerint* (Budapest: Dobrowsky és Franke, 1896).
37. Kőváry, *A millennium lefolyásának története*, 172–206.

38. "A millennium megünneplése Pozsonyban," *Nyugatmagyarországi Hiradó*, 12 May 1896.
39. Bertalan Schönvitzky, *A "Pozsonyi Toldy-Kör" 1896. évi szeptember hó 26. és 27. napján tartott millenáris ünnepségeinek emléklapjai* (Pozsony: Eder István könyvnyomdája, 1896).
40. "Nyitramegye ezredévi díszgyűlése," *Nyitramegyei Közlöny*, 24 May 1896; "A nyitramegyei tisztelt házból," *Nyitramegyei Szemle*, 24 May 1896; "Unsere Festtage," *Nyitrai Lapok (Neutra-Trenchiner Zeitung)*, 24 May 1896.
41. *Die Millenniumsfeierlichkeiten im Kronstädter Komitate* (Kronstadt: Schlandt, n. d.), 32–51; "Vármegyénk ünnepe," *Brassói Lapok*, 18 May 1896.
42. "Győrmegye ünnepe," *Győri Hirlap*, 12 May 1896.
43. "A millennium megünneplése Pozsonyban," *Nyugatmagyarországi Hiradó*, 12 May 1896.
44. *Annual Report of the Pressburg Roman Catholic Gymnasium*, 1895/96, 7–14; *Annual Report of the Pressburg Lutheran Lyceum*, 1895/96, 1–8.
45. "A millennium megünneplése Pozsonyban," *Nyugatmagyarországi Hiradó*, 12 May 1896; "Die Millenniums-Feier in Pressburg," *Preßburger Zeitung*, 11 May 1896; "Die Feier des Millenniums in Pressburg," *Westungarischer Grenzbote*, 11 May 1896; "Különfélék," *Nyugatmagyarországi Hiradó*, 10 May 1896.
46. "Millennáris napok," *Nyitramegyei Szemle*, 17 May 1896.
47. *Annual Report of the Roman Catholic Gymnasium in Nitra*, 1895/96, 128; *Annual Report of the Roman Catholic Elementary Schools in Nitra*, 1895/96, 1–10; *Annual Report of the Roman Catholic Middle School for Girls in Nitra*, 1895/96, 19–20; "A nyitrai ezredéves iskolai ünnepélyek," *Nyitramegyei Közlöny*, 17 May 1896; "Millenniums-Schul und Kirchenfeier," *Nyitrai Lapok (Neutra-Trenchiner Zeitung)*, 17 May 1896.
48. "Nyitramegye ezredévi díszgyűlése," *Nyitramegyei Közlöny*, 24 May 1896; "A magyar állam ezeréves fennállásának történelmi méltatása," *Nyitramegyei Közlöny*, 24 May 1896.
49. *Annual Report of the State Gymnasium in Munkács*, 1895/96, 5–10.
50. "A g. kath. elemi iskolában" and "Zászlószentelés Oroszvégen," *Munkács*, 24 May 1896; "Ezredévi ünnepségek," *Munkács és vidéke*, 24 May 1896.
51. "Az izraelita egyházban" and "Ezredévi fohász," *Munkács*, 10 May 1896.
52. "Az egyházak ünnepe," *Brassói Lapok*, 12 May 1896.
53. *Annual Report of the State Realschule in Brassó*, 1895/96, 3–16 and 25–26.
54. "Millenniumi fa-ültetés," *Brassói Lapok*, 9 May 1896; "A róm. kath. főelemi iskola ezredévi ünnepe," *Brassói Lapok*, 23 May 1896.
55. *Annual Report of the State Commercial Academy in Brassó*, 1895/96, 29–30.
56. "Az iparos ifjak ünnepe," *Brassói Lapok*, 7 and 9 May 1896; "A tanitók ünnepe," *Brassói Lapok*, 16 May 1896; "A brassóvármegyei tanítótestület ezredéves ünnepe," *Brassói Lapok*, 18 May 1896; "A Brassói Magyar Dalárda estélye," *Brassói Lapok*, 11 June 1896.
57. "A dicsőség napja," *Brassói Lapok*, 9 June 1896.
58. "A zászlódisz," *Brassói Lapok*, 12 June 1896. This symbolic conquest was reported by the *Kronstädter Zeitung* in a mocking article: "Irgendein Millenniumsfestivität," *Kronstädter Zeitung*, 8 June 1896.
59. *Annual Report of the Saxon Lutheran Gymnasium in Brassó*, 1895/96, 43; "Millenniumsfeier der Kronstädter evang. Schulanstalten," *Kronstädter Zeitung*, 9 May 1896; Minutes of the (Saxon) Lutheran presbytery and the extended parish council, 21 April 1896, 63–64, AH, IV. Ba. 54.
60. *Annual Report of the Romanian Orthodox Gymnasium, Commercial School and Realschule in Brassó*, 1895/96, 163. The *Gazeta Transilvaniei* reported exclusively about the celebration of the Saxon schools: "Saşii din Braşov şi Mileniul," *Gazeta Transilvaniei*, 30 April/12 May 1896.
61. "Helyi és vidéki hírek," *Brassói Lapok*, 14 May 1896.

62. "896–1000–1896," *Preßburger Zeitung*, 1 January 1896; "An der Schwelle eines Jahrtausends," *Preßburger Zeitung*, 10 May 1896.
63. "Tausend Jahre!" *Preßburger Tagblatt*, 10 May 1896.
64. "896–1896," *Westungarischer Grenzbote*, 10 May 1896; "Die Landesausstellung 1896," *Westungarischer Grenzbote*, 9 May 1896.
65. Imre Szabó, "1896," *Nyugatmagyarországi Hiradó*, 1 January 1896; "Pozsony ünnepe," *Nyugatmagyarországi Hiradó*, 10 May 1896.
66. "Millenniums-Betrachtungen," *Westungarische Volkszeitung*, 24 May 1896.
67. "A haza nagy ünnepére," *Nyitramegyei Szemle*, 10 May 1896.
68. "A nyitramegyei t. házból," *Nyitramegyei Szemle*, 24 May 1896.
69. "Nem illik," *Nyitramegyei Közlöny*, 31 May 1896.
70. "A második évezred küszöbén," *Nyitramegyei Közlöny*, 5 January 1896; "Az ünneprontók," *Nyitramegyei Közlöny*, 3 May 1896.
71. Hugó Dombay, "A nemzet ünnepe" and Leopold Erdélyi, "Zum tausendjährigen Feste," *Nyitrai Lapok (Neutra-Trenchiner Zeitung)*, 3 May 1896; Erdélyi, "Zum Festtage," *Nyitrai Lapok (Neutra-Trenchiner Zeitung)*, 17 May 1896.
72. "Millennium," *Neutraer Zeitung-Nyitrai Hírlap*, 2 May 1896.
73. "Millenniumsfeier der Kronstädter evang. Schulanstalten," *Kronstädter Zeitung*, 9 May 1896.
74. "Die Millenniumsfeier der ev. Schulanstalten," *Kronstädter Tageblatt*, 9 May 1896.
75. "A dicsőség napja," *Brassói Lapok*, 9 June 1896; "Sachsentag," *Kronstädter Zeitung*, 8 June 1896; "Grünen Größenwahns jüngste Blüte," *Kronstädter Tageblatt*, 8 June 1896; "Defecte administrațonali?" *Gazeta Transilvaniei*, 28 May/9 June 1896.

Chapter 11

SIGNS FOR ETERNITY

The Millennial Monuments

❧

The bulk of the millennial festivities, a series of large-scale, splendid celebrations held throughout the country, was over by the beginning of June 1896. Emotions calmed down and life was back on track. Although these celebrations definitely challenged local elite groups, they passed without leaving permanent traces, with the exception of some new buildings, located mostly in Budapest. The event that had a far deeper impact and that proved more of a challenge, foreshadowed by the reception of the May festivities, was the inauguration of the millennial memorials in the following months. Unlike some school or church celebrations, the millennial artifacts initiated by Kálmán Thaly did not fade away, but were intended to be permanent signs to remind Hungarian citizens of the "correct" reading of the past and its logical consequences in the presence and the future. "Thou shalt stand as long as the homeland stands," the festive document placed in the foundation stone of each of the monuments solemnly stated.[1] Moreover, the local celebrations in the spring were managed by local actors, which opened the possibility of adapting the message of the government to local conditions. In contrast, it was the government only that decided the monuments' locations, design, and unveiling ceremonies and it also financed the project. The budget—325,800 florins for the entire project—was covered by the government, whereas the costs of inauguration ceremonies were partially financed by the host counties and municipalities. The construction of the monuments was supervised directly by the Prime Minister's Office. Local authorities participated in the project only as managers of practical issues. As shown in Chapter 2, the final decision about the locations was made in February 1894. As the government ran out of time, an open call for artists (the standard process at the time)[2] was not possible;

instead, the government commissioned the sculptors directly. The task to design the monuments was given to Gyula Berczik, an unknown architect and employee at the Technical Department of the Ministry of Trade.[3] Accompanied and guided by Thaly, Berczik inspected all the locations during the year 1895 and in September he submitted his drafts to a commission of artists. This commission had been delegated by the National Council of Fine Arts at the request of Prime Minister Wekerle in the previous year to comment the plans of the central Millennial Memorial and the St. Stephen statue in Budapest.[4] The members included painters Gyula Benczúr and Károly Lotz (both were leading representatives of historicist painting), sculptor János Fadrusz, politician and chairman of the Hungarian Association of Applied Arts Béla Lipthay, urbanistic expert Lajos Lechner and Budapest Vice-Mayor Károly Gerlóczy. Further invited members were Gyula Pauler, a leading medievalist and director of the Hungarian National Archives and State Secretary József Tarkovich, who was in charge of the execution of the project. The chairman of the committee was Prime Minister Bánffy.

The committee had a mixed opinion of Berczik's plans. Regarding Theben, Lipthay disapproved of the shape of the monument. Berczik planned a thin column and a figure standing on it but according to Lipthay the massive hill would dwarf the monument. He therefore suggested a more substantial monument. Sharing this opinion, Fadrusz recommended a monument carved into the hill itself. The second disputed case was Pusztaszer, where Berczik designed a Greek porticus (an allegory of the Parliament), on which the figure of Árpád sits. To use a porticus as a plinth was an awkward idea according to Lipthay. Furthermore, Fadrusz criticized the Greek style which had no connection to ancient Magyars; instead, he preferred a 'rougher' style. Yet Pauler defended the Greek style, as it fitted into the tranquility of the puszta. The third controversy emerged concerning the location of the Munkács monument. Lipthay was unhappy with the castle: since the castle itself was a historical monument, an 'artificial' monument did not fit into it. Furthermore, the planned obelisk resembled more a flue than a monument. Instead of using the castle, Lipthay suggested to re-locate the monument to the nearby Lovácska hill. The other plans were accepted by the commission. Bánffy promised to forward the commission's recommendations to the Millennial Commission of the Parliament.[5] However, the opinion of the experts was completely disregarded: in Theben the needle-like monument was built on the hill, the sitting Árpád was put on a Greek porticus, and the castle hosted the chimney-like monument in Munkács.

Once the design of the monuments was finalized, sculptors could start their work. Compared to Berczik, more known sculptors were employed to carve the sculptures themselves: Gyula Jankovits (Theben, Brassó), Ede Kallós (Nitra, Pusztaszer), Gyula Bezerédy (Munkács, Pannonhalma, Semlin), and József Róna (Semlin).[6] Thaly was also consulted about stylistic questions: sculptors presented their models to the committee and to him, and he decided about the topics for the inner decorative paintings of the Pannonhalma monument.[7] Commissioned by Bánffy, Thaly also contributed to the festive documents, which were placed in the foundation stone of each monument.[8]

The artistic quality of the monuments remained rather mediocre: contemporary journals and accounts of art history acknowledged their "patriotic" function but failed to praise their beauty. According to historian László Kőváry, who recalled the millennial achievements in an enthusiastic monograph, "the seven monuments are not like pyramids of Cheops, Khafre and Menkaure on the shores of the Nile ..., neither are they wonders of the world, but they are places of pilgrimage driven by patriotic feelings."[9] The technical quality was also imperfect: even Thaly had to acknowledge that the Nitra memorial was simply too small to properly dominate the landscape and both the Pusztaszer and Pannonhalma monuments had to be renovated just a few years after their inauguration.[10] Otherwise, Thaly was satisfied: similar to his poetry and historical works, the sentimental and clichéd monuments fit in well with his aesthetic preferences.

To anchor the monuments' message—the Hungarian state doctrine—in the minds of the masses, splendid inauguration festivities were held in each location. The date of these events was set pragmatically without connecting them to local festive culture. To avoid political debates and thus to represent "national unity," the celebrations had to be held before the parliamentary elections in October 1896. The sculptors and the construction teams, however, did not manage to complete all the monuments before this date. Some memorials therefore had to be inaugurated before being completed: in Pannonhalma, only a foundation stone was laid (the monument was finalized as late as 1898); in Pusztaszer, only the plinth was ready at the time of the solemn festivity (the statue was completed the following year); and in Nitra minor amendments were necessary after the inauguration.

The ceremonies were quite similar to each other: in the presence of the political elite of the country (both houses of Parliament, the Hungarian Academy of Sciences, universities, and churches sent delegates), a minister and a local politician delivered speeches and a priest blessed the monument. Before and after the inauguration, exclusive banquets were held in the towns. Local authorities organized relatively large crowds as audiences, comprising schoolchildren, associations, as well as peasants from the countryside.

The Theben Monument

Kálmán Thaly chose not the center of Pressburg but the ruins of the Theben castle approximately twelve kilometers west of the downtown to build an

Figure 11.1. The millennial monument in Theben. Courtesy of the National Széchényi Library, Budapest. Detail: *Vasárnapi Ujság* 43, no. 42 (1896).

artifact of the Hungarian state doctrine. The monument displayed an old Magyar warrior, facing west, holding the coat of arms of Hungary in his left hand and a lowered, downward-pointing sword in his right. According to Thaly, the coat of arms made it clear to all travelers that they had arrived in a different country, while the sword meant that Árpád's Magyars had conquered the country but had not aimed to expand further. However, in case of need, the lowered sword could be raised again to make it clear that "to this point, German [i.e. Austrian], but not further [may you come]".[11] Nowhere else was the depiction of Hungarian independence stronger than at the inner border of the Austro-Hungarian Monarchy.

The Slavic origins of the castle did not play a relevant role in the monument's location. As the Moravians were seen as victims of the Magyar conquest, a secondary reason for Thaly's choice to locate the monument in Theben was the ruined castle itself, as a reminder of Magyar rule over the indigenous Slavs. However, as it was principally the monument on Zobor Hill that reminded Slovak speakers of the millennium, the Moravian aspect of the Theben memorial was less emphasized and the border with Austria was stressed by the symbolic language and unveiling ceremony.[12]

The inauguration celebration was similar to those of the other millennial memorials in that it almost completely lacked local references. The main speaker at the event, *Minister a Latere*[13] Sámuel Jósika, delivered a speech full of commonplaces about the liberal virtues of Hungary, without any local references. In a romantic speech, the local lawyer Gyula Zsigárdy explained the military defeat of the Moravians, and then surprisingly also discussed the accommodation of the Slavs and the Magyars.[14]

The unveiling ceremony was attended by a number of invited guests, meaning that the participants represented mostly the upper and middle classes of the city. Some workers, members of the petite bourgeoisie, and peasantry were also present; the volunteer firemen, the typographers' choral society, and representatives of the villages in the county, covering Slovak-, Magyar-, and German-speaking communes, also accepted the invitation. The organizers were unlucky, as heavy rain discouraged a larger audience.

Unsurprisingly, the Magyar press welcomed the monument enthusiastically. The Budapest papers stressed that the border function of Theben was strengthened by the millennial memorial.[15] *Nyugatmagyarországi Hiradó* joined the Budapest papers in emphasizing the national importance of the memorial, which was seen as a model for teaching patriotism.[16] The local German press was less delighted; none of them produced a festive editorial on the day of the inauguration, although all of them reported on the ceremony in detail the next day. Both liberal papers, *Preßburger Zeitung* and *Westungarischer Grenzbote*, welcomed the monument; the former saw the city as being honored to host the ceremony, while the latter was happy to learn that the celebration was not blemished by the absence of any of the invited guests (referring here to the Catholic clergy).[17] The Catholic *Preßburger Tagblatt*, although it also delivered a detailed report on the ceremony, avoided any comments on the monument.[18] Nonetheless, the reports of all three papers hinted that the Theben monument was an artifact not belonging to the city in an organic way, therefore in their view it did not influence the public space of the city directly.

Open discontent could have emerged from two sides: the social democrats and the Slovak nationalists. The opinion of *Westungarische Volksstimme*, the local socialist paper, was presumably negative (since it criticized the May festivities too), but since the October 1896 copies are lost, this assumption cannot be verified. The local Slovak reception of the monument is also unknown. *Národnie noviny* failed to report on the celebration, focusing instead on the forthcoming elections. Whether *Národnie noviny* consciously boycotted the Theben ceremony or just did not find it interesting enough to cover is hard to decide; nevertheless, the potential members of the Slovak nation in Pressburg could not learn about the "correct" Slovak interpretation of the monument. Instead, they had to rely on the short report in *Slovenské noviny*, which also failed to deliver an ideological interpretation, as the approaching elections again proved more interesting for the editors.[19] How the millennial monument was received by the most open rivals of the liberal order (if it was received at all) is thus not known. What is certain is that neither the authorities nor newspapers reported any incidents during the festivities. The inauguration of the symbol of liberal Magyar nationalism was not challenged directly but genuine and honest support was fairly limited.

The Nitra Monument

As Nitra played only a marginal role in the Magyar national historical imagination, to locate a millennial monument in the town was only justified by the large Slovak-speaking environment in Nitra County. The monument was erected on Zobor Hill, approximately six kilometers north of the downtown. As Zobor Hill rises above the surrounding plain, the monument, a 22-meter-high obelisk decorated with four *turuls* taking flight, was clearly visible from the town. Thaly had planned a far larger, 36-meter-high obelisk but architect Berczik changed this plan to cut costs. This displeased Thaly, who found that the monument failed to properly rule the countryside due to its small size.[20]

The inauguration day started with a festive meeting of the municipal assembly, where Mayor Pál Kostyál praised the present cultural achievements of the town and its historical contribution to Magyar national history.[21] The festivity at the monument began with a mass celebrated by Bishop Imre Bende. Following the mass, he delivered a speech combining liberal and Catholic elements and praising the Hungarian state doctrine. The main speaker and leader of the governmental delegation, Minister of the Interior Dezső Perczel, did not differ from his counterparts involved in other unveiling ceremonies: his speech was a collection of liberal-nationalist commonplaces lacking local references. The official ceremony was followed by a popular festival, attended by a large crowd. According to *Nyitramegyei Közlöny*, the whole event attracted six to eight thousand people, while *Nyitrai Lapok (Neutra-Trenchiner Zeitung)* estimated the crowd at two thousand.[22]

According to the liberal papers, Minister Perczel was received by an enthusiastic gathering at the railway station and accompanied to the town center by applauding crowds.[23] The Catholic press, however, claimed that people were ordered to receive the minister; most of them remained silent, and the few applauding were either governmental employees or Jews. The reason for their discontent was the religious legislation of the previous years and the local branch of the Liberal Party, which had earned questionable fame for corruption.[24]

The question of whether or not the Catholic population of the town welcomed the liberal minister cannot be answered precisely. What is certain is that the majority of the Catholic clergy persisted in their discontent, expressed

Figure 11.2. The millennial monument in Nitra. Reprinted from Mór Erdélyi, *A Magyar Állam ezeréves fennállását megörökítő hét vidéki emlékmű: 896–1896* (Budapest: Hornyánszky, 1896), n. p.

in May by ignoring the local festivities. The clergy, despite the explicit order of Bende, failed to pay a festive visit to the minister and also boycotted the banquet following the inauguration ceremony. It was only Bende, some of his immediate clerical circle, and some teachers of the Piarist gymnasium who fulfilled the governmental demands and participated in the entire course of festive events.[25]

Beyond this conflict, all sides were able to dissociate themselves from petty political issues and treat the millennial monument and celebrations as a national cause with the potential to integrate society. The Catholic *Nyitramegyei Szemle* printed enthusiastic articles about the monument; at the same time, following the standards of political Catholicism, it highlighted the Church and Christian virtues as the most positive forces in Hungarian history. The editors also justified the local clergy's boycott of any meeting with the representative of the Liberal Party and at the same time explained their participation in the unveiling ceremony. The difference lay precisely in the monument's supra-political meaning: to greet the liberal minister was a political question, while the memorial was seen as a politically neutral, patriotic artifact, even a reminder of Christian values.[26] For the local Magyar nationalist liberal press, the monument served as a justification of the Hungarian state doctrine, and in particular Magyar dominance over Hungary. For *Nyitramegyei Közlöny* the memorial represented the Magyar dominance on the one hand, and on the other hand proclaimed Magyar generosity toward the Slavs by having tolerated their language since the conquest.[27] The liberal but nationally less engaged *Nyitrai Lapok (Neutra-Trenchiner Zeitung)* praised the patriotism of the polyglot county.[28] *Neutraer Zeitung-Nyitrai Hírlap* praised the town's contribution to Hungary's historical achievements and the progress witnessed in the previous decades; the monument also reminded the columnist of the loyalty of the town's multilingual population to the country.[29]

This means that, similar to the May festivities, the inauguration of the millennial monument satisfied all the local actors' needs. The Catholics read the memorial in Christian terms, the nationalist liberals employed an ethnic Magyar discourse, while the nationally more moderate, mostly Jewish liberals found equality of the country's citizens and religious tolerance the most appealing message of the sculpture.

In the shadow of the Catholic–liberal conflict, Slovak national activity was hardly visible. The millennial memorial definitely challenged the town's Slovak reading, as it was erected on the very hill where a Moravian leader had been allegedly executed by Magyar conquerors. For Slovak national activists, the memorial could be interpreted only in terms of a Slovak–Magyar conflict, yet the complete absence of Slovak national activists prevented any Slovak counteraction. *Národnie noviny* ignored the monument entirely and did not even discourage its readers from the monument's inauguration, probably realizing that any call for a boycott was doomed to fail. This omission left Slovak speakers to be influenced solely by the government-supported *Slovenské noviny*. The editors of *Slovenské noviny* found themselves in a complicated situation, as the explicit ethnic Magyar message of the Zobor monument had to be combined with Slovak cultural values. Thus, the article reporting on the monument's inauguration called the memorial a symbol of the Hungarian state. An article from *Budapesti Hirlap* was translated, which confirmed a moderate version of the Hungarian state doctrine. In order to make the monument plausible for Slovak-speaking readers, too, it even questioned the accuracy of the story of Prince Zobor's execution, and argued for the advantages of the Hungarian state for all of its citizens regardless of their mother tongue.[30]

The Munkács Monument

While Theben and Nitra were rather marginal in the ideal Magyar past, Munkács had already been firmly settled as a central place in the Magyar historical imagination. The monument itself was a high obelisk with a *turul* on the top, located in the castle, approximately five kilometers north of the downtown. The local public was slightly disappointed by the monument's location, as it would have preferred the monument to be built in the downtown instead of within the castle.[31] Thaly disregarded this demand, since he was convinced of the importance of the castle more than the town.

The foundation stone of the millennial memorial in Munkács was laid on 19 July 1896 in the presence of Minister of Justice Sándor Erdélyi, Calvinist Bishop of Debrecen Áron Kiss, and Greek Catholic Bishop of Ungvár Gyula Firczák. The festivity included a mass celebrated by Firczák and a prayer by Kiss. According to the rules of the Greek Catholic Church, the liturgical part of the mass was said in Church Slavonic; the songs were performed partly in Church Slavonic, partly in Magyar. Kiss's solemn prayer was reported by many papers as the climax of the celebration.[32] The festive speech by the minister included the usual points of its genre, focusing on the patriotism of all the peoples of Hungary.[33]

The unveiling ceremony was attended by thousands of people from Munkács and all over Bereg County, whose travel to the festivity was organized by the government. Due to the relatively small size of the castle terrace where the monument stood, most of the audience could neither see nor hear the festivity, nevertheless the guests gave a frenetic ovation, at least according to the liberal papers. The festive inauguration was followed by a popular celebration at the castle, where thousands of "ordinary" guests were invited at the expense of the county. The festivities were accompanied in the town by floodlights and concerts on the promenade and in a music hall. The large

Figure 11.3. The millennial monument in Munkács. Courtesy of the National Széchényi Library, Budapest.

number and the enthusiastic spirit of the audience, consisting of both Magyars and Rusyns representing numerous villages in the county, was highlighted by all newspapers.[34]

On the following day, other monuments were inaugurated. A memorial plaque was unveiled at Veretsky Pass, through which the ancient Magyars had allegedly entered the Carpathian basin, and another obelisk was inaugurated on the Hungarian-Galician border. The local Greek Catholic priests delivered speeches at both ceremonies praising the eternal loyalty of Rusyn speakers to

Figure 11.4. Scenes from the inauguration festivity in Munkács. Reprinted from *Vasárnapi Ujság* 43, no. 30 (1896).

Hungary and stressing the Rusyn participation in the conquest. Similar to the Munkács festivities, the ceremonies in these frontier villages were also attended by many local inhabitants wearing their Sunday best, applauding the delegation, and singing patriotic songs.

There were certainly many motivations that explain the large masses celebrating the millennium. Local Greek Catholic priests could easily identify with the festivities. The obedience of the poor and uneducated peasants could easily be assured by the orders of local governmental officials.[35] Furthermore, Greek Catholic priests explained the millennial idea to peasants in a way they could easily identify with. The concept that the forefathers of the Rusyns had been allies to Árpád's Magyars and that they had conquered Hungary together was widely shared among Greek Catholic intellectuals. A report in a local paper confirms this idea: a correspondent claimed that Rusyn-speaking peasants of the villages near Veretsky Pass became proud, even arrogant after the

Figure 11.5. The festivity at the Veretsky Pass. Reprinted from *Vasárnapi Ujság* 43, no. 31 (1896).

celebrations. He explained this by the successful spread of the millennial idea: the splendid governmental delegation, the presence of their bishop, and the speeches of their own priests made local peasants imagine themselves as heirs of a splendid past.[36] The "patriotic" behavior of Rusyn speakers was warmly praised by the liberal papers of Budapest.[37]

Discontent over the festivities was reported only from the local Jewry. As was usual in the age, the day before the inauguration all authorities, associations, and church congregations paid a ceremonial visit to Minister Erdélyi. The only institution that failed to send its representatives to the minister was the Jewish congregation. The reason for this was a disagreement about the proper form of delegation between the majority Hasidim and the minority reform-minded Jews. Each party denounced the other to the minister, which led to Erdélyi refusing to receive any Jewish delegation. The absence of Munkács Jewry from the ceremonial visit to the minister was, according to the standards of the age, an outstandingly rude act and provoked deep criticism. Liberal papers of Budapest accused the Jewish community of a lack of patriotism as they had failed to prove their honest loyalty to a high representative of the government.[38] *Egyenlőség*, the leading paper of Neolog Jewry, followed the same argumentation and even blamed Munkács Jews for making the Hungarian Jewry feel ashamed. The Orthodox press, however, accused the aggressive Neologs of not accepting their minority position in the delegation and causing discord and also blamed the minister for not recognizing this destructive effort. Refuting the accusations of disloyalty, the Orthodox *Zsidó Hiradó* referred to the leaders of the Munkács community who demanded that congregation members decorate their houses even though the unveiling ceremony coincided with Tisha B'Av, the most important mourning day in the Jewish calendar.[39]

Budapest papers also criticized the low participation of Jews in the unveiling ceremony and thus questioned again their true loyalty to the country.[40] This time *Egyenlőség* protested too; this paper routinely criticized Orthodoxy but did not tolerate the accusation of disloyalty of Jews in general. A detailed article claimed that, despite the strict fast and prohibition of any entertainment during Tisha B'Av, all Jews decorated their houses, many of them participated in the festivities, and the "more intelligent Jews" (in the terminology of *Egyenlőség* this meant the liberal reform-minded) even wore their Sunday best. *Egyenlőség* thus claimed that many Jews broke the rules of their religion on the altar of their true Magyar national identity and this proved the loyalty of the entire Munkács Jewry. The absence of Jews wearing traditional caftans and speaking in Yiddish, an observation of many Budapest papers, was explained by the *Egyenlőség* columnist claiming that the majority of Munkács Jewry preferred modern clothes and spoke Magyar, making them appear similar to the Christians. Furthermore, *Egyenlőség* noted that the Munkács Jews had demanded that the unveiling ceremony be moved to another day to avoid conflict with Tisha B'Av and also initiated the idea of a rabbi blessing the monument.[41]

In fact, the arguments of *Egyenlőség* were clearly not true. With the exception of the few reform-minded, Munkács Jews firmly insisted on their Hasidim traditions, including wearing the caftan and speaking Yiddish.[42] This means that the correspondents failed to see Hasidim Jews at the celebration not because of their assimilation in clothing and language, but because of their actual absence. The Hasidic Jews of Munkács chose to observe Tisha B'Av instead of the millennium and this fact surprised only a few.

The Brassó Monument

In theory, the Brassó monument commemorated Árpád's Magyars. They, however, had never been to the town, hence the memorial in fact represented the power of the Hungarian state over the traditional rulers of the town. Located on the Cenk peak over the downtown, the Brassó memorial was identical to the one in Theben (an old Magyar warrior was set on a high column) and they were both inaugurated on the same day. The boycott of the May festivities by Romanian and Green Saxon politicians, the disregard of the Romanian and Saxon press and associations, and the particular format of the school festivities foreshadowed the conflicts over the far more provocative erection of the millennial monument in Brassó. Although the final decision to erect a millennial memorial was made long before, local papers did not consider the monument in detail until the late summer of 1896, when it seemed to be inevitable. The first conflict to have a deep impact on the local public emerged on 16 September 1896 at the meeting of the town council. The government requested the transfer of the territory of Cenk peak and the town's financial contribution to the unveiling festivity. The government also demanded that the town council receive the monument officially, meaning they would need to not only accept it but also assume the future maintenance in the municipal budget.[43]

The government's demand provoked a bitter fight in the town council and in local papers. Backed by Mayor Karl Jacobi, council member Ernst Hintz, the rapporteur on the issue, came forward with the suggestion to accept the governmental demands. This proposal was supported by the Magyar and moderate Saxon representatives, but vehemently rejected by the Green Saxons and Romanians. *Kronstädter Zeitung* summarized well the arguments against the monument and municipal involvement:

> The town could use its money more wisely than financing a project that challenges and insults the Saxons of the town. … The further growth of chauvinism cannot be supported. The erection of the Árpád monument in Kronstadt is nonsense, a historical lie, a deliberate insult of the ruling German elements in Burzenland.[44]

The opponents of the memorial used historical-ideological and practical (financial) arguments. Karl Lurtz, a prominent leader of the Green Saxons, criticized the exclusive role of the government in planning the monument, ignoring the town council and in a broader sense municipal autonomy. Another critical remark by Lurtz noted that the monument failed to refer to the "cultural work" of the Saxons in the region. Another Saxon councilman, Eugen Lassel, argued against the monument, consciously realizing the importance of public space:

> The monument was located consciously on the Zinne [the German name of Cenk], the point dominating the Burzenland; it will be breathing down our necks; every day it will propagate the increasing impediment of the Saxons by the Magyars. This is the decisive point. The idea embodied in this monument is the violent spread of Magyardom here in the old Saxon land. As we condemn the idea, we also condemn the monument and cannot contribute to its promotion. ... The government should be urged to remove the monument as soon as possible, for its existence is a constant provocation to Saxons and Romanians.[45]

Similar arguments were made by Romanian politicians. The lawyer Iosif Puşcariu warned of the financial burden of maintaining the memorial, while the gymnasium teacher Arsenie Vlaicu accused the government of abusing its power to force the town to accept the monument.

At the same time, several Saxon politicians argued in favor of the monument. The lawyer Karl Schnell, also a member of the Green Saxon group, claimed that a memorial outside of the town did not disturb anyone and its official reception had no financial consequences. As it turned out, none of these arguments were realistic.[46] Doctor Eduard Gusbeth recalled the peaceful coexistence of the Magyars and Saxons and urged the acceptance of the monument. Born in 1839, Gusbeth belonged to an older generation and his argument was quite anachronistic; he did not or did not want to understand the character of modern nationalism, which aimed at integrating an imagined population but did not tolerate multiple identities. The Magyar alderman Nándor Otrobán chose a historical argument, claiming that Saxons had not been present in Transylvania in the times of Árpád, therefore failing to resemble Saxon history in the monument's symbolic language was correct. He, together with all the Magyar representatives, favored the complete fulfillment of the government's demands. The bitter rhetorical fight at the council meeting ended with a vote in favor of the request of the government, supported by Magyar and moderate Saxon councilmen.[47]

This meeting outraged all political sides, and in the following days all local papers delivered angry articles accusing the other parties of betrayal. *Kronstädter Zeitung* blamed the moderate Saxons for betraying the Saxon interest:

> Like the character and visible landmark of the Rhineland at Rüdesheim and Bingen is marked by the national monument on the top of the Niederwald, so will the

Burzenland stay under the sign of this millennial memorial in the future and the traveler will look first at the Árpád statue when entering the Burzenland. But we cannot answer, gnashing our teeth, the traveler's astonished question that the monument was forced on us. No, voluntarily have we Kronstadters, i.e., the moderates, given place, blind and deaf towards all warnings have we let the monument be given to us as a present and we repay the generous Magyars for this Greek gift with glittering celebrations.[48]

Similar arguments were employed by the Romanian press; *Gazeta Transilvaniei* labeled the moderate Saxons opportunists since, in its view, the monument was simply propaganda for the violent spread of Magyar chauvinism.[49]

The vote of the moderate Saxon councilmen was justified in *Kronstädter Tageblatt* by an argument combining ideological and practical elements. The columnist claimed that Saxons must take a moderately positive stand toward the millennium. The importance of Saxons should be demonstrated by partaking in the celebration since the festivity commemorated the common Hungarian fatherland and not only the Magyars. The *Kronstädter Tageblatt* editorial condemned the Green Saxon speakers for being braggarts and argued in favor of fulfilling the demands of the government for practical reasons.[50] Another article in *Kronstädter Tageblatt* criticized the choice of figure for the memorial, since Árpád represented the Magyars exclusively, but otherwise agreed with the idea of commemorating Hungary on the Cenk peak.[51]

Brassói Lapok published a reprimanding editorial claiming that the radical Saxons damaged the interests of the Saxon people the most.[52] The scandal was not confined to Brassó: József Pótsa, lord lieutenant of neighboring Háromszék County, sent an outraged letter to the minister of the interior about the hostility of Brassó to the millennium. Háromszék County was officially invited to the unveiling ceremony and, according to the original plan, its Szekler delegation was to stay in Brassó for some days. But the scandalous meeting outraged the Háromszék lord lieutenant so much that he demanded a special train for his delegation to leave the hostile town as early as possible after the inauguration ceremony, because "Magyars do not need forced hospitality."[53] However, the wish for an early departure was not fulfilled, as the ministry declined to send the special train. The explanation of the Ministry of Trade, responsible for the railway system, was quite surprising: the train could easily fall victim to non-Magyar terrorists during the night, therefore the delegation's safety could only be guaranteed by staying in Brassó for the night of the festivity.[54] Needless to say, the idea of terrorism was complete nonsense, as terrorist attacks were not part of the repertoire of any political group in fin-de-siècle Hungary. The very fear, however, demonstrates that the Hungarian state administration took the discontent over the millennium into serious consideration.

A further problem causing problems for the government was the Catholic Church. According to the standard protocol, the unveiling celebrations started with a festive church service. For obvious reasons, in Brassó, it was not the oldest, largest, most central, and honored Saxon Lutheran Black Church that was chosen for this festive service, but the Catholic church (the parish with the most Magyar believers). Archdeacon Ede Möller was willing to celebrate the festive mass in his church and to pray "for our sweet homeland and beloved crowned king."[55] However, he refused to pay a ceremonial visit to the main speaker of the unveiling ceremony, Minister of the Interior Dezső Perczel, and to participate in the inauguration celebration. Lord Lieutenant Mihály Maurer therefore asked Ferenc Lönhárt, Transylvanian Catholic bishop, to order Möller to participate in the whole celebration, claiming that the unveiling ceremony was purely "patriotic" and had no political character and that Möller's discontent would outrage the local Magyars.[56] In a detailed letter, Möller explained to the bishop the reasons for his discontent, referring to civil marriage and religious laws, for which he blamed Perczel.[57] Despite the political pressure by the lord lieutenant, the bishop accepted Möller's argument and left the decision to the priest. The incident was further exacerbated by the fact that Lönhárt could not participate in the ceremony due to a serious illness, delegating his role to Möller, who, as archdeacon, was the highest ranking ecclesiastical figure in the town.

Thus, the absence of Romanians, Green Saxons, and high-ranking representatives of the Catholic Church at the unveiling ceremony was predictable. To elevate the boycott to a higher level, intensive agitation started before the unveiling ceremony. *Kronstädter Zeitung* argued for a boycott by claiming that the millennial festivities served exclusively the Magyar idea of the nation ("*magyarische Nationalidee*") and Magyar chauvinism. The call for a boycott did not remain solely on paper; the question of whether a particular Saxon choir would participate in the inauguration ceremony seriously divided the membership.[58] The *Gazeta Transilvaniei* did not even issue a direct call to boycott the "millennial uproar" ("*tămbălăul milenar*"), as non-participation was self-evident for its readers.

The absence of the Green Saxon and Romanian guests and a proper representative of the Catholic Church did not disturb the splendid pageantry of the unveiling ceremony. Although the issue of the monument seriously divided the local Saxon community, the inauguration festivity was attended by the two most important Saxon leaders, Bishop Friedrich Müller and Karl Wolff, chairman of the Saxon People's Party. Müller, as the highest spiritual leader of the Transylvanian Saxons, received a particularly warm welcome from the town's mayor and Saxon youth, as he was visiting Brassó for the first time since becoming bishop in 1893.[59]

The governmental delegation, led by Minister of the Interior Dezső Perczel, was received by Deputy Lord Lieutenant Friedrich Jekel and Lord Lieutenant Mihály Maurer. The Saxon Jekel delivered a speech emphasizing the importance of the Cenk monument, which embodied the miseries and achievements of a thousand years, while Maurer discussed the equal loyalty of all citizens to Hungary. From the railway station they paraded to the county hall, accompanied by Saxon and Magyar horsemen in national dress, while the road was lined with members of the Magyar craftsmen's associations and students.[60] During the evening a festive serenade was performed in honor of the minister by the Saxon and Magyar choral societies.[61]

The next day the unveiling ceremony started in the Catholic church with the festive mass said by Ede Möller. Following the mass, the participants marched to the monument, where Perczel delivered a speech. Perczel expressed the glory of Hungarian history and also praised the Saxons, who had contributed significantly to the development of the country. Following the decision of the town council of 16 September, Mayor Karl Jacobi talked about Saxon loyalty to Hungary and officially accepted the monument.[62]

In the afternoon a festive banquet took place, where additional speeches were delivered. The most interesting speech was offered by Müller. Although Müller had some conflicts with the Magyar public when criticizing the Magyarizing aims of the millennial conference on education, at this moment he forgot his reservations and surpassed all other speeches. He spoke in German, arguing that Saxons participated in the ceremony of their own will with no element of coercion. According to Müller, the Cenk monument showed the just expression of the consciousness of Hungary and the coherence of the people inhabiting it. He worried about those who did not want to partake in the ceremony.[63] Wolff praised the people who worked in favor of the cooperation of Saxons and Magyars in his speech. Franz Oberth, priest of the Black Church, proposed a toast to the Liberal Party and the town's Saxon-friendly Magyar parliamentary representative, András Bethlen. The banquet was followed by floodlights and concerts in the town.[64]

The editorial of the local Magyar *Brassói Lapok* expressed all the enthusiasm felt by the town's Magyar national activists:

> Let this monument be our hope, the column of our trust. Like the biblical pillar of fire let it lead us to the yet unreached land of promise, which this country will become when all its people, without regard to differences of language or religion, with one heart, with one spirit, with true fraternal love will prostrate themselves at the holy altar of patriotism. You are such an altar, dignified column. Steadily stand, rule this beautiful land, preach the power and glory of the millennium-old Hungarian state. Even if the time eroding your stone base for countless millennia were to finally succeed in destroying you, or if the lightning of the enraged heavens were to smite and fell you, or if patricidal hands were to strike against you in such a horrendous

Figure 11.6. The millennial monument in Brassó. Courtesy of the National Széchényi Library, Budapest.

act ... the idea that you represent is irrefutable and will live in our hearts firmly and will assure for our glorious nation the blessed homeland and this beautiful land for the following millennia.[65]

The monument's frenetic reception seems to have spread to a relatively large Magyar audience. Besides the official guests, approximately seven hundred Szeklers representing Háromszék County and members of the Magyar associations, including several craftsmen clubs and students of the Magyar high schools, participated in the ceremony by lining the streets, escorting the minister on his walk to the monument, and so on. The limited space at the memorial did not discourage Magyar participants: pupils of the state Realschule could not participate directly in the unveiling celebration at the small peak of the Cenk, so they stood nearby at the ruins of the former castle. Since they were able neither to hear nor see anything of the ceremony, they sang the national anthem.[66]

While the monument completely fulfilled the demands of local Magyar national activists, it seriously challenged the Saxon understanding of the town. Its symbolic language, the Magyar warrior, and its shape being identical to the Theben memorial at the very opposite corner of the country recalled the integrated space of the Kingdom of Hungary and the Magyar ethnic reading of Hungarian history, thus de-emphasizing the particular Saxon territory and past.

In response to this challenge, two answers were given. On the one hand, the majority of the Saxon elite, both at the local and the top level, tried to find a compromise with the Hungarian government. This group included Müller, Wolff, Jacobi, and majority of the councilmen. Though definitely critical of the millennial festivities, this group preferred to avoid conflicts with the government as its members believed that loyalty to the state ensured the maintenance of the Saxon people. The festive article in *Kronstädter Tageblatt* on the unveiling ceremony demonstrated this idea well:

> Therefore, we have the idea that love of fatherland or the entire state is and must remain a moral inevitability for the Saxon people, unless we want to sign our death sentence. However, this love of the fatherland cannot mean that we Magyarize the name of our fathers or forget the language of our mothers. ... As we would like to be truthful citizens of the Hungarian state, we shall be prepared to stay and fall with the Hungarian state. Even though we are full of this consciousness, such a time will not come in the second millennium that we Saxons would have to be nationalized in the interest of the Hungarian state.[67]

The reports of both moderate and pro-governmental papers, the local *Kronstädter Tageblatt* and *Siebenbürgisch-Deutsches Tageblatt* (the central paper of the Saxon People's Party published in Hermannstadt), emphasized the visit and speech of Bishop Müller and the Saxon contribution to Hungarian history, thus making an attempt to "Saxonize" the inauguration ceremony just as they had the school festivity in May.[68]

On the other hand, the second possible answer was that of the mostly younger generation, open to German nationalism. Their answer to the monument was national and modern: refuse it, as according to their understanding, the memorial was a tool in the process of Magyar nationalism in the town. Following the Black Saxon and Magyar representatives voting to fulfill the government's demands, their tools became limited. Besides some critical and ironic articles in *Kronstädter Zeitung*, Green Saxon representatives could only boycott the ceremony.

Romanians also refused to share in the festivities and *Gazeta Transilvaniei* failed to report on the inauguration ceremony. Instead of being present at the unveiling ceremony, Romanian Orthodox believers welcomed the new priest of the St. Nicholas Church. The priest was received and escorted by a mass of believers from the train station through the downtown to the church. The mass included festively decorated horse riders who used the colors of the Romanian flag. This procession met Minister Perczel as he was walking in the town center. The minister and his delegation were outraged to see that the colors of Romania were openly used in a Hungarian town; the police even initiated minor offense proceedings.[69] Although direct sources do not prove that the new priest's arrival was deliberately timed for the very day of the unveiling ceremony, there is good reason to suppose that the Romanian Orthodox Church, using its wide autonomy, organized this procession as a sort of counter-demonstration against the millennium.

The Pannonhalma Monument

The Pannonhalma monument was built near the abbey in the form of a chapel in the style of historicism using some neo-Renaissance elements, with the Holy Crown of Hungary on top. In the following years the chapel's interior was decorated with an allegorical fresco, painted by students of the celebrated academic painter Károly Lotz. The fresco displayed the installation of Árpád as prince of the Magyars and the allegory of the reign of Francis Joseph, and some other scenes and kings related to the monastery (St. Stephen receives the Holy Crown, the meeting of Godfrey of Bouillon and King Coloman, the siege of Pannonhalma by the Mongols).[70]

While the erection of a millennial monument was welcomed by the Benedictine Order without any reservations, the details of the construction of the memorial led to some discontent. First, the memorial occupied a particular hill where, until the millennial year, an often-used calvary stood. In order to build the monument, the calvary had to be removed, which was an unusual and insensitive act. The government declared that the monument could be located only on that particular hill, so the failure to remove the calvary would have resulted in choosing another location for the millennial memorial. As the Order understood the millennial memorial as a confirmation of its national role, it had to give up the calvary.[71] This act was then legitimized by the standard Benedictine reading of history, claiming that the millennial monument's Christian character improved the holiness of the place and the cross on the Holy Crown of Hungary, to be placed on top of the monument, replaced the original crosses of the calvary.[72]

A further issue was the memorial devoted to the first abbot, Astrik, which had already been planned as the Order's own contribution to the millennium. Thaly promised the Order that Astrik's sculpture would be placed within the millennial chapel, but in the end this did not happen and Astrik's statue was erected in the courtyard of the abbey.[73] Furthermore, the style of the monument was also criticized, as the dominant neo-Renaissance elements of the chapel were not only meaningless for both the conquest and the Benedictine Order, but even referred to the darkest age of the abbey's history, the sixteenth century, when the monastery fell under Ottoman rule. Nevertheless, the proposal to replace neo-Renaissance elements with neo-Romanesque,

Figure 11.7. The millennial monument in Pannonhalma. Reprinted from Mór Erdélyi, *A Magyar Állam ezeréves fennállását megörökítő hét vidéki emlékmű: 896–1896* (Budapest: Hornyánszky, 1896), n. p.

representing both the age of the conquest and the foundation of the abbey, was not accepted.[74]

The inauguration celebration started with a grandiose mass, celebrated by Abbot Ipoly Fehér, which was followed by speeches delivered by Döme Vojnits, prior and director of the Benedictine gymnasium in Esztergom, and canon Cziprián Halbik. Vojnits focused on Prince Árpád's visit and employed an ethnic Magyar reading of history, while Halbik provided the standard Benedictine historical narrative, making the past and fate of Pannonhalma and Hungary identical.[75] Minister of Culture and Religion Gyula Wlassics delivered a speech praising the Hungarian state doctrine and the cultural achievements of the country symbolized by the abbey. The speakers on behalf of Győr County shared the same ideas.[76] As all the speakers, including the representatives of the Catholic Church, shared the same vision, the festivity passed without conflict. Compared to the other locations, the question of popular participation was slightly different, as, lacking an urban environment, large masses of people were not expected. Győr County nevertheless organized a delegation from each of its villages, intended to transmit the message of the memorial to their countrymen.[77]

The Pusztaszer Monument

Just as in the case of Munkács, Pusztaszer had been settled as an outstanding location in the Magyar national phantasies well before the millennial year. Magyar national protagonists were firmly convinced that Pusztaszer had long been deserving of a monument financed by the government. As a symbol of the eternal Hungarian constitution, choosing Pusztaszer to house a millennial memorial was thus natural.

The monument, a portico in Greek style with Árpád seated on the top, was erected near the ruins of the monastery. The monument was an awkward artifact: the leader of a nation of nomadic horsemen sat on a Greek portico. Furthermore, the portico is far larger than the sculpture of Árpád, thus the Greek structure dwarfs the figure. The location of the monument lacked any kind of built environment but the ruins, therefore seven trees symbolizing Árpád's Magyar tribes were planted there. Despite this, the monument remained a lone building in the middle of a vast, desolate area.

The inauguration ceremony took place on 27 June, although only the portico was finished by that time; the sculpture of Árpád was completed the following year. The inauguration festivity began with a Catholic mass celebrated by the Abbot of Pusztaszer, which was followed by a speech by Minister of

Figure 11.8. The millennial monument in Pusztaszer. Courtesy of the
National Széchényi Library, Budapest.

Agriculture Ignác Darányi. Darányi praised the eternal Hungarian constitution and the Hungarian state doctrine, a topic particularly fitting for the environment.

Lacking any group contesting the Hungarian state doctrine, the celebration proceeded without any conflict. Szeged and the surrounding Csongrád County, completely Magyar speaking, were not targeted by any non-Magyar national elite and the Catholic People's Party's influence was also quite limited. Szeged and its vicinity were in fact famous for their support of the Party of Independence, which promoted sometimes radical Magyar nationalist ideas.[78] The middle classes of Szeged and the nearby city of Hódmezővásárhely were proud to participate in the celebration and financially supported the festival: they understood the monument as an artifact displaying their identity. The local liberal-national consensus is well illustrated by the reports of the Szeged dailies: the speech of Minister Darányi was so compatible with the local concept of the nation that not only the pro-governmental *Szegedi Hiradó* but also *Szegedi Napló*, the paper of the Party of Independence, praised it without any criticism.[79] The idea of Pusztaszer being the cradle of Hungarian constitutionalism was so firmly believed by all the Magyar political parties that not only the Budapest liberal papers but also the Catholic, otherwise aggressively critical *Magyar Állam* celebrated it.[80]

Whereas the audience of most monuments was confined to the middle class, the Pusztaszer memorial was successful beyond that. The unveiling ceremony of the semi-completed monument attracted an outstandingly large audience. Thousands of inhabitants from the nearby towns and villages participated in the festivity, including a large number of peasants. The papers estimated the total number of participants at around twenty to twenty-five thousand; all the reports agreed on the large number of people taking carts and boats, and even walking to the festivity.[81] Darányi's solemn speech was hardly audible due to heavy rain; still, peasants could read the monument as a confirmation of their membership in the Magyar nation without the guidelines of the minister. The well-known myth of the *puszta* and its genuine Magyar inhabitants seemed enough to win over a large number of people for Árpád.

The Semlin Monument

Obeying the terms of the 1868 Croatian-Hungarian Compromise, Magyar nationalism did not target the territory and population of Croatia-Slavonia. This principle was disregarded only occasionally and these attempts had to be restricted mostly to the symbolic sphere, as the Hungarian government lacked any practical means to intervene in nationally sensitive matters in the territory of Croatia-Slavonia. The erection of the millennial monument in Semlin was one of the few examples of such efforts. Having power in local politics, Mayor Kosovac and his pro-governmental and pro-Hungarian party were partners in Thaly's effort, as their cooperation was an apt means to demonstrate their loyalty toward the government, which was believed to be the main patron of the local economy.

The Semlin monument was the most impressive and the most expensive in Thaly's project. It was a 35-meter-high neo-Renaissance, majolica-covered tower, built at the ruins of the castle. A sitting *Hungaria* statue, accompanied by two stone lions, occupied the upper floor. The top of the monument was crowned by a 4.5-meter-wide bronze *turul*, holding a sword in its rostrum. The structure faced Belgrade; it was deliberately located on the hill above the town in order to be visible from the Serbian capital and from the Constantinople–Paris railway line.

The festive inauguration was attended by a number of representatives of the Croatian political elite, including the speaker of the Croatian Parliament, the lord lieutenants of Srem, Požega, and Virovitica counties, the mayor of the regional center Esseg, and several other high-ranking pro-Hungarian politicians. During the celebration, the town, and particularly the castle ruins, were decorated with Hungarian and Croatian flags. The state-owned Hungarian Danube Steamboat Company flew several large Hungarian flags. The festivity started with a festive mass in the Roman Catholic church and then in the Serbian Orthodox church; both services were celebrated by high-ranking

Figure 11.9. The millennial monument in Semlin. Courtesy of the National Széchényi Library, Budapest.

priests (a Catholic abbot, and an Orthodox archimandrite and an archdeacon, respectively). The main speaker of the event, Emerik Josipović, Minister of Croatian Affairs in the Hungarian government, delivered a bilingual (Croatian-Magyar) speech, praising the common past and equal partnership of Croatia and Hungary. Josipović, a conservative Croatian-Hungarian magnate, framed his speech in the unionist Croatian narrative: the freedom-loving ancient Magyars allied with the Croats to defend Christianity, their common homeland, and ancient liberties, symbolized by the achievement of John Hunyadi. The other speeches, delivered by Ervin Čeh (Lord Lieutenant of Srem County) and Kosovac, emphasized the eternal alliance of the two nations, and in particular the loyalty of the region and the town. All institutions, civil, economic, and confessional, paid a ceremonial visit to the minister, and the crowd often cheered both in Croatian and in Magyar. *Oestlicher Grenz-Bote*, a local German paper, stressed the friendly and conflict-free environment.[82]

The monument inspired the pro-governmental Croatian press to praise the equal partnership of Hungary and Croatia-Slavonia. The leading paper of the government, *Narodne novine*, and the influential *Agramer Zeitung* indeed thought that the two nations' alliance was based on their common contribution to the defense of Western Christianity and therefore the town was the best chosen symbol.[83] A similar view was shared by local and regional German papers: the Semlin-based *Oestlicher Grenz-Bote* and the *Slavonische Presse*, printed in Esseg, declared Croatian loyalty to the alliance with Hungary.[84] *Die Drau*, another German paper published in the regional center of Esseg, even held the millennial memorial to be a symbol of the integration of Croatia-Slavonia and Hungary, which in its view was in the inevitable interest of both countries.[85] The liberal papers of Budapest interpreted the monument as a symbol of the Hungarian state doctrine; some of them also solemnly declared the partnership of Croatia and Hungary.[86]

At first glance, one could consider that the celebration passed in complete harmony. However, the town's very commitment to the celebration seems questionable, as the town council did not convene for a festive meeting, unlike the other municipalities.[87] The municipal documents furthermore reveal that the town's administration dealt mainly with the participation of local entrepreneurs at the Millennial Exhibition in Budapest, which was a great marketing opportunity, while the issue of the millennial monument was ignored.[88] Just like in the other locations, the organization of the inauguration ceremony was almost exclusively the task of the central authorities and the Lord Lieutenant of Srem County.[89] The top-level organization of the celebration then led to some discontent, as a correspondent of *Oestlicher Grenz-Bote* claimed that several local notables were not invited to the festivities, including former mayor Panajot Morphy.[90]

Popular participation in the inauguration ceremony seems ambiguous. The pro-governmental papers reported a large crowd following the events. This information, however, contradicts the fact that, unlike the other inauguration ceremonies, pupils of the Semlin schools did not participate collectively in the festivity, and a popular festival following the official event was not held either. Although open conflicts did not emerge, it is more than probable that discontent appeared under the surface. *Budapesti Hírlap* reported some negative incidents. Its correspondent saw the Orthodox church being decorated with the imperial black and yellow flag, which the paper interpreted as a clear sign of discontent with Hungary's autonomy within the Austro-Hungarian Monarchy. Furthermore, the local Catholic dean, allegedly a supporter of Bishop Josip Strossmayer and the oppositional Independent People's Party, deliberately left town in order to escape the festive church service. Nevertheless, other reports did not affirm this.[91]

Open criticism rather came from Zagreb, as basically all parties of the opposition were outraged by the memorial, claiming that the monument violated the Croatian constitution and the Croatian-Hungarian Compromise. *Obzor*, the paper of the Party of State Right, a major oppositional party, interpreted the celebration as a purely Magyar act on Croatian soil, inspired by a deliberate falsification of history. Its editor contrasted the high level of Croatian civilization with the pagan ancient Magyars. The fact that Minister Josipović gave a bilingual speech on the territory of Croatia-Slavonia was seen by the commentator as the most aggressive violation of Croatian law. The speech of the minister was further criticized as he referred to the common fight of Croatia and Hungary with the Ottoman Empire. In contrast, *Obzor* felt that this fight gave Hungary the chance to undermine the equality of Croatia within the Croatian-Hungarian union. Therefore, the millennial monument represented the unlawful subjection of Croatia to Budapest. As its final argument, *Obzor* also claimed that the trade policy of the Hungarian government explicitly hindered the development of the town's economy, providing one more reason to condemn the millennial monument.[92] A similar argumentation was employed by another paper close to the Party of State Right, *Hrvatska domovina*. The commentator of this paper also accused the Hungarian government of creating a past that never happened and forcing Croatia to give up its autonomy.[93]

The leader of the Party of State Right, Josip Frank, interpellated *Banus* Khuen-Héderváry in late November. Frank claimed that the *Hungaria* statue and "the bird of Árpád" on the Semlin monument and the Magyar inauguration speech by Minister Josipović outraged the Croatian audience. "Croatia has existed for more than a thousand years," argued Frank, and King Tomislav "struck Magyar hordes several times," therefore the Croatian state was well established before the Hungarian one. The Semlin monument therefore violated Croatian state law. "The sword in the rostrum of the eagle," continued

Frank, "means not love but it is the symbol of tyranny and means: I will subjugate you." Finally, Frank urged the Croatian government to remove the monument.[94]

As the town municipality, led mostly by Serbian politicians, had some minor role in the organization of the millennial celebration, and the Serbian Kosovac officially took over the monument, Croatian nationalists accused local Serbs of betraying the Croatian state by cooperating with the Hungarian government to erect a memorial to the Hungarian state doctrine on Croatian soil. Some Croatian papers charged the Serbian Orthodox priests with delivering bilingual speeches during the inauguration ceremony as a sign of their Magyarophilia; this claim was strongly denied by the editors of *Novo vreme*, the Serbian radical paper in Semlin.[95]

Serbian nationalists were certainly not supportive of the millennial memorial. The Radical Party's paper *Novo vreme* failed to publish a festive editorial or a detailed report of the inauguration ceremony. *Srbobran*, the paper of the Serbian Independent National Party published in Zagreb, harshly condemned the monument and the Croatian government. According to the editor of *Srbobran*, Semlin was a true Serbian town liberated from the Ottomans by overwhelmingly Serbian power; the article also held John Hunyadi to be a Serb. It furthermore criticized the Croatian government for supporting the Magyars instead of promoting the common Serbo-Croatian nation. The title of the report ("Zagorci u Zemunu") referred to the Zagore region in north Croatia, whose inhabitants spoke the Kajkavian dialect, in contrast to the Štokavian dialect, which was spoken in Semlin and was promoted by Serbian and Yugoslavist national leaders. The sources do not reveal in which dialect Minister Josipović delivered his speech but as he was born in north Croatia, he could be portrayed as a stranger in the town by stressing the difference between the vernaculars. For *Srbobran*, the monument thus symbolized the Magyarophilia of the Croatian government, a fake past, and ultimately the denial of the Serbian nation in Croatia.[96]

Carving the Magyar Nation in Stone and Bronze, 1896

Kálmán Thaly, a backward-looking prophet *per definitionem*, was successful in inscribing his historical and political vision onto the Hungarian landscape. Marked by the millennial signposts, the landscape now turned from ahistorical to historic, from an open, endless, and meaningless space into a closed and significant territory, from neutral to national. Whether people around these signposts became national was certainly another question; yet Thaly and his contemporaries firmly believed in the impact of memorials and the importance of the past to the people. Whether Thaly knew of Ernest Renan's lecture on the nation is not known but their thoughts coincided strikingly. Renan claimed that a nation was constituted of past and present, which mingle inseparably:

[The past] is the possession in common of a rich legacy of memories; the other [the present] is present-day consent, the desire to live together, the will to perpetuate the value of the heritage that one has received in an undivided form. ... The nation, like the individual, is the culmination of a long past of endeavours, sacrifice, and devotion. Of all cults, that of the ancestors is the most legitimate, for the ancestors have made us what we are. A heroic past, great men, glory (by which I understand genuine glory), this is the social capital upon which one bases a national idea. To have common glories in the past and to have a common will in the present; to have performed great deeds together, to wish to perform still more—these are the essential conditions for being a people.[97]

Thaly's millennial memorials indeed connected the past and the present and had a clear agenda for the future: they had to forge a single and united memory in order to ensure "the desire to live together" and to "perform great deeds together."

Invention was a key concept in this process in two stages. First, the past and the territory had to be invented; this had been already done by historians, authors, geographers, and all other intellectuals working on the national master narratives of history and space. Second, the very spaces which hosted the monuments were Thaly's own innovations. By building monuments on the margins of cities, Thaly created new public spaces, intended to be used for national purposes only. Their existence was justified by their attributed historic importance. In fact, they only pretended to be historic by their design and the references to events that had allegedly occurred during the Magyar conquest. The most innovation was needed in Nitra and Brassó: the Zobor and Cenk hills were certainly scenic places but were not even pseudo-historic; their only raison d'être was the millennial monument. Significant creativeness was needed in Pusztaszer, too, to make the metaphor of the Hungarian constitution material in the physical world. After all, until 1896, Pusztaszer was physically an empty and meaningless spot; it gained meaning only with the statue of Prince Árpád. The abandoned ruins in Theben and Semlin, the Munkács castle, and a side-hill in Pannonhalma could count as historic spaces but they were certainly outside of the public space used by the local populations. Hence, it was the millennial monuments that turned Theben and Semlin into "proper" national shrines. In fact, before 1896 only the Munkács castle and the Pannonhalma abbey were meaningful enough to need not invention but rather confirmation of their position as national shrines. Still, ways of national utilization had to be invented there too (closing up the prison and establishing a museum in the Munkács castle).

While various ways of invention were needed to create the new public space around the monuments, their symbolism was, despite the eclectic usage of historicist elements, univocal. The monuments demarcated the imagined Magyar national space and represented the monopoly of the Hungarian nation-state over the public space and the hegemony of the Hungarian state doctrine without any compromise or local alteration. Their features were not adjusted to local circumstances: Thaly and the organizers disregarded local initiatives about location (downtown instead of the castle in Munkács), symbols (Saxon symbols in Brassó), and style (neo-Romanesque instead of neo-Renaissance in Pannonhalma). The government paid attention only to the selection of the speakers at the inauguration ceremonies. Ministers with a locally meaning-ful portfolio were delegated (if such a connection could be justified). Thus, at the Austro-Hungarian border, the minister responsible for Hungary's relations with Austria was present; in Semlin the minister for Croatian affairs delivered a speech; at the Pannonhalma Archabbey the minister in charge of church affairs was the main speaker; and in Pusztaszer the minister of agriculture represented the government.[98]

Given the distance between urban spaces and the monuments, the inaugu-ration festivities were organized as a form of modern pilgrimage. The delega-tion of national notables and local guests convened in the towns. The historic space of the towns was used as a mere departure point, from where the delega-tion departed to the unveiling ceremony and returned afterwards. It is quite ironic that before the inauguration festivals of these millennial monuments, it was only the excursion of Ľudovít Štúr to Theben in 1836 that followed a somewhat similar pattern in constructing the national territory; in that case, the physical body of the Slovak nation was demarcated.

The inauguration rituals confirmed the status quo of fin-de-siècle Hungary. They echoed the liberal, Magyar nationalist middle class and its allies (in Pressburg the genuine German middle class, in Nitra moderate Catholics and Jews, in Munkács and at the Veretsky Pass Greek Catholic clergymen, in Brassó moderate Saxons, in Semlin conservative Croats and pragmatic Serbs). The organizers frequently labeled the ceremonies nonpartisan and serving only "patriotic" (in fact, Magyar nationalist) goals: that was how supporters of po-litical Catholicism and the Party of Independence were able to join the millen-nial rituals. This rhetoric was actually employed by Kálmán Thaly, too, who was able to lead the entire project according to his preferences, despite being a member of the parliamentary opposition. In the rhetoric of the festivities, two discourses, an ethnic Magyar and a state patriotic, intermingled inseparably.

The univocal millennial project was vulnerable from its very beginning. Not only did these monuments represent a single concept but their audience was necessarily limited too. Locating the monuments outside inhabited places, the main audience for Thaly's monument project was the middle class, whose members had enough time and resources to visit such places. Indeed, Thaly and the executors of the monument project sometimes even disregarded the demands of the local middle class: in Munkács the location of the monument caused some discontent while in Pannonhalma the relocation of the calvary and the style of the monument were somewhat criticized. Nonetheless, the very construction of a millennial monument was seen as confirmation of the national importance of the town and the abbey, respectively, and so these minor discontents did not seriously challenge the positive reception of the millennial project.

The participation of the lower classes is a more difficult issue, as exact numbers of guests are obviously not available. The government actively facilitated the participation of the masses: it organized transportation to and from the festivities, provided popular feasts after the ceremonies, while local authorities illuminated the streets and commissioned orchestras to play music. These tools were certainly apt to make the rural and small-town guests remember the millennial events. The abundance of food during the feasts and meeting (or at least seeing) the political and church leaders were a special treat for social classes which were used to the shortage of food and great distance between them and the elites. Forms of urban entertainment, such as orchestra music on the streets, were also exceptional and worth remembering. Certainly, within the limits of mass mobilization of the age, the Hungarian government managed to attract the largest possible audience to educate them on the ideal Magyar past of Hungary and the subsequent "correct" form of national identity. Press reports give the highest estimations at Pusztaszer and agree that the other ceremonies were also attended by thousands (with the exception of Semlin and Pannonhalma). The government and local authorities took an active role in attracting audiences by providing free travel, food, and entertainment; this was certainly enough to recruit some thousands. Furthermore, both press and governmental reports agree that the crowds in Munkács, at the Veretsky Pass, and at Pusztaszer sincerely shared enthusiasm for the past as represented on the monuments. In these locations, pre-modern conditions did not facilitate the formation of pillarized sub-societies; the Magyar past was plausible and the Magyar way of modernity appealing. Therefore, it can be supposed that the national education of the masses was efficient there.

Other groups, whose skepticism the Hungarian government was aware of, were consciously marginalized. Anthropologist Jan Kubik claims that "[i]n situations in which it is conceivable that the sociopolitical order can be contested and could fall apart or be replaced—but is temporarily invulnerable because of the overwhelming power of the ruler(s)—ceremonies can directly challenge the status quo."[99] In the year 1896, the overwhelming power in Hungary was in the hands of the liberal and Magyar nationalist elite. A direct challenge to the millennial festivities, i.e. straightforward representation of the counter-hegemonic discourse, was hardly possible. As freedom of the press was practically granted, papers could publish outraged editorials but more concrete deeds were limited by the authorities. Therefore, boycott seemed the best strategy to express discontent, as happened in the most extreme case, that of the Romanians in Brassó. Due to the pillarized society of Brassó, a Romanian-Orthodox sub-society came into being, whose elite elaborated a profoundly different historical narrative from the Magyar and strove for modernity within its own group. The government could neither convince nor force either the Romanian elite or the masses; thus, the Romanian absence at the millennial festivities aptly demonstrates the limits of Magyar national integration.

A number of individuals strikingly differed from the general patterns. In Nitra, Bishop Bende and some priests were active participants in the festivities, in sharp contrast to the majority of local clergy. In Brassó, Archdeacon Möller refused to cooperate with the government because of his Catholic political views. Bishop Lönhárt supported his decision, despite the absence of an organized Catholic party in Transylvania. In Munkács, some Jews decided to participate in the joyful millennial celebration instead of the Jewish mourning festivity. These cases do not challenge the picture drawn here but rather demonstrate the limits of social history when confronted with individual stories.

Notes

1. Kőváry, *A millennium lefolyásának története*, 124–66.
2. Márta Kovalovszky, "'Bronzba öntött halhatatlan': A historizmus emlékműszobrászata," in *A historizmus művészete Magyarországon: Művészettörténeti tanulmányok*, ed. Anna Zádor (Budapest: Magyar Tudományos Akadémia Művészettörténeti Kutató Intézet, 1993), 82.
3. Before 1896, Berczik constructed a handful of mansions only. János Szendrei and Gyula Szentiványi, *Magyar képzőművézek lexikona: Magyar és magyarországi vonatkozású művészek életrajzai a XII. századtól napjainkig* (Budapest: M. Kir. Vallás- és Közoktatásügyi Minisztérium, 1915), s.v. "Berczik Gyula."
4. Ferenc Pulszky to Sándor Wekerle, 19 December 1894. MNL OL, K 26 1895-22.I.A.623, box 333, 64–65.
5. "Jegyzőkönyv az ezredéves emlékmű és a Szent István szobor kivitelének ellenőrzésére hivatott művészbizottságnak Budapesten, 1895. szeptember hó 17-én tartott negyedik üléséről." MNL OL, K 26, 1895-22.I.A.712, box 332, 60–67.
6. Anna Zádor and István Gentheon, eds., *Művészeti lexikon* (Budapest: Akadémiai Kiadó, 1966), s.vv. "Bezerédi Gyula," "Jankovits Gyula," "Kallós Ede," and "Róna József."
7. Gyula Berczik to Kálmán Thaly, 8 October 1896, MNL OL P 1747, box 3, 7156; Gyula Wlassics to Kálmán Thaly, 18 October 1897, MNL OL P 1747, box 3, 8865.
8. Dezső Bánffy to Kálmán Thaly, 8 February 1896, MNL OL P 1747, box 2.
9. Kőváry, *A millennium lefolyásának története*, 126.
10. Thaly, *Az ezredévi*, 36–37.
11. Ibid., 21.
12. *Nyugatmagyarországi Hiradó* downplayed the importance of Theben's Slavic origin by denying its function as a Moravian capital, following the argumentation of Šafařík, cited in Chapter 3. György Valentényi, "Dévény vára," *Nyugatmagyarországi Hiradó*, 18 October 1896.

13. The *minister a latere* represented the Hungarian government at the imperial and royal court in Vienna. His main duty was mediation between the monarch and the government.

14. "Das Fest in Theben," *Preßburger Zeitung*, 19 October 1896; Gyula Zsigárdy, *Beszéd, melyet Zsigárdy Gyula a dévényi millenáris szobor leleplezésénél mondott* (Galánta: Első Galánthai Nyomda, 1896). Zsigárdy published his speech in Slovak too.

15. "Ünnep a zajban," *Pesti Napló*, 18 October 1896; "Az utolsó millenniumi emlékek," *Pesti Napló*, 19 October 1896.

16. "A dévényi ünnep," *Nyugatmagyarországi Hiradó*, 18 October 1896; "A dévényi ezre-déves emlékmű felavatása," *Nyugatmagyarországi Hiradó*, 19 October 1896; Ernő Radó, "Dévény: A dévényi ünnep," *Nyugatmagyarországi Hiradó*, 21 October 1896.

17. "Das Fest in Theben," *Preßburger Zeitung*, 19 October 1896; "Die Einweihung des Thebener Millenniumsdenkmales," *Westungarischer Grenzbote*, 19 October 1896.

18. "Die Einweihung des Thebener Millenniums-Denkmales," *Preßburger Tagblatt*, 19 October 1896.

19. "Millennárne pomniky," *Slovenské noviny*, 20 October 1896.

20. Thaly, *Az ezredévi*, 35–37.

21. ŠANPN, 181. Minutes of the assembly of the town of Nyitra, 30 August 1896.

22. "A honalapítás zobori emlékművének leleplezése," *Nyitramegyei Közlöny*, 6 September 1896; "A zoborhegyi ünnep," *Nyitramegyei Szemle*, 3 September 1896; "Der 30-te August," *Nyitrai Lapok (Neutra-Trenchiner Zeitung)*, 6 September 1896.

23. "Az ünnepély lefolyása," *Nyitramegyei Közlöny*, 30 August 1896; "Die Einweihungsfeier der Zoborer Millenniums-Denkmales," *Nyitrai Lapok (Neutra-Trenchiner Zeitung)*, 30 August 1896.

24. "A nyitra-zoborhegyi ünnep," *Magyar Állam*, 2 September 1896; "Perczel miniszter Nyitrán," *Nyitramegyei Szemle*, 3 September 1896.

25. "A millenniumi emlék leleplezése," *Nyitramegyei Szemle*, 30 August 1896; "Der 30-te August," *Nyitrai Lapok (Neutra-Trenchiner Zeitung)*, 6 September 1896. The archives of the Nitra diocese are not available for research, therefore in-depth analysis of the clergy's concerns is not possible.

26. "Fel a szivekkel," *Nyitramegyei Szemle*, 30 August 1896.

27. "A honalapítás zobori műemlékének leleplezése," *Nyitramegyei Közlöny*, 30 August 1896.

28. "Willkommen!" *Nyitrai Lapok (Neutra-Trenchiner Zeitung)*, 30 August 1896.

29. "Eine tausendjährige Geschichte," *Neutraer Zeitung-Nyitrai Hírlap*, 29 August 1896.

30. "Slávnost' na Zobore," *Slovenské noviny*, 1 September 1896.

31. Popovics, *Munkács kultúrtörténete*, 90–91.

32. The bibliographer József Szinnyei even claimed that this prayer saved the Magyar character of the festivity's ecclesiastical section, probably referring to the Greek Catholic mass. Szinnyei, *Magyar írók*, s.v. "Kiss Áron."

33. Kőváry, *A millennium lefolyásának története*, 128–29.

34. "A munkácsi Árpád-ünnep," *Budapest Hírlap*, 20 July 1896.

35. Sándor Lónyay to Mór Balajthy, 26 June 1896, DAZO, 10, 5–211, 133.

36. Endre Kiss, "Utóhangok: Milleniumi beszámoló," *Bereg*, 9 August 1896.

37. "Magyarok utja," *Pesti Hirlap*, 23 July 1896; "A rutének," *Pesti Napló*, 22 July 1896.

38. "Munkács ünnepe," *Pesti Hirlap*, 19 July 1896; "A munkácsi emlék-ünnep," *Pesti Hirlap*, 20 July 1896; "A munkácsi ünnepek," *Alkotmány*, 19 July 1896; "A munkácsi ünnepségek," *Alkotmány*, 21 July 1896.

39. Lajos Hartstein, "Munkácsi levél," and Viador, "A munkácsi eset," *Zsidó Hiradó*, 23 July 1896; "A munkácsi 'magyar párt'," *Zsidó Hiradó*, 30 July 1896; "Der Munkatscher Fall," *Allgemeine Jüdische Zeitung*, 22 July 1896.

40. "A munkácsi ünnepségek," *Alkotmány*, 21 July 1896; "A munkácsi emlék-ünnep," *Pesti Hirlap*, 20 July 1896.
41. Mardochai Hajehudi, "A munkácsi zsidók magukviselete," *Egyenlőség*, 31 July 1896.
42. A film shot in 1933, more than forty years after the millennial year and more than a decade after the establishment of the modernizing Czechoslovak Republic, proves that local Jews still wore their traditional caftans. See "Jewish Life in Munkatch—March 1933," YouTube, http://www.youtube.com/watch?v=rp1OeIf0D0w (accessed 25 March 2012).
43. Dezső Bánffy to the Council of Brassó, 13 June 1895, DJBAN, 1, VI–1895/85–3; Memo of the Council of Brassó to Mihály Maurer, 5 October 1895, DJBAN, 1, VI–1895/85–4; Mihály Maurer to the Council of Brassó, 7 September 1896, DJBAN, 1, VI–1895/85–9; Dezső Bánffy to Mihály Maurer, 15 September 1896, DJBAN, 2, 1896/8.
44. "Die Einweihung des Millenniumsdenkmals auf der Zinne," *Kronstädter Zeitung*, 15 September 1896.
45. "Ein schmachvoller Tag," *Kronstädter Zeitung*, 17 September 1896.
46. The reasons for Schnell's vote are unclear; in his memoirs, he emphasized only that the Greens rejected the millennial memorial without highlighting his own position. Moreover, he stressed his initiative as a mayor to build a large monument to commemorate the German colonization of the town. Karl Ernst Schnell, *Aus meinem Leben: Erinnerungen aus alter und neuer Zeit* (Kronstadt: Honterusdruckerei, 1934), 45–46.
47. Minutes of the assembly of Brassó, 16–17 September 1896, 306–16, DJBAN, 1, IV. A 152.
48. "Ein schmachvoller Tag," *Kronstädter Zeitung*, 17 September 1896.
49. "Afacerea monumentului lui Arpad," *Gazeta Transilvaniei*, 6/18 September 1896.
50. "Zur Millenniumsdebatte in unserer Stadtvertretung," *Kronstädter Tageblatt*, 19 September 1896.
51. "Noch einmal das Zinnendenkmal: Eine Stimme vom Lande," *Kronstädter Tageblatt*, 25 September 1896.
52. "A gyalázat napja," *Brassói Lapok*, 24 September 1896.
53. József Pótsa to Dezső Perczel, 25 September 1896, MNL OL, K 148, 1896–II–20.
54. Ibid.
55. Ede Möller to Ferenc Lönhardt, 20 September 1896, GYÉL, I. 1/a, 1896–4–3584.
56. Mihály Maurer to Ferenc Lönhardt, 15 September 1896, DJBAN, 2, 1896/7.
57. Ede Möller to Ferenc Lönhardt, 20 September 1896, GYÉL, I. 1/a, 1896–4–3584.
58. "Die Einweihung des Zinnendenkmals und unsere Frauenvereine," *Kronstädter Zeitung*, 17 October 1896.
59. "Willkommen!" *Kronstädter Zeitung*, 16 October 1896; "Bischof Dr. Müller in Kronstadt," *Kronstädter Zeitung*, 17 October 1896.
60. *Gazeta Transilvaniei* claimed that among the horsemen there were also four riders in Romanian dress, but three of them were Roma wearing borrowed dress and the fourth lived in the neighboring, mostly Magyar-speaking Hétfalu district, and was thus a potential renegade. If it was true, this is a telling sign of the illusion organized by the authorities to prove the comprehensive support for the celebration. See "Tămbălăul milenar din Brașov," *Gazeta Transilvaniei*, 6/18 October 1896. The Roma of the region spoke Romanian. See August Jekelius, *Die Burzenländer Zigeuner im Jahre 1893* (Kronstadt: J. Gött's Sohn, n. d.).
61. "Perczel Dezső belügyminiszter Brassóban," *Brassói Lapok*, 20 October 1896.
62. Ibid.
63. *Rede Sr. Hochwürden des Herrn Bischofs Dr. Friedrich Müller, gehalten bei dem zu seinen Ehren Freitag den 17. Oktober 1896 in Kronstadt veranstalteten Bankette* (Kronstadt: Schlandt, n. d.).
64. "Perczel Dezső belügyminiszter Brassóban," *Brassói Lapok*, 20 October 1896.

65. "Áll a szobor…" *Brassói Lapok*, 20 October 1896.
66. *Annual Report of the State Realschule in Brassó*, 1896/97, 16–17.
67. "Treue um Treue: Zur Einweihung des Zinnendenkmals," *Kronstädter Tageblatt*, 17 October 1896.
68. "Unser Bischof," *Kronstädter Tageblatt*, 16 October 1896; "Willkommen!" *Kronstädter Zeitung*, 16 October 1896; "Bischof Dr. Müller in Kronstadt," *Kronstädter Zeitung*, 17 October 1896; "Unser Bischof in Kronstadt," *Kronstädter Tageblatt*, 17 October 1896; "Unser Bischof in Kronstadt," *Kronstädter Tageblatt*, 19 October 1896; "Das Fest in Kronstadt," *Siebenbürgisch-Deutsches Tageblatt*, 20 October 1896; "Unser Bischof in Kronstadt," *Siebenbürgisch-Deutsches Tageblatt*, 21 October 1896.
69. "Állam elleni kihágás," *Brassói Lapok*, 27 October 1896.
70. Ernő Mihályi, *Pannonhalma részletes kalauza* (Budapest: Turistaság és Alpinizmus, 1923), 5.
71. Minutes of the Archabbey Convent, 23 April 1895, 79–82, PFL, I.1.g.
72. Thaly, *Az ezredévi*, 23–26; Samu Wargha, *Pannonhalmán a Kálvária áthelyezése alkalmával 1896. évi julius 26-án tartott beszéd* (Győr: Győregyházmegye Könyvnyomtató Intézete, 1896).
73. Thaly, *Az ezredévi*, 24.
74. "Kifogások a pannonhalmi emlékmű ellen," *Magyar Állam*, 30 August 1896.
75. Halbik, *Pannonhalma a milleniumon*; Döme Vojnits, *Pannonhalmán 1896. aug. 26-án, az országos millenniumi ünnepélyen tartott beszéd* (Esztergom: Laiszky János, 1896).
76. *Győrvármegye törvényhatósági bizottságának*.
77. "A pannonhalmi orsz. ünnep," *Győri Hirlap*, 27 August 1896; "Pannonhalmi ünnep," *Dunántúli Hirlap*, 27 August 1896; "Wlassics Gyula beszéde," *Győri Közlöny*, 27 August 1896.
78. In spite of serious electoral manipulations, the Party of Independence dominated both the city of Szeged and Congrád County. Fodor, "A magyarországi országgyűlési képviselőválasztási kerületek"; Toth, *Parteien und Reichstagswahlen*, 161.
79. "A pusztaszeri orsz. Árpád-ünnep," *Szegedi Hiradó*, 28 June 1896; "A pusztaszeri ünnepek," *Szegedi Napló*, 28 June 1896.
80. "Árpád felmagasztalása," *Budapesti Hirlap*, 27 June 1896; "Pusztaszer," *Magyar Állam*, 28 June 1896; "A pusztaszeri ünnepély," *Magyar Állam*, 1 July 1896.
81. Kőváry, *A millennium lefolyásának története*, 141–46.
82. "Das Millenniums-Denkmal in Semlin," *Agramer Zeitung*, 21 September 1896; "Die Millenniumsfeier," *Oestlicher Grenz-Bote*, 26 September 1896; "Odkriće milenijskog spomenika u Zemunu," *Narodne novine*, 21 September 1896; "Semliner Festtage," *Die Drau*, 22 September 1896.
83. "Odkriće milenijskog spomenika u Zemunu," *Narodne novine*, 21 September 1896.
84. "Die Enthüllung des Millennium-Denkmals in Semlin," *Slavonische Presse*, 22 September 1896; "Die Millenniumsfeier," *Oestlicher Grenz-Bote*, 26 September 1896.
85. "Die Enthüllung des Millennium-Denkmals in Semlin," *Die Drau*, 20 September 1896.
86. "Határkövek," *Budapesti Hirlap*, 20 September 1896; "A zimonyi ünnep," *Pesti Napló*, 21 September 1896.
87. Minutes of the town assembly, 1896–97, IAB, 1180.
88. Minutes of the meeting of the Semlin magistracy, 28 April 1896, IAB, 10, box 3477, 5295/96, and box 3601, 5 and 14.
89. The file "Millennial monument in Semlin of the Presidency of the Provincial Government, Zagreb" (1391/1895, box 6–14, HDA, 78) deals almost exclusively with the purchase of the memorial's territory. More practical issues were probably delegated to the Lord Lieutenant of Srem County, but I have been unable to locate these documents.

90. "Eine Stimme zur Millenniums-Feier," *Oestlicher Grenz-Bote*, 26 September 1896.
91. What is sure is that the festive mass in the Catholic church was celebrated by a Novi Sad priest. "A zimonyi ünnep," *Budapesti Hirlap*, 21 September 1896.
92. "Magjarska slava na hrvatskom zemljištu," *Obzor*, 22 September 1896.
93. "Uviek nešto nova," *Hrvatska domovina*, 21 September 1896.
94. "Kroatischer Landtag," *Agramer Zeitung*, 24 November 1896.
95. "Kakvi su naši Srbi," *Novo vreme*, 26 September 1896.
96. "'Zagorci' u Zemunu," *Srbobran*, 10/22 September 1896.
97. Ernest Renan, "What Is a Nation?" Unknown translator. http://web.archive.org/web/20110827065548/http://www.cooper.edu/humanities/core/hss3/e_renan.html (accessed 14 January 2014).
98. Vadas, "Programtervezetek," 29.
99. Jan Kubik, *The Power of Symbols against the Symbols of Power: The Rise of Solidarity and the Fall of State Socialism in Poland* (University Park, PA: The Pennsylvania State University Press, 1994), 247.

Chapter 12

THE MILLENNIAL MONUMENTS IN THE PUBLIC SPACE, 1896–1918

∞

By the end of the festive year, 1896, the splendid inauguration celebrations had passed and emotions had calmed down. The Hungarian government achieved its goal of carving its main political principles in stone and bronze at several distinguished locations; whether locals accepted these ideas or not, they had to tolerate the erection of the memorials. The task of the millennial monuments, however, was far from being fulfilled, as they were intended to distribute and strengthen Magyar national identity in the long term and to remind locals of the "correct" reading of the past and of its consequences. The crucial question was how these monuments functioned in the following years.

To complicate things, the millennial ardor opened Pandora's Box and provoked the construction of memorials throughout the country, leading to symbolic competition for the public space.[1] Until the millennial year there were hardly any modern public monuments in the provincial towns of Hungary, but the two decades between 1896 and World War I witnessed a mushrooming of memorials. Most of these new public monuments were initiated, designed, and financed by local actors, and represented the topics most meaningful to the local audience.[2]

Due to the power relations in the country, these new symbols had to be compatible with the Magyar historical master narrative, even if they expressed a different identity. One of the few such cases was a monument to the Saxon Lutheran bishop and historian Georg Daniel Teutsch, erected in 1898 in Hermannstadt. Teutsch was an honored church leader and promoted a historical narrative partly compatible with the Magyar one, therefore his memory served as a useful tool for Saxon self-understanding, while not directly challenging the Hungarian state doctrine.[3]

Árpád and Maria Theresa

The Theben monument quickly became part of the Magyar national canon. A typical popular booklet started:

> The traveler coming by boat from Vienna reaches the Hungarian border at Dévény. One cannot imagine a more uplifting view than the steep and great rock at the border which, as a warning sign made by God's hand, draws the traveler's attention to the fact that here begins the empire of St. Stephen, whose borders shall be respected.[4]

The monument was also often depicted in publications, for instance in the Pressburg County chapter of the *Kronprinzenwerk*[5] and in the historical chapter of the official county monograph, which opened with a picture of Theben castle and its millennial memorial.[6]

Besides publications, the millennial memorial of Theben also attracted a large number of visitors. A day after its unveiling, eleven hundred high school students visited the memorial, performing the usual national songs, poems, and so on.[7] Until 1918, similar national excursions on a smaller scale were part of the everyday practice of national education in Pressburg high schools, as at least twenty-eight trips were made to the castle.[8] In 1898 a few members of the Hungarian Tourist Association visited the Theben and the Zobor monuments. In Pressburg, the tourists met some members of the Magyar middle class of the city, among them Gábor Pávai Vajna, the doctor whose arguments for a local university were analyzed in Chapter 3, and Gyula Zsigárdy, the lawyer who delivered a speech at the inauguration festival of the monument.[9] These excursions were made despite the shortcomings of the monument and its environment. The governmental project in 1896 had erected a memorial only, but due to insufficient time and money it failed to turn the ruins into a proper tourist destination. The millennial monument stood literally in the middle of a ruined area. The situation was made even worse by the ambiguous legal position of the monument: it was built by the government and then passed to the county without defining the exact duties of each party. Finally, in 1907, a governmental agency, the National Committee of Art Relics, took over all seven millennial monuments. In 1910, the original owner of the castle, Count Miklós Pálffy, donated a large sum, twenty thousand crowns, for comprehensive development of the castle. However, these plans were never completed, probably due to the outbreak of World War I.[10]

The Theben monument failed to fulfill the demands of the elites of Pressburg both to commemorate the millennium and to represent local identity and the local reading of the past. The most immediate example of local statuomania came from Pressburg itself. The city insisted on building its own millennial memorial, which would better represent the local reading of the past and refer more to the city itself. This task was achieved by the monument dedicated to Queen Maria Theresa, unveiled in 1897.

Figure 12.1. The Maria Theresa monument in Pressburg. Courtesy of the Zemplén Museum, Szerencs.

The idea for a monument to Maria Theresa emerged in 1892. A local politician, Karl Neisidler, proposed celebrating the twenty-fifth anniversary of the coronation of Francis Joseph in 1892 by erecting a monument to Maria Theresa. Neisidler's idea was endorsed by the entire municipal assembly. The construction of the monument was delayed due to financial problems, but the millennial year provided enough inspiration to complete the project. The memorial represented the overlapping layers of Pressburg identity well. The monument sought to illustrate the importance of the city in the past and the present, to highlight its eternal loyalty to the royal family, and to confirm its love for the homeland. The memorial showed Queen Maria Theresa in her full glory, reminding viewers that Pressburg had flourished under her reign.

The monument completely fulfilled these expectations. First, it confirmed the royal loyalty of the city by the figure of the glorious queen and the main inscription, which was written in Latin: *Vitam et sanguinem*. This is a clear reference to the famous Pressburg Diet in 1741, when the Hungarian estates offered their "life and blood" as an oath of allegiance to Maria Theresa in the ongoing War of Austrian Succession. The loyalty of the city to the Habsburg family was appreciated by Francis Joseph, who participated in the unveiling ceremony.

Second, the monument displayed the loyalty of the city to Hungary. The monument's dedication was scheduled for the millennial celebrations as a local contribution to the national festivities, but its inauguration had to be delayed because of problems at the marble mine in Carrara. The actual foundation of the memorial contained soil from every Hungarian county, including soil from historically important places such as the field of the tragic 1526 battle of Mohács, and several other battlefields and *lieux de mémoire*. The right-side figure, a Hungarian aristocrat pointing south, was interpreted by everyone as a symbol of the country's loyalty to its queen.[11]

Finally, the monument proudly displayed Pressburger self-confidence. According to the official leaflet from the ceremony, the left-side figure was an armed citizen, displaying the city's contribution to national history and culture. Together, the two side figures represented the unity and the equal contributions of the Hungarian nobility and the city-dwellers.[12] Furthermore, the memorial represented the city's vast financial resources, since it cost eighty-five thousand florins, almost three times more than the state-sponsored one in Theben. *Preßburger Zeitung* proudly remarked that this monument was the first large-scale memorial in Hungary to be financed by a city rather than the central government. It also showcased local artistic talent, as the sculptor was Pressburg-born János Fadrusz, whereas Budapest artists designed and built the Theben monument. Since no other Hungarian cities except for Budapest planned such a huge project for the millennium, the memorial seemed to reconfirm the "second capital of Hungary" concept.[13]

The city-centered narrative was strengthened by the festive theatrical performance following the unveiling ceremony. The performance was produced by city archivist Johann Batka, a representative of the city's traditional German-speaking middle class. It displayed six scenes from the history of the city, all of them having dynastic or national significance, such as the election of Ferdinand I in 1526 and the 1741 Diet. All of these scenes referred to the overlapping strata of Pressburg's identity, especially its historical relevance throughout the course of Hungarian history and its plural loyalties, meaning national and royal.[14] German dailies celebrated the monument as the embodiment of Pressburg's multilevel identity, emphasizing both the historical importance of the city and its loyalties to the Habsburgs and Hungary. In their understanding, the *city* was the main actor.[15]

The Magyar national press, however, offered a slightly different interpretation of the events, putting the *nation* at the center. Most of the Magyar press, including the local *Nyugatmagyarországi Hiradó*, held that the left-side figure was an ordinary Magyar soldier who represented the different strata of the Magyar noble nation but downplayed the importance of the local bourgeoisie.[16] The inscription also displayed the country's loyalty to the monarch. The monument reminded *Nyugatmagyarországi Hiradó* of the Magyarization of the city because the memorial was built in "true Magyar" artistic style. This differentiated it from the works of Viktor Tilgner, the other famous Pressburg-born sculptor of the period, whose sculptures on the Vienna Ringstraße led to accusations of cosmopolitanism. Moreover, *Nyugatmagyarországi Hiradó* vigorously emphasized the generosity of the Hungarian nation (as opposed to the city), which had helped the empire in times of trouble. One of the articles anachronistically attributed the development of Magyar national culture to Maria Theresa, which would have allowed for the placement of the queen in the Magyar national pantheon. Another article inspired by the monument argued that the founding of a university in Pressburg was necessary to Magyarize the city sufficiently.[17] The annual report of the state-run Realschule delivered the clearest example of this nation-centered narrative: the participation of the students in the ceremonies for the monument was offered as evidence of the faithfulness of the nation but the city's role in building the monument was not mentioned at all.[18]

The reports of the German papers show that for the German-speaking Pressburgers the Maria Theresa monument, financed by the city and built by a local artist, was the artifact to represent their own identity. The Theben memorial remained an object on the margin of their world, being constructed outside of the city, financed by the central government, and carved by a Budapest sculptor. At the same time, the local Magyar public interpreted both monuments as representations of the Magyar national idea and used them for national purposes. The Maria Theresa memorial could be read as a monument to both local and Magyar national identity.

In the following years, the Magyarization of the urban space of Pressburg went further, preventing such overlapping artifacts. In 1911, the memorial to Johann Nepomuk Hummel was removed from the promenade to a side street, in order to be replaced by a monument to Sándor Petőfi, the most celebrated Magyar romantic poet. Petőfi's Magyar national importance was beyond doubt, although his direct connection to the city was rather marginal and definitely weaker than that of the Pressburg-born Hummel.[19]

The Lonely *Turul*

The millennial monument in Nitra seemed to have a relatively low impact on the town's urban space. Even local Magyar national activists did not use the monument actively, nor can commitment be seen in publications about the town. One of the few examples is related to the Hungarian Tourist Association. In the course of an organized tour in 1898, A mere six Budapest-based members were interested enough to visit the monument; they, however, were even received by the mayor.[20]

Of the towns investigated here, Nitra was the only one where no local initiative for another monument emerged. In the years following 1896, a few streets were renamed, representing the different readings of the town. These new street names included several local bishops, St. Stephen and St. Ladislaus I, politicians with local attachments who were also active on a national level (János Bottyán, general of Francis II Rákóczi and citizen of the town, and Vilmos Tóth, lord lieutenant and later minister of the interior), Francis Joseph and Queen Elisabeth, and Lajos Kossuth and Ferenc Deák, two outstandingly important figures in the Magyar national pantheon who nevertheless lacked particular local references.[21] Large-scale public celebrations were also absent. The commemoration of Francis II Rákóczi in 1906 was held for an exclusive audience in the town's assembly hall.[22] It seems that any national identity in the town remained superficial and the millennial memorial definitely failed to challenge this.

The Monopoly of Árpád

The public of Munkács was convinced of the town's importance in the history of Hungary and wished to see it represented in a tangible way. At first glance, the millennial monument seemed to have satisfied this need. Yet the monument itself was not enough. The prison was removed from the castle but none of the planned developments, except the millennial memorial, were actually carried out; neither a national historical museum nor the shrine of the Rákóczi family were built in the fortress. As the mortal remains of the Rákóczi family were reburied in Kassa and Käsmark in 1906, the hope of turning Munkács castle into a national museum and an often-visited shrine had to be given up. The castle stood empty in the following years; large-scale national usage remained a dream.

The Magyar national elite of Munkács understood this threat early on and argued for location of the millennial memorial in the main square. As Kálmán Thaly insisted on locating the millennial monument in the castle, the public of Munkács decided to build its own monument downtown. Initiatives to build an Árpád monument in the town had already been discussed; this idea

Figure 12.2. The model of the planned Árpád monument in Munkács. Courtesy of the Museum of Hungarian Agriculture, Budapest.

was revitalized during the millennial year. In March 1896, donations for the Árpád memorial downtown started to be collected to keep pace with the state-sponsored monument. However, the middle class of Munkács was weak and it took almost two decades to raise enough funds. Finally, sufficient money was gathered by the eve of World War I and the statue was almost finished in the atelier of György Vastagh Jr., a Budapest sculptor. Vastagh was known for his animal sculptures and a few historic works, such as a statue of the Transylvanian prince Gabriel Bethlen in Budapest (1903) and an equestrian statue of Francis II Rákóczi in Szeged (1912).[23] The memorial would have been erected on the Árpád square and it would have displayed the glorious Prince Árpád riding a horse. It would have carried the same historical narrative as the state-sponsored millennial memorial. The outbreak of the war, however, prevented this achievement. For patriotic reasons, part of the money collected over two decades was offered for a war loan; the town never regained this sum and the memorial was never built. Ironically, meanwhile, an electric pylon was constructed on the planned site of the monument, contributing to the modern urban development of the town but disregarding the protest of the patrons of the Árpád memorial.[24]

Árpád and Honterus

It is not surprising that the Brassó millennial monument provoked great emotional reactions long after its inauguration. Due to its location, its visibility from most of the streets downtown, and its explicit Magyar national symbolism, the memorial could not be overlooked. The monument was used extensively by the local Magyar public. The Magyar media also commemorated the inauguration of the memorial. The Catholic schools frequently held festivities at the statue; they made processions around 18 October in the following years to commemorate its inauguration. During these processions, patriotic speeches, songs, and poems were performed.[25] These excursions meant an important shift in the use of public space, as demonstrations in the town and subsequent excursions to the mountains were part of the routines of both the Saxon and the Romanian youth; now Magyar students joined this practice too.[26] The Transylvanian Carpathian Association (Erdélyrészi Kárpát-Egyesület), dedicated to promoting local tourism, held its general assembly in 1903 in Brassó; part of the program was an excursion to the millennial monument.[27] The Transylvanian Museum Association (Erdélyi Múzeum Egyesület), an association promoting regional research, held its annual meeting in Brassó in 1907 and also made an excursion to the memorial, where the national anthem and other songs were performed, and a patriotic speech was delivered.[28] The well-known fairytale collector and author, Elek Benedek, expressed well the sentiments of many Magyar national activists when, climbing the hill and looking at the monument, he turned, astonished:

> The eye and spirit cannot have enough of the splendor. Who desires to leave for another country from here? And who would dare to take a fancy to this precious territory sanctified by blood, since here stands Árpád, the monument to the conqueror Árpád. The heroic figure of the conqueror stands on the top of a great column and it seems to me that he not only conquered this land, but keeps guard over it, too. … I feel my heart swell and I spontaneously begin to recite *Szózat*: To your homeland …[29]

Local Saxons and Romanians did not share the same feelings. The town council, still dominated by Saxons, refused to offer any kind of financial support for the monument. In 1898, the town council rejected co-financing a metal fence around the monument, referring to the former town decision giving over the territory of the monument to the state, and refused to make any contribution to the maintenance costs. The government and local Magyar council members tried to persuade the town council to change its decision. Following a long debate, the council was willing to take moral guard over the memorial but still refused to make any financial contribution.[30] Saxons in fact never regarded the monument as their own. Local author Adolf Meschendörfer juxtaposed the governmental monument and his local identity: "The lords in Budapest plan for their millennial festivity to erect an Árpád monument on the Zinne above the town—in our city!"[31]

The Romanian reception of the monument was even more radical. The memorial had such a deep impact on the minds of local Romanian national activists that it was condemned by several authors even decades after its inauguration and demolition. The booklet *Brașov: Romanians and Saxons* by the Romanian nationalist author Andrei Popovici, published in 1923, opens with:

> The face of Brașov changed in the course of only one day, became Magyar, from a peaceful German-Romanian town became a Magyar nest, above which on the top of the Tâmpa [the Romanian name of Cenk] the most Mongolian figure stood, who never even entered Brașov, a Magyar idol, a Magyar stone symbol.[32]

Another example of condemnation of the millennial memorial is the collection of Hungarian government documents published by Ion Bozdog. Bozdog aimed to denounce the "oppressive" policy of dualist Hungary toward the Romanians; the millennial memorial was seen as so important that no less than one-seventh of this collection was dedicated to the monument and the celebrations.[33]

The monument was an object not only of verbal condemnation, but also of various physical attacks. In 1901 an unknown person shot at it, damaging the top of the figure,[34] and in 1902 it was damaged by metal tools.[35] The Magyar press routinely blamed Romanians for these attacks, but as the perpetrators were never found, this suspicion could not be proved. To protect the memorial, an iron fence was built around it in 1903, financed by donations from local Magyar citizens.[36]

In 1913, the memorial was damaged by a bomb attack by the Bessarabian Romanian adventurer Ilie Cătărău and his companion Tomiftei Kirilov.[37] Although the perpetrators were not identified for some months, the Magyar public immediately blamed local Romanians. Local Magyars were outraged; on the day following the attack, *Brassói Lapok* claimed that the monument symbolized the nation and the Hungarian state, and therefore the attack was a direct assault on all of Hungary.[38] On the next day, pupils of the Roman Catholic elementary schools and gymnasium marched to the monument, where a priest said a prayer; this was followed by recitations of patriotic poems. The attack had not ruined only the statue itself, but also its function as a shrine; this ritual re-sacralized the monument.[39]

However, the "re-consecration" of the monument could not protect it; a couple of months after the attack a storm caused the figure to fall and only the column remained standing. The reaction of Brassó citizens was predictable, as reported in *Brassói Lapok*: "The monument was visited by curious people during the morning and its view provoked different reactions in visitors, *depending on their nationality* [my emphasis]. Many of them stood there awed by seeing the terrible view of ruin, while some others could not hide their malicious joy."[40] Although the reconstruction of the memorial was initiated immediately, World War I put an end to this plan. When the Romanian army conquered Brassó temporarily in 1916, it demolished the ruins further.

The millennial memorial thus remained alien for the non-Magyars and it soon provoked a symbolic response. The Saxon elite, possessing wide resources and power to manipulate the urban space, made an attempt to reconquer the town by symbolic means shortly after the millennial year. The year 1898 provided a good occasion for this re-conquest, as it marked the four hundredth anniversary of the birth of the great church reformer Johannes Honterus. The first idea for a Honterus memorial emerged as early as 1845, during the celebration of the three hundredth anniversary of the opening of the local Lutheran gymnasium. In 1857, a memorial plaque was inaugurated at Honterus's birthplace in the town center. The idea of celebrating the four hundredth anniversary of Honterus's birth emerged in 1882 and a year later the first donations for the monument were collected.[41] These anniversary celebrations finally provided enough inspiration to complete the project.

The monument, a work by Harro Magnussen (a Berlin sculptor famous for his statues of Bismarck), made a great impression on the public.[42] The monument was mostly financed by the Transylvanian Saxon public, church congregations, schools, and private donations. Some other donations came from Austrian and German contributors.[43] The festive inauguration was attended by

Kronstadt

Honterus-Denkmal

Figure 12.3. The Honterus monument in Brassó. Courtesy of the Zemplén Museum, Szerencs.

the entire Saxon elite: Bishop Müller, many Lutheran pastors, elders, teachers, politicians, all the major Saxon associations, and thousands of "ordinary" Saxon people from all over the Transylvanian Saxon counties wearing traditional costumes also participated in the celebration. Local non-Saxon politicians, including the lord lieutenant, clerks of Brassó County, ministers of other religions, and representatives of non-governmental institutions, also took part. The day of the celebration started with a march of Saxon youth and associations through the town center. The celebratory speeches emphasized the extraordinary importance of Honterus, and Protestantism in general, in preserving the Saxon people throughout the centuries. For a whole week Saxon associations held festive meetings in the town, conquering the urban space of Brassó with public events such as singing or athletic performances.[44] A festive drama by the best-known contemporary Saxon author, Traugott Teutsch, was also performed.[45] To anchor Honterus and the Saxon historical narrative in the minds of the people, numerous articles and biographies were published in newspapers, popular calendars, and books, addressing both popular and academic audiences.[46]

The Saxon papers emphasized the religious character of the celebration. When discussing the Saxon identity related to the monument, it was stressed that Saxon national feeling was not hostile toward any other ethnic group.[47] As open national messages were not expressed, both the Magyar and Romanian press welcomed the new statue. *Brassói Lapok*, although previously suspicious of the Saxon celebrations because of the invitation of some pan-German associations and their Austrian leader Georg Schönerer, also emphasized the religious character of the festivities and argued that the monument was proof of Hungarian tolerance.[48] *Gazeta Transilvaniei* also reported on the celebrations in a positive manner.[49]

Although the Honterus project started long before 1896 and there was no direct reference to the millennial monument, the Honterus memorial may still be interpreted as a response to the millennial challenge. The monument was erected by the Lutheran Church and it demonstrated the organic and historical legitimation of the Saxons, in contrast to the millennial memorial, which was considered to be ahistorical and externally forced. The Honterus memorial was financed by Saxon society, demonstrating its civil values, again in contrast to the governmental Cenk memorial.

Árpád and Astrik

The Pannonhalma monument was completed in the years following the inauguration. Although its inner decorations were painted by disciples of Károly Lotz, a prestigious painter of the time, the millennial monument was dwarfed by the complex of the abbey, which was greater in size and historically far more interesting. Contemporary descriptions focused on the abbey itself and mentioned the millennial chapel only as an auxiliary building.[50] The millennial chapel, even though its message was compatible with the Benedictine reading of the place, thus remained quite peripheral.

In order to demonstrate its patriotic feelings, the Benedictine Order donated three hundred crowns for the maintenance of the monument each year. This donation is in sharp contrast to Győr County, which was in charge of the maintenance of the millennial chapel. In fact, Győr County hardly paid the costs of the monument's maintenance, not on principle but for financial reasons, leading to a serious deterioration of the building. The Benedictine donation was paid each year until 1906, when the government took over the complete maintenance of the monument and financed some renovation works.[51]

The millennial chapel did not satisfy the symbolic needs of the Order. As has been discussed above, an initiative to erect a monument to Astrik, the first abbot of the abbey, who was also known as the person who brought the Holy Crown from Rome to St. Stephen, had already emerged before the idea of the state-sponsored millennial memorial. In 1895, the Order requested the inclusion of the statue of Astrik in the millennial memorial but this wish was rejected, as a figure did not fit into the temple-like design of the millennial monument. The Order then erected the monument to Astrik on its own in the courtyard of the monastery a year later, in 1897.[52]

A Race for Árpád

Due to its peripheral location, direct use of the monument in Pusztaszer was so complicated that even public bodies ignored it after the final unveiling ceremony. Instead, a gentlemen's club in Szeged, founded in 1895 with the exclusive aim of going out on Saturday evenings in search of gastronomic pleasures and heavy drinking, began to make annual excursions to the memorial from 1897. To combine national commitment with gastronomy, food believed to be traditionally Magyar was served during these excursions. Needless to say, the particular food was a recent invention. Nonetheless, the excursions attracted an increasing audience from year to year. In 1901, guests from Budapest participated, and in 1907 the excursion was turned into a national memorial festival and it soon became known as the Árpád pilgrimage, attracting large crowds each year. Meanwhile, in 1902, the Pusztaszer Árpád Association came into being from the original gentlemen's club, with 369 members instead of the genuine 21. Replacing the former gastronomic goals, the association now aimed to cultivate the heritage of Árpád and Pusztaszer. The fact that renewed archeological excavations failed to find ultimate evidence of Árpád's constitutional assembly did not disturb either the Árpád Association or the Magyar public in general, and the invention of Pusztaszer's heritage developed further.[53]

Besides the annual excursions of the Árpád Association, the memorial was rarely used by anyone else.[54] This shortcoming apparently inspired local national activists to bring together Pusztaszer's envisioned national importance and its actual usage. Several initiatives emerged in order to give Pusztaszer a proper function. As early as 1893, the idea of rebuilding the village at Pusztaszer was initiated by the mayor of Szentes, a nearby town.[55] However, Csongrád County was forced to reject this idea, as the proposed site was private property and the establishment of a completely new village would have exceeded the financial possibilities of the county.[56] The idea, however, did not disappear. In 1907, the establishment of a grand "national city" was initiated by a local landholder. This fantastic plan never became a reality but instead provoked bitter criticism from the influential journalist and outstanding representative of modern Magyar poetry, Endre Ady, for whom Pusztaszer became the metaphor of anti-democratic, gentry-led Hungary.[57]

Besides the foundation of a village or a city in Pusztaszer, other ideas concerned the establishment of a more appropriate memorial. The actual millennial memorial was often criticized by contemporaries; the sandstone material was not regarded as elegant enough, and the illogical shape, the small size, and the poor artistic quality all fed discontent.[58] To give Pusztaszer a proper artistic representation, the proposal to rebuild the medieval monastery was published in 1900, and a Catholic church dedicated to Árpád was even proposed. The architectural style and the symbolism to be used in this building were never defined in detail, so it is still unknown what kind of Christian building could have been built to commemorate a pagan prince.[59]

As the Árpád Association was rich in ideas but not in money, it requested donations from the government and the Hungarian Parliament several times. These requests were never met due to the government's lack of financial resources, so the idea of developing Pusztaszer into a living commune with a more appropriate memorial failed. The Pusztaszer memorial remained an artifact of low artistic quality in the middle of a vast unpopulated area, used for political purposes only once a year.

Still, this single annual festival was enough to win the legacy of Pusztaszer for Szeged in the competition with Kecskemét. As has been discussed, Kecskemét failed to erect a monument in its own part of Pusztaszer in the 1860s and thus to ensure the heritage as its own. As the millennial year approached, the demand to build a monument emerged once again. Regarding the state-sponsored monument at Pusztaszer, the government's decision favored a location lying outside of Kecskemét's territory, disappointing the city's public. In the end, the city's angry and envious representatives even failed to attend the inauguration ceremony of the state-sponsored monument.[60]

Instead, in 1894, students of the Calvinist College of Law in Kecskemét convinced the National Students' Association (Országos Diákszövetség) to hold its annual meeting in 1896 in Kecskemét and to celebrate the millennium there. The initiative of the students gained immediate support from the city. The mayor, members of the city's millennial committee, professors of the college, representatives of the student's millennial committee, and a delegation from the University of Budapest drafted the plans in May 1894. The delegations agreed on an impressive program: all Hungarian universities and colleges were invited to the National Student Congress in Kecskemét. They were to travel together from Kecskemét to Pusztaszer to commemorate the first Hungarian constitution by erecting a monument on a field that belonged to the city of Kecskemét. The costs of this monument were to be covered by public donations collected by the students: the main targets were universities, schools, counties and towns, companies, and private funders. Kecskemét promised to bear the costs of the festival.[61]

However, the students were able to collect only 9,400 crowns, which was not enough to cover the costs of the monument. The students turned to the assembly of Kecskemét for help. The assembly regretted that "disregarding accurate historical data, the government assigned the location of the state-sponsored monument of Pusztaszer not on the property of Kecskemét but, without asking the city's public, on the Pallavicini estate."[62] Therefore, Kecskemét appreciated the students' initiative and supplemented the budget in order to ensure a memorial on its own territory. The location, Árpád Hill (which, as mentioned earlier, had only received this name in 1861), was deliberately chosen to represent Kecskemét as the heir of ancient Magyar constitutionalism.

On 20 June 1896, just a week before the inauguration celebration of the state-sponsored millennial monument, the foundation stone of Kecskemét's Pusztaszer memorial was laid. The ceremony was attended mostly by representatives of the Students' Association and a delegation from the city. Being responsible for higher education, Minister Wlassics was also invited but he did not join the festivity. Nor was a larger audience invited.[63]

The city's public was dissatisfied with the proposed monument: it had an awkward location (far from any inhabited place) and was clearly inferior to its state-sponsored rival. Kecskemét therefore decided to complete the monument within the city itself and not in the *puszta*. Yet the plans by sculptor Lajos Lovas were ambitious and the costs seriously exceeded the original estimations. As further attempts to ensure the increased budget through public donations failed, the city and Lovas engaged in a bitter argument about the finances. Lovas was dismissed and Imre Pataky, a teacher of drawing in local schools, who had some higher training in arts, was commissioned to design a less complex monument, to be erected in Pusztaszer.[64] Finally, the monument, a plain obelisk with a *turul* on top, was completed in 1900.

The goal of this artifact was to compete with the state-sponsored monument and the city of Szeged, but Kecskemét's memorial, of low artistic quality, became even more peripheral and attracted even fewer visitors. No source verifies that this memorial was ever used for political purposes on behalf of either Kecskemét or any other public body. Thus, the rivalry was ultimately won by Szeged, as the governmental monument was built closer to the ruins of the monastery, completed earlier, legitimized by governmental sponsorship, and accepted by the wealthier Szeged middle class. The outcome of the rivalry between the two cities was two peripheral artifacts lacking high artistic quality standing in the middle of the Hungarian Great Plain and rarely attracting any visitors.

The Metamorphosis of Árpád

The Semlin monument was rarely used by Magyar national activists—given the lack of a Magyar society in the town, this is easy to explain.[65] In spite of the lack of genuine local enthusiasm, the millennial monument soon became a popular artifact in Semlin. Locals rarely referred to the memorial as the millennial monument; it was known rather as the Hunyadi tower (Kula Sibinjanin Janka). The memory of John Hunyadi, the great warlord who fought the Ottomans, seems to have been the most positive for all layers of the local population, therefore a monument commemorating him was acceptable to the local public. Due to its excellent location and the beautiful panorama, it was often targeted by small excursions. The town used the tower in a practical way. Fire watchmen occupied its terrace to guard the town, and it was illuminated during celebrations.[66]

Semlin also erected a monument on its own. In 1901, a memorial to Francis Joseph was unveiled, built by the most important contemporary Croatian sculptor, Ivan Rendić. In 1903, another monument, dedicated to the late Queen Elisabeth, was initiated, although it was never finished due to insufficient funding. Explicit national monuments were not built; a Serbian national hero would have provoked the Croatian government, and a Croatian one would have been unpopular with the local Serbs. Thus, imperial loyalty, a particularly important factor on the former Military Frontier, was the framework that best satisfied local needs.[67]

Epilogue: After the Great War

"Thou shalt stand as long as the homeland stands," stated the festive document placed in the foundation stone of each monument. No one in 1896 expected to witness the power of this sentence in less than a quarter of century. Those millennial memorials that stood on the territory of the successor states of Austria-Hungary became the subjects of immediate and radical reinterpretation after World War I.

The most radical course of action took place in Theben. After 1921, the Magyar national monument was replaced several times by an often-changing understanding of (Czecho-)Slovak national memory. The Czechoslovak army demolished the monument in 1921 in order to turn the castle into a Czechoslovak shrine based on the Moravian legacy.[68] In 1938, the Munich Agreement transferred Theben to Nazi Germany, which used the castle to host a festival for Germans living east of the Third Reich. In 1945, the castle was the site of a popular celebration of anti-fascist Slavic nations, an obvious reference to Soviet dominance in Central Europe. During the 1950s, the castle was cut off from Bratislava in order to prevent illegal border crossings to Austria. From the 1970s, it slowly became a national shrine once more, but this time a Slovak reading replaced the Czechoslovak one, particularly after sovereign Slovakia came into being in 1993.[69]

The Maria Theresa monument was also demolished in 1921. In the place of the former Maria Theresa memorial, a large statue dedicated to Štúr was built in 1973. Štúr was seen by Slovak communists as a "progressive" intellectual fighting for the people, and he therefore fit into the national-communist pantheon well. Since the 2000s, a new trend has appeared on the streets of the Slovak capital, as several monuments have been erected reflecting local traditions rather than national ones.[70] Recently the Bratislava Beautification Association (Bratislavský okrášľovácí spolok) has initiated the re-erection of the Maria Theresa monument as a way to reaffirm local traditions.[71]

The memorial on Zobor Hill was demolished in 1921 too.[72] This act was necessary to "purge" Nitra of the symbolic Magyar domination and to replace it with a representation of the Czechoslovak, then later Slovak, national narrative. The town hosted several important national festivals, including large-scale festivities in 1933 commemorating the one thousandth anniversary of the first Christian church in the town.[73] In 1938, negotiations over the new border between Hungary and Czechoslovakia also affected Nitra; a large monument to Cyril and Methodius was built in the nearby village of Berencs to symbolically strengthen Czechoslovak rule in the region.[74] The town remained in Czecho-Slovakia, so not even brief Hungarian rule could prevent its emergence as one of the most important national locations in Slovakia.[75] Today the plinth still stands on Zobor Hill and some remains of the millennial monument are scattered in the nearby forest. Visitors often go to the hill to enjoy the panorama and very few Slovaks today know what the plinth once supported. Members of the local Magyar community still remember the memorial. Including some remains of the original memorial, in 2015 a new *turul* monument was built in Alsóbodok, a nearby village where Magyars still outnumber Slovaks. The monument was erected in the courtyard of a private high school, which operates in Magyar and is supported by local Magyar businessmen.[76]

The monument in Munkács was removed by the Czechoslovak army in 1924. The sculpture itself was kept in the castle cellar and was found by the Hungarian army when they reconquered the town in 1938. An initiative to re-erect the monument immediately emerged but World War II prevented this from happening.[77] Following the Soviet conquest of the town and its incorporation into Soviet Ukraine, the bronze material was melted down and used, ironically, for a memorial commemorating the fallen soldiers of the Red Army. Then, somewhat surprisingly, the millennial memorial was rebuilt in 2008. The initiative and the financing came from Imre Pákh, a Magyar-American millionaire who was born in the town and migrated first to Hungary and later to the United States.[78] Today the castle of Munkács is a popular destination for both Ukrainian and Hungarian travelers.

The ruins of the millennial monument in Brassó were not used for any political purpose in the interwar period. During the 1950s, however, when the town was renamed Oraşul Stalin (Stalin City), several deciduous trees on the Cenk Hill were replaced by several darker pines in a pattern that could be read as Stalin from the downtown streets. Many of these trees were removed following the Romanian de-Stalinization, although some of them can be seen even today.[79] The hill preserved its popularity as a tourist resort, particularly since a cableway was built. Today the wind above the town blows a huge Romanian flag on the top of the hill just a short walk from the still existing plinth of the millennial memorial. Locals have long forgotten the memorial of the Hungarian millennium, but the Magyar minority community remembers it well. The local Magyar media occasionally publishes articles commemorating the memorial, while the original head of the monument, decorated by the Hungarian tricolor, is kept in the Magyar Lutheran parish.

In the interwar period, the millennial chapel in Pannonhalma had to be renovated and some parts were demolished. The original fresco had to be removed and was replaced by the work of Vilmos Aba-Novák, a representative of modern Hungarian painting,[80] but even Aba-Novák's monumental picture was not enough to turn the chapel into a central place in Pannonhalma. Today the chapel stands closed and most tourist guides mention it only briefly; the masses of tourists visiting the abbey mostly ignore it.

While all other millennial monuments have been either destroyed or abandoned, Pusztaszer became a true success story. During the interwar period, several nationalist and far-right organizations participated in the annual Árpád festivities. However, another attempt to rebuild the medieval village failed in 1935 and the proposed church also remained only on paper. The place received a completely new meaning in 1945, when the national land re-allotment campaign started symbolically in Pusztaszer as the first step of the "new conquest of the country," this time by the peasantry. The communist regime soon realized that the already well-known cult of Pusztaszer could be used for its own purposes with a slight reinterpretation. From 1957, Pusztaszer hosted an annual communist festival, officially called a national worker-peasant meeting, commemorating the land re-allotment and in a broader sense praising the results of the new order, trying to forget the fact that the redistributed lands were soon forced into Soviet-style collective farms. In order to combine the "progressive" heritage of Hungarian history with the "second conquest," the annual Pusztaszer festivals were moved from the neutral early September date to the national holiday of 20 August, which in the communist interpretation commemorated the 1949 constitution and the "new bread" baked from the recently harvested wheat. The area surrounding the millennial memorial was developed into a National Heritage Park. An initiative to build a memorial commemorating the "second conquest" also emerged, although this monument was never built.

The cult of Pusztaszer became so deeply fixed in Hungarian minds that post-1989 democratic Hungary could not renounce it either. The National Heritage Park was developed further: today the National Historical Memory Park covers a vast area and includes an eclectic collection of the millennial memorial, several other historical statues, the restored ruins of the monastery, the Feszty panorama, a museum, an open-air ethnographic exhibition, and a nomad park, which are visited by thousands of mostly Hungarian travelers each year. At the same time, political utilization of Pusztaszer has continued. In 1996 the Hungarian government coined a quasi-Latin term, *millecentenarium*, to celebrate the 1100th anniversary of the conquest; the National Heritage Park hosted some events during these commemorations. Four years later, large-scale celebrations took place again: Hungary now celebrated the one thousandth anniversary of the coronation of St. Stephen and the foundation of the Kingdom of Hungary. In both 1996 and 2000, nationwide celebrations were organized, and comparisons to the 1896 festivities were commonplace. The overlapping myths of Pusztaszer, Prince Árpád, and St. Stephen became an everyday reality.[81]

As an artifact of Magyar nationalism, the Semlin monument was bombarded by Serbian artillery during World War I. The town was conquered by Serbian troops and incorporated into the South Slav state in 1918, providing an opportunity to destroy the millennial monument just as in Czechoslovakia and Romania. However, the monument was kept as a sign of victory over Austria-Hungary and only the explicit Magyar symbols were removed.[82] Since then the monument has had various functions; it has served as a museum, a restaurant, and an atelier. Locals have forgotten the original meaning of the artifact and call it the Hunyadi tower; as such, it has become a symbol of the town. As a local landmark, the monument today serves as a popular lookout tower and hosts a small gallery.

Árpád and the City: In or Above?

Contemporaries ascribed to the millennial monuments an almost magical power to disseminate the ideal Magyar past and identity. This power, however, showed remarkable limits. As most of the millennial memorials were established on the edges of urban space, their utilization was rather accidental; this is best shown by the almost complete abandonment of the Pusztaszer monument. Sources suggest that the millennial monuments were used mostly in organized form, most frequently by (secondary) schools and national associations, in other words by institutions of the middle class. This, in fact, entirely corresponded to Thaly's vision. He never hid that he meant the middle class as the main audience of the monuments. When arguing with Munkács about the exact location of the monument, he rejected the downtown plan, because

> people on the market would profane [the monument]: during unloading goods, it would be surrounded by various vegetables, tomato and rotten fruit; but pumpkin, parsley and carrot are certainly not appropriate around the millennial monument. On the contrary, if it is built on the battlement of the castle, youth and their teachers can visit it on 15 March, St. Stephen Day or at other national festivals, they can deliver patriotic speeches and the effect of these scenes on that holy spot will be engraved into the young souls forever.[83]

Others, less educated, less wealthy, less urban, and women particularly, were unlikely to have been affected by the millennial artifacts, as they participated in the national pilgrimages less often, if at all.[84] Rudy Koshar's argument explains these limits well: "Nineteenth-century monuments were products of that 'bourgeois public' that had gained power and influence, and even where governments and monarchs built monuments, as they often did in Germanophone Europe, they did so with reference to the ideas and values of architects, nationalist groups, literary societies, and other typical representatives of bourgeois society."[85]

Yet the success of symbolic means of national integration also seems questionable with the middle class and local elites. The legal position of the monuments was ambiguous; their territory belonged to the central government, which financed their construction, but during the inauguration ceremony they were handed over to municipalities and counties as well. Their maintenance proved problematic in several cases. Bereg County and Szeged did not have the resources to turn the Munkács castle and the Pusztaszer memorial into proper national shrines. The Pannonhalma abbey contributed a considerable sum to the chapel but it was not enough to replace the failing contribution of Győr County and the artifact suffered serious deterioration, while Saxon-dominated Brassó refused to make any contribution to the monument for political reasons. The result was that, in the end, the central government had to take over the maintenance of the monuments, but plans for further development were never completed.[86] The shortcomings in regard to maintenance and further development demonstrate the high costs of national integration, which local players could definitely not cover, and which the central government was reluctant to finance.

In response to the millennial monuments, artifacts of local memory were built. These local monuments were inspired by the millennial achievements and were true representatives of the Zeitgeist of the late nineteenth and early twentieth centuries. Similar to several Western European countries, fin-de-siècle Hungary also witnessed statuomania, even in provincial towns, whose elites regarded these memorials as proof of their advanced culture. In locations where the Magyar national narrative coincided with the local reading of history, these monuments transmitted the same message as the state-sponsored millennial memorials. The envisioned-but-never-completed Árpád memorial in Munkács, the statue of Astrik in Pannonhalma, and the obelisk at Pusztaszer erected by Kecskemét all confirmed the conformity of national and local readings of history. In these places, the millennial monuments fulfilled the intentions of Thaly and the local elites: they merged national and local visions of the past. In cities where local and Magyar national ideas did not intertwine completely, local monuments challenged the millennial artifacts. This challenge, however, differed from location to location. The Maria Theresa memorial in Pressburg was intended to demonstrate local values and loyalty to Hungary at the same time. It could have been read both in local, *Hungarus*-Pressburger and Magyar national terms. The Honterus memorial in Brassó and the Teutsch statue in Hermannstadt had a profoundly different goal. They represented the cultural, economic, and political superiority and the historical primacy of the Saxons over any other group. Nevertheless, in order to avoid open conflict with the Hungarian authorities and the Magyar public, figures having rather an ecclesiastical legacy were chosen. Imperial figures were depicted in public memorials in Semlin in order to represent the town's traditional Habsburg loyalty, and at the same time to avoid conflicts among the town's competing elite groups.

At first glance, the millennial *panem et circenses* worked well. Prince Árpád and the conquest of the Magyars as fundamental myths had been invented and refined for more than a century; now the myth materialized, became tangible and well known to wide sections of the country. In Budapest, the millennial monument seems to have achieved its goal, as it is still regarded as a highlight of the city in the eyes of many locals, despite the many alterations since its construction.[87] Local elites in Munkács, Pannonhalma, and Szeged found the monuments to be a confirmation of their plentiful services to the nation. In Brassó, the Magyar elite read the monument as a sign of the protection of the Hungarian state against local Saxon hegemony. Greek Catholics in Munkács, Orthodox Jews in Nitra, and liberal Jews throughout the country could celebrate the millennium in their own terms, too, as a sign of a virtual social contract giving them the perspective of modernity in exchange for their loyalty and assimilation. Further dissemination of a uniform Hungarian state doctrine was, despite all the state support, rather vulnerable. Pre-national conditions influenced whether *circus* (emotions and the perception of the past) and *panis* (modernity) were attractive and plausible for local elites, who were responsible for transmitting ideas further down.

The state-sponsored monuments became relevant and meaningful only in the cases where they were able to mirror local values, best shown in Munkács, Pannonhalma, and Pusztaszer. Ironically, in Semlin the state-sponsored monument became a local symbol, but this phenomenon can be explained only by a radical reinterpretation and the complete eradication of the original intention behind the millennial tower. Wherever local memorials differed in their meaning from state-sponsored monuments, the former turned out to be more successful. Thus, the most popular symbol of Pressburg became the Maria Theresa memorial and not the Theben monument. In Brassó, also, it was the Honterus memorial that became important enough for the local public to save it from destruction, despite the fact that it was meant to represent only the Saxons of the town.

A comparison between the millennial and the local monuments illustrates well the difference between the central and local symbolic politics. The millennial memorials were only accidentally compatible with local ideas. These government-sponsored monuments were initiated, planned, carried out, and inaugurated by outsiders without any dialogue with the representatives of the communities in which they were built. It was a result of a well-elaborated strategy that all of the millennial monuments were erected outside of the urban space *above* the towns to symbolically rule them. The historic spaces of the towns and the artificial extension of these spaces by the millennial monuments were connected by the festivities, yet this connection frequently vanished after the ceremonies. The local monuments, on the contrary, were built *in the middle of* the historic space, fit smoothly into their environment, and inscribed themselves almost automatically into the public space. The initiators, the executors, and in the case of Pressburg even the sculptor himself, were locals or representatives of the region. As grassroots artifacts representing local values, they mostly found a far wider consensus with the local elite groups' historical and spatial concepts.

Thus, the most important lesson of the millennial monuments' construction, usage, and afterlife was a need for dialogue, which the top-level Magyar national activists often did not realize. The more the national elite was able to include local elites in decision making and to include their narratives in the national vision, the better the chances were for the spread of national identity in the particular local context. And vice versa; if a particular national narrative was incompatible with the local understanding of past and space, the local elites tended to refuse the top concept of national integration and maintained their own particular identities. National integrative projects had to meet local demands; if this failed, the integration process was doomed to fail. The fact that no local input was taken into consideration about the monuments themselves or about the inauguration festivities, and all the celebrations transmitted the very same message, meant that Budapest completely ignored the regional and local levels of Hungarian society. This meant that Magyar national integration could only succeed in locations where the content accidentally coincided with local demands and ideas. The less this favorable condition dominated, the less chance Magyar national activists had to disseminate their vision of national integration.

Comparing the Magyar millennial monuments to monuments in Germany, probably the country best known to contemporary Hungarian politicians and intellectuals outside the Habsburg Monarchy, the lack of dialogue becomes even more striking. The Hungarian millennial monuments condensed the exclusive Magyar national reading of Hungarian history on a scale that was unknown in contemporary Germany and Western Europe. The German statuomania, in fact the primary example for Magyar national activists, had clear grassroots dimensions. German national monuments thus can be read as artifacts of the negotiation between macro- and micro-levels. In spite of the several differences between German and French national monuments, the grassroots dimension of the memorials was also present in France, where initiatives came from the local level, and representation of local values was given high importance. Compared to Hungary, the limited role played by the government in constructing national monument both in Germany and in France is even more pronounced (though the superiority of the French bourgeoisie to its German counterpart is clear in using its own resources and managing the construction of a national monument independently of the state level).[88] Furthermore, both the German and French nations could be read as a symbiosis of regions and localities. These nations worked well on the micro-level because they could be seen as a "local metaphor," with local communities mirroring the abstract macro-level of the nation.[89]

From a retrospective point of view, the reluctance of Magyar national activists to conform to local needs indeed seems irrational given the country's deep fragmentation along linguistic, religious, and social lines and taking into consideration the largely limited set of integrative means of the center (due to the incomplete sovereignty, limited financial resources, and so on). The outcome of this ignorance proved lethal for Magyar national integration. As most of the national elites of the country could not find their place within the Kingdom of Hungary, they sought other solutions. The sudden and complete collapse of the Austro-Hungarian Monarchy in the autumn of 1918 gave the non-Magyar national activists an unexpected chance to establish their visions of national integration and thus prevented the Magyar national protagonists' dream of a homogenous Magyar-Hungarian nation having the same historical memory and looking to Budapest as its center of modernity. The central will of the Hungarian government was able to put Prince Árpád above the city, but did not manage to bring him down to its streets.

Notes

1. It is telling that in 1898 Francis Joseph tried to increase his popularity among Hungarians by donating ten monuments to Budapest which depicted figures of the Hungarian national pantheon who were also loyal subjects of the Habsburg monarchs. Iván Bertényi d. J., "Zehn Denkmäler, ein Herrscher und eine Nation: Ein Ausgleichsversuch zwischen der dynastischen Loyalität und den ungarischen nationalen Emotionen," in *Jahrtausendwende 2000*, ed. Ferenc Glatz (Budapest: Europa Institut, 2001), 246–55.
2. Károly Lyka, *Szobrászatunk a századfordulón 1896–1914* (Budapest: Képzőművészeti Alap, 1954).
3. Thomas Wolfes, "Adolf Harnack und Ernst Troeltsch in Siebenbürgen: Zur Reise deutscher Wissenschaftler nach Hermannstadt anläßlich der Enthüllung des G. D. Teutsch-Denkmals 1899," *Zeitschrift für Siebenbürgische Landeskunde* 27 (2004): 143–55.
4. Gyula Déri, *Pozsony és Pozsony vármegye* (Budapest: Hornyánszky Viktor, 1909), 1.
5. Theodor Ortvay, "Pressburg und das Pressburger Comitat," in *Die Österreichisch-Ungarische Monarchie in Wort und Bild: Ungarn V/1* (Vienna: Verlag der kaiserlich-königlichen Hof- und Staatsdruckerei, 1898), 177.
6. Lajos Dedek Crescens, "Pozsony vármegye története," in *Magyarország vármegyéi és városai: Pozsony vármegye, Pozsony sz. kir. város, Nagyszombat, Bazin, Modor, és Szentgyörgy r. t. városok*, ed. Samu Borovszky (Budapest: Apollo, n. d.), 502–3. Further examples: *Illustrierte Führer durch Pozsony (Pressburg) und Umgebung: Mit 52 Abbildungen, Stadtplan, Karten der Umgebung und des Komitates Pozsony in Farbendruck* (Pozsony: Sigmund Steiner, n. d.), 125–26; János Györffy and Andor Zellinger, *Földrajzi előismeretek: Pozsony vármegye és Pozsony város rövid földrajza* (Budapest: Szent István Társulat, 1913), 32.
7. "A dévényi emlék második ünnep napja," *Nyugatmagyarországi Hiradó*, 20 October 1896; "Die vier Mittelschulen bei dem Thebener Millenniums-Denkmal," *Preßburger Tagblatt*, 20 October 1896.
8. This number relies on the aggregate data of the yearly high school reports.
9. Mihály Benkó, "A dévényi és zobori kirándulás," *Turisták lapja* 10 (1898): 116–119.
10. Gyula Forster, ed., *Magyarország műemlékei* (Budapest: Hornyánszky Viktor, 1905–15), 3: 256 and 281.
11. Jenő Engyeli and Alajos Langer, *Emléklapok a pozsonyi koronázó emlékszobor leleplezésének ünnepére 1897. évi május hó 16-án* (Pozsony: Eder István, 1897). Also in German: Eugen Engyeli and Alois Langer, *Festschrift zur Enthüllung des Preßburger Krönungsdenkmales am 16. Mai 1897* (Pressburg: Stefan Eder, 1897).

12. Engyeli and Langer, *Emléklapok*, 13.

13. "Sr. Majestät dem Könige und seinem Hause Heil!" *Preßburger Zeitung*, 16 May 1897.

14. *Programmbuch der unter dem hohen Protectorate Ihrer kaiserlichen und königlichen Hoheit der durchlauchtigen Frau Erzherzogin Isabelle stattfindenden Fest-Vorstellungen vom 16., 17. und 18. Mai 1897 zu wohltätigen Zwecken anlässlich der feierlichen Enthüllung des Krönungsdenkmales* (Pressburg: Königl. freistädt. Theater in Pressburg, 1897).

15. "Der Preßburger Krönungshügel und seine Geschichte," *Preßburger Zeitung*, 16 May 1897; "Der Enthüllungstag," *Preßburger Zeitung*, 17 May 1897; "Vitam et Sanguinem!" *Westungarischer Grenzbote*, 16 May 1897; "Zur Enthüllungs-Feier unseres Krönungs-Denkmales," *Westungarischer Grenzbote*, 16 May 1897; "Die Enthüllungs-Feier unseres Krönungs-Denkmales," *Westungarischer Grenzbote*, 17 May 1897; "16. Mai 1897," *Preßburger Tagblatt*, 16 May 1897.

16. Mózes Gaal, "A mit ez a szobor beszél," *Nyugatmagyarországi Hiradó*, 16 May 1897. The German newspapers either interpreted the side figures in the same way as the *Nyugatmagyarországi Hiradó* ("Der Preßburger Krönungshügel und seine Geschichte," *Preßburger Zeitung*, 16 May 1896) or did not go into such details.

17. Bertalan Plachy, "A 'Sedes sacrae coronae' ékességének leleplezése előtt," *Nyugatmagyarországi Hiradó*, 15 May 1897; Mózes Gaal, "A mit ez a szobor beszél," *Nyugatmagyarországi Hiradó*, 16 May 1897; Sándor Vutkovich, "Király és nemzet," *Nyugatmagyarországi Hiradó*, 16 May 1897; Bertalan Schönvitzky, "Pozsony jövője," *Nyugatmagyarországi Hiradó*, 16 May 1897.

18. *Annual Report of the Pressburg State Realschule*, 1896/97, 58–59.

19. Mannová, "Von Maria Theresia zum schönen Náci," 207.

20. Mihály Benkó, "A dévényi és zobori kirándulás," *Turisták lapja* 10 (1898): 119–20.

21. Géza Rédeky, *Nyitra rend. tan. város köztereinek, utainak és utcáinak valamint bel- és külterületi lakóházainak jegyzéke* (Nyitra: Neugebauer Nándor, 1912).

22. *Nyitra r. t. város képviselőtestülete részéről 1906. évi október 28-án II. Rákóczi Ferencz dicső emlékű fejedelmünk és bujdosó társai hamvainak hazahozatala alkalmából megtartott díszközgyűlés jegyzőkönyve* (Nyitra: Neugebauer Nándor, 1906).

23. László Barla-Szabó, *A Vastagh művészcsalád* (Budapest: Ernst Múzeum, 2004), 6.

24. Bay, *A munkácsi Árpád-szobor*.

25. "Az Árpád szobor," *Brassói Lapok*, 18 October 1906; "A kaszinó ösztöndija," *Brassói Lapok*, 19 October 1902; "Évforduló," *Brassói Lapok*, 17 October 1898.

26. This observation was made by Gábor Egry, whom I thank for bringing it to my attention.

27. József Orosz, "A brassói Millenniumi emlékoszlop története," *Erdélyi gyopár* 9, no. 1 (2001): 3–5.

28. Lajos Schilling, ed., *Az Erdélyi Múzeum-Egyesület Brassóban 1908 június 7-9. napjain tartott negyedik vándorgyűlésének emlékkönyve* (Kolozsvár: Erdélyi Múzeum-Egyesület, 1908), 4–5.

29. Elek Benedek, *Szent Anna tavától a Cenk-tetőig* (Budapest: Franklin, n. d.), 62. *Szózat* (Appeal) is a Magyar national anthem, written by poet Mihály Vörösmarty in 1836.

30. Mihály Maurer to the Council of Brassó, 21 September 1898, DJBAN, 1, VI–1895/85–44.

31. Adolf Meschendörfer, *Die Stadt im Osten* (Munich: Albert Langen, 1934), 170–71.

32. Andrei Popovici, *Brașovul: Românii și Sașii* (Brașov: Ziarul Carpații, 1923), 1. The author was born in the town in 1856 and published several books and articles, mainly on the economic aspect of the Magyar–Romanian conflict.

33. Ion Bozdog, ed., *Statul polițist: Material documentar dintr'o arhivă secretă brașoveană* (Brașov: ASTRA, 1944).

34. Bogdan Florin Popovici, "Muntele Tâmpa și simbolurile sale," *Magazin istoric* 34, no. 6 (2001): 40–47.

35. "Merénylet a czenki emlék ellen," *Brassói Lapok*, 19 December 1902.

36. This was the fence that the town refused to co-finance. Orosz, "A brassói Millenniumi emlékoszlop."

37. Ioan Vlad, *Cărturarii brașoveni pentru România Mare* (Brașov: Academia Aviației și Apărării Antiaeriene „Henri Coandă," 1999), 298.

38. "Merénylet a magyar állam ellen," *Brassói Lapok*, 30 September 1913.

39. "A cenki emlékoszlop megkoszoruzása," *Brassói Lapok*, 3 October 1913.

40. "Elpusztult az Árpád szobor!" *Brassói Lapok*, 31 December 1913.

41. *Zur Geschichte des Honterus-Denkmals* (Kronstadt: Johann Gött's Sohn, 1895).

42. Harro Magnussen (1861–1908) studied in Munich and Berlin with Reinhold Begas, a major representative of German neo-Baroque art. Besides his Bismarck statues, Magnussen made several German national monuments throughout Germany. Hans Vollmer, *Allgemeines Lexikon der bildenden Künstler von der Antike bis zur Gegenwart* (Leipzig: E. A. Seemann, 1929), s.v. "Harro Magnussen."

43. *Gaben-Verzeichnis: Enthaltend die für das Honterus-Denkmal gespendeten Beträge an Geld und Geldeswert* (Kronstadt: Honterus-Denkmal-Ausschuss, 1898).

44. Lutz Korodi, *Die Honterus-Jubelfeier und die sächsischen Vereinstage in Kronstadt* (Kronstadt: H. Zeidner, 1898).

45. Traugott Teutsch, *Johannes Honterus: Drama in drei Aufzügen* (Kronstadt: Heinrich Zeidner, 1897).

46. Theochar Alexi, *Johannes Honterus: Volksschrift* (Kronstadt: Gabony, 1897); W. Morres, *Johannes Honterus: Zu seiner 400. Geburtsfeier der sächsischen Jugend* (Kronstadt: H. Zeidner, 1898); E[mil] N[eugeboren], "Johannes Honterus," *Neuer Volkskalendar* 9 (1898): 117–29; Emil Neugeboren, "Johannes Honterus," *Kronstädter Zeitung*, 19 August 1898; Theobald Wolf, *Johannes Honterus der Apostel Ungarns* (Kronstadt: Ausschuß zur Errichtung eines Honterusdenkmals, 1894).

47. "Zum Willkommen!" *Kronstädter Zeitung*, 19 August 1898.

48. "A szászok ünnepe," *Brassói Lapok*, 23 August 1898.

49. "Serbările săsescï," *Gazeta Transilvaniei*, 11/23 August 1898.

50. Récsey, *Győr és Pannonhalma*, 20; *Pannonhalma a multban*, 53–54.

51. Minutes of the Archabbey Convent, 26 October 1899, 156–58, PFL, I.1.g; Sándor Wekerle to Ipoly Fehér, 11 July 1906, PFL, I.1.d, 1906/393; Forster, *Magyarország műemlékei*, 3: 273; Gábor Sonkoly, "Pannonhalma újkori territorializációja," in *Terek, tervek, történetek: Az identitás történetének térbeli keretei 2*, ed. András Cieger (Budapest: Atelier, 2011), 194–95.

52. Minutes of the Archabbey Convent, 23 April 1895, 79–82, PFL, I.1.g; Sörös, *A pannonhalmi főapátság története*, 146.

53. Ákos Kovács, *A kitalált hagyomány* (Pozsony: Kalligram, 2006), 23–33; *Pusztaszer község újratelepítése: Emlékirat* (Szeged: Pusztaszeri Árpád Egyesület, 1935), 24–27.

54. The Pusztaszer excursion of the Hungarian Tourist Association in 1904 was certainly a rare event. Ten members traveled from Budapest to Kistelek, the nearest train station, from where they were brought to the monument by the cart of the Pallavicini estate and they were also hosted by the estate manager. Needless to say, this was rather an exclusive way of tourism limited to a low number of people. Béla Mihalovics, "Pusztaszer," *Turisták lapja* 16 (1904): 135–38.

55. "Az ezredéves ünnepély vármegyénkben," *Szentesi Lap*, 13 August 1893.

56. Minutes of the council of Csongrád County, 15 February 1895, no. 23–27, MNL CSML, IV. B. 402.

57. Kovács, *A kitalált hagyomány*, 37–40.

58. Ibid., 25–26.

59. Pál Hegedűs, *Pusztaszer* (Szeged: Lipsitz Sándor, 1903).

60. "Az országos emlék Pusztaszeren," *Kecskemét*, 21 June 1896; "A pusztaszeri országos emlék," *Kecskemét*, 28 June 1896.

61. "Jogadémiai millenniumi bizottság," *A Kecskeméti Ev. Ref. Jogakadémia* Évkönyve 20 (1895): 81–90.

62. "Jogadémiai millenniumi bizottság," *A Kecskeméti Ev. Ref. Jogakadémia* Évkönyve 21 (1896): 108.

63. "A diákkongresszus," *Kecskemét*, 28 June 1896; "Az országos Diák-Kongresszusról," *Pestmegyei Hirlap*, 20 June 1896; "Egy beszéd a pusztaszeri ünnepen," *Pestmegyei Hirlap*, 27 June 1896; "A pusztaszeri emlék alapkő letétele," *Kecskeméti lapok*, 28 June 1896; *Az Országos Magyar Diákszövetség 1896. junius 17., 18., 19., 20. és 21. napjain Kecskemét th. városban megtartott kongresszusának jegyzőkönyve* (Budapest: Valter Ernő, 1897), 40–41.

64. *A pusztaszeri millenáris emlékszobor ügye* (Kecskemét: Ottinger Ede, 1898).

65. For instance, members of the Hungarian Tourist Association visited it in 1902. István Kőszeghy, "A Magyar Turista-Egyesületnek 1902. évben Budapesten tartott közgyűlése alkalmából rendezett kirándulásai," *Turisták lapja* 14 (1902): 118.

66. Branko Najhold, *Stoleće milenijumske kule 1896–1996* (Zemun: Trag, 1996), 28.

67. Najhold, *Hronika Zemuna 1871–1918*, 95–96.

68. In his memories, historian Branislav Varsik claims to have participated in the demolition of the Maria Theresa memorial. As an eighteen-year-old gymnasium student, he identified the monument as the symbol of Magyar and Habsburg oppression of the Slavs. Peter Machos's nuanced analysis shows that Varsik, too young to participate directly in the 1918 establishment of Czechoslovakia, could show his loyalty to the new state by taking part in this act. Peter Macho, "Branislav Varsik a bratislavský pomník Márie Terézie," in *Miles Sempes Honestus: Zborník štúdií vydaný pri príležitosti život ného jubilea Vojtecha Dangla*, ed. Vladimír Segeš and Božena Šedová (Bratislava: Vojenský historický ústav, 2007), 161–67.

69. Kiliánová, *Identität und Gedächtnis*, 59–137.

70. Mannová, "Von Maria Theresia zum schönen Náci." At the same time, new artifacts of Slovak nationalism have also been built, such as a monument to the Moravian ruler Svatopluk, depicting him ahistorically as a Slovak king.

71. "Súsošie Márie Terézie," Bratislavský okrašľovácí spolok, http://bos-bratislava.sk.data12. websupport.sk/projekt/16/susosie–marie–terezie (accessed 22 October 2014).

72. Ferenc Olay, "A magyar emlékművek és a magyar művészet sorsa az elszakított területeken," *Budapesti Szemle* 58, no. 628 (1930): 355.

73. *Pribinova Nitra 833–1933* (Nitra: Pribinov Fond, 1933).

74. Juraj Zajonc, "Mesto a spoločensko-historické procesy: Východiská analýzy. Niekoľko príladov z mesta Nitra," *Slovenský narodopis* 51, no. 2 (2003): 184–85.

75. Zajonc, "Prečo je Nitra staroslávne mesto."

76. "Idén is: Generációk Találkozása 2011. aug. 19," Magyar Koalíció Pártja, http://www. mkp.sk/node/17291 (accessed 30 May 2012); "Alsóbodok: Felröppent a zoborhegyi turulmadár a szoboravatással," Felvidék.ma, http://www.felvidek.ma/felvidek/regio/52504-alsobodok-felroppent-a-zoborhegyi-turulmadar-a-szoboravatassal (accessed 11 January 2016).

77. Aladár R. Vozáry, *Munkács* (Budapest: Officina, 1943), 4–9.

78. "Visszaszállt a turul a munkácsi várra," *Kárpáti Igaz Szó*, 13 March 2008.

79. Márk László-Herbert, "Sztálingrádok Kelet-Európában: Orașul Stalin, 1950–1960," *Korunk* 3/14 no. 2 (February 2003): 64–74.

80. Magdolna B. Supka, *Aba-Novák Vilmos* (Budapest: Corvina, 1966), appendix 79.

81. Kovács, *A kitalált hagyomány*, 64–88.

82. Memo of the Ministry of Education of the Kingdom of Serbs, Croats, and Slovenes, 12 April 1921, AJ, 66, 627.

83. Thaly, *Az ezredévi*, 29.

84. Even the Hermannsdenkmal, one of Germany's largest national monuments, was annually visited by only around two thousand people during the 1880s. Kirsten Belgum, "Displaying the Nation: A View of Nineteenth-Century Monuments through a Popular Magazine," *Central European History* 26, no. 4 (1993): 458.

85. Koshar, *From Monuments to Traces*, 30.

86. Forster, *Magyarország műemlékei*, passim; *Magyarország fenntartandó műemlékei hivatalos jegyzékének tervezete* (Budapest: Műemlékek Országos Bizottsága, 1916). It is noteworthy that the seven millennial memorials were the only modern monuments in the country maintained by the government. All the other important contemporary artifacts, including the St. Stephen monument in Budapest, the Mathias Corvinus monument in Kolozsvár, and the 1848 memorial in Arad, were absent from the list of art relics maintained by the government. Their maintenance was financed by the respective cities.

87. Gerő, *Modern Hungarian Society*, 203–22.

88. Tacke, *Denkmal im sozialen Raum*.

89. Alan Confino, *The Nation as a Local Metaphor: Württemberg, Imperial Germany, and National Memory, 1871–1918* (Chapel Hill: University of North Carolina Press, 1997).

Appendix 1

TABLES

❧

13.1. Denomination of the civil population of Pressburg, 1869–1900.
Source: *Magyar statisztikai közlemények* 27 (1909): 84–85, 92–93.

Year	Roman Catholic		Lutheran		Calvinist		Jew		Other		Total
1869	34,714	74.6%	7,038	15.1%	178	0.4%	4,552	9.8%	58	0.1%	46,540
1880	35,308	73.5%	6,939	14.5%	509	1.1%	4,966	10.3%	284	0.6%	48,006
1890	39,020	74.5%	7,347	14.0%	525	1.0%	5,396	10.3%	123	0.2%	52,411
1900	45,644	74.2%	7,868	12.8%	1,020	1.7%	6,808	11.1%	197	0.3%	61,537

13.2. Mother tongue of the civil population of Pressburg, 1880–1900.
Source: *Magyar statisztikai közlemények* 27 (1909): 114–115.

Year	German		Magyar		Slovak		Other		Total
1880	31,492	65.6%	7,537	15.7%	7,537	15.7%	1,440	3.0%	48,006
1890	31,404	59.9%	10,433	19.9%	8,709	16.6%	1,865	3.6%	52,411
1900	32,104	52.2%	18,744	30.5%	9,004	14.6%	1,685	2.7%	61,537

13.3. Denomination of the civil population of Nitra, 1869–1900.
Sources: Gusztáv Thirring, ed., *A magyar városok statisztikai* évkönyve (Budapest: Budapest székesfőváros házinyomdája, 1912), 67 (for 1869–1890); *Magyar statisztikai közlemények* 27 (1909): 92–93 (for 1900). The data covers both Nitra proper and Párovce.

Year	Roman Catholic		Lutheran		Calvinist		Jew		Other		Total
1869	7,433	69.6%	81	0.8%	27	0.3%	3,141	29.4%	1	0.0%	10,683
1880	8,331	69.2%	142	1.2%	43	0.4%	3,501	29.1%	16	0.1%	12,033
1890	9,538	70.5%	166	1.2%	67	0.5%	3,757	27.8%	10	0.1%	13,538
1900	10,663	72.3%	241	1.6%	172	1.2%	3,648	24.7%	28	0.2%	14,752

13.4. Mother tongue of the civil population of Nitra, 1880–1900.
Source: Magyar statisztikai közlemények 27 (1909): 114–115. The data covers both Nitra proper and Párovce.

Year	Magyar		Slovak		German		Other		Total
1880	3,403	28.3%	4,780	39.7%	3,743	31.1%	107	0.9%	12,033
1890	5,002	36.9%	5,205	38.4%	3,234	23.9%	97	0.7%	13,538
1900	7,035	47.7%	5,340	36.2%	2,279	15.4%	98	0.7%	14,752

13.5. Denomination of the civil population of Munkács, 1869–1900.
Sources: Thirring, *A magyar városok,* 67 (for 1869–1890); *Magyar statisztikai közlemények* 27 (1909): 94–95 (for 1900).

Year	Roman Catholic		Greek Catholic		Lutheran		Calvinist		Jew		Other		Total
1869	1,579	18.4%	2,353	27.4%	110	1.3%	957	11.1%	3,602	41.9%	1	0.0%	8,602
1880	1,848	19.2%	2,339	24.3%	116	1.2%	872	9.0%	4,468	46.3%	1	0.0%	9,644
1890	1,976	18.8%	2,456	23.3%	91	0.9%	956	9.1%	5,049	47.9%	3	0.0%	10,531
1900	2,539	18.6%	3,201	23.5%	137	1.0%	1,240	9.1%	6,513	47.7%	10	0.1%	13,640

13.6 Mother tongue of the civil population of Munkács, 1880–1900.
Source: Magyar statisztikai közlemények 27 (1909): 116–117.

Year	Magyar		Rusyn		German		Other		Total
1880	5,451	56.5%	1,648	17.1%	2,358	24.5%	187	1.9%	9,644
1890	5,737	54.5%	1,632	15.5%	3,009	28.6%	153	1.5%	10,531
1900	8,344	61.2%	1,402	10.3%	3,782	27.7%	112	0.8%	13,640

13.7. Denomination of the civil population of Brassó, 1857–1900. * Standing population.
Sources: Árpád E. Varga, Erdély etnikai és felekezeti statisztikája: Népszámlálási adatok 1850 és 2002 között. V.: Brassó, Hunyad és Szeben megye (Csík-szereda: Pro Print, 2011), 95 (for 1857–1890); Magyar statisztikai közlemények 27 (1909): 96–97 (for 1900).

Year	Roman Catholic		Greek Catholic		Orthodox		Lutheran		Calvinist		Unitarian		Jew		Other		Total
1857*	3,710	16.6%	80	0.4%	9,873	44.2%	7,817	35.0%	798	3.6%	9	0.0%	39	0.2%	18	0.1%	22,344
1869	7,472	26.9%	127	0.5%	9,489	34.2%	8,446	30.4%	1,816	6.5%	138	0.5%	217	0.8%	61	0.2%	27,766
1880	7,438	25.1%	280	0.9%	9,523	32.2%	8,637	29.2%	2,658	9.0%	405	1.4%	610	2.1%	33	0.1%	29,584
1890	8,357	27.2%	378	1.2%	9,733	31.7%	8,399	27.3%	2,674	8.7%	412	1.3%	769	2.5%	17	0.1%	30,739
1900	8,569	24.8%	567	1.6%	1,0449	30.3%	9,359	27.1%	3,669	10.6%	705	2.0%	1,171	3.4%	22	0.1%	34,511

13.8. Mother tongue of the civil population of Brassó, 1880–1900.
Source: Magyar statisztikai közlemények 27 (1909): 118–119.

	German		Magyar		Romanian		Other		Total
1880	9,919	33.5%	9,827	33.2%	9,382	31.7%	458	1.5%	29,584
1890	9,578	31.2%	10,441	34.0%	9,758	31.7%	962	3.1%	30,739
1900	10,272	29.8%	13,162	38.1%	10,477	30.4%	600	1.7%	34,511

13.9. Denomination of the civil population of Semlin, 1869–1900.
Source: Magyar statisztikai közlemények 27 (1909): 86–87, 98–99.

Year	Roman Catholic		Orthodox		Lutheran		Calvinist		Jew		Other		Total
1869	4,991	49.7%	4,359	43.4%	28	0.3%	7	0.1%	661	6.6%	0	0.0%	10,046
1880	6,568	55.5%	4,386	37.1%	210	1.8%	53	0.4%	589	5.0%	30	0.3%	11,836
1890	7,171	55.9%	4,622	36.0%	229	1.8%	111	0.9%	662	5.2%	28	0.2%	12,823
1900	8,384	57.8%	5,057	34.8%	333	2.3%	63	0.4%	638	4.4%	42	0.3%	14,517

13.10. Mother tongue of the civil population of Semlin, 1880–1900.
Source: Magyar statisztikai közlemények 27 (1909): 120–121.

Year	German		Serbian		Croatian		Magyar		Other		Total
1880	5,254	44.4%	5,268	(44.5%)			520	4.4%	794	6.7%	11,836
1890	6,046	47.1%	4,458	34.8%	1,099	8.6%	648	5.1%	572	4.5%	12,823
1900	6,908	47.6%	4,949	34.1%	1,461	10.1%	739	5.1%	460	3.2%	14,517

NAME LOCATOR

Alsóbodok → Dolné Obdokovce, Slovakia

Altstadt → part of Braşov, Romania

Arad → Arad, Romania

Banat region → divided among Csongrád County, Hungary, Arad, Caraş-Severin and Timiş Counties, Romania, and Vojvodina Autonomous Province, Serbia

Banská Bystrica → Banská Bystrica, Slovakia

Banská Štiavnica → Banská Štiavnica, Slovakia

Bereg County → divided between Szabolcs-Szatmár-Bereg County, Hungary, and Zakarpatska County, Ukraine

Beregszász → Beregovo, Ukraine

Berencs → Branč, Slovakia

Bistriţa-Năsăud → divided between Bistriţa-Năsăud and Suceava Counties, Romania

Blaj → Blaj, Romania

Bolonya → part of Braşov, Romania

Brassó → Braşov, Romania

Burzenland → part of Braşov County, Romania

Černova → Černova, part of Ružomberok, Slovakia

Csongrád County → part of Csongrád County, Hungary

Debrecen → Debrecen, Hungary

Esseg → Osijek, Croatia

Esztergom → Esztergom, Hungary

Fiume → Rijeka, Croatia

Franzenstal → part of Zemun, Belgrade, Serbia

Gornja varoš → part of Zemun, Belgrade, Serbia

Győr County → part of Győr-Moson-Sopron County, Hungary

Gyula → Gyula, Hungary

Háromszék County → part of Covasna County, Romania

Hermannstadt → Sibiu, Romania

Hermannstadt County → part of Sibiu County, Romania

Hétfalu → Săcele, Romania

Hódmezővásárhely → Hódmezővásárhely, Hungary

Holič → Holič, Slovakia

Karlovci → Karlovci, Serbia

Käsmark → Kežmarok, Slovakia

Kassa → Košice, Slovakia

Kecskemét → Kecskemét, Hungary

Kolozsvár → Cluj, Romania

Kubin → Kovin, Serbia

Levoča → Levoča, Slovakia

Liptovský Svätý Mikuláš → Liptovský Mikuláš, Slovakia

Lugoj → Lugoj, Romania

Munkács → Mukacheve, Ukraine

Nagyvárad → Oradea, Romania

Nitra → Nitra, Slovakia

Nitra County → divided between Nitra and Trenčin Counties, Slovakia

Nógrád County → divided between Nógrád County, Hungary, and Banská Bystrica County, Slovakia

Novi Sad → Novi Sad, Serbia

Orava County → divided between Małopolskie County, Poland, and Žilina County, Slovakia

Ostratice → Ostratice, Slovakia

Pannonhalma → Pannonhalma, Hungary

Párovce → part of Nitra, Slovakia

Pest → part of Budapest, Hungary

Požega County → divided between Brod-Posavina and Požega-Slavonia Counties, Croatia

Prešov → Prešov, Slovakia

Pressburg → Bratislava, Slovakia

Prievidza → Prievidza, Slovakia

Pusztaszer → Ópusztaszer, Hungary

Raiding → Raiding, Austria

Riga → Rīga, Latvia

Royal Land → divided among Bistrița-Năsăud, Brașov, Mureș, and Sibiu Counties, Romania

Șchei → part of Brașov, Romania

Semlin → Zemun, part of Belgrade, Serbia

Solnoc-Dăbâca County → divided among Bistrița-Năsăud, Cluj, Maramureș, and Sălaj Counties, Romania

Spiš County → divided between Małopolskie County, Poland, and Prešov County, Slovakia

Srem County → divided between Vukovar-Srijem County, Croatia, and Vojvodina Autonomous Province, Serbia

Szeged → Szeged, Hungary

Székelyudvarhely → Oderheiu Secuiesc, Romania

Szentes → Szentes, Hungary

Szombathely → Szombathely, Hungary

Tekov County → divided between Banská Bystrica and Nitra Counties, Slovakia

Theben → Devín, Slovakia

Tiszaeszlár → Tiszaeszlár, Hungary

Trenčin County → part of Trenčin County, Slovakia

Trnava → Trnava, Slovakia

Turčiansky Svätý Martin → Martin, Slovakia

Turiec County → part of Žilina County, Slovakia

Újkigyós → Újkígyós, Hungary

Ungvár → Uzhgorod, Ukraine

Virovitica County → divided between Osijek-Baranja and Virovitica-Podravina Counties, Croatia

Werschetz → Vršac, Serbia

Zagreb → Zagreb, Croatia

Zvolen County → part of Banská Bystrica County, Slovakia

BIBLIOGRAPHY

Unpublished Sources

Archival Sources

AH
Archiv der Honterusgemeinde A. B. in Kronstadt (Archives of the Honterus Lutheran Parish in Braşov)
  – IV. Ba. 54. Minutes of the presbytery and the extended parish council
  – Stenner collection

AJ
Arhiv Jugoslavije (Archives of Yugoslavia, Belgrade)
  – 66 Documents of the Ministry of Education of the Kingdom of Yugoslavia

DAZO
Derzhavnii Arhiv Zakarpatskoi Oblasti (State Archives of the Transcarpathian County, Beregovo)
  – 10 Documents of the Lord Lieutenant of Bereg County
  – 890 Minutes of the assembly of Bereg County

DJBAN
Direcţia Judeţeană Braşov a Arhivelor Naţionale (Braşov County Filiale of the National Archives, Braşov)
  – 1 Municipal documents of Brassó
  – 2 Documents of the lord lietunant of Brassó County

GYÉL
Gyulafehérvári Érseki Levéltár (Archives of the Alba Iulia Diocese, Alba Iulia)
  – I. 1/a Registered documents of the Office of the Bishop (Archbishop)

HDA
Hrvatski državni arhiv (Croatian State Archives, Zagreb)
  – 367 Statistical Office of the Socialist Republic of Croatia

IAB
Istorijski arhiv Beograda (Historic Archives of Belgrade)
  – 10 Documents of the Semlin magistracy
  – 1180 Minutes of the Semlin assembly

MNL CSML
Magyar Nemzeti Levéltár Csongrád Megyei Levéltár Szentesi Levéltára (Hungarian National Archives, Archives of Csonrád County in Szentes)

– IV. B. 402 Minutes of the council of Csongrád County

MNL OL
Magyar Nemzeti Levéltár Országos Levéltár (Hungarian National Archives, Budapest)
 – K 26 Centrally registered documents of the Prime Minister of Hungary
 – K 148 Presidential documents, Hungarian Ministry of Interior
 – K 149 Reserved documents, Hungarian Ministry of Interior
 – P 1747 Documents of the Thaly family
 – XXXII-23-h Census documents of the Hungarian Central Statistical Office

OSZK K
Országos Széchényi Könyvtár Kézirattár (Manuscript Collection of the Széchényi Hungarian National Library, Budapest)
 – Fol. Lat. Latin manuscripts

PFL
Pannonhalmi Főapátság Levéltára (Archives of the Pannonhalma Archabbey, Pannonhalma)
 – I.1.d Documents of the archabbot
 – I.1.g Minutes of the Archabbey Convent

ŠANPN
Štatny archív v Nitre pobočka Nitra (Nitra Filial of the Nitra State Archives)
 – 181 Documents of Nitra Town

SNA
Slovenský národný archív (Slovak National Archives, Bratislava)
 – 46 Documents of the Hungarian Ministry of Interior

ŠOAB
Štátny oblastný archív v Bratislave (State County Archives in Bratislava)
 – 1052 Documents of Pressburg County I

ŠOAN
Štátny oblastný archív v Nitre (State County Archives in Nitra)
 – 11 Documents of Nitra County I

Unpublished Doctoral Dissertations

Bertényi, Iván Jr. "Bánffy Dezső és a nemzetiségi kérdés." PhD diss., Eötvös Loránd Tudományegyetem, Budapest, 2005.

Schöck, Andreas. "Brassó, Braşov, Kronstadt. Beiträge zur Stadtentwicklung, Bevölkerungs- und Berufsgruppenstruktur." PhD diss., Freie Universität Berlin, 1995.

Szabó, Dániel. "A Néppárt 1895–1914." PhD diss., Magyar Tudományos Akadémia, Budapest, 1983.

Papers Presented at Conferences

Wilke, Carsten. "Orthodoxy's Stronghold: The Educational Policies of the Pressburg Yeshiva and Their Bearing on the Hungarian Jewish Schism." Paper presented at the conference Schism, Sectarianism and Jewish Denominationalism: Hungarian Jewry in a Comparative Perspective, Budapest, 14 October 2009.

Published Sources

Periodicals

Agramer Zeitung 1895, 1896

Alkotmány 1896

Allgemeine Jüdische Zeitung 1896

Bereg 1893, 1896

Brassói Lapok 1896, 1898, 1902, 1906, 1913

Budapesti Hirlap 1896

Der ungarische Israelit 1896

Die Drau 1896

Dunántúli Hirlap 1896

Egyenlőség 1896

Egyetértés 1890

Gazeta Transilvaniei 1896, 1898

Győri Hirlap 1896

Győri Közlöny 1896

Hrvatska domovina 1896

Kárpáti Igaz Szó 2008

Kecskemét 1896

Kecskeméti lapok 1896

Kronstädter Tageblatt 1896, 1898

Kronstädter Zeitung 1896, 1898

Lipa 1864

Magyar Állam 1896

Magyar-Zsidó Szemle 1886

Munkács 1889, 1890, 1892, 1893, 1896

Munkács és vidéke 1896

Narodne novine 1896

Národnie noviny 1896

Nemzeti Társalkodó 1839

Nemzeti Ujság 1896

Népszava 1896

Neutraer Zeitung-Nyitrai Hírlap 1896

Novo vreme 1895, 1896

Nyitrai Lapok (Neutra-Trenchiner Zeitung) 1896

Nyitramegyei Közlöny 1886, 1896

Nyitramegyei Szemle 1896

Nyugatmagyarországi Hiradó 1896, 1897

Obzor 1896

Oestlicher Grenz-Bote 1896

Ország tükre 1863, 1865

Pester Lloyd 1895

Pesti Hirlap 1896

Pesti Napló 1894, 1896

Pestmegyei Hirlap 1896

Preßburger Tagblatt 1896, 1897

Preßburger Zeitung 1896, 1897

Semliner Wochenblatt 1895

Semliner Zeitung 1896

Siebenbürgisch-Deutsches Tageblatt 1896

Sokol: Časopis pre zábavu a poučenie 1853

Slavonische Presse 1896

Slovenské noviny 1896

Srbobran 1896

Szegedi Hiradó 1896

Szegedi Napló 1896

Szentesi Lap 1893

Vasárnapi Ujság 1856, 1860, 1874, 1883, 1886, 1896

Vlast' a Svet 1887

Westungarische Volkszeitung 1896

Westungarischer Grenzbote 1896, 1897

Zsidó Hiradó 1896

School Reports

As the title of school reports frequently varied, the signatures of the School Report Collection of the Széchényi Hungarian National Library are provided in parentheses following the school names.

Brassó, Roman Catholic Elementary School in the Downtown (ért. 186) 1901/02

Brassó, Roman Catholic Gymnasium (ért. 202) 1895/96

Brassó, Romanian Orthodox Gymnasium, Commercial School and Realschule (ért. 204) 1895/96

Brassó, Saxon Lutheran Gymnasium (ért. 203) 1868/69–1896/97

Brassó, State Commercial Academy (ért. 197) 1895/96

Brassó, State Elementary Schools (ért. 187) 1895/96, 1900/1901

Brassó, State Realschule (ért. 201) 1895/96, 1896/97

Munkács, State Elementary School (ért. 1278-1279) 1883/84, 1885/86, 1886/87, 1887/88

Munkács, State Gymnasium (ért. 1284) 1868/69–1914/15

Munkács, State Middle School for Girls (ért. 1282) 1882/83, 1895/96

Munkács, State Trade and Commercial Apprentice School (ért. 1281) 1885/86

Nitra, Jewish Elementary School (ért. 1467) 1908/09

Nitra, Municipal Trade and Commercial Apprentice School (ért. 1468) 1885/86–1917/18

Nitra, Roman Catholic Elementary Schools (ért. 1466) 1895/96

Nitra, Roman Catholic Gymnasium (ért. 1471) 1877/78–1917/18

Nitra, Roman Catholic Middle School for Girls (ért. 1470) 1895/96

Pressburg, Commercial Academy (ért. 1603) 1885/86

Pressburg, Lutheran Lyceum (ért. 1610) 1840/41, 1853/54, 1857/58, 1864/65, 1895/96

Pressburg, Roman Catholic Elementary Schools (ért. 1582) 1895/96, 1900/1901

Pressburg, Roman Catholic Gymnasium (ért. 1609) 1895/96

Pressburg, State Female Teachers' Training College (ért. 1598) 1873/74

Pressburg, State Realschule (ért. 1608) 1896/97

Pressburg, State Upper Grammar School for Girls (ért. 1607) 1894/95

Pressburg, Ursuline Middle School for Girls (ért. 1593) 1893/94

Semlin, State Realgymnasium and Upper School of Commerce (ért. 2164), 1897/98

Other Printed Sources

Die 50jährige Tätigkeit des Kronstädter Männer-Gesangvereins 1859 bis 1909. Kronstadt: Johann Gött's Sohn, 1909.

Ábrahám, Barna. "Urbanizáció, urbanitás az erdélyi románoknál a dualizmus korában." In *Erdélyi várostörténeti tanulmányok*, edited by Judit Pál and János Fleisz, 224–53. Csíkszereda: Pro Print, 2001.

Abshoff, Fritz. *Deutschlands Ruhm und Stolz: Unsere hervorragendsten vaterländischen Denkmäler in Wort und Bild.* Berlin: Universum, n. d.

Adressenbuch der Stadt Kronstadt 58 (1896).

Albert, Réka. "A nemzet tájképe: Történeti-antropológiai elemzés." In *Nemzeti látószögek a 19. századi Magyarországon: 19. századi magyar nemzetépítő diskurzusok*, edited by Réka Albert, Gábor Czoch, and Péter Erdősi, 179–211. Budapest: Atelier, 2010.

Aleksov, Bojan. "One Hundred Years of Yugoslavia: The Vision of Stojan Novaković Revisited." *Nationalities Papers* 39, no. 6 (November 2011): 997–1010.

Alexi, Theochar. *Johannes Honterus: Volksschrift.* Kronstadt: Gabony, 1897.

Ambruš, Jozef. "Slovenské národné obrodenie v Nitre." In *Nitra*, edited by Juraj Fojtík, 69–79. Bratislava: Obzor, 1977.

Angermayer, Károly. *A Preßburger Zeitung Magyarország legrégebbi hirlapja története: Geschichte der Preßburger Zeitung.* Pozsony: Angermayer Károly, 1896.

Ansted, D. T. *A Short Trip in Hungary and Transylvania in the Spring of 1862.* London: Wm. H. Allen & Co., 1862.

Baár, Monika. *Historians and Nationalism: East-Central Europe in the Nineteenth Century.* Oxford: Oxford University Press, 2010.

Babejová, Eleonóra. *Fin-de-Siècle Pressburg: Conflict and Cultural Coexistence in Bratislava 1897–1914.* Boulder, CO: East European Monographs, 2003.

Baiulescu, Bartolomeu. *Monografia comunei bisericesci gr. ort. române a Sfintei Adormiri din Cetatea Braşovului cu acte şi dovezi.* Braşov: Ciurcu, 1898.

Bak, János M. "From the Anonymous *Gesta* to the *Flight of Zalán* by Vörösmarty." In *Manufacturing a Past for the Present: Forgery and Authenticity in Medievalist Texts and Objects in Nineteenth-Century Europe*, edited by János M. Bak, Patrick J. Geary, and Gábor Klaniczay, 96–106. Leiden and Boston: Brill, 2015.

Bak, János M., and Anna Gara-Bak. "The Ideology of a 'Millennial Constitution' in Hungary." *East European Quarterly* 15, no. 3 (1981): 307–26.

Balajthy, József. *Munkács. Azaz: Munkács várának és városának topographiai, geographiai, históriai és statistikai leírása.* Debreczen: Tóth Lajos, 1836.

Bálint, Zoltán. *Die Architektur der Millenniumsausstellung.* Vienna: Kunstverlag Anton Schroll, 1897.

Balogh, János. *Munkács-vár története.* Munkács: szerző kiadása, 1890.

Balogh, Pál. *A népfajok Magyarországon.* Budapest: M. Kir. Vallás- és Közoktatásügyi Ministerium, 1902.

Băltescu, Mircea. "Contribuţii la istoricul 'Reuniunii Femeilor Române' din Braşov." *Cumidava* 1 (1967): 191–211.

Banac, Ivo. *The National Question in Yugoslavia: Origins, History, Politics.* Ithaca: Cornell University Press, 1984.

Bariţiu, Georgie. *Parti alese din Istori'a Transilvaniei: Pe doue sute de ani din urma.* 3 vols. Sibiu: W. Krafft, 1889–91.

Barla-Szabó, László. *A Vastagh művészcsalád.* Budapest: Ernst Múzeum, 2004.

Bârseanu, Andreiŭ. *Istoria Şcólelor Centrale Române Gr. Or. din Braşov.* Braşov: Ciurcu, 1902.

Bartha, Miklós. *Kazár földön.* 2 vols. Kolozsvár: Ellenzék, 1901.

Batka, Johann, and Emerich Wodiáner. *Zur Enthüllung des Hummel-Denkmals 16. October 1887. Joh. Nep. Hummel: Biographische Skizze. Geschichte des Denkmals und Rechnungsausweis.* Pressburg: Denkmal-Comité, 1887.

Bax, E. H. "Modernization and Cleavage in Dutch Society: A Study of Long Term Economic and Social Change." PhD diss., University of Groningen, 1988. Quoted in Paul Dekker and Peter Ester, "Depillarization, Dedenominationalization, and De-Ideologization: Empirical Trends in Dutch Society 1958–1992." *Review of Religious Research* 37, no. 4 (June 1996): 327–28.

Bay, Gábor, ed. *A munkácsi Árpád-szobor regénye.* Munkács: Munkácsi Árpád-szobor bizottság, 1942.

Beksics, Gusztáv. *Magyarosodás és magyarosítás: Különös tekintettek városainkra.* Budapest: Athenaeum, 1883.

Belgum, Kirsten. "Displaying the Nation: A View of Nineteenth-Century Monuments through a Popular Magazine." *Central European History* 26, no. 4 (1993): 457–74.

Beluszky, Pál, and Róbert Győri. *The Hungarian Urban Network in the Beginning of the 20th Century.* Pécs: Centre for Regional Studies of the Hungarian Academy of Sciences, 2005.

Benedek, Elek. *Szent Anna tavától a Cenk-tetőig.* Budapest: Franklin, n. d.

Benkó, Mihály. "A déványi és zobori kirándulás." *Turisták lapja* 10 (1898): 117–20.

Benyovszky, Karl, and Josef Grünsfeld. *Preßburger Ghettobilder.* Bratislava-Pressburg: Sigmund Steiner, 1932.

Benyovszky, Károly. *A pozsonyi magyar szinészet története 1867-ig.* Bratislava-Pozsony: Steiner Zsigmond, 1928.

Berecz, Ágoston. *The Politics of Early Language Teaching: Hungarian in the Primary Schools of the Late Dual Monarchy.* Budapest: Pasts, Inc., Central European University, 2013.

Berger, Benő. "A pozsonyi kong. izr. hitközség fiuiskolájának monográfiája." In *A magyarzsidó felekezet elemi és polgári iskoláinak monográfiája*, edited by Jónás Barna and Fülöp Csukási, 1: 331–52. Budapest: Corvina, 1896.

Berger, Stefan. "The Invention of European National Traditions in European Romanticism." In *The Oxford History of Historical Writing, vol. 4: 1800–1945*, edited by Stuart Macintyre, Juan Maiguashca, and Attila Pók, 19–40. Oxford: Oxford University Press, 2011.

Bergner, Rudolf. *Eine Fahrt duch's Land der Rastelbinder: Bilder und Skizzen aus Nordungarn.* Leipzig: S. L. Morgenstern, 1883.

Bertényi, Iván Jr. "A nevetségesség öl? Adalékok a magyarországi sovinizmusfogalom századfordulós értelmezéséhez." In *Magyar-szlovák terminológiai kérdések*, edited by Barna Ábrahám, 118–36. Piliscsaba: Pázmány Péter Katolikus Egyetem Bölcsészettudományi Kar Szlavisztika Közép-Európa Intézet Szent Adalbert Közép-Európa Kutatócsoport, 2008.

―――. "Zehn Denkmäler, ein Herrscher und eine Nation: Ein Ausgleichsversuch zwischen der dynastischen Loyalität und den ungarischen nationalen Emotionen." In *Jahrtausendwende 2000*, edited by Ferenc Glatz, 246–55. Budapest: Europa Institut, 2001.

Bettelheim, Samuel. "Geschichte der Preßburger Jeschiba." In *Die Juden und die Judengemeinde Bratislava in Vergangenheit und Gegenwart: Ein Sammelwerk*, edited by Hugo Gold, 61–67. Brünn: Jüdischer Buchverlag, 1932.

Beudant, F. S. *Travels in Hungary in 1818*. London: Richard Phillips, 1823.

Bielicky, Elek. *Nyitra vármegye földrajza: A Nyitra vármegyei népiskolák III-ik osztálya számára segédkönyvül*. Nyitra: Huszár István, 1908.

Bielz, E. A. *Handbuch der Landeskunde Siebenbürgens eine physikalisch-statistisch-topographische Beschreibung dieses Landes*. Hermannstadt: S. Filtsch, 1857.

Bjork, James E. *Neither German nor Pole: Catholicism and National Indifference in a Central European Borderland*. Ann Arbor: University of Michigan Press, 2008.

Boia, Lucian. *Relationships between Romanians, Czechs and Slovaks 1848–1914*. Bucharest: Edituria Academiei Republicii Socialiste România, 1977.

Boner, Charles. *Transylvania: Its Products and Its People*. London: Longmans, Green, Reader, and Dyer, 1865.

Borbély, János. "Heinrich Hentzi Magyarországon: 'Sárkányölő Szent Györgytől' a "vaskísértetig." *Aetas* 21, no. 4 (2006): 88–113.

Borovszky, Samu. *A honfoglalás története: A művelt közönség számára*. Budapest: Franklin-Társulat, 1894.

Botka, Tivadar. "Nyitrai emlékek." *Századok* 7, no. 9 (November 1873): 642–45.

Bozdog, Ion, ed. *Statul polițist: Material documentar dintr'o arhivă secretă brașoveană*. Brașov: ASTRA, 1944.

Bozóky, Endre, and Károly Antolik. *A pozsonyi állami főreáliskola története 1850-1893 és az intézet jelenlegi állapota*. Pozsony: Eder István, 1895.

Brandt, Juliane. "Die ungarischen Protestanten und das Millennium: Nationale und konfessionelle Identität bei Reformierten und Evangelischen im Spiegel der Tausendjahr-Feiern der Landnahme." *Jahrbücher für Geschichte und Kultur Südosteuropas* 1 (1999): 57–93.

Brock, Peter. *The Slovak National Awakening: An Essay in the Intellectual History of East Central Europe*. Toronto: University of Toronto Press, 1976.

Brophy, James M. *Popular Culture and the Public Sphere in the Rhineland, 1800–1850*. Cambridge: Cambridge University Press, 2010.

Brusanowski, Paul. *Învățământul confesional ortodox din Transilvania între anii 1848–1918: Între exigențele statului centralizat și principiile autonomiei bisericești*. Cluj-Napoca: Presa Universitară Clujeană, 2005.

Bucur, Maria, and Nancy M. Wingfield, eds. *Staging the Past: The Politics of Commemoration in Habsburg Central Europe, 1848 to the Present*. West Lafayette, IN: Purdue University Press, 2001.

Burke, Peter. "Lay History: Official and Unofficial Representations, 1800–1914." In *The Oxford History of Historical Writing, vol. 4: 1800–1945*, edited by Stuart Macintyre, Juan Maiguashca, and Attila Pók, 115–32. Oxford: Oxford University Press, 2011.

Buxbaum, Heinrich. *Geschichte der israel. öffentlichen Gemeinde-Primär-Hauptschule, und des Hermann Todesco'schen Stiftungsgebäudes in Pressburg: Von ihrem Entstehen bis auf den heutigen Tag (1820–1884)*. Pressburg: Selbstverlag des Verfassers, 1884.

Carlyle, Thomas. *On Heroes, Hero-worship, and the Heroic in History: Six Lectures*. London: James Fraser, 1841.

Ćelap, Lazar. *Zemun u srpskom pokretu 1848–1849*. Novi Sad: Matica Srpska, 1960.

———. *Zemunski vojni komunitet*. Beograd: Izdavačka Ustanova Naučno Delo, 1967.

Cercel, Cristian. "Transylvanian Saxon Symbolic Geographies." *Civilisations* 60, no. 2 (2012): 83–101.

Cesnaková-Michalcová, Milena. *Geschichte des deutschsprachigen Theaters in der Slowakei*. Cologne: Böhlau, 1997.

Cieger, András. "A Bereg megyei politikai elit a dualizmus időszakában." *Szabolcs-Szatmár-Beregi Levéltári Évkönyv* 12 (1997): 213–81.

———. "A hatalomra jutott liberalizmus és az állam a dualizmus első felének magyar politikai gondolkodásában." *Századvég*, no. 20 (2001): 95–118.

———. "A közigazgatás autonómiájának nézőpontjai 1848–1918." In *Autonómiák Magyarországon 1848–2000*, edited by Jenő Gergely, 1: 25–62. Budapest: ELTE Történettudományi Doktori Iskola – L'Harmattan, 2005.

Clogg, Richard. "The Greek Merchant Companies in Transylvania." In *Minderheiten, Regionalbewusstsein und Zentralismus in Ostmitteleuropa*, edited by Heinz-Dietrich Löwe, Günther H. Tontsch, and Stefan Troebst, 161–69. Cologne: Böhlau, 2000.

Colan, Ion. *Casina Română din Braşov (1835–1935)*. Braşov: Institutul de Arte Grafice "ASTRA," 1935.

———. "După cincizeci de ani: Librăria Ciurcu din Braşov." *Ţara Bârsei* 2, no. 6 (1930): 547–50.

Confino, Alan. *The Nation as a Local Metaphor: Württemberg, Imperial Germany, and National Memory, 1871–1918*. Chapel Hill: University of North Carolina Press, 1997.

Csáky, Moritz. "'Hungarus' oder 'Magyar': Zwei Varianten des Nationalbewusstseins zu Beginn des 19. Jahrhunderts." *Annales Universitatis Scientiarium Budapestinensis: Sectio Historica* 22 (1982): 71–84.

Csapodi, Csaba. *Az Anonymus-kérdés története*. Budapest: Magvető, 1978.

Cserei, József. *Szentbeszéd: Az ezredév alkalmával a tanuló ifjúságnak*. Temesvár: Uhrmann Henrik, 1896.

Cserenyey, István. *Palugyay Imre püspök és a nyitrai irgalmas nővérek emlékezete*. Nyitra: Risnyovszky János, 1911.

Csősz, Imre. *A kegyes-tanító-rend nyitrai gymnasiumának történeti vázlata*. Nyitra: Neugebauer E., 1876.

———. *A kegyes-tanító-rendiek Nyitrán: Magyar műveltségtörténelmi rajz*. Nyitra: Siegler M., 1879.

Čulen, Konštantin. *Slovenské študentské tragédie*. Bratislava: Slovenska Liga, 1935.

Czinár, Mór. "Győr vármegyei Sabáriáról." *Magyar Akadémiai Értesítő* 19, no. 6 (1859): 515–26.

———. "Sacer Mons Pannoniae aevo vetere et cunabula benedictina monasterii S. Martini super eo siti." *Status personalis, officialis et localis religiosorum antiquissimi, celeberrimi, regii, nullius dioeceseos, sedi apostolicae immediate subiecti Archi-coenobii Sancti Martini in Sacro Monte Pannoniae ordinis S. Benedictini congregationes cassinensis alias S. Iustinae de Padua* (1846): 7–29.

Czobor, Béla. *Egyházi emlékek a történelmi kiállításon*. Budapest: Pesti Könyvnyomda, 1896.

Czobor, Béla, and Imre Szalay, eds. *Magyarország történeti emlékei az 1896. évi országos kiállításon*. Budapest: Gerlach Márton, 1903.

Dabižić, Miodrag A., and Stevan S. Radovanović. *Zemunska biblioteka 1825–1975*. Zemun: Matična Biblioteka Jovan Popović, 1975.

Dabrowski, Patrice M. *Commemorations and the Shaping of Modern Poland*. Bloomington: Indiana University Press, 2004.

Dalfüzér nagyságos és főtisztelendő Göndöcs Benedek Ujkigyósi lelkésznek Zeer monostori apáttá lett örvendetes kineveztetése alkalmára szerkesztve. N. p.: Első magyar egyesületi könyvnyomda, 1869.

Dankó, József. *Győrmegyei Sabaria vagyis Pannonhalmi Szent-Márton toursi Sz. Mártonnak születéshelye: Történeti tanulmány.* Esztergom: Horák Egyed, 1868.

Danneberg, Stephanie. "Die Verbrüderungsbewegung und Partei 'Nemere': Ein besonderer Moment im politischen Leben Kronstadts der 1870er Jahre." *Forschungen für Volks- und Landeskunde* 54 (2011): 107–20.

Dariu, Ión. *Geografia comitatului "Brasso": Precedată de elementele introductive în geografia universală pentru școlele poporale, anul al III-lea de școlă.* Brassó: Ciurcu, 1901.

Deac, Augustin. *Mișcarea muncitorească din Transilvania 1890–1895.* Bucharest: Editura Științifică, 1962.

Dedek Crescens, Lajos. "Nyitravármegye története." In *Magyarország vármegyéi és városai: Nyitravármegye,* edited by Samu Borovszky and János Sziklay, 466–680. Budapest: Apollo, 1898.

———. "Pozsony vármegye története." In *Magyarország vármegyéi és városai: Pozsony vármegye, Pozsony sz. kir. város, Nagyszombat, Bazin, Modor, és Szentgyörgy r. t. városok,* edited by Samu Borovszky, 503–637. Budapest: Apollo, n. d.

Demmel, József. *"Egész Szlovákia elfért egy tutajon...": Tanulmányok a 19. századi Magyarország szlovák történelméről.* Pozsony: Kalligram, 2009.

———. *Pánszlávok a kastélyban: Justh József és a szlovák nyelvű magyar nemesség elfeledett története.* Pozsony: Kalligram, 2014.

Déri, Gyula. *Pozsony és Pozsony vármegye.* Budapest: Hornyánszky Viktor, 1909.

Diachonovich, C., ed. *Enciclopedia română.* 3 vols. Sibiu: Krafft, 1898–1900.

Egry, Gábor. "Nemzet és gazdaság: A Brassói Általános Takarékpénztár társadalmi-gazdasági szerepfelfogása (1835–1914)." *Pro Minoritate* (Spring 2003): 59–68.

Eliáš, Michal. "Pobočka stánok Slovenského učeného tovarišstva v Nitre." In *Kapitoly z dejín Nitry: Sborník štúdií k 1100. výročiu príchodu Cyrila a Metóda,* edited by Alexander Csanda, 68–80. Bratislava: Slovenské Pedagogické Nakladateľstvo, 1963.

Emlékkönyv: Fennállásának tizedik évfordulója alkalmából kiadta a Nyitrai nagyobb papnevelőintézet magyar egyházirodalmi iskolája. Nyitra: Huszár István, 1899.

Encyclopedia Judaica. Jerusalem: Encyclopedia Judaica, 1971.

Endrődi, Sándor, ed. *Az 1887. szeptember hó 26-ára hirdetett országgyűlés képviselőházának naplója.* Budapest: Pesti Könyvnyomda, 1892.

Engyeli, Eugen, and Alois Langer. *Festschrift zur Enthüllung des Preßburger Krönungsdenkmales am 16. Mai 1897.* Pressburg: Stefan Eder, 1897.

Engyeli, Jenő, and Alajos Langer. *Emléklapok a pozsonyi koronázó emlékszobor leleplezésének ünnepére 1897. évi május hó 16-án.* Pozsony: Eder István, 1897.

Erdélyi, László, ed. *A pannonhalmi főapátság története: Első korszak. A megalapítás és terjeszkedés kora 996–1243,* vol. 1 of *A Pannonhalmi Szent-Benedek-Rend története.* Budapest: Stephaneum, 1902.

Erdélyi, Lipót, ed. *Emléklap a nyitrai izr. hitközségi népiskola új épületének felavatása alkalmából.* Nyitra: Iritzer, 1898.

Erdélyi, Mór. *A Magyar Állam ezeréves fennállását megörökítő hét vidéki emlékmű: 896–1896.* Budapest: Hornyánszky, 1896.

Ezeréves Magyarország: XIII. Leó pápa és a magyar katholikus főpásztorok ünneplő szava papjaik- és hiveikhez a magyar honfoglalás ezredik évfordulója alkalmából. Budapest: Szent-István-Társulat, 1896.

Fehér, Ipoly. "Pannonhalma." In *Győr megye és város egyetemes leírása,* edited by Ipoly Fehér, 659–70. Budapest: Franklin-Társulat, 1874.

Feischmidt, Margit. "Lehorgonyzott mítoszok: Kőbe vésett sztereotípiák? A lokalizáció jelentősége az aradi vértanúk emlékműve és a millenniumi emlékoszlopok kapcsán." In *Mindennapi előítéletek: Társadalmi távolságok és etnikai sztereotípiák*, edited by Boglárka Bakó, Richárd Papp, and László Szarka, 370–91. Budapest: Balassi, 2006.

Fényes, Elek. *Magyarország geographiai szótára, mellyben minden város, falu és puszta, betürendben körülményesen leiratik.* 4 vols. Pest: Kozma Vazul, 1851.

Fogel, Danilo. *The Jewish Community in Zemun: Chronicle (1739–1945).* Zemun: Jewish Community in Zemun, 2007.

Forster, Gyula, ed. *Magyarország műemlékei.* 4 vols. Budapest: Hornyánszky Viktor, 1905–15.

Fraknói, Vilmos. "Előszó." In *Magyarország vármegyéi és városai: Nyitravármegye*, edited by Samu Borovszky and János Sziklay, ix–xv. Budapest: Apollo, 1898.

Francsics, Norbert. "Das Raaber Comitat." In *Die Österreichisch-Ungarische Monarchie in Wort und Bild: Ungarn IV*, 461–83. Vienna: Verlag der kaiserlich-königlichen Hof- und Staatsdruckerei, 1896.

Freifeld, Alice. *Nationalism and the Crowd in Liberal Hungary, 1848–1914.* Washington, DC: Woodrow Wilson Center Press, 2000.

Gaben-Verzeichnis: Enthaltend die für das Honterus-Denkmal gespendeten Beträge an Geld und Geldeswert. Kronstadt: Honterus-Denkmal-Ausschuss, 1898.

Gerő, András. *The Hungarian Parliament, 1867–1918: A Mirage of Power.* Boulder, CO: Social Science Monographs, 1997.

———. *Modern Hungarian Society in the Making: The Unfinished Experience.* Budapest: Central European University Press, 1995.

Ghibu, Onosofir. *Viaţa şi organizaţia bisericească şi şcolară in Transilvania şi Ungaria.* Bucharest: Nicolae Stroilă, 1915.

Gillis, John R. "Memory and Identity: The History of a Relationship." In *Commemorations: The Politics of National Identity*, edited by John R. Gillis, 3–24. Princeton: Princeton University Press, 1994.

Gleig, G. R. *Germany, Bohemia and Hungary: Visited in 1837.* London: John W. Parker, 1839.

Glettler, Monika. "Ethnische Vielfalt in Pressburg und Budapest um 1910." *Ungarn Jahrbuch* 16 (1988): 46–71, and 17 (1989): 95–152.

Göllner, Carl. "Abwehr von Magyarisierungsversuchen 1877–1900." In *Die Siebenbürger Sachsen in den Jahren 1848–1918*, edited by Carl Göllner, 170–205. Cologne-Vienna: Böhlau Verlag, 1988.

———. "Die Auflösung der Sächsischen Nationsuniversität (1876): Vorgeschichte und Folgen." In *Gruppenautonomie in Siebenbürgen: 500 Jahre siebenbürgisch-sächsische Nationsuniversität*, edited by Wolfgang Kessler, 355–66. Cologne: Böhlau, 1990.

Gologan, N. G. V. *Cercetări privitoare la trecutul comerţului românesc din Braşov.* Bucharest: Lupta, 1928.

Göndöcs, Benedek. *Pusztaszer és az évezredes ünnepély.* Budapest: szerző kiadása, 1883.

Gracza, György. *Az 1848–49-iki magyar szabadságharcz története.* 5 vols. Budapest: Lampel, 1895.

Greenfeld, Liah. *Nationalism: Five Roads to Modernity.* Cambridge, MA: Harvard University Press, 1992.

Groß, David. "Äusserer Verlauf der Geschichte der Juden." In *Die Juden und die Judengemeinde Bratislava in Vergangenheit und Gegenwart: Ein Sammelwerk*, edited by Hugo Gold, 3–10. Brünn: Jüdischer Buchverlag, 1932.

———. "Zionistisches Leben in Bratislava." In *Die Juden und die Judengemeinde Bratislava in Vergangenheit und Gegenwart: Ein Sammelwerk*, edited by Hugo Gold, 141–46. Brünn: Jüdischer Buchverlag, 1932.

Groß, Julius. "Aus der Geschichte des Burzenlandes." In *Das sächsische Burzenland*, 1–70. Kronstadt: Honterusdruckerei, Joh. Gött's Sohn, 1898.

———. *Geschichte des evangelischen Gymnasiums A. B. in Kronstadt: Festschrift zur Honterusfeier*. Kronstadt: Honterusdruckerei J. Gött's Sohn, 1898.

Gross-Hoffinger, A. J. *Die Donau vom Ursprung bis in das schwarze Meer: Ein Handbuch for Donaureisende von Ulm, Linz, Wien, Pesth, Galatz über das shwarze Meer nach Constantinopel*. Breslau: Eduard Trewendt, 1846.

Grünfeld, Náthán. "Nyitra és vidéke." In *Magyar zsidók a millenniumon: Művelődéstörténeti tanulmány*, edited by Hermán Zichy and Gy. M. Derestye, 91–108. Budapest: Miljković Dragutin, 1896.

Grünsfeld, Josef. "Geschichte der orth. israelitischen Kultusgemeinde." In *Die Juden und die Judengemeinde Bratislava in Vergangenheit und Gegenwart: Ein Sammelwerk*, edited by Hugo Gold, 109–18. Brünn: Jüdischer Buchverlag, 1932.

———. "Neue Geschichte der Jeschiba." In *Die Juden und die Judengemeinde Bratislava in Vergangenheit und Gegenwart: Ein Sammelwerk*, edited by Hugo Gold, 67–69. Brünn: Jüdischer Buchverlag, 1932.

Grünwald, Béla. *A Felvidék: Politikai tanulmány*. Budapest: Ráth Mór, 1878.

Gudewitz, Thorsten. "Performing the Nation: The Schiller Centenary Celebrations of 1859 and the Media." *European Review of History* 15, no. 6 (2008): 587–601.

Gusbeth, Eduard. *Die Bewegung der Bevölkerung im Kronstädter Komitat in den Jahren 1876–1887*. Kronstadt: Albrecht & Zillich, 1888.

Gyáni, Gábor. "A középosztály és a polgárság múltja különös tekintettel a dualizmus kori Erdélyre." In *Erdélyi várostörténeti tanulmányok*, edited by Judit Pál and János Fleisz, 157–77. Csíkszereda: Pro Print, 2001.

Györffy, János, and Arnold Zellinger. *Földrajzi előismeretek: Nyitravármegye rövid földrajza. Vezérkönyv a nyitravármegyei római kath. népiskolák III. osztályú tanítói számára*. Budapest: Szent István Társulat, 1913.

———. *Földrajzi előismeretek: Pozsony vármegye és Pozsony város rövid földrajza*. Budapest: Szent István Társulat, 1913.

Győrvármegye törvényhatósági bizottságának Pannonhalmán az országos ezredéves emlékmű alapkövének letétele alkalmával 1896. évi augusztus hó 26-án tartott ünnepélyes közgyűléséről felvett jegyzőkönyv. Győr: Gross testvérek, 1896.

Gyurgyák, János. *Ezzé lett magyar hazátok…: A magyar nemzeteszme és nacionalizmus története*. Budapest: Osiris, 2007.

Halász, Sándor. *Horvát-, Szlavon-, Dalmátországnak Magyarországhoz való viszonya a történelmi és közjogi alapon*. Pápa: Debreczeny Károly, 1885.

Halbik, Ciprián. "Adatok Pannonhalma múltjához." *A pannonhalmi Sz. Benedekrend névtára 1880-ik évre* (1880): ix–cix.

———. *Pannonhalma a milleniumon: Ünnepi beszéd*. Budapest: Hunyady Mátyás Intézet, 1896.

Hanák, Péter. "Die Parallelaktion von 1898: Fünfzig Jahre ungarische Revolution und fünfzig Jahre Regierungsjubiläum Franz Josephs." In *Der Garten und der Werkstatt: Ein kulturgeschichtlicher Vergleich Wien und Budapest um 1900*, 101–15. Vienna: Böhlau, 1992.

Handler, Andrew. *An Early Blueprint for Zionism: Győző Istóczy's Political Anti-semitism.* Boulder, CO: East European Monographs, 1989.

Hanebrink, Paul A. *In Defense of Christian Hungary: Religion, Nationalism, and Antisemitism, 1890–1944.* Ithaca: Cornell University Press, 2006.

Hannak, Christof. "Die alten Kronstädter Gassennamen." In *Kronstadt: Eine siebenbürgische Stadtgeschichte,* edited by Harald Roth, 268–85. Munich: Universitas, 1999.

Haslinger, Peter. "Das Ungarnbild der Wiener Presse am Vorabend des Millenniums: Der Nationalitätenkongress 1895 und die kroatische Frage." In *Nationalitäten und Identitäten in Ostmitteleuropa: Festschrift aus Anlaß des 70. Geburtstages von Richard Georg Plaschka.* Edited by Walter Lukan and Arnold Suppan, 133–46. Vienna: Böhlau Verlag, 1995.

————. *Hundert Jahre Nachbarschaft: Die Beziehungen zwischen Österreich und Ungarn 1895–1994.* Frankfurt am Main: Peter Lang, 1996.

————. *Nation und Territorium im tschechischen politischen Diskurs 1880–1938.* Munich: Oldenbourg, 2010.

Hefner, Nikolaus, Franz Egger, and Josef Braschel. *Franztal 1816–1944.* Salzburg: Verein der Franztaler Ortsgemeinschaft, 1984.

Hegedűs, Pál. *Pusztaszer.* Szeged: Lipsitz Sándor, 1903.

Heksch, Alexander F. *Die Donau von ihrem Ursprung bis an die Mündung: Eine Schilderung von Land und Leuten des Donaugebietes.* Vienna: A. Hartleben, 1881.

————. *Illustrirter Führer durch Pressburg und seine Umgebungen.* Vienna-Pressburg: C. Stampel, 1884.

————. *Illustrirter Führer durch Ungarn und seine Nebenländer (Siebenbürgen, Croatien, Slavonien und Fiume.* Vienna: A. Hartleben, 1882.

————. *Neuester Führer durch Pressburg und Umgebungen.* Pressburg: Selbstverlag des Verfassers, 1880.

Hermann, Gusztáv Mihály. *Az eltérített múlt: Oklevél- és krónikahamisítványok a székelyek történetében.* Csíkszereda: Pro-Print, 2007.

Hitchins, Keith. "Austria-Hungary, Rumania, and the Nationality Problem in Transylvania, 1894–1897." *Rumanian Studies* 4 (1979): 75–126.

————. "The Romanians of Transylvania and the Congress of Nationalities." *The Slavonic and East European Review* 48, no. 112 (July 1970): 388–402.

Hodinka, Antal. *A munkácsi görög-katholikus püspökség története.* Budapest: Magyar Tudományos Akadémia, 1909.

Holec, Roman. *Tragédia v Černovej a slovenské spoločnost'.* Martin: Matica slovenská, 1997.

Holly, Eugen. *Im Lande der Kabbalisten, der Religionskämpfe und des Hungers: Quer durch Karpatorussland.* Pressburg: Grenzbote, 1927.

"A honfoglalás." In *Népszava naptár 1896. szökő évre a magyar munkásnép számára,* 128–33. Budapest: Boruth E., 1896.

Hornik, Solomon. "Misrachi in Pressburg und in der Slowakei." In *Die Juden und die Judengemeinde Bratislava in Vergangenheit und Gegenwart: Ein Sammelwerk,* edited by Hugo Gold, 147–50. Brünn: Jüdischer Buchverlag, 1932.

Hornyik, János. *Pusztaszer, a honalapító magyar nemzet első törvényhozási közgyűlése színhelyének története.* Kecskemét: Gallia Fülöp, 1865.

Horvát- és Szlavónország a Magyarország ezeréves fennállásának megünneplésére Budapesten 1896.-évben rendezett országos kiállításon. Zágráb: Narodne Novine, 1896.

Horvát, Sándor, ed. *Okmánytár a piaristák Sz. László királyról czímzett nyitrai kollegiumának történetéhez 1698–1849.* Nyitra: Huszár István, 1896.

Horváth, Mihály. *Magyarország függetlenségi harczának története 1848 és 1849-ben.* 3 vols. Genf: Puky Miklós, 1865.

———. *Magyarország történelme.* 8 vols. Pest: Heckenast Gusztáv, 1871–73.

Horváth, Vladimír. "Preßburger Bürger in der inneren Stadt (1740–1916)." In *Städtisches Alltagsleben in Mitteleuropa vom Mittelalter bis zum Ende des 19. Jahrhunderts: Die Referate des internationalen Symposions in Časta-Píla vom 11.-14. September 1995,* edited by Viliam Čičaj and Othmar Pickl, 225–30. Bratislava: Academic Electronic Press, 1998.

Hunfalvy, János. *Magyarország és Erdély eredeti képekben.* 3 vols. Darmstadt: Lange Gusztáv György, 1864.

Hurban, Miloslaw Jos., ed. *Nitra: Dar dcerám a syňŭm Slowenska, Morawy, Čech a Slezka obětowaný.* Prešporok: Antonjn Šmid, 1842.

Hurban Vajanský, Svetozár. *Storočná pamiatka narodenia Štefana Moysesa, biskupa bańskobystrického: Jeho veličenstva skutočného tajného radcu, doktora filosofie, predsedu Matice Slovenskej 1797–1897.* Turčiansky Sv. Martin: Kníhkupecko-nakladateľský spolok, 1897.

Ilić, Nikola. *Zemunska Gornja Varoš.* Zemun: Mostart, 2000.

Illustrierte Führer durch Pozsony (Pressburg) und Umgebung: Mit 52 Abbildungen, Stadtplan, Karten der Umgebung und des Komitates Pozsony in Farbendruck. Pozsony: Sigmund Steiner, n. d.

Imendörffer, A., W. Gerlai, and J. Sziklay. *Nach und durch Ungarn: Von Wien nach Budapest.* Zürich: Orell Füssli, n. d.

"I my v Evropi: Protest halyts'kyh Rusyniv proty madiars'koho tysiacholitia." *Zhyte i slovo: Vistnyk literatury, polityky i nauky* 3, no. 1 (1896): 1–9.

Iorga, Nicolae. *Brașovul și romînii: Scrisorĭ și lămuririĭ.* Bucharest: I. V. Socecu, 1905.

Jabukovich, Sándor. "A nyitrai róm. kath. elemi fiúiskola multja és jelene." In *A nyitrai városi róm. kath. elemi fiú- és leányiskolák értesítője az 1896–97. tanévről,* 3–163. Nyitra: Huszár István nyomdája, 1897.

Jászi, Oscar. *The Dissolution of the Habsburg Monarchy.* Chicago: University of Chicago Press, 1929.

Jekelfalussy, József, ed. *A Magyar Korona Országainak Helységnévtára 1900.* Budapest: Pesti Könyvnyomda-Részvénytársaság, 1900.

Jekelius, August. *Die Burzenländer Zigeuner im Jahre 1893.* Kronstadt: J. Gött's Sohn, n. d.

———. *Der Grund- und Hausbesitz im Burzenland.* Kronstadt: n. p., 1904.

Jelinek, Yeshayahu A. *The Carpathian Diaspora: The Jews of Subcarpathian Rus' and Mukachevo, 1848–1948.* Boulder, CO: East European Monographs, 2007.

Jeschke, Felix. "Dracula on Rails: The *Preßburgerbahn* between Imperial Space and National Body, 1867–1935." *Central Europe* 10, no. 1 (May 2012): 1–17.

Jeszenszky, Alajos, ed. *Bende Imre püspök beszédei: Ötven éves áldozárságának emlékére.* Nyitra: Huszár István, 1897.

Jeszenszky, Géza. *Az elveszett presztízs: Magyarország megítélésének változása Nagy-Britanniában (1894–1918).* Budapest: Magvető, 1986.

"Jogadémiai millenniumi bizottság." *A Kecskeméti Ev. Ref. Jogakadémia Évkönyve* 20 (1895): 81–90, and 21 (1896): 106–23.

Johnson, Owen V. *Slovakia 1918–1938: Education and the Making of a Nation.* Boulder, CO: East European Monographs, 1985.

Jónás, Johannes. *Rückblick auf die fünfzigjährige Thätigkeit der Preßburger ersten Sparcassa in den Jahren 1842–1891.* Pressburg: Stampfel, Eder, 1892.

Judson, Pieter M. *Guardians of the Nation: Activists on the Language Frontiers of Imperial Austria.* Cambridge, MA: Harvard University Press, 2006.

Kaindl, Raimund Friedrich. *Geschichte der Deutschen in den Karpathenländern.* 3 vols. Gotha: Friedrich Andreas Perthes, 1911.

Kajtár, István. *Magyar városi önkormányzatok (1848–1918).* Budapest: Akadémiai Kiadó, 1992.

Kálal, Karel. *Na krásném Slovensku.* Praha: Jos. R. Vilímek, n. d.

Karady, Victor. *The Jews of Europe in the Modern Era: A Socio-historical Outline.* Budapest: Central European University Press, 2004.

Katona, József. "A Kecskeméti Pusztákról." *Tudományos Gyűjtemény* 7, no. 4 (1823): 50–58.

Katz, Jacob. "Towards a Biography of the Hatam Sofer." In idem., *Divine Law in Human Hands: Case Studies in Halakhic Flexibility,* 403–43. Jerusalem: Magnes Press, Hebrew University, 1998.

————. *With My Own Eyes: The Autobiography of an Historian.* Hanover, NH: Brandeis University Press, 1995.

Katzburg, Nathaniel. *Antisemitism in Hungary, 1867–1914.* Tel-Aviv: Dvir, 1969.

Kaval, Hillel J. "Texts and Contest: Myths of Origin and Myths of Belonging in Nineteenth-Century Bohemia." In *Jewish History and Jewish Memory: Essays in Honor of Yosef Hayim Yerushalmi,* edited by Elisheva Carlebach, John M. Efron, and David N. Myers, 348–68. Hanover, NH: Brandeis University Press, 1998.

Kelecsény, József, and Imre Vahot. "Nyitra jelen állapota." In *Nyitra és környéke képes albuma,* 13–22. Pest: Vahot Imre, 1854.

Kemény, Gábor G., ed. *Iratok a nemzetiségi kérdés történetéhez Magyarországon a dualizmus korában.* 7 vols. Budapest: Tankönyvkiadó, 1952–99.

Kiliánová, Gabriela. *Identität und Gedächtnis in der Slowakei: Die Burg Devín als Erinnerungsort.* Frankfurt am Main: Peter Lang, 2012.

Kincses, Katalin Mária. "Minden különös ceremonia nélkül: A Rákóczi-kultusz és a fejedelem hamvainak hazahozatala." In idem., *Kultusz és hagyomány: Tanulmányok a Rákóczi-szabadságharc 300. évfordulóján,* 132–77. Budapest: Argumentum, 2003.

King, Jeremy. *Budweisers into Czechs and Germans: A Local History of Bohemian Politics 1848–1948.* Princeton: Princeton University Press, 2003.

Kirschbaum, Joseph M. "The Role of the Cyrilo-Methodian Tradition in Slovak National and Political Life." *Slovak Studies* 3 (1963): 153–72.

Klaić, Vj[ekoslav]. *Opis zemalja u kojih obitavaju hrvati.* Zagreb: Dionička tiskare, 1881.

————. *Slavonija od X. do XIII. stoljeća.* Zagreb: Dionička tiskare, 1882.

Klaniczay, Gábor. "The Myth of Scythian Origin and the Cult of Attila in the Nineteenth Century." In *Multiple Antiquities—Multiple Modernities: Ancient Histories in Nineteenth Century European Cultures,* edited by Gábor Klaniczay, Michael Werner, and Ottó Gecser, 185–212. Frankfurt: Campus, 2011.

Kohl, J. G. *Austria: Vienna, Prague, Hungary, Bohemia, and the Danube; Galicia, Styria, Moravia, Bukovina and the Military Frontier.* London: Chapman and Hall, 1843.

Kohn, Sámuel. *A zsidók története Magyarországon: A legrégebbi időktől a mohácsi vészig.* Budapest: Athenaeum, 1884.

Komlos, John. *The Habsburg Monarchy as a Customs Union: Economic Development in Austria-Hungary in the Nineteenth Century.* Princeton: Princeton University Press, 1983.

Komora, Pavol. "Milenárne oslavy v Uhorsku roku 1896 a ich vnímanie v slovenskom prostredí." *Historický Časopis* 44, no. 1 (1996): 3–16.

Kompánek, Jozef. *Nitra: Nástin dejepisný, miestopisný a vzdelanostný*. Ružomberok: Karol Salva, 1895.

Könyöki, József. *Kleiner Wegweiser Pressburg's und seiner Umgebung mit einer Karte von Pressburg*. Pressburg: Angermayer, 1873.

Koós, Ferenc. *Az 1848 márczius 15-iki ünnepély hét éves története Brassóban*. Brassó: Közművelődés, 1892.

Korać, Gordana. "Zemun i Zemunci u Prvom srpskom ustanku." *Godišnjak Grada Beograda* 55–56 (2008–2009): 129–205.

Korodi, Lutz. *Die Honterus-Jubelfeier und die sächsischen Vereinstage in Kronstadt*. Kronstadt: H. Zeidner, 1898.

Kőrösy, József. *A Felvidék eltótosodása: Nemzetiségi tanulmányok. Pozsony és Nyitra megyék külön lenyomata*. Budapest: Grill Károly, 1898.

Koshar, Rudy. *From Monuments to Traces: Artifacts of German Memory, 1870–1990*. Berkeley: University of California Press, 2000.

Kőszeghy, István. "A Magyar Turista-Egyesületnek 1902. évben Budapesten tartott közgyűlése alkalmából rendezett kirándulásai." *Turisták lapja* 14 (1902): 108–26.

Kovács, Ákos. *A kitalált hagyomány*. Pozsony: Kalligram, 2006.

Kovalovszky, Márta. "'Bronzba öntött halhatatlan': A historizmus emlékműszobrászata." In *A historizmus művészete Magyarországon: Művészettörténeti tanulmányok*, edited by Anna Zádor, 79–98. Budapest: Magyar Tudományos Akadémia Művészettörténeti Kutató Intézet, 1993.

Kőváry, László. "Barczaság." In *Erdély képekben*, edited by Károly Szathmári Pap, 55–62. Kolosvár: Kir. Lyceum, 1842.

———. *Erdély története 1848–49-ben*. Pest: Emich, 1861.

———. *A millennium lefolyásának története és a millenáris emlékalkotások*. Budapest: Athenaeum, 1897.

Kövér, György. "Inactive Transformation: Social History of Hungary from the Reform Era to World War I." In *Social History of Hungary from the Reform Era to the End of the Twentieth Century*, edited by Gábor Gyáni, György Kövér, and Tibor Valuch, 3–267. Boulder, CO: Social Science Monographs, 2004.

———. "A magyar középosztály-teremtés programjai és kudarcai: Fogalomtörténeti áttekintés a reformkor végétől a nagy válság kezdetéig." In *Zsombékok: Középosztályok és iskoláztatás Magyarországon a 19. század elejétől a 20. század közepéig*, edited by György Kövér, 77–160. Budapest: Századvég, 2006.

———. *A tiszaeszlári dráma: Társadalomtörténeti látószögek*. Budapest: Osiris, 2011.

Krajčovič, Milan. *Slovenská politika v Strednej Európe 1890–1901: Spolupráca Slovákov, Rumunov a Srbov*. Bratislava: Vydavateľstvo Slovenskej Akadémie Vied, 1971.

Krestić, Vasilije. *Istorija srpske štampe u Ugarskoj 1791–1914*. Novi Sad: Matica Srpska, 1980.

Krickel, Adalbert Joseph. *Wanderung von Wien über Pressburg und Tyrnau in die Bergstädte Schemnitz, Kremnitz und Neusohl, und von da in die Turoß und das Waagthal*. Vienna: M. Ehr Adolph, 1831.

Kubik, Jan. *The Power of Symbols against the Symbols of Power: The Rise of Solidarity and the Fall of State Socialism in Poland*. University Park, PA: The Pennsylvania State University Press, 1994.

Kubinszky, Judit. *Politikai antiszemitizmus Magyarországon 1875–1900*. Budapest: Kossuth, 1976.

Kubinyi, Ferencz and Imre Vahot, eds. *Magyarország és Erdély képekben*. 4 vols. Pest: Emich Gusztáv, 1853–1854.

Kukk, Kristi. "Stubborn Histories: Overcoming Pagan Brutality Narrative in Estonian 19th-Century National-Romantic Historiography in the Nordic and Baltic Context." *Scandinavian Journal of History* 38, no. 2 (2013): 135–53.

Kumlik, Emil. *Adalékok a pozsonyi országgyűlések történetéhez (1825–1848)*. Pozsony: Stampfel Hugó, 1908.

———. *Pozsony und der Freiheitskampf 1848/49*. Pozsony: Karl Stampfel, 1905.

———. *A szabadságharc pozsonyi vértanui*. Pozsony: Stampfel Károly, 1905.

Kuncz, Aladár. *Thököly a francia irodalomban*. Budapest: Fritz Ármin, 1914.

Kuppis, Uzor. *Jelentés a Pozsonyi Dalárda huszonöt évi művészeti tevékenységéről 1857–1882*. Pozsony: Stampfel, Eder és társai, 1882.

Kyllien, Hansgeorg. "Die ethnische und konfessionelle Zusammensetzung der Schülerschaft am Kronstädter deutschen Gymnasium von 1856/57 bis 1946/47." *Zeitschrift für Siebenbürgische Landeskunde* 29, no. 1 (2006): 37–43.

Lajtai, László L. *"Magyar nemzet vagyok": Az első magyar nyelvű és hazai tárgyú történelemtankönyvek nemzetdiskurzusa*. Budapest: Argumentum, 2013.

Lăpědatu, Ioan I. *Probleme sociale și economice: Ajută-te și Dumnedău te va ajuta*. Brașov: A. Mureșianu, 1904.

László-Herbert, Márk. "Sztálingrádok Kelet-Európában: Orașul Stalin, 1950–1960." *Korunk* 3/14, no. 2 (February 2003): 64–74.

Leerssen, Joep. *When Was Romantic Nationalism? The Onset, the Long Tail, the Banal*. Antwerp: NISE, 2014.

Lees, Andrew, and Lynn Hollen Lees. *Cities and the Making of Modern Europe, 1750–1914*. Cambridge: Cambridge University Press, 2007.

Lehmann, Michael. "Die katholischen Donauschwaben in Kroatien und Slawonien (1867–1918)." In *Die katholischen Donauschwaben in der Doppelmonarchie 1867–1918: Im Zeichen des Liberalismus*, edited by Michael Lehmann, 426–96. Stuttgart: Buch und Kunst Kepplerhaus, 1977.

"Lehoczky Tivadar." *Archeologiai értesítő* 35 (1915): 366–67.

Lehoczky, Tivadar. *A beregmegyei görögszertartású katholikus lelkészsége története a XIX. század végéig*. Munkács: Grünstein Mór, 1904.

———. *Beregvármegye monographiája*. 3 vols. Ungvár: Pollacsek Miksa, 1881.

———. *Munkács város uj monografiája*. Munkács: Grünstein Mór, 1907.

Lexen, Friedrich. *Zur wirtschaftlichen Entwicklung Kronstadts in den letzten 50 Jahren*. Kronstadt: Separatdruck aus Nr. 78, 79, 80 und 81 der *Kronstädter Zeitung*, n. d.

Liber, Endre. *Budapest szobrai és emléktáblái*. Budapest: n. p., 1934.

Libertiny, Gusztáv. *Nyitravármegye népoktatásügye 1895-ben: Nyitravármegye közigazgatási bizottsága elé terjesztett tanfelügyelői jelentés*. Nyitra: Neugebauer Nándor, 1896.

Lipták, Ľubomír. "Nehlavné hlavné mesto?" *OS* 4, no. 8 (2000): 3–7.

Lombardini, Alexander. "Zoborské opátstvo." *Tovaryšstvo* 2 (1895): 115–24.

Lőrinczy, György. "Nyitravármegye társadalma." In *Magyarország vármegyéi és városai: Nyitravármegye*, edited by Samu Borovszky and János Sziklay, 216–23. Budapest: Apollo, 1898.

Loring Brace, Charles. *Hungary in 1851; with an Experience of the Austrian Police*. New York: Charles Scribner, 1852.

Lumperdean, Ioan. *Romanian Economic Journalism in Transylvania in the First Half of the Nineteenth Century.* Cluj-Napoca: Romanian Cultural Institute, 2005.

Luz, Ehud. *Parallels Meet: Religion and Nationalism in the Early Zionist Movement (1882–1904).* Philadelphia: Jewish Publication Society, 1988.

Lyka, Károly. *Szobrászatunk a századfordulón 1896–1914.* Budapest: Képzőművészeti Alap, 1954.

Macho, Peter. "Branislav Varsik a bratislavský pomník Márie Terézie." In *Miles Sempes Honestus: Zborník štúdií vydaný pri príležitosti život ného jubilea Vojtecha Dangla,* edited by Vladimír Segeš and Božena Šedová, 161–67. Bratislava: Vojenský historický ústav, 2007.

Magocsi, Paul Robert. *The Shaping of a National Identity: Subcarpathian Rus', 1848–1948.* Cambridge, MA: Harvard University Press, 1978.

Magyar statisztikai közlemények 1 (1893), 2 (1904), 16 (1906), 27 (1909), 42 (1912), and 56 (1915).

"Magyarország ezeréves fennállásának megünneplésére vonatkozó ministerelnöki előterjesztés tárgyalására kiküldött bizottság jelentése." In *Az 1892. február hó 18-ára hirdetett országgyűlés képviselőházának irományai,* 17: 360–65. Budapest: Pesti Könyvnyomda, 1894.

Magyarország fenntartandó műemlékei hivatalos jegyzékének tervezete. Budapest: Műemlékek Országos Bizottsága, 1916.

Manațe, Carmen, Sami Fiul, and Viorica Oprea. *Comunitatea evreilor din Brașov: Secolele XIX–XX.* Brașov: Transilvania Expres, 2007.

Mannová, Elena. "Associations in Bratislava in the Nineteenth Century: Middle Class Identity or Identities in a Multiethnic City?" In *Civil Society, Associations and Urban Places: Class, Nation and Culture in Nineteenth-Century Europe,* edited by Graeme Morton, Boudien de Vries, and R. J. Morris, 77–85. Aldershot: Ashgate, 2006.

———. "Elitné spolky v Bratislave v 19. a 20. storočí." In *Diferenciácia mestského spoločenstva v každodennom živote,* edited by Zuzana Beňušková and Peter Salner, 52–69. Bratislava: Ústav etnológie SAV, 1999.

———. "Die Entstehung einer neuen Hauptstadt und der Wandel der Vereinsöffentlichkeit: Pressburg 1900–1939." In *Stadt und Öffentlichkeit in Ostmitteleuropa 1900–1939,* edited by Andreas R. Hofmann and Anna Veronika Wendland, 185–92. Stuttgart: Franz Steiner, 2002.

———. "Identitätsbildung der Deutschen in Pressburg/Bratislava im 19. Jahrhundert." *Halbasien: Zeitschrift für deutsche Literatur und Kultur Südosteuropas* 5, no. 2 (1995): 60–76.

———. "Vereinsbälle der Preßburger Bürger im 19. Jahrhundert." In *Städtisches Alltagsleben in Mitteleuropa vom Mittelalter bis zum Ende des 19. Jahrhunderts: Die Referate des internationelen Symposions in Časta-Píla vom 11.-14. September 1995,* edited by Viliam Čičaj and Othmar Pickl, 251–57. Bratislava: Academic Electronic Press, 1998.

———. "Von Maria Theresia zum schönen Náci: Kollektive Gedächtnisse und Denkmalkultur in Bratislava." In *Die Besetzung des öffentlichen Raumes. Politische Plätze, Denkmäler und Straßennamen im europäischen Vergleich,* edited by Rudolf Jaworski and Peter Stachel, 203–17. Berlin: Frank & Timme, 2007.

Marczali, Henrik. "A vezérek kora és a királyság megalapítása." In *A magyar nemzet története,* edited by Sándor Szilágyi, 1: 1–311. Budapest: Athenaeum, 1895.

Marienburg, Lucas Joseph. *Geographie des Großfürstenthums Siebenbürgen.* Hermannstadt: Martin Hochmeister, 1813.

Marković, Petar St. *Zemun: Od najstariji vremena pa do danas.* Zemun: Jovan Karamat, 1896.

Markusovszky, Sámuel. *A pozsonyi ág. hitv. evang. Lyceum története kapcsolatban a pozsonyi ág. hitv. evang. egyház multjával.* Pozsony: Wigand F. K., 1896.

Marosi, István. "Firczák Gyula (1836–1912) munkácsi püspök élete és munkásságának súlypontjai." *Acta Beregsasiensis* 9, no. 2 (2010): 75–89.

Masznyik, Endre. *A "Pozsonyi Toldy-Kör" hivatásáról: Különlenyomat a "Nyugatmagyarországi Hiradó" 253. számából.* Pozsony: Wigand F. K., 1905.

Matula, Vladimír. *Devín, milý Devín: Národná slávnosť štúrovcov na Devíne 1836. História a tradícia.* Martin: Matica slovenská, 2008.

Maxwell, Alexander. *Choosing Slovakia: Slavic Hungary, the Czechoslovak Language and Accidental Nationalism.* London: Tauris Academic Series, 2009.

———. "Multiple Nationalism: National Concepts in Nineteenth-Century Hungary and Benedict Anderson's 'Imagined Communities'." *Nationalism and Ethnic Politics* 11 (2005): 385–414.

Mayer, Mária. *The Rusyns of Hungary: Political and Social Developments 1860–1910.* Boulder, CO: East European Monographs, 1997.

Mayer, Sigmund. *Die Wiener Juden: Kommerz, Kultur, Politik 1700–1900.* Vienna: K. Löwit, 1917.

Mednyánszky, Alajos. "Nyitravár- és város története." In *Nyitra és környéke képes albuma,* 2–9. Pest: Vahot Imre, 1854.

Medvigy, Cyrill. *Munkács geográfiája.* Budapest: Globus, 1917.

Meschendörfer, Adolf. *Die Stadt im Osten.* Munich: Albert Langen, 1934.

Mihalovics, Béla. "Pusztaszer." *Turisták lapja* 16 (1904): 135–38.

Mihályi, Ernő. *Pannonhalma részletes kalauza.* Budapest: Turistaság és Alpinizmus, 1923.

Mikos, Éva. *Árpád pajzsa: A magyar honfoglalás-hagyomány megszerkesztése és népszerűsítése a XVIII-XIX. században.* Budapest: MTA Néprajzi Kutatóintézete – PTE Néprajz – Kulturális Antropológia Tanszék – L'Harmattan, 2010.

Mikszáth, Kálmán. "Nyitra." In *Isten hóna alatt,* edited by Csaba Gy. Kiss and Karol Wlachovsky, 143–47. Miskolc: Felsőmagyarország, 2003.

"A millenarium az Akadémiában: A Történelmi Bizottság jelentése." *Századok* 17, no. 2 (1883): 185–215.

Die Millenniumsfeierlichkeiten im Kronstädter Komitate. Kronstadt: Schlandt, n. d.

Miller, Michael Laurence. "A Monumental Debate in Budapest: The Hentzi Statue and the Limits of Austro-Hungarian Reconciliation, 1852–1918." *Austrian History Yearbook* 40 (2009): 215–37.

Miller, Nicholas J. *Between Nation and State: Serbian Politics in Croatia before the First World War.* Pittsburgh: University of Pittsburgh Press, 1997.

"Ministerelnök előterjesztése, az államalapítás ezredik évfordulójának megünneplése tárgyában." In *Az 1892. február hó 18-ára hirdetett országgyűlés képviselőházának irományai,* 16: 28–30. Budapest: Pesti Könyvnyomda, 1894.

Miskolczy, Ambrus. *A brassói román levantei kereskedőpolgárság kelet-nyugati közvetítő szerepe (1780–1860).* Budapest: Magyar Tudományos Akadémia, 1987.

Moldovan, Silvestru. *Ţara nóstră: Descrierea părţilor Ardélului dela Mureş spre médă-di şi valea Mureşului.* Sibiu: Tipografia archidiecesană, 1894.

Mollenhauer, Daniel. "Die Grenzen der Germanisierung: Identitätsentwürfe im Elsass um 1900." *Comparativ* 15, no. 2 (2005): 22–44.

Molnár, János. *A brassói magyarság és ev. ref. egyház története.* Brassó: Brassói Ev. Ref. Egyházkebli Tanács, 1887.

Morphy, Panajot. *Rechenschaftsbericht des Landtagsabgeordneten Panajot P. Morphy an die Wählerschaft Semlins.* Semlin: Selbstverlag, 1892.

Morres, Eduard. "Die kleinen Kirchen." In *Kronstadt*, vol. 3 of *Das Burzenland*, edited by Erich Jekelius, 153–62. Kronstadt: Burzenländer Sächs. Museum, 1928.

Morres, W. *Johannes Honterus: Zu seiner 400. Geburtsfeier der sächsischen Jugend.* Kronstadt: H. Zeidner, 1898.

Moskovits, Aron. *Jewish Education in Hungary (1848–1948).* New York: Bloch, 1964.

Mosse, George L. *The Nationalization of the Masses: Political Symbolism and Mass Movements in Germany from the Napoleonic Wars through the Third Reich.* New York: New American Library, 1975.

Mudroň, Mihály. *A Felvidék: Felelet Grünwald Béla hasonnevű politikai tanulmányára.* Pozsony: Stampfel, 1878.

Nadler, Allan L. "The War on Modernity of R. Hayyim Elazar Shapira of Munkacz." *Modern Judaism* 14 (1994): 233–64.

Nagy, Ferencz. *A brassói magyar polgári kör története az 1873. évtől, az 1893. év végéig.* Brassó: Alexi, 1894.

Nagy, Gereben. *Album: Nyitramegye nagy férfiainak fény és árnyképei.* Nyitra: Kapsz és Kramár, 1904.

Najhold, Branko. *Hronika Zemuna 1871–1918.* Zemun: Trag, 1994.

———. *Hronika Zemuna 1918–1941.* Zemun: Trag, 1991.

———. *Stoleće milenijumske kule 1896–1996.* Zemun: Trag, 1996.

Nemes, Robert. "Obstacles to Nationalization on the Hungarian-Romanian Language Frontier." *Austrian History Yearbook* 43 (2012): 28–44.

Neudorfl, Marie L. "Slovakia in the Czech Press at the Turn of the Nineteenth and Twentieth Centuries." In *The Czech and Slovak Experience: Selected Papers from the Fourth World Congress for Soviet and East European Studies, Harrogate, 1990*, edited by John Morrison, 38–61. New York: St. Martin's Press, 1992.

Das neue Straßen und Häuser-Schema der Stadt Kronstadt. Kronstadt: Johann Gött & Sohn Heinrich, 1890.

N[eugeboren], E[mil]. "Johannes Honterus." *Neuer Volkskalender* 9 (1898): 117–29.

Niederle, Lubor. *Národopisná mapa uherských slováků na základě sčítání lidu z roku 1900.* Praha: Národopisná Společnost Československanske, 1903.

Nikodemusz, Károly. *A brassói magyar ág. h. ev. egyházmegye megalakulásának története.* Kolozsvár: Concordia, n. d.

Nikolić, Ilija. *Zemunska bibliografija: Knjige, listovi i časopisi štampani u Zemuni.* Zemun: Narodna biblioteka Jovan Popović, 1976.

Nipperdey, Thomas. "Nationalidee und Nationaldenkmal in Deutschland im 19. Jahrhundert." *Historische Zeitschrift* 206, no. 3 (June 1968): 529–85.

Nyitramegyei közállapotok. Nyitra: n. p., 1885.

Nyitra r. t. város képviselőtestülete részéről 1906. évi október 28-án II. Rákóczi Ferencz dicső emlékű fejedelmünk és bujdosó társai hamvainak hazahozatala alkalmából megtartott díszközgyűlés jegyzőkönyve. Nyitra: Neugebauer Nándor, 1906.

Nyitra rend. tan. város utczái-, és házszámainak és külterületeinek jegyzéke. Nyitra: Huszár István, 1890.

Oberkersch, Valentin. *Die Deutschen in Syrmien, Slawonien und Kroatien bis zum Ende des Ersten Weltkrieges: Ein Beitrag zur Geschichte der Donauschwaben.* Stuttgart: Selbstverlag, 1972.

Olay, Ferenc. "A magyar emlékművek és a magyar művészet sorsa az elszakított területeken." *Budapesti Szemle* 58, no. 628 (1930): 348–85.

Olsen, Donald J. *The City as a Work of Art: London, Paris, Vienna.* New Haven: Yale University Press, 1986.

Orbán, Balázs. *A Székelyföld leírása: Történelmi, régészeti, természetrajzi s népismereti szempontból.* 6 vols. Budapest: Tettey Nándor, 1868–73.

Orosz, József. "A brassói Millenniumi emlékoszlop története." *Erdélyi gyopár* 9, no. 1 (2001): 3–5.

Az Országos Magyar Diákszövetség 1896. junius 17., 18., 19., 20. és 21. napjain Kecskemét th. városban megtartott kongresszusának jegyzőkönyve. Budapest: Valter Ernő, 1897.

Ortvay, Tivadar. *Pozsony város utcái és terei: A város története utca- és térnevekben.* Pozsony: Wigand F. K., 1905.

———. "Pressburg und das Pressburger Comitat." In *Die Österreichisch-Ungarische Monarchie in Wort und Bild: Ungarn V/1,* 177–228. Vienna: Verlag der kaiserlich-königlichen Hof- und Staatsdruckerei, 1898.

———. *Száz év egy hazai főiskola életéből: A pozsonyi Kir. Akadémiának 1784-től 1884-ig való fennállása alkalmából.* Budapest: Magyar Kir. Egyetemi Könyvnyomda, 1884.

Ottův slovník naučný: Illustrovaná encyklopaedie obecných vědemostí. 28 vols. Praha: J. Otto, 1888–1909.

Öze, Sándor, and Norbert Spannenberger. "Zur Reinterpretation der mittelalterlichen Staatsgründung in der ungarischen Geschichtsschreibung des 19. und 20. Jahrhunderts." *Jahrbücher für Geschichte und Kultur Südosteuropas* 2 (2000): 61–77.

Paget, John. *Hungary and Transylvania; with Remarks on their Condition, Social, Political and Economical.* 2 vols. London: John Murray, 1839.

Pajić, Sima. *Ein wahrheitsgetreues Bild des Herrn Panajot Morphy, Bürgermeister, Landtags- und Reichstagsabgeordneten, Besitzers des königl. Serb. Takova-Ordens, etc., etc.* Semlin: S. Pajić, 1891.

Pál, Judit. *Unió vagy "unificáltatás"? Erdély uniója és a királyi biztos működése (1867–1872).* Kolozsvár: Erdélyi Múzeum Egyesület, 2010.

A Pallas nagy lexikona: Az összes ismeretek enciklopédiája. 18 vols. Budapest: Pallas Irodalmi és Nyomdai Részvénytársaság, 1893–1904.

Pálóczi Horváth, Lajos. *Álompákász: Egy dzsentri gyermekkora.* Budapest: Magvető, 1986.

Panajot P. Morphy an die Wähler der Stadt Semlin. Semlin: S. Pajić, 1892.

Pannonhalma a multban és napjainkban. Ungvár: Székely és Illés, 1913.

Papadrianos, Ioannis A. "Die Spirtas: Eine Familie klissuriotischer Auswanderer in der jugoslawischen Stadt Zemun während des 18. und 19. Jahrhunderts." *Balkan Studies* 16, no. 1 (1975): 116–25.

Pávai Vajna, Gábor. *Hol állítsuk fel a harmadik egyetemet?* Pozsony: Wigand F. K., 1887.

———. *Pozsony és a harmadik egyetem.* Pozsony: Stampfel Károly, 1884.

———. *A pozsonyi színügyi kérdésről.* Pozsony: Wigand F. K., 1901.

Peéry, Rezső. "Pista bátyám és a nemzetiségi kérdés." In *A magyar esszé antológiája,* edited by Mátyás Domokos, 2: 139–41. Budapest: Osiris, 2006.

Pernold, Adolf Emmanuel. *Magyarország' Távcső-földképe: Első Osztály magában foglalván Pozsonyt a' környékeivel.* Bécs: szerző saját kiadása, 1839.

Pesty, Frigyes. *Die Entstehung Croatiens.* Budapest: Friedrich Kilian, 1882.

———. *Száz politikai és történeti levél Horvátországról.* Budapest: Akadémiai könyvkereskedés, 1885.

Péter, László. "The Holy Crown of Hungary, Visible and Invisible." *Slavonic and East European Review* 81, no. 3 (July 2003): 421–510.

Petrovics, László. *Zobor vezér: Költői elbeszélés.* Budapest: szerző kiadása, 1884.

Philippi, Friedrich. *Aus Kronstadt's Vergangenheit und Gegenwart: Begleitwort zum Plan von Kronstadt.* Kronstadt: Gött, 1874.

———. *Die deutschen Ritter im Burzenlande: Ein Beitrag zur Geschichte Siebenbürgens.* Kronstadt: Johann Gött, 1861.

Phillippi, Kurt. "Kurze Geschichte der 'Kronstädter Philharmonischen Gesellschaft' (1878–1944)." *Zeitschrift für Siebenbürgische Landeskunde* 5, no. 2 (1982): 144–85.

Phillippi, Maja. "Die Anfänge der industriellen Entwicklung in Kronstadt (1872–1900)." *Forschungen zur Volks- und Landeskunde* 36, no. 1 (1993): 66–77.

Pisztóry, Mór. *Pozsony: Közgazdasági, közművelődési és közegészségügyi állapotok ismertetése. Különlenyomat a Nemzetgazdasági Szemle 1887. évi XI. évfolyamának 5. 6. és 7. füzetéből.* Budapest: Athenaeum, 1887.

Plămădeală, Antonie. *Lupta împotriva deznaționalizării Românilor din Transilvania în timpul dualismului austro-ungar în vremea lui Miron Romanul 1874–1898 după acte, documente și corespondențe inedite.* Sibiu: Typografiei Eparhiale, 1986.

Plody zboru Učencû Řeči Československé Prešporského. Prešporok: Landerer, 1836.

Podhradczky, József. *Szlavóniáról mint Magyarországnak alkotmányos részéről.* Buda: Gyurián és Bagó, 1837.

Podrimavský, Milan. "Slovenská národná strana vo volebnej aktivite r. 1901." *Historický Časopis* 26, no. 3 (1978): 409–36.

Pohlsander, Hans A. *National Monuments and Nationalism in 19th Century Germany.* New German-American Studies, vol. 31. Oxford: Peter Lang, 2008.

Polonyi, Heinrich. "Das 'Deutsche Kasino' in Kronstadt: Zur Geschichte des 'Kronstädter Lese- und Geselligkeitsvereins' kurz 'Deutsches Kasino' genannt." *Siebenbürgisch-sächsischer Hauskalender* 16 (1971): 97–99.

Popis kuća u gradu Zemunu sa novom numeracijom i nacrtom novih naziva ulica. Zemun: Semliner Tagblatt, 1897.

Popovici, Andrei. *Brașovul: Românii și Sașii.* Brașov: Ziarul Carpații, 1923.

Popovici, Bogdan Florin. "Muntele Tâmpa și simbolurile sale." *Magazin istoric* 34, no. 6 (2001): 40–47.

Popovics, Béla. *Munkács kultúrtörténete a korabeli sajtó tükrében.* Munkács: Kárpátaljai Magyar Cserkészszövetség, 2005.

Pór, Antal. *Hunyadi János: Élet- és korrajz.* Budapest: Szent István Társulat, 1873.

Pozsony Sz. Kir. Város Törvényhatóságának a Magyar Országgyűlés Képviselőházához intézett emlékirata a Pozsonyban fölállítandó egyetem tárgyában. Pozsony: Angermayer Károly, 1880.

"A pozsonyi Talmud-tórával egyesitett orth. izraelita elemi fiuiskola keletkezésének és fejlődésének története." In *A magyar-zsidó felekezet elemi és polgári iskoláinak monográfiája,* edited by Jónás Barna and Fülöp Csukási, 1: 414–28. Budapest: Corvina, 1896.

A pozsonyi Toldy-Kör harmincéves története. Pozsony: Wigand F. K., 1905.

Prepuk, Anikó. "A zsidóság a millenniumon." *Századvég* 17 (Summer 2000): 89–117.

Pribinova Nitra 833-1933. Nitra: Pribinov Fond, 1933.

Programmbuch der unter dem hohen Protectorate Ihrer kaiserlichen und königlichen Hoheit der durchlauchtigen Frau Erzherzogin Isabelle stattfindenden Fest-Vorstellungen vom 16., 17. und 18. Mai 1897 zu wohltätigen Zwecken anlässlich der feierlichen Enthüllung des Krönungsdenkmales. Pressburg: Königl. freistädt. Theater in Pressburg, 1897.

P. Szathmáry, Károly, ed. *Az 1881. évi szeptember hó 24-ére hirdetett országgyűlés képviselőházának naplója*. 17 vols. Budapest: Pesti Könyvnyomda, 1881–1884.

Pusztaszer község újratelepítése: Emlékirat. Szeged: Pusztaszeri Árpád Egyesület, 1935.

A pusztaszeri millenáris emlékszobor ügye. Kecskemét: Ottinger Ede, 1898.

Quellen zur Geschichte der Stadt Brassó: Chroniker und Tagebücher. 7 vols. Kronstadt: Heinrich Zeidner, 1896–1915.

La question des trois nationalités en Hongrie. Paris: Édition du Comité des Trois Nationalités, 1896.

Quitzmann, Ernst Anton. *Reisebriefe aus Ungarn, dem Banat, Siebenbürgen, den Donaufürstenthümern, der Europäischen Türkei und Griechenland*. Stuttgart: J. B. Müller's Verlagsbuchhandlung, 1850.

Radnóti, Dezső, ed. *Erdélyi kalauz: Utmutató Magyarország erdélyi részében*. Kolozsvár: Erdélyi Kárpát-Egyesület, 1901.

Radváni, Hadrián. "Nitra a Spolok sv. Vojtecha." In *Nitra v slovenských dejinách*, edited by Richard Marsina, 293–300. Martin: Matica slovenska, 2002.

Rakovszky, István. "Adatok Pozsony történetéből." In *Pozsony és környéke*, 1–73. Pozsony: Wigand Károly Frigyes, 1865.

Récsey, Viktor. *Győr és Pannonhalma nevezetességei*. Budapest: Hornánszky Viktor, 1897.

Rede Sr. Hochwürden des Herrn Bischofs Dr. Friedrich Müller, gehalten bei dem zu seinen Ehren Freitag den 17. Oktober 1896 in Kronstadt veranstalteten Bankette. Kronstadt: Schlandt, n. d.

Rédeky, Géza. *Nyitra rend. tan. város köztereinek, utainak és utcáinak valamint bel- és külterületi lakóházainak jegyzéke*. Nyitra: Neugebauer Nándor, 1912.

Reich Milton, Oszkár. *Erdély térképmellékletekkel és képekkel*. Budapest: Eggenberger, 1910.

Révész, Imre. "Pusztaszer." *Sárospataki füzetek: Protestáns tudományos folyórat* 10 (1866): 97–115.

Rízner, Ľudovít V. *Krátky Zemepis so zvláštnym ohľadom na Kráľovstvo Uhorské: Pre III., IV., a V. triedu slov. ľudových škôl*. Uh. Skalice: Jozef Škarnicl, 1876.

Rómer, Flóris. "A történeti érzék keltése a közönségnél, ünnepi menetek, színpadi előadások, nemzeti képek, történeti kiállítások és muzeumok által." *Századok* 19, no. 8 (1885): 114–135.

Roth, Harald. "Autostereotype als Identifikationsmuster: Zum Selbstbild der Siebenbürger Sachsen." In *Das Bild des Anderen in Siebenbürgen: Stereotype in einer multiethnischen Region*, edited by Konrad Gündisch, Wolfgang Höpken, and Michael Markel, 179–91. Cologne: Böhlau, 1998.

———. "Von der Nation zum Volk der Nation: Ethnische Identitäten im Siebenbürgen des 18. und 19. Jahrhunderts." In *Ethnische und soziale Konflikte im Neuzeitlichen Osteuropa: Festschrift für Heinz-Dietrich Löwe zum 60. Geburtstag*, edited by Ralph Tuchtentagen and Christoph Gassenschmidt, 233–45. Hamburg: Dr. Kovač, 2004.

Róth, József. *A pozsonymegyei tankerület valamint külön Pozsony szab. kir. városa népoktatásának 1877. évi állapota (tekintettel a városi iskolák történeti fejlődésére)*. Pozsony: Nirschy Ferenc könyvnyomdája, 1878.

Rothkirchen, Livia. "Deep-Rooted Yet Alien: Some Aspects of the History of the Jews in Subcarpathian Ruthenia." *Yad Vashem Studies* 12 (1977): 147–91.

Rózsa, Mária. "Pozsony a német nyelvű helyi sajtóban (1850–1920)." In *Fejezetek Pozsony történetéből magyar és szlovák szemmel*, edited by Gábor Czoch, 420–36. Pozsony: Kalligram, 2005.

Rukavina, Vlatko. *Hrvati stvaraoci u Zemunu*. Zemun: Hrvatska matica iseljenika, 1999.

R. Várkonyi, Ágnes. *Thaly Kálmán és történetírása*. Budapest: Akadémiai Kiadó, 1961.

R. Vozáry, Aladár. *Munkács*. Budapest: Officina, 1943.

Rybářová, Petra. *Antisemitizmus v Uhorsku v 80. rokoch 19. storočia*. Bratislava: Pro Historia, 2010.

Das sächsische Burzenland. Kronstadt: Honterusdruckerei, Joh. Gött's Sohn, 1898.

Šafařjk, Pawel Josef. *Slowanské starožitnosti*. Praha: Jan Spurný, 1837.

Samarjay, Karl. *Das 50-jährige Jubiläum der Preßburger Casino am 1. Juli 1887*. N. p.: n. d.

———. *A pozsonyi régi és új színház: Töredékek Pozsony multja és jelenéből*. Pozsony: Wigand F. K., 1886.

———. *Vázlatok a pozsonyi társas körök a Toldy-kör, Casino és Magyar Kör ügyében*. Pozsony: Wigand F. K., 1885.

Samassa, János, ed. *Bartha Miklós összegyűjtött munkái*. 6 vols. Budapest: Benkő Gyula, 1908–12.

Sándor, István. "Szvatoplugról 's Divin Váráról." *Sokféle* 6 (1799): 19–24.

Sand, Wolfgang. *Kronstadt: Das Musikleben einer multiethnischen Stadt bis zum Ende des Habsburgerreiches*. Kludenbach: Gehann-Musik-Verlag, 2004.

Sasinek, Fr[antišek] V[ítazoslav]. *Arpád a Uhorsku*. Turč. Sv. Martin: Kníhtlačiarsko účastinársky spolok, 1885.

———. "Biskupstvo v Nitre." *Tovaryšstvo* 1 (1893): 119–22.

———. *Dejepis slovákov*. Ružomberok: Karol Salva, 1895.

———. *Slováci v Uhorsku*. Turčiansky Sv. Martin: Kníhtlačiarsko-účastinársky spolok, 1902.

Savu, Ovidiu. "Situaţia învătământului românesc din Braşov la jumătatea secolului al XIX-lea." *Ţara Bârsei* 5, no. 5 (2006): 63–84.

Schaser, Angelika. *Josephinische Reformen und soziale Wandel in Siebenbürgen: Die Bedeutung des Konzivilitätsreskriptes für Hermannstadt*. Stuttgart: Franz Steiner, 1989.

Schilling, Lajos, ed. *Az Erdélyi Múzeum-Egyesület Brassóban 1908 június 7–9. napjain tartott negyedik vándorgyűlésének emlékkönyve*. Kolozsvár: Erdélyi Múzeum-Egyesület, 1908.

"Das Schloss Neutra." *Taschenbuch für die vaterländische Geschichte* 3 (1822): 191–210.

Schmidl, Adolf. *Reisehandbuch durch das Königreich Ungarn mit den Nebenländern und Dalmatien, nach Serbien, Bukarest und Constantinopel*. Vienna: Carl Gerold, 1835.

Schnell, Karl Ernst. *Aus meinem Leben: Erinnerungen aus alter und neuer Zeit*. Kronstadt: Honterusdruckerei, 1934.

Schönvitzky, Bertalan. *A pozsonyi kir. kath. főgymnasium története: Hazánk ezeréves fennállásának emlékére*. Pozsony: Eder István, 1896.

———. *A "Pozsonyi Toldy-Kör" 1896. évi szeptember hó 26. és 27. napján tartott millenáris ünnepségeinek emléklapjai*. Pozsony: Eder István könyvnyomdája, 1896.

Schorske, Carl E. *Fin-de-Siècle Vienna: Politics and Culture*. New York: Vintage Books, 1981.

"Die Schulen der orth. israelitischen Gemeinde." In *Die Juden und die Judengemeinde Bratislava in Vergangenheit und Gegenwart: Ein Sammelwerk*, edited by Hugo Gold, 121–25. Brünn: Jüdischer Buchverlag, 1932.

Schuller, Josef. *Kronstadt: Neuer illustrierter Führer durch die Stadt und deren Umgebung.* Kronstadt: Heinrich Zeidner, 1898.

Schulpe, György. *Pozsony és a harmadik egyetem: Értekező felhívás.* Pozsony: Drodtleff Rezső, 1893.

Schuster, Karl Ludwig, ed. *Leben und Wirken der Kronstädter Freiwilligen Feuerwehr im ersten Vierteljahrhundert 1874–1899: Festgabe zum 25-jährigen Jubiläum des Vereines.* Kronstadt: Schlandt, 1899.

Sčítánie l'udu v Republike československej zo dňa 15. februára 1921. Praha: Státni uřad statistický, 1925.

Scotus Viator [Robert William Seton-Watson]. *Racial Problems in Hungary.* London: Archibald Constable, 1908.

Seewann, Gerhard. *Geschichte der Deutschen in Ungarn.* 2 vols. Marburg: Herder-Institut, 2012.

———. "Siebenbürger Sachse, Ungarndeutscher, Donauschwabe? Überlegungen zur Identitätsproblematik des Deutschtums in Südosteuropa." In *Minderheitenfragen in Südosteuropa: Beiträge der internationalen Konferenz: The Minority Question in Historical Perspective 1900–1990. Inter University Center, Dubrovnik, 8.-14. April 1991,* edited by Gerhard Seewann, 139–55. Munich: Oldenbourg Verlag, 1992.

Seton-Watson, R. W. *Corruption and Reform in Hungary: A Study of Electoral Practice.* London: Constable, 1911.

Shanes, Joshua. *Diaspora Nationalism and Jewish Identity in Habsburg Galicia.* Cambridge: Cambridge University Press, 2012.

Sindel, Friedrich. "Die Vermögensverhältnisse der Kirchengemeinden." In *Das sächsische Burzenland,* 273–80. Kronstadt: Joh. Gött's Sohn, 1898.

Sinkó, Katalin. "'A História a mi erős várunk': A millenniumi kiállítás mint Gesamtkunswerk." In *A historizmus művészete Magyarországon: Művészettörténeti tanulmányok,* edited by Anna Zádor, 132–147. Budapest: Magyar Tudományos Akadémia Művészettörténeti Kutató Intézet, 1993.

———. "A millenniumi emlékmű mint kultuszhely." *Medvetánc* 7, no. 2 (1987): 29–50.

———. "Árpád kontra Szent István." *Janus* 6, no. 1 (Winter 1989): 42–52.

Skalský, J. J. "Vývin mesta Bratislavy po stránke národnostnej, administratívnej a politickej." In *Zlatá kniha mesta Bratislavy,* 17–22. Bratislava: Čechoslovakia, 1928.

Smith, Anthony D. *National Identity.* London: Penguin Books, 1991.

Sokcsevits, Dénes. "A magyar millennium a horvát közvélemény szemében." In *Croato-Hungarica: Uz 900 godina hrvatsko-mađarskih povijesnih veza,* edited by Milka Jauk-Pinhak, Csaba Gy. Kiss, and István Nyomárkay, 437–50. Zagreb: Katedra za hungarologiju Filozofskoga fakulteta Sveučilišta u Zagrebu i Matica hrvatska, 2002.

Sonkoly, Gábor. "Pannonhalma újkori territorializációja." In *Terek, tervek, történetek: Az identitás történetének térbeli keretei 2,* edited by András Cieger, 191–209. Budapest: Atelier, 2011.

Soppron, Ignaz. *Monographie von Semlin und Umgebung: Zumeist nach handschriftlichen Quellen.* Semlin: Selbstverlage des Verfassers, 1890.

Sörös, Pongrácz. *A pannonhalmi főapátság története: Hatodik korszak. A rend új kora, új munkaköre. 1802-től napjainkig.* Vol. 6, bk. A of *A Pannonhalmi Szent-Benedek-Rend története.* Budapest: Stephaneum, 1916.

Sretvizer, Lajos. *Ezer esztendő: A milleniumi ünnepségek anyaga a népiskolákban a Vallás és Közoktatásügyi M. Kir. Minister tervezete szerint.* Budapest: Dobrowsky és Franke, 1896.

Stampfer, Shaul. "Hungarian Yeshivot, Lithuanian Yeshivot and Joseph Ben-David." *Jewish History* 11, no. 1 (Spring 1997): 131–41.

Stekl, Hannes, and Hans Heiss. "Klein- und mittelstädtische Lebenswelten." In *Soziale Strukturen*, ed. Ulrike Harmat, vol. 9/1 of *Die Habsburgermonarchie 1848–1918*, ed. Helmut Rumpler and Peter Urbanitsch, 1: 561–9. Vienna: Verlag der Österreichischen Akademie der Wissenschaften, 2010.

Stinghe, Sterie, ed. *Istoriïa bešéreceï Şchéilor Braşovuli (manuscript dela Radu Témpé)*. Braşov: Ciurcu, 1899.

———. *Die Schkejer oder Trokanen in Kronstadt*. Leipzig: Johann Ambrosius Barth, 1900.

Stojčić, Isidor, ed. *Znameniti zemunski Srbi u 19. veku*. Zemun: Isidor Stojčić, 1913.

Strevoiu, Nicolaus. *Aktenmässiger Sachverhalt des Kirchenstreites der gr.-or. Bürger rumänischer Nationalität gegen die gr.-or. Bürger griechischer Zunge wegen der Dreifaltigkeitskirche in der innern Stadt Kronstadt*. Kronstadt: J. Gött & Sohn, 1881.

Struve, Kai, and Philipp Ther, eds. *Die Grenzen der Nationen: Identitänwandel in Oberschlesien in der Neuzeit*. Marburg: Herder-Institut, 2002.

Sundhausen, Holm. *Der Einfluss der Herderschen Ideen auf die Nationsbildung bei den Völkern der Habsburgermonarchie*. Munich: Oldenbourg, 1973.

Supka, Magdolna B. *Aba-Novák Vilmos*. Budapest: Corvina, 1966.

Szabó, Dániel. "A Néppárt az 1896. évi országgyűlési választásokon." *Századok* 112, no. 4 (1978): 730–56.

Szabó, Eumén, ed. *Orosz nyelvtan és olvasókönyv: A magyarországi oroszok irodalmi nyelvének tanulásához*. Ungvár: Kelet Könyvnyomda, 1890.

Szalay, László. *Magyarország története*. 6 vols. Lipcse: Geibel Károly, 1852–58.

Szász, Zoltán. "A brassói román iskolák ügye a századvég nemzetiségi politikájában." *Történelmi Szemle* 19, no. 1 (1976): 35–63.

Szekcső, Tamás. "Sz. Kir. Pozsony városának és környékének helyrajzi és statistikai ismertetése." In *Pozsony és környéke*, 76–196. Pozsony: Wigand Károly Frigyes, 1865.

Szendrei, János, and Gyula Szentiványi. *Magyar képzőművézek lexikona: Magyar és magyarországi vonatkozású művészek életrajzai a XII. századtól napjainkig*. Budapest: M. Kir. Vallás- és Közoktatásügyi Minisztérium, 1915.

Sziklay, János. "Nyitra." In *Magyarország vármegyéi és városai: Nyitravármegye*, edited by Samu Borovszky and János Sziklay, 28–41. Budapest: Apollo, 1898.

———. "Nyitravármegye lakossága." In *Magyarország vármegyéi és városai: Nyitravármegye*, edited by Samu Borovszky and János Sziklay, 169–215. Budapest: Apollo, 1898.

Szinnyei, József. *Magyar írók élete és munkái*. 14 vols. Budapest: Hornyánszky Viktor, 1891–1914.

Tabódy, József. *Munkács múltja és jelene Magyarország történetében*. Pest: Winter, 1860.

Tacke, Charlotte. *Denkmal im sozialen Raum: Nationale Symbole in Deutschland und Frankreich im 19. Jahrhundert*. Göttingen: Vandoeck & Ruprecht, 1995.

Tancer, Josef. *Im Schatten Wiens: Zur deutschsprachigen Presse und Literatur im Pressburg des 18. Jahrhunderts*. Bremen: Lumière, 2008.

Tarnóczy, Gusztáv. *A nyitrai választás*. Budapest: Márkus Samu, 1895.

Tatay, János. "A Haza Tudósaihoz." *Tudományos Gyűjtemény* 15, no. 3 (1831): 126–27.

Teleki, Domonkos. *Egynéhány hazai utazások' le-irása Tót és Horváthországoknak rövid esmertetésével egygyütt*. Vienna: n. p., 1791.

Teleki, József. *Hunyadiak kora Magyarországon*. 5 vols. Pest: Emich Gusztáv, 1852–57.

Teutsch, Georg Daniel. *Geschichte der Siebenbürger Sachsen für das sächsische Volk*. 6 vols. Kronstadt: Johann Gött, 1852–58, 2nd ed. Leipzig: G. Hirzel, 1874.

Teutsch, Traugott. *Johannes Honterus: Drama in drei Aufzügen*. Kronstadt: Heinrich Zeidner, 1897.

Thaly, Kálmán. *Az ezredévi országos hét emlékoszlop története*. Pozsony: Wigand F. K., 1898.

"Theben." *Taschenbuch für die vaterländische Geschichte* 9 (1828): 352–65.

Thiele, J. C. v. *Das Königreich Ungarn: Ein topographisch-historisch-statistisches Kundgemälde. Das ganze dieses Landes in mehr denn 12,400 Artikeln umfassend*. 6 vols. Kaschau: Thiele'schen Erben, 1833.

Thim, József. *A magyarországi 1848–49-iki szerb fölkelés története*. 3 vols. Budapest: Magyar Történelmi Társulat, 1930–40.

Thirring, Gusztáv, ed. *A magyar városok statisztikai évkönyve* 1 (1912).

Thuróczy, Károly. *Nyitra megye: Felolvastatott a Magyar Tudományos Akadémia II. osztályának 1895. évi deczember hó 9-én tartott ülésében*. Budapest: Magyar Tudományos Akadémia, 1896.

A Toldy-Kör a pozsonyi egyetemért. Pozsony: Angermayer Károly, 1908.

Toma, Simion. *Monografia Colegiului Național "Andrei Șaguna"*. Brașov: Cocordia, 2000.

A történelmi főcsoport hivatalos katalogusa. Budapest: Történelmi Főcsoport Igazgatósága, 1896.

Toth, Adalbert. *Parteien und Reichstagswahlen in Ungarn 1848 bis 1892*. Munich: R. Oldenbourg, 1973.

Tóth, János. *Adatok a nyitrai papnevelde történetéhez*. Nyitra: Huszár István, 1905.

Tóth, Zoltán. "A rendi norma és a 'keresztény polgárosodás': Társadalomtörténeti esszé." *Századvég*, no. 2–3 (1991): 75–130.

Turczynski, Emanuel. *Konfession und Nation: Zur Frühgeschichte der serbischen und rumänischen Nationsbildung*. Düsseldorf: Pädagogischer Verlag Schwann, 1976.

Turda, Marius. *The Idea of National Superiority in Central Europe, 1880–1918*. Lewiston: Edwin Mellon Press, 2004.

Ujes, Alojz. *Zemunska pozorja: Iz pozorišne istorije Zemuna*. Zemun: Festival Monodrame i Pantomine Zemun, 2007.

Ujvári, Péter, ed. *Magyar Zsidó Lexikon*. Budapest: Magyar Zsidó Lexikon, 1929.

Unowsky, Daniel L. *The Pomp and Politics of Patriotism: Imperial Celebrations in Habsburg Austria, 1848–1916*. West Lafayette, IN: Purdue University Press, 2005.

Vadas, Ferenc. "Programtervezetek a millennium megünneplésére (1893)." *Ars Hungarica* 24, no. 1 (1996): 3–55.

Vagner, József. *Adatok a nyitrai székes-káptalan történetéhez*. Nyitra: Huszár István, 1896.

———. *Adatok a Nyitra-városi plebániák történetéhez*. Nyitra: Huszár István, 1902.

Vályi, Katalin, and István Zombori. *Ópusztaszer*, ed. László Blazovich. Budapest: Száz magyar falu könyvesháza, 2000.

van Duin, Pieter C. *Central European Crossroads: Social Democracy and National Revolution in Bratislava (Pressburg), 1867–1921*. New York: Berghahn Books, 2009.

Varga, Árpád F. *Erdély etnikai és felekezeti statisztikája V.: Brassó, Hunyad és Szeben megye. Népszámlálási adatok 1850–2002 között*. Csíkszereda: Pro Print, 2011.

Varga, Bálint. "A barbár múlt és a nemzeti dicsőség." *Történelmi Szemle* 57, no. 2 (2015): 319–332.

Varga, Lajos, ed. *A magyar szociáldemokrácia kézikönyve*. Budapest: Napvilág Kiadó, 1999.

Vaszary, Kolos. "Pannonhalma helytörténete." In *Győr megye és város egyetemes leírása*, edited by Ipoly Fehér, 580–602. Budapest: Franklin-Társulat, 1874.

Veliz, Fernando. *The Politics of Croatia-Slavonia 1903–1918: Nationalism, State Allegiance and the Changing International Order*. Wiesbaden: Harrasowitz, 2012.

Veritas [pseud.]. *A magyarországi románok egyházi, iskolai, közművelődési, közgazdasági intézményeinek és mozgalmainak ismertetése*. Budapest: Uránia, 1908.

Vlad, Ioan. *Cărturarii brașoveni pentru România Mare*. Brașov: Academia Aviației și Apărării Antiaeriene "Henri Coandă," 1999.

Vlaicu, Arsène. *Monographie de l'École Supérieure de Commerce Gréco-Orientale Roumaine de Brassó*. Brassó: Ciurcu, 1913.

Vojnits, Döme. *Pannonhalmán 1896. aug. 26-án, az országos millenniumi ünnepélyen tartott beszéd*. Esztergom: Laiszky János, 1896.

Vollmer, Hans. *Allgemeines Lexikon der bildenden Künstler von der Antike bis zur Gegenwart*. Leipzig: E. A. Seemann, 1929.

von Ballus, Paul. *Presburg und seine Umgebungen*. Presburg: Andreas Schwaiger und I. Landes, 1823.

von Engel, Johann Christian. *Geschichte des Ungrischen Reichs*. 5 vols. Vienna: Camesinasche Buchhandlung, 1813–14.

von Gogolák, Ludwig. "Ungarns Nationalitätengesetze und das Problem des magyarischen National- und Zentralstaates." In *Die Völker des Reiches*, vol. 3 of *Die Habsburgermonarchie 1848–1918*, edited by Adam Wandruszka and Peter Urbanitsch, 1207–303. Vienna: Verlag der Österreichischen Akademie der Wissenschaften, 1980.

von Hirschhausen, Ulrike. *Die Grenzen der Gemeinsamkeit: Deutsche, Letten, Russen und Juden in Riga 1860–1914*. Göttingen: Vandenhoeck & Ruprecht, 2006.

von Klimó, Árpád. *Nation, Konfession, Geschichte: Zur nationalen Geschichtskultur Ungarns im europäischen Kontext (1860–1948)*. Munich: Oldenbourg, 2003.

von Puttkamer, Joachim. "Kein europäischer Sonderfall: Ungarns Nationalitätenproblem im 19. Jahrhundert und die jüngere Nationalismusforschung." In *Das Ungarnbild der deutschen Historiographie*, edited by Márta Fata, 84–98. Stuttgart: Franz Steiner, 2004.

———. "Die EMKE in Siebenbürgen und die FEMKE in Oberungarn: Die Tätigkeiten zweier ungarischer Schutzvereine in ihrem nationalen Umfeld." In *Schutzvereine in Ostmitteleuropa: Vereinswesen, Sprachenkonflikte und Dynamiken nationaler Mobilisierung 1860–1939*, edited by Peter Haslinger, 158–69. Marburg: Herder-Institut, 2009.

———. "Mehrsprachigkeit und Sprachenzwang in Oberungarn und Siebenbürgen 1867–1914: Eine statistische Untersuchung." *Zeitschrift für Siebenbürgische Landeskunde* 26, no. 1 (2003): 7–40.

———. *Schulalltag und nationale Integration in Ungarn: Slowaken, Rumänen und Siebenbürger Sachsen in der Auseinandersetzung mit der ungarischen Staatsidee 1867–1914*. Munich: Oldenbourg, 2003.

von Taube, Friedrich Wilhelm. *Historische und geographische Beschreibung des Königreiches Slavonien und des Herzogthumes Syrmien, sowol nach ihrer natürlichen Beschaffenheit, als auch nach ihrer itzigen Verfassung und neuen Einrichtung in kirchlichen, bürgerlichen und militarischen Dingen*. 3 vols. Leipzig: n. p., 1777–1778.

Vragaš, Stefan. "Augustin Roškovány Bischof von Nitra (1807–1892): Sein Leben und Werk." *Slovak Studies* 19 (1979): 167–75.

Vranešević, Branislav. "Die aussenpolitische Beziehungen zwischen Serbien und der Habsburgermonarchie." In *Die Habsburgermonarchie im System der internationalen*

Beziehungen, vol. 6 of *Die Habsburgermonarchie 1848–1918*, edited by Adam Wandruszka and Peter Urbanitsch, 319–75. Vienna: Verlag der Österreichischen Akademie der Wissenschaften, 1989.

Vutkovich, Ödön. "Pozsony." In *Magyarország vármegyéi és városai: Pozsony vármegye, Pozsony sz. kir. város, Nagyszombat, Bazin, Modor, és Szentgyörgy r. t. városok*, edited by Samu Borovszky, 131–72. Budapest: Apollo, n. d.

Wagner, Lajos. *A pozsonyi m. kir. állami tudomány-egyetem tervezete*. Pozsony: Stampfel Károly, 1900.

Wargha, Samu. *Pannonhalmán a Kálvária áthelyezése alkalmával 1896. évi julius 26-án tartott beszéd*. Győr: Győregyházmegye Könyvnyomtató Intézete, 1896.

Weber, Petru. "The Nationalities and the Millennium in Dualist Hungary." *Transylvanian Review* 6, no. 4 (1997): 97–105.

———. "Das ungarische Millennium bei den Rumänen." In *Interethnische- und Zivilisationsbeziehungen im siebenbürgischen Raum: Historische Studien*, edited by Sorin Mitu and Florin Gogâltan, 256–71. Cluj: Verein der Historiker aus Siebenbürgen und dem Banat, 1996.

Weinberger, Maxmilian. *Vzpomínky z cest*. Brno: Papežská Knihtiskárna Benedektinů Rajhradských, 1899.

Weiss, Ignácz. *Az Erdélyi Magyar Közművelődési Egylet és a brassói magyarság: Hirlapi czikkek*. Brassó: Alexi, 1885.

———. *A zsidók és a nemzetiségek*. Brassó: Brassó Könyvnyomda, 1894.

Wittstock, Oscar. *Grün oder Schwarz? Eine Beleuchtung der gegenwärtigen politischen Verhältnisse der Siebenbürger Sachsen*. Hermannstadt: G. U. Seraphim, 1896.

Wolf, Theobald. *Johannes Honterus der Apostel Ungarns*. Kronstadt: Ausschuß zur Errichtung eines Honterusdenkmals, 1894.

Wolfes, Thomas. "Adolf Harnack und Ernst Troeltsch in Siebenbürgen: Zur Reise deutscher Wissenschaftler nach Hermannstadt anläßlich der Enthüllung des G. D. Teutsch-Denkmals 1899." *Zeitschrift für Siebenbürgische Landeskunde* 27 (2004): 143–55.

Wühr, Hans. "Die Zinne und die Kronstädter Maler." *Klingsor* 3, no. 4 (April 1926): 128–34.

Zach, Krista. "'Wir wohnten auf dem Königsboden...' Identitätsbildung bei den Siebenbürger Sachsen im historischen Wandel." In *Minderheitenfragen in Südosteuropa: Beiträge der internationalen Konferenz: The Minority Question in Historical Perspective 1900–1990. Inter University Center, Dubrovnik, 8.-14. April 1991*, edited by Gerhard Seewann, 115–37. Munich: Oldenbourg, 1992.

Zádor, Anna, and István Gentheon, eds. *Művészeti lexikon*. 4 vols. Budapest: Akadémiai Kiadó, 1965–68.

Zahra, Tara. "Imagined Noncommunities: National Indifference as a Category of Analysis." *Slavic Review* 69, no. 1 (Spring 2010): 93–119.

Zajonc, Juraj. "Mesto a spoločensko-historické procesy: Východiská analýzy. Niekol'ko príkladov z mesta Nitra." *Slovenský národopis* 51, no. 2 (2003): 178–92.

———. "Prečo je Nitra staroslávne mesto." In *Mýty naše Slovenské*, edited by Eduard Krekovič, Elena Mannová, and Eva Krekovičová, 134–49. Bratislava: Academic Electronic Press, 2005.

Zamfir, Anca Maria. "Un posibil model vienez pentru Braşovul celei de-a doua jumătăţi a secolului al XIX-lea." *Cumidava* 22–24 (1998–2000): 321–60.

Zăstroiu, Remus. "Einige Beobachtungen hinsichtlich des sozialen und beruflichen Status' des rumänischen Journalisten im 19. Jahrhundert." In *Deutschsprachige Öffentlichkeit und*

Presse in Mittelost- und Südeuropa (1848–1948), edited by Andrei Ciorbea-Hoişie, Ion Lihaciu, and Alexander Rubel, 75–82. Iaşi: Editura Universităţii "Al. I. Cuza," 2008.

Zichy, Hermán, and Gy. M. Derestye, eds. *Magyar zsidók a millenniumon: Művelődéstörténeti tanulmány.* Budapest: Miljković Dragutin, 1896.

Zima, András. "Cult or Spirit? Integration Strategies and History of Memory in Jewish Groups in Hungary at the turn of the 19th-20th century." *Acta Ethnographica Hungarica* 53, no. 2 (2008): 243–263.

Zoltvány, Irén L. *Guzmics Izidor életrajza.* Budapest: Franklin-Társulat, 1884.

Zoltvány, Irén L., and Antal Klemm. "A magyarországi benczés irodalom." In *A pannonhalmi főapátság története: Hatodik korszak. A rend új kora, új munkaköre. 1802-től napjainkig,* vol. 6, bk. B of *A Pannonhalmi Szent-Benedek-Rend története,* 134–889. Budapest: Stephaneum, 1916.

Zsigárdy, Gyula. *Beszéd, melyet Zsigárdy Gyula a dévényi millenáris szobor leleplezésénél mondott.* Galánta: Első Galánthai Nyomda, 1896.

Zubácka, Ida. *Nitra za prvej Československej republiky.* Nitra: Univerzita Konštantina, 1997.

Zur Geschichte des Honterus-Denkmals. Kronstadt: Johann Gött's Sohn, 1895.

Websites

"1892. évi II. törvényczikk az 1895. évben Budapesten tartandó országos nemzeti kiállításról." http://1000ev.hu/index.php?a=3&param=6452 (accessed 25 April 2011).

"1893. évi III. törvényczikk az országos nemzeti kiállitás költségeinek fedezéséről." http://1000ev.hu/index.php?a=3&param=6486 (accessed 25 April 2011).

"1896. évi VIII. törvényczikk a honalapitás ezredik évfordulójának megörökitésére alkotandó müvekről." http://1000ev.hu/index.php?a=3&param=6625 (accessed 25 April 2011).

"Alsóbodok: Felröppent a zoborhegyi turulmadár a szoboravatással." Felvidék.ma. http://www.felvidek.ma/felvidek/regio/52504-alsobodok-felroppent-a-zoborhegyi-turulmadar-a-szoboravatassal (accessed 11 January 2016).

Fodor, Ferenc. "A magyarországi országgyűlési képviselőválasztási kerületek térképei 1861-1915-ig." Országgyűlési Könyvtár. http://www.ogyk.hu/e-konyvt/mpgy/valasztasiterkep/ (accessed 25 May 2012).

"Idén is: Generációk Találkozása 2011. aug. 19." Magyar Koalíció Pártja. http://www.mkp.sk/node/17291 (accessed 30 May 2012).

"Jewish life in Munkatch—March 1933." YouTube. http://www.youtube.com/watch?v=rp1OeIf0D0w (accessed 25 March 2012).

Renan, Ernest. "What is a Nation?" Unknown translator. http://web.archive.org/web/20110827065548/http://www.cooper.edu/humanities/core/hss3/e_renan.html (accessed 14 January 2014).

"Petőfi Sándor összes költeményei." Magyar Elektronikus Könyvtár. http://mek.oszk.hu/01000/01006/html/vs184704.htm (accessed 25 May 2012).

"Súsošie Márie Terézie." Bratislavský okrašľovácí spolok. http://bos-bratislava.sk.data12.websupport.sk/projekt/16/susosie-marie-terezie (accessed 22 October 2011).

INDEX

AUSTRIAN AND HABSBURG STUDIES

General Editor: Gary B. Cohen, Center for Austrian Studies,
University of Minnesota

Before 1918, Austria and the Habsburg lands constituted an expansive
multinational and multiethnic empire, the second largest state in Europe and
a key site for cultural and intellectual developments across the continent. At
the turn of the twentieth century, the region gave birth to modern psychology,
philosophy, economics, and music, and since then has played an important
mediating role between Western and Eastern Europe, today participating as
a critical member of the European Union. The volumes in this series address
specific themes and questions around the history, culture, politics, social, and
economic experience of Austria, the Habsburg Empire, and its successor states
in Central and Eastern Europe.

www.ingramcontent.com/pod-product-compliance
Lightning Source LLC
Chambersburg PA
CBHW070912030426
42336CB00014BA/2379